Prese

On the occasion of

from

Date

Church

The Book
of
Common Prayer

for everyday use

LARGE PRINT

Adapted from the
1979 Book of Common Prayer

1

Saint Austin's Press
world wide web: www.austinspress.com
email: info@austinspress.com

Publication: January 7, 2017

Errata corrected March 27, 2017

The Book of Common Prayer for Everyday Use
Large print edition

Editor: McCalister, Van

The Book of Common Prayer is in the Public Domain

Scripture quotations and Psalter are from: The Book of Common Prayer (1979), except where otherwise noted.

Table of Contents

Introduction

The Book of Common Prayer for Everyday Use is an edited adaptation of the 1979 Book of Common Prayer used in many Anglican and Episcopalian churches in the United States. This edition includes only those Rites most commonly used by the average parishioner. The goal of which is to to provide an inexpensive large print Book of Common Prayer (BCP) that can be used for personal prayer, home groups, camps, youth groups, travel, nursing homes and pastoral visitations. As an aid to nursing home use and pastoral visitations (and for those of us who can't always find their reading glasses), it is offered in a type considerably larger than what is found in the 1,000 page editions of the BCP.

In order to achieve these goals, *The Book of Common Prayer for Everyday Use* only includes the Daily Office, Holy Eucharist (Contemporary), Communion Under Special Circumstances, Collects, Prayers for the Sick, The Reconciliation of a Penitent (Form One), Psalter and Lectionary (1979). In addition to the Collects, a short section of devotional prayers has been added as an aid to preparation for Holy Eucharist. Also, a traditional *Gloria Patri* is substituted for the contemporary version:

Glory be to the Father, and to the Son, and to the Holy Spirit: as it was in the beginning, is now, and ever shall be, world without end. Amen.

The Traditional Eucharistic Prayers (Rite One), Seasonal Services, Eucharistic Prayer C, the Pastoral Services: Baptism, Confirmation, Matrimony, Burial, Ordination, and the Revised Common Lectionary, are omitted from this edition.

With the goal of using this edition of the Book of
Common Prayer in settings outside of the church,
Eucharistic Prayer A has been included in a complete
format with Prayers of the People, Form III, and the
Ordinary Time Prefaces, absolution and concluding
blessings embedded in the Liturgy. This makes it simple
for the Celebrant to offer the Eucharist with minimal
page turns and reduces confusion in settings where there
may be visitors or others unfamiliar with the Liturgy.

Daily Morning Prayer:
Contemporary Rite

The Officiant begins the service with one or more of these sentences of Scripture, or with the versicle "Lord, open our lips" on page 7.

Advent

Watch, for you do not know when the master of the house will come, in the evening, or at midnight, or at cockcrow, or in the morning, lest he come suddenly and find you asleep. *Mark 13:35, 36*

In the wilderness prepare the way of the Lord, make straight in the desert a highway for our God. *Isaiah 40:3*

The glory of the Lord shall be revealed, and all flesh shall see it together. *Isaiah 40:5*

Christmas

Behold, I bring you good news of a great joy which will come to all the people; for to you is born this day in the city of David, a Savior, who is Christ the Lord. *Luke 2:10, 11*

Behold, the dwelling of God is with mankind. He will dwell with them, and they shall be his people, and God himself will be with them, and be their God. *Revelation 21:3*

Epiphany

Nations shall come to your light, and kings to the brightness of your rising. *Isaiah 60:3*

I will give you as a light to the nations, that my salvation may reach to the end of the earth. *Isaiah 49:6b*

From the rising of the sun to its setting my Name shall be great among the nations, and in every place incense shall be offered to my Name, and a pure offering; for my Name shall be great among the nations, says the Lord of hosts. *Malachi 1:11*

Lent

If we say we have no sin, we deceive ourselves, and the truth is not in us, but if we confess our sins, God, who is faithful and just, will forgive our sins and cleanse us from all unrighteousness. *1 John 1:8, 9*

Rend your hearts and not your garments. Return to the Lord your God, for he is gracious and merciful, slow to anger and abounding in steadfast love, and repents of evil. *Joel 2:13*

I will arise and go to my father, and I will say to him, "Father, I have sinned against heaven and before you; I am no longer worthy to be called your son."*Luke 15:18, 19*

To the Lord our God belong mercy and forgiveness, because we have rebelled against him and have not obeyed the voice of the Lord our God by following his laws which he set before us. *Daniel 9:9, 10*

Jesus said, "If anyone would come after me, let him deny himself and take up his cross and follow me." *Mark 8:34*

Holy Week

All we like sheep have gone astray; we have turned every one to his own way; and the Lord has laid on him the iniquity of us all. *Isaiah 53:6*

Is it nothing to you, all you who pass by? Look and see if there is any sorrow like my sorrow which was brought upon me, whom the Lord has afflicted. *Lamentations 1:12*

Easter Season, including Ascension Day and the Day of Pentecost

Alleluia! Christ is risen.
The Lord is risen indeed. Alleluia!

On this day the Lord has acted; we will rejoice and be glad in it. *Psalm 118:24*

Thanks be to God, who gives us the victory through our Lord Jesus Christ. *1 Corinthians 15:57*

If then you have been raised with Christ, seek the things that are above, where Christ is, seated at the right hand of God. *Colossians 3:1*

Christ has entered, not into a sanctuary made with hands, a copy of the true one, but into heaven itself, now to appear in the presence of God on our behalf. *Hebrews 9:24*

You shall receive power when the Holy Spirit has come upon you; and you shall be my witness in Jerusalem, and in all Judea, and Samaria, and to the ends of the earth. *Acts 1:8*

Trinity Sunday

Holy, holy, holy is the Lord God Almighty, who was, and is, and is to come! *Revelation 4:8*

All Saints and other Major Saints' Days

We give thanks to the Father, who has made us worthy to share in the inheritance of the saints in light. *Colossians 1:12*

You are no longer strangers and sojourners, but fellow citizens with the saints and members of the household of God. *Ephesians 2:19*

Their sound has gone out into all lands, and their message to the ends of the world. *Psalm 19:4*

Occasions of Thanksgiving

Give thanks to the Lord, and call upon his Name; make known his deeds among the peoples. *Psalm 105:1*

At any Time

Grace to you and peace from God our Father and the Lord Jesus Christ. *Philippians 1:2*

I was glad when they said to me, "Let us go to the house of the Lord." *Psalm 122:1*

Let the words of my mouth and the meditation of my heart be acceptable in you sight, O Lord, my strength and my redeemer. *Psalm 19:14*

Send out your light and your truth, that they may lead me, and bring me to your holy hill and to your dwelling. *Psalm 43:3*

The Lord is in his holy temple; let all the earth keep silence before him. *Habakkuk 2:20*

The hour is coming, and now is, when the true worshipers will worship the Father in spirit and truth, for such the Father seeks to worship him. *John 4:23*

Thus says the high and lofty One who inhabits eternity, whose name is Holy, "I dwell in the high and holy place and also with the one who has a contrite and humble spirit, to revive the spirit of the humble and to revive the heart of the contrite." *Isaiah 57:15*

The following Confession of Sin may then be said; or the Office may continue at once with "Lord, open our lips."

Confession of Sin

The Officiant says to the people

Dearly beloved, we have come together in the presence of Almighty God our heavenly Father, to set forth his praise, to hear his holy Word, and to ask, for ourselves and on behalf of others, those things that are necessary for our life and our salvation. And so that we may prepare ourselves in heart and mind to worship him, let us kneel in silence, and with penitent and obedient hearts confess our sins, that we may obtain forgiveness by his infinite goodness and mercy.

or this

Let us confess our sins against God and our neighbor.

Officiant and People together, all kneeling

Most merciful God, we confess that we have sinned against you in thought, word, and deed, by what we have done, and by what we have left undone. We have not loved you with our whole heart; we have not loved our neighbors as ourselves. We are truly sorry and we humbly repent. For the sake of your Son Jesus Christ, have mercy on us and forgive us; that we may delight in your will, and walk in your ways, to the glory of your Name. Amen.

The Priest stands and says

Almighty God have mercy on you, forgive you all your sins through our Lord Jesus Christ, strengthen you in all goodness, and by the power of the Holy Spirit keep you in eternal life. *Amen.*

A deacon or lay person using the preceding form remains kneeling, and substitutes "us" for "you" and "our" for "your."

The Invitatory and Psalter

All stand

Officiant	Lord, open our lips.
People	And our mouth shall proclaim your praise.

Officiant and People

Glory be to the Father, and to the Son, and to the Holy Spirit: *
as it was in the beginning, is now, and ever shall be, world
without end. Amen.

Except in Lent, add Alleluia.

Then follows one of the Invitatory Psalms, Venite or Jubilate.

One of the following Antiphons may be sung or said with the Invitatory Psalm

In Advent
Our King and Savior now draws near: Come let us adore him.

On the Twelve Days of Christmas
Alleluia. To us a child is born: Come let us adore him. Alleluia.

From the Epiphany through the Baptism of Christ, and on the Feasts of the Transfiguration and Holy Cross
The Lord has shown forth his glory: Come let us adore him.

In Lent
The Lord is full of compassion and mercy: Come let us adore him.

From Easter Day until the Ascension
Alleluia. The Lord is risen indeed: Come let us adore him. Alleluia.

From Ascension Day until the Day of Pentecost
Alleluia. Christ has ascended into heaven: Come let us adore him. Alleluia.

On the Day of Pentecost
Alleluia. The Spirit of the Lord renews the face of the earth: Come let us adore him. Alleluia.

On Trinity Sunday
Father, Son, and Holy Spirit, one God: Come let us adore him.

On other Sundays and weekdays
The earth is the Lord's for he made it: Come let us adore him.

> *or this*

Worship the Lord in the beauty of his holiness: Come let us adore him.

> *or this*

The mercy of the Lord is everlasting: Come let us adore him.

The Alleluias in the following Antiphons are used only in Easter Season.

On Feasts of the Incarnation
[Alleluia] The Word was made flesh and dwelt among us:
Come let us adore him. [Alleluia]

On all Saints and other Major Saints' Days
[Alleluia.] The Lord is glorious in his saints: Come let us adore him. [Alleluia.]

Venite *Psalm 95:1-7*　　　　*or Psalm 95*

Come let us sing to the Lord; *
　let us shout for joy to the Rock of our salvation.
Let us come before his presence with thanksgiving *
　and raise a loud shout to him with psalms.
For the Lord is a great God, *
　and a great King above all gods.
In his hand are the caverns of the earth, *
　and the heights of the hills are his also.
The sea is his, for he made it, *
　and his hands have molded the dry land.
Come, let us bow down, and bend the knee, *
　and kneel before the Lord our Maker.
For he is our God, and we are the people of his pasture
and the sheep of his hand. *
　Oh, that today you would hearken to his voice!

Jubilate *Psalm 100*

Be joyful in the Lord, all you lands; *
　serve the Lord with gladness
　and come before his presence with song.
Know this: The Lord himself is God; *
　he himself has made us, and we are his;
　we are his people and the sheep of his pasture.
Enter his gates with thanksgiving;
　go into his courts with praise; *
　give thanks to him and call upon his Name.
For the Lord is good;
　his mercy is everlasting; *
　and his faithfulness endures from age to age.

In Easter Week, in place of an Invitatory Psalm, the following is sung or said. It may also be used daily until the Day of Pentecost.

Christ our Passover *Pascha nostrum*
1 Corinthians 5:7-8; Romans 6:9-11; 1 Corinthians 15:20-22

Alleluia.
Christ our Passover has been sacrificed for us; *
   therefore let us keep the feast,
Not with the old leaven, the leaven of malice and evil, *
   but with the unleavened bread of sincerity and truth.
Alleluia.
Christ being raised from the dead will never die again; *
   death no longer has dominion over him.
The death that he died, he died to sin, once for all; *
   but the life he lives, he lives to God.
So also consider yourselves dead to sin, *
   and alive to God in Jesus Christ our Lord. Alleluia.
Christ has been raised from the dead, *
   the first fruits of those who have fallen asleep.
For since by a man came death, *
   by a man has come also the resurrection of the dead.
For as in Adam all die, *
   so also in Christ shall all be made alive. Alleluia.

Then follows

The Psalm or Psalms Appointed

At the end of the Psalms is sung or said

Glory be to the Father, and to the Son, and to the Holy Spirit: *
as it was in the beginning, is now, and ever shall be, world
without end. Amen.

The Lessons

One or two lessons, as appointed, are read, the Reader first saying

A Reading (Lesson) from _____.

A citation giving chapter and verse may be added.

After each Lesson the Reader may say
> The Word of the Lord.

Answer   Thanks be to God.

Or the Reader may say
> Here ends the Lesson (Reading).

Silence may be kept after each Reading. One of the following Canticles is sung or said after each Reading. If three lessons are used, the Lesson from the Gospel is read after the second Canticle.

Canticle 8 The Song of Moses   *Cantemus Domino*
Exodus 15:1-6, 11-13, 17-18

Especially suitable for use in Easter Season

I will sing to the Lord, for he is lofty and uplifted; *
   the horse and its rider has he hurled into the sea.
The Lord is my strength and my refuge; *
   the Lord has become my Savior.
This is my God and I will praise him, *
   the God of my people and I will exalt him.
The Lord is a mighty warrior; *
   Yahweh is his Name.
The chariots of Pharoah and his army has he hurled into
the sea;*
   the finest of those who bear armor have been drowned in
the Red Sea.
The fathomless deep has overwhelmed them; *
   they sank into the depths like a stone.
Your right hand, O Lord, is glorious in might; *
   your right hand, O Lord, has overthrown the enemy.
Who can be compared with you, O Lord, among the gods? *
   who is like you, glorious in holiness,
   awesome in renown, and worker of wonders?
You stretched forth your right hand; *
   the earth swallowed them up.
With your constant love you led the people you redeemed; *
   with your might you brought them in safety to your holy
dwelling.
You will bring them in and plant them *
   on the mount of your possession,
The resting-place you have made for yourself, O Lord, *
   the sanctuary, O Lord, that your hand has established.
The Lord shall reign *
   for ever and for ever.

Glory be to the Father, and to the Son, and to the Holy Spirit: *
as it was in the beginning, is now, and ever shall be, world
without end. Amen.

Canticle 9 The First Song of Isaiah *Ecce, Deus*
Isaiah 12:2-6

Surely, it is God who saves me; *
  I will trust in him and not be afraid.
For the Lord is my stronghold and my sure defense, *
  and he will be my Savior.
Therefore you shall draw water with rejoicing *
  from the springs of salvation.
And on that day you shall say, *
  Give thanks to the Lord and call upon his Name;
Make his deeds known among the peoples; *
  see that they remember that his Name is exalted.
Sing praises of the Lord, for he has done great things, *
  and this is known in all the world.
Cry aloud, inhabitants of Zion, ring out your joy, *
  for the great one in the midst of you is the Holy One
of Israel.

Glory be to the Father, and to the Son, and to the Holy Spirit: *
as it was in the beginning, is now, and ever shall be, world
without end. Amen.

Canticle 10 The Second Song of Isaiah
Quaerite Dominum   *Isaiah 55:6-11*

Seek the Lord while he wills to be found; *
  call upon him when he draws near.
Let the wicked forsake their ways *
  and the evil ones their thoughts;

And let them turn to the Lord, and he will have
compassion, *
  and to our God, for he will richly pardon.
For my thoughts are not your thoughts, *
  nor your ways my ways, says the Lord.
For as the heavens are higher than the earth, *
  so are my ways higher than your ways,
  and my thoughts than your thoughts.
For as rain and snow fall from the heavens *
  and return not again, but water the earth,
Bringing forth life and giving growth, *
  seed for sowing and bread for eating,
So is my word that goes forth from my mouth; *
  it will not return to me empty;
But it will accomplish that which I have purposed, *
  and prosper in that for which I sent it.

Glory be to the Father, and to the Son, and to the Holy Spirit: *
as it was in the beginning, is now, and ever shall be, world
without end. Amen.

Canticle 11 The Third Song of Isaiah
Surge, illuminare Isaiah 60:1-3, 11a, 14c, 18-19

Arise, shine, for your light has come, *
  and the glory of the Lord has dawned upon you.
For behold, darkness covers the land; *
  deep gloom enshrouds the peoples.
But over you the Lord will rise, *
  and his glory will appear upon you.
Nations will stream to your light, *
  and kings to the brightness of your dawning.
Your gates will always be open; *
  by day or night they will never be shut.

They will call you, The City of the Lord, *
  The Zion of the Holy One of Israel.
Violence will no more be heard in your land, *
  ruin or destruction within your borders.
You will call your walls, Salvation, *
  and all your portals, Praise.
The sun will no more be your light by day; *
  by night you will not need the brightness of the
moon.
The Lord will be your everlasting light, *
  and your God will be your glory.

Glory be to the Father, and to the Son, and to the Holy Spirit: *
as it was in the beginning, is now, and ever shall be, world
without end. Amen.

Canticle 12 A Song of Creation
Benedicite, omnia opera Domini
  Song of the Three Young Men, 35-65

*One or more sections of this Canticle may be used. Whatever
the selection, it begins with the Invocation and concludes with
the Doxology.*

Invocation

Glorify the Lord, all you works of the Lord, *
  praise him and highly exalt him for ever.
In the firmament of his power, glorify the Lord, *
  praise him and highly exalt him for ever.

I The Cosmic Order

Glorify the Lord, you angels and all powers of the Lord, *
  O heavens and all waters above the heavens.
Sun and moon and stars of the sky, glorify the Lord, *
  praise him and highly exalt him for ever.

Glorify the Lord, every shower of rain and fall of dew, *
    all winds and fire and heat.
Winter and Summer, glorify the Lord, *
    praise him and highly exalt him for ever.
Glorify the Lord, O chill and cold, *
    drops of dew and flakes of snow
Frost and cold, ice and sleet, glorify the Lord, *
    praise him and highly exalt him for ever.
Glorify the Lord, O nights and days, *
    O shining light and enfolding dark.
Storm clouds and thunderbolts, glorify the Lord, *
    praise him and highly exalt him for ever.

II The Earth and its Creatures

Let the earth glorify the Lord, *
    praise him and highly exalt him for ever.
Glorify the Lord, O mountains and hills,
    and all that grows upon the earth, *
    praise him and highly exalt him for ever.
Glorify the Lord, O springs of water, seas, and streams, *
    O whales and all that move in the waters.
All birds of the air, glorify the Lord, *
    praise him and highly exalt him for ever.
Glorify the Lord, O beasts of the wild, *
    and all you flocks and herds.
O men and women everywhere, glorify the Lord, *
    praise him and highly exalt him for ever.

III The People of God

Let the people of God glorify the Lord, *
    praise him and highly exalt him for ever.
Glorify the Lord, O priests and servants of the Lord, *
    praise him and highly exalt him for ever.

Glorify the Lord, O spirits and souls of the righteous, *
  praise him and highly exalt him for ever.
You that are holy and humble of heart, glorify the Lord, *
  praise him and highly exalt him for ever.

Doxology

Let us glorify the Lord: Father, Son, and Holy Spirit; *
  praise him and highly exalt him for ever.
In the firmament of his power, glorify the Lord, *
  praise him and highly exalt him for ever.

Canticle 13 *Benedictus es, Domine*
Song of the Three Young Men, 29-34

Glory to you, Lord God of our fathers; *
  you are worthy of praise; glory to you.
Glory to you for the radiance of you holy Name; *
  we will praise you and highly exalt you for ever.
Glory to you in the splendor of you temple; *
  on the throne of your majesty, glory to you.
Glory to you, seated between the Cherubim; *
  we will praise you and highly exalt you for ever.
Glory to you, beholding the depths; *
  in the high vault of heaven, glory to you.

Glory to you, Father, Son, and Holy Spirit; *
  we will praise you and highly exalt you for ever.

Canticle 14 A Song of Penitence *Kyrie Pantokrator*
Prayer of Manasseh 1-2, 4, 6-7, 11-15

Especially suitable in Lent, and on other penitential occasions

O Lord and Ruler of the hosts of heaven, *
  God of Abraham, Isaac, and Jacob,
  and of all their righteous offspring:
You made the heavens and the earth, *
  with all their vast array.
All things quake with fear at your presence; *
  they tremble because of your power.
But your merciful promise is beyond all measure; *
  it surpasses all that our minds can fathom.
O Lord, you are full of compassion, *
  long-suffering, and abounding in mercy.
You hold back your hand; *
  you do not punish as we deserve.
In your great goodness, Lord,
  you have promised forgiveness to sinners, *
  that they may repent of their sin and be saved.
And now, O Lord, I bend the knee of my heart, *
  and make my appeal, sure of your gracious goodness.
I have sinned, O Lord, I have sinned, *
  and I know my wickedness only too well.
Therefore I make this prayer to you: *
  Forgive me, Lord, forgive me.
Do not let me perish in my sin, *
  nor condemn me to the depths of the earth.
For you, O Lord, are the God of those who repent, *
  and in me you will show forth your goodness.
Unworthy as I am, you will save me,
  in accordance with your great mercy, *
  and I will praise you without ceasing all the days of my life.
For all the powers of heaven sing your praises, *
  and yours is the glory to ages of ages. Amen.

Canticle 15 The Song of Mary *Magnificat*
Luke 1:46-55

My soul proclaims the greatness of the Lord,
    my spirit rejoices in God my Savior; *
    for he has looked with favor on his lowly servant.
From this day all generations will call me blessed: *
    the Almighty has done great things for me,
    and holy is his Name.
He has mercy on those who fear him *
    in every generation.

He has shown the strength of his arm, *
    he has scattered the proud in their conceit.
He has cast down the mighty from their thrones, *
    and has lifted up the lowly.
He has filled the hungry with good things, *
    and the rich he has sent away empty.
He has come to the help of his servant Israel, *
    for he has remembered his promise of mercy,
The promise he made to our fathers, *
    to Abraham and his children for ever.

Glory be to the Father, and to the Son, and to the Holy Spirit: *
as it was in the beginning, is now, and ever shall be, world
without end. Amen.

Canticle 16 The Song of Zechariah
Benedictus Dominus Deus   *Luke 1: 68-79*

Blessed be the Lord, the God of Israel; *
    he has come to his people and set them free.
He has raised up for us a mighty savior, *
    born of the house of his servant David.

Through his holy prophets he promised of old,
  that he would save us from our enemies, *
  from the hands of all who hate us.
He promised to show mercy to our fathers *
  and to remember his holy covenant.
This was the oath he swore to our father Abraham, *
  to set us free from the hands of our enemies,
Free to worship him without fear, *
  holy and righteous in his sight all the days of our life.
You, my child, shall be called the prophet of the Most High, *
  for you will go before the Lord to prepare his way,
To give his people knowledge of salvation *
  by the forgiveness of their sins.
In the tender compassion of our God *
  the dawn from on high shall break upon us,
To shine on those who dwell in darkness and the shadow of death, *
  and to guide our feet into the way of peace.

Glory be to the Father, and to the Son, and to the Holy Spirit: *
as it was in the beginning, is now, and ever shall be, world
without end. Amen.

Canticle 17 The Song of Simeon *Nunc Dimittis*
Luke 2:29-32

Lord, you now have set your servant free *
  to go in peace as you have promised;
For these eyes of mine have seen the Savior, *
  whom you have prepared for all the world to see:
A Light to enlighten the nations, *
  and the glory of your people Israel.

Glory be to the Father, and to the Son, and to the Holy Spirit: *
as it was in the beginning, is now, and ever shall be, world
without end. Amen.

Canticle 18 A Song to the Lamb *Dignus es*
Revelation 4:11, 5:9-10, 13

Splendor and honor and kingly power *
   are yours by right, O Lord our God,
For you created everything that is, *
   and by your will they were created and have their
being;
And yours by right, O Lamb that was slain, *
   for with your blood you have redeemed for God,
From every family, language, people, and nation, *
   a kingdom of priests to serve our God.

And so, to him who sits upon the throne, *
   and to Christ the Lamb,
Be worship and praise, dominion and splendor, *
   for ever and for evermore.

Canticle 19 The Song of the Redeemed
Magna et mirabilia   *Revelation 15:3-4*

O ruler of the universe, Lord God,
   great deeds are they that you have done, *
   surpassing human understanding.
Your ways are ways of righteousness and truth, *
   O King of all the ages.
Who can fail to do you homage, Lord,
   and sing the praises of your Name? *
   for you only are the Holy One.
All nations will draw near and fall down before you, *
   because your just and holy works have been
revealed.

Glory be to the Father, and to the Son, and to the Holy Spirit: *
as it was in the beginning, is now, and ever shall be, world
without end. Amen.

Canticle 20 Glory to God *Gloria in excelsis*

Glory to God in the highest,
  and peace to his people on earth.
Lord God, heavenly King,
almighty God and Father,
  we worship you, we give you thanks,
  we praise you for your glory.
Lord Jesus Christ, only Son of the Father,
Lord God, Lamb of God,
you take away the sin of the world:
  have mercy on us;
you are seated at the right hand of the Father:
  receive our prayer.
For you alone are the Holy One,
you alone are the Lord,
you alone are the Most High,
  Jesus Christ,
  with the Holy Spirit,
  in the glory of God the Father. Amen.

Canticle 21 You are God *Te Deum laudamus*

You are God: we praise you;
You are the Lord; we acclaim you;
You are the eternal Father:
All creation worships you.
To you all angels, all the powers of heaven,
Cherubim and Seraphim, sing in endless praise:
  Holy, holy, holy Lord, God of power and might,
  heaven and earth are full of your glory.

The glorious company of apostles praise you.
The noble fellowship of prophets praise you.
The white-robed army of martyrs praise you.

The Book of Common Prayer 22

Throughout the world the holy Church acclaims you;
Father, of majesty unbounded,
your true and only Son, worthy of all worship,
and the Holy Spirit, advocate and guide.

You, Christ, are the king of glory,
the eternal Son of the Father.
When you became man to set us free
you did not shun the Virgin's womb.
You overcame the sting of death
and opened the kingdom of heaven to all believers.
You are seated at God's right hand in glory.
We believe that you will come and be our judge.
Come then, Lord, and help your people,
bought with the price of your own blood,
and bring us with your saints
to glory everlasting.

The Apostles' Creed

Officiant and People together, all standing

I believe in God, the Father almighty, creator of heaven and earth.

I believe in Jesus Christ, his only son, our Lord. He was conceived by the power of the Holy Spirit and born of the Virgin Mary. He suffered under Pontius Pilate, was crucified, died, and was buried. He descended to the dead. On the third day he rose again. He ascended into heaven, and is seated at the right hand of the Father. He will come again to judge the living and the dead.

I believe in the Holy Spirit, the holy catholic Church, the communion of saints, the forgiveness of sins, the resurrection of the body, and the life everlasting. Amen.

The Prayers

The People stand or kneel

Officiant	The Lord be with you.
People	And also with you.
Officiant	Let us pray.

Officiant and People

Our Father, who art in heaven, hallowed be thy Name, thy kingdom come, thy will be done, on earth as it is in heaven. Give us this day our daily bread. And forgive us our trespasses, as we forgive those who trespass against us. And lead us not into temptation, but deliver us from evil. For thine is the kingdom, and the power, and the glory, for ever and ever. Amen.

Or this

Our Father in heaven, hallowed be your Name, your kingdom come, your will be done, on earth as in heaven. Give us today our daily bread. Forgive us our sins as we forgive those who sin against us. Save us from the time of trial, and deliver us from evil. For the kingdom, the power, and the glory are yours, now and for ever. Amen.

Then follows one of these sets of Suffrages

Suffrages A

V. Show us your mercy, O Lord;
R. And grant us your salvation.
V. Clothe your ministers with righteousness;
R. Let your people sing with joy.
V. Give peace, O Lord, in all the world;
R. For only in you can we live in safety.

V. Lord, keep this nation under your care;

R. And guide us in the way of justice and truth.

V. Let your way be known upon earth;

R. Your saving health among all nations.

V. Let not the needy, O Lord, be forgotten;

R. Nor the hope of the poor be taken away.

V. Create in us clean hearts, O God;

R. And sustain us by your Holy Spirit.

Suffrages B

V. Save your people, Lord, and bless your inheritance;

R. Govern and uphold them, now and always.

V. Day by day we bless you;

R. We praise your name for ever.

V. Lord, keep us from all sin today;

R. Have mercy on us, Lord, have mercy.

V. Lord, show us your love and mercy;

R. For we put our trust in you.

V. In you, Lord, is our hope;

R. And we shall never hope in vain.

The Officiant then says one or more of the following Collects

The Collect of the Day

A Collect for Sundays

O God, you make us glad with the weekly remembrance of the glorious resurrection of you Son our Lord: Give us this day such blessing through our worship of you, that the week to come may be spent in your favor; through Jesus Christ our Lord. *Amen.*

A Collect for Fridays

Almighty God, whose most dear Son went not up to joy but first he suffered pain, and entered not into glory before he was crucified: Mercifully grant that we, walking in the way of the cross, may find it none other than the way of life and peace; through Jesus Christ your Son our Lord. *Amen.*

A Collect for Saturdays

Almighty God, who after the creation of the world rested from all you works and sanctified a day of rest for all your creatures: Grant that we, putting away all earthly anxieties, may be duly prepared for the service of your sanctuary, and that our rest here upon earth may be a preparation for the eternal rest promised to your people in heaven; through Jesus Christ our Lord. *Amen.*

A Collect for the Renewal of Life

O God, the King eternal, whose light divides the day from the night and turns the shadow of death into the morning: Drive far from us all wrong desires, incline our hearts to keep your law, and guide our feet into the way of peace; that, having done your will with cheerfulness during the day, we may, when night comes, rejoice to give you thanks; through Jesus Christ our Lord. *Amen.*

A Collect for Peace

O God, the author of peace and lover of concord, to know you is eternal life and to serve you is perfect freedom: Defend us, your humble servants, in all assaults of our enemies; that we, surely trusting in your defense, may not fear the power of any adversaries; through the might of Jesus Christ our Lord, *Amen.*

A Collect for Grace

Lord God, almighty and everlasting Father, you have brought us in safety to this new day: Preserve us with your mighty power, that we may not fall into sin, nor be overcome by adversity; and in all we do, direct us to the fulfilling of your purpose; through Jesus Christ our Lord. *Amen.*

A Collect for Guidance

Heavenly Father, in you we live and move and have our being: We humbly pray you so to guide and govern us by your Holy Spirit, that in all the cares and occupations of our life we may not forget you, but may remember that we are ever walking in your sight; through Jesus Christ our Lord. *Amen.*

Then, unless the Eucharist or a form of general intercession is to follow, one of these prayer for mission is added.

Almighty and everlasting God, by whose Spirit the whole body of your faithful people is governed and sanctified: Receive our supplications and prayers which we offer before you for all members of you holy Church, that in their vocation and ministry they may truly and devoutly serve you; through our Lord and Savior Jesus Christ. *Amen.*

or this

O God, you have made of one blood all the peoples of the earth, and sent your blessed Son to preach peace to those who are far off and to those who are near: Grant that people everywhere may seek after you and find you; bring the nations into your fold; pour out your Spirit upon all flesh, and hasten the coming of your kingdom; through Jesus Christ our Lord. *Amen.*

or the following

Lord Jesus Christ, you stretched out your arms of love on the hard wood of the cross that everyone might come within the reach of your saving embrace: So clothe us in your Spirit that we, reaching forth our hands in love, may bring those who do not know you to the knowledge and love of you; for the honor of your Name. *Amen.*

Here may be sung a hymn or anthem.

Authorized intercessions and thanksgivings may follow.

Before the close of the Office one or both of the following may be used

The General Thanksgiving

Officiant and People

Almighty God, Father of all mercies, we your unworthy servants give you humble thanks for all your goodness and loving-kindness to us and to all whom you have made. We bless you for our creation, preservation, and all the blessings of this life; but above all for your immeasurable love in the redemption of the world by our Lord Jesus Christ; for the means of grace, and for the hope of glory. And, we pray, give us such an awareness of your mercies, that with truly thankful hearts we may show forth your praise, not only with our lips, but in our lives, by giving up our selves to your service, and by walking before you in holiness and righteousness all our days; through Jesus Christ our Lord, to whom, with you and the Holy Spirit, be honor and glory throughout all ages. *Amen.*

A Prayer of St. Chrysostom

Almighty God, you have given us grace at this time with one accord to make our common supplication to you; and you have promised through your well-beloved Son that when two or three are gathered together in his Name you will be in the midst of them: Fulfill now, O Lord, our desires and petitions as may be best for us; granting us in this world knowledge of your truth, and in the age to come life everlasting. *Amen.*

Then may be said

Let us bless the Lord.
Thanks be to God.

From Easter Day through the Day of Pentecost "Alleluia, alleluia" may be added to the preceding versicle and response.

The Officiant may then conclude with one of the following

The grace of our Lord Jesus Christ, and the love of God, and the fellowship of the Holy Spirit, be with us all evermore. *Amen.*
        2 Corinthians 13:14

May the God of hope fill us with all joy and peace in believing through the power of the Holy Spirit. *Amen.*
        Romans 15:13

Glory to God whose power, working in us, can do infinitely more than we can ask or imagine: Glory to him from generation to generation in the Church, and in Christ Jesus for ever and ever. *Amen.*
        Ephesians 3:20,21

An Order of Service
for Noonday

Officiant	O God, make speed to save us.
People	O Lord, make haste to help us.

Officiant and People
Glory be to the Father, and to the Son, and to the Holy Spirit: *
as it was in the beginning, is now, and ever shall be, world
without end. Amen.

Except in Lent, add Alleluia.

A suitable hymn may be sung.

*One or more of the following Psalms is sung or said. Other
suitable selections include Psalms 19,67, one or more sections
of Psalm 119, or a selection from Psalms 120 through 133.*

Psalm 119   *Lucerna pedibus meis*

105 Your word is a lantern to my feet *
  and a light upon my path.
106 I have sworn and am determined *
  to keep your righteous judgments.
107 I am deeply troubled; *
  preserve my life, O Lord, according to your word.
108 Accept, O LORD, the willing tribute of my lips, *
  and teach me your judgments.
109 My life is always in my hand, *
  yet I do not forget your law.
110 The wicked have set a trap for me, *
  but I have not strayed from your commandments.
111 Your decrees are my inheritance for ever; *
  truly, they are the joy of my heart.
112 I have applied my heart to fulfill your statues *
  for ever and to the end.

Psalm 121 *Levavi oculos*

1 I lift up my eyes to the hills; *
   from where is my help to come?
2 My help comes from the LORD, *
   the maker of heaven and earth.
3 He will not let your foot be moved *
   and he who watches over you will not fall asleep.
4 Behold, he who keeps watch over Israel *
   shall neither slumber nor sleep;
5 The LORD himself watches over you; *
   the LORD is your shade at your right hand,
6 So that the sun shall not strike you by day, *
   nor the moon by night.
7 The LORD shall preserve you from all evil; *
   it is he who shall keep you safe.
8 The LORD shall watch over your going out and
your coming in, *
   from this time forth for evermore.

Psalm 126 *In convertendo*

1 When the LORD restored the fortunes of Zion, *
   then were we like those who dream.
2 Then was our mouth filled with laughter, *
   and our tongue with shouts of joy.
3 Then they said among the nations, *
   "The LORD has done great things for them."
4 The LORD has done great things for us, *
   and we are glad indeed.
5 Restore our fortunes, O LORD, *
   like the watercourses of the Negev.
6 Those who sowed with tears *
   will reap with songs of joy.
7 Those who go out weeping, carrying the seed, *
   will come again with joy, shouldering their sheaves.

Glory be to the Father, and to the Son, and to the Holy Spirit: *
as it was in the beginning, is now, and ever shall be, world
without end. Amen.

*One of the following, or some other suitable passage of
Scripture, is read*

The love of God has been poured into our hearts through the
Holy Spirit that has been given to us. *Romans 5:5*

People   Thanks be to God.

     or the following

If anyone is in Christ he is a new creation; the old has
passed away, behold the new has come. All this is
from God, who through Christ reconciled us to himself
and gave us the ministry of reconciliation.
2 Corinthians 5:17-18

People   Thanks be to God.

     or this

From the rising of the sun to its setting my Name shall
be great among the nations, and in every place incense
shall be offered to my Name, and a pure offering; for
my Name shall be great among the nations, says the
Lord of Hosts. *Malachi 1:11*

People   Thanks be to God.

A meditation, silent or spoken, may follow.

The Officiant then begins the Prayers

Lord, have mercy.
Christ, have mercy.
Lord, have mercy.

Our Father, who art in heaven, hallowed be thy Name, thy kingdom come, thy will be done, on earth as it is in heaven. Give us this day our daily bread. And forgive us our trespasses, as we forgive those who trespass against us. And lead us not into temptation, but deliver us from evil. For thine is the kingdom, and the power, and the glory, for ever and ever. Amen.

or this

Our Father in heaven, hallowed be your Name, your kingdom come, your will be done, on earth as in heaven. Give us today our daily bread. Forgive us our sins as we forgive those who sin against us. Save us from the time of trial, and deliver us from evil. For the kingdom, the power, and the glory are yours, now and for ever. Amen.

Officiant	Lord, hear our prayer;
People	And let our cry come to you.
Officiant	Let us pray.

The Officiant then says one of the following Collect. If desired, the Collect of the Day may be used.

Heavenly Father, send your Holy Spirit into our hearts, to direct and rule us according to your will, to comfort us in all our afflictions, to defend us from all error, and to lead us into all truth; through Jesus Christ our Lord. *Amen.*

Blessed Savior, at this hour you hung upon the cross, stretching out your loving arms: Grant that all the peoples of the earth may look to you and be saved; for your tender mercies' sake. *Amen.*

Almighty Savior, who at noonday called your servant Saint Paul to be an apostle to the Gentiles: We pray you to illumine the world with the radiance of your glory, that all nations may come and worship you; for you live and reign for ever and ever. *Amen.*

Lord Jesus Christ, you said to your apostles, "Peace I give to you; my peace I leave with you:" Regard not our sins, but the faith of your Church, and give to us the peace and unity of that heavenly city, where with the Father and the Holy Spirit you live and reign, now and for ever. *Amen.*

Free intercessions may be offered.

The service concludes as follows

Officiant	Let us bless the Lord.
People	Thanks be to God.

Daily Evening Prayer:
Contemporary Rite

*The Officiant begins the service with one or more of the
following sentences of Scripture, or of those from Morning
Prayer, and continuing with the appointed Psalmody; or with the
versicle "O God, make speed to save us" on page 39*

Let my prayer be set forth in your sight as incense, the
lifting up of my hands as the evening sacrifice. *Psalm
141:2*

Grace to you and peace from God our Father and from
the Lord Jesus Christ. *Philippians 1:2*

Worship the Lord in the beauty of holiness; let the
whole earth tremble before him. *Psalm 96:9*

Yours is the day, O God, yours also the night; you
established the moon and the sun. You fixed all the
boundaries of the earth; you made both summer and
winter. *Psalm 74:15,16*

I will bless the Lord who gives me counsel; my heart
teaches me, night after night. I have set the Lord
always before me; because he is at my right hand, I
shall not fall. *Psalm 16:7,8*

Seek him who made the Pleiades and Orion, and turns
deep darkness into the morning, and darkens the day
into night; who calls for the waters of the sea and
pours them out upon the surface of the earth: The Lord
is his name. *Amos 5:8*

If I say, "Surely the darkness will cover me, and the light around me turn to night," darkness is not dark to you, O Lord; the night is as bright as the day; darkness and light to you are both alike.   *Psalm 139:10,11*

Jesus said, "I am the light of the world; whoever follows me will not walk in darkness, but will have the light of life."   *John 8:12*

The following Confession of Sin may then be said; or the Office may continue at once with "O God make speed to save us."

Confession of Sin

The Officiant says to the people

Dear friends in Christ, here in the presence of Almighty God, let us kneel in silence, and with penitent and obedient hearts confess our sins, so that we may obtain forgiveness by his infinite goodness and mercy.

> *or this*

Let us confess our sins against God and our neighbor.

Silence may be kept.

Officiant and People together, all kneeling

Most merciful God, we confess that we have sinned against you in thought, word, and deed, by what we have done, and by what we have left undone. We have not loved you with our whole heart; we have not loved our neighbors as ourselves. We are truly sorry and we humbly repent. For the sake of your Son Jesus Christ, have mercy on us and forgive us; that we may delight in your will, and walk in your ways, to the glory of your Name. Amen.

Almighty God have mercy on you, forgive you all
your sins through our Lord Jesus Christ, strengthen
you in all goodness, and by the power of the Holy
Spirit keep you in eternal life. *Amen.*

*A deacon or lay person using the preceding form remains
kneeling, and substitutes "us" for "you" and "our" for "your."*

The Invitatory and Psalter

All stand

Officiant	O God, make speed to save us..
People	O Lord, make haste to help us..

Officiant and People

Glory be to the Father, and to the Son, and to the Holy Spirit: *
as it was in the beginning, is now, and ever shall be, world
without end. Amen.

Except in Lent, add Alleluia.

*The following, or some other suitable hymn, or an Invitatory
Psalm, may be sung or said*

O Gracious Light *Phos hilaron*

O gracious Light,
    pure brightness of the everliving Father in heaven,
    O Jesus Christ, holy and blessed!

Now as we come to the setting of the sun,
    and our eyes behold the vesper light,
    we sing your praises, O God: Father, Son, and Holy Spirit.

You are worthy at all times to be praised by happy voices,
   O Son of God, O Giver of life,
   and to be glorified through all the worlds.

Then follows

The Psalm or Psalms Appointed

At the end of the Psalms is sung or said

Glory be to the Father, and to the Son, and to the Holy Spirit: *
as it was in the beginning, is now, and ever shall be, world
without end. Amen.

The Lessons

*One or two lessons, as appointed, are read, the Reader first
saying*

A Reading (Lesson) from _____.

A citation giving chapter and verse may be added.

After each Lesson the Reader may say
                The Word of the Lord.
Answer   Thanks be to God.

Or the Reader may say
                Here ends the Lesson (Reading).

*Silence may be kept after each Reading. One of the following
Canticles, or one of those from Morning Prayer is sung or said
after each Reading. If three Lessons are used, the Lesson from
the Gospel is read after the second Canticle.*

The Song of Mary *Magnificat*   *Luke 1:46-55*

My soul proclaims the greatness of the Lord,
   my spirit rejoices in God my Savior; *
   for he has looked with favor on his lowly servant.
From this day all generations will call me blessed: *
   the Almighty has done great things for me,
   and holy is his Name.
He has mercy on those who fear him *
   in every generation.
He has shown the strength of his arm, *
   he has scattered the proud in their conceit.
He has cast down the mighty from their thrones, *
   and has lifted up the lowly.
He has filled the hungry with good things, *
   and the rich he has sent away empty.
He has come to the help of his servant Israel, *
   for he has remembered his promise of mercy,
The promise he made to our fathers, *
   to Abraham and his children for ever.

Glory be to the Father, and to the Son, and to the Holy Spirit: *
as it was in the beginning, is now, and ever shall be, world
without end. Amen.

The Song of Simeon *Nunc Dimittis*
Luke 2:29-32

Lord, you now have set your servant free *
   to go in peace as you have promised;
For these eyes of mine have seen the Savior, *
   whom you have prepared for all the world to see:
A Light to enlighten the nations, *
   and the glory of your people Israel.

Glory be to the Father, and to the Son, and to the Holy Spirit: *
as it was in the beginning, is now, and ever shall be, world
without end. Amen.

The Apostles' Creed

Officiant and People together, all standing

I believe in God, the Father almighty, creator of
heaven and earth.

I believe in Jesus Christ, his only son, our Lord. He
was conceived by the power of the Holy Spirit and
born of the Virgin Mary. He suffered under Pontius
Pilate, was crucified, died, and was buried. He
descended to the dead. On the third day he rose again.
He ascended into heaven, and is seated at the right
hand of the Father. He will come again to judge the
living and the dead.

I believe in the Holy Spirit, the holy catholic Church,
the communion of saints, the forgiveness of sins, the
resurrection of the body, and the life everlasting.
Amen.

The Prayers

The People stand or kneel

Officiant	The Lord be with you.
People	And also with you.
Officiant	Let us pray.

Officiant and People

Our Father, who art in heaven, hallowed be thy Name, thy kingdom come, thy will be done, on earth as it is in heaven. Give us this day our daily bread. And forgive us our trespasses, as we forgive those who trespass against us. And lead us not into temptation, but deliver us from evil. For thine is the kingdom, and the power, and the glory, for ever and ever. Amen.

Or this

Our Father in heaven, hallowed be your Name, your kingdom come, your will be done, on earth as in heaven. Give us today our daily bread. Forgive us our sins as we forgive those who sin against us. Save us from the time of trial, and deliver us from evil. For the kingdom, the power, and the glory are yours, now and for ever. Amen.

Then follows one of these sets of Suffrages

Suffrages A

V. Show us your mercy, O Lord;
R. And grant us your salvation.
V. Clothe your ministers with righteousness;
R. Let your people sing with joy.
V. Give peace, O Lord, in all the world;
R. For only in you can we live in safety.
V. Lord, keep this nation under your care;
R. And guide us in the way of justice and truth.
V. Let your way be known upon earth;
R. Your saving health among all nations.
V. Let not the needy, O Lord, be forgotten;
R. Nor the hope of the poor be taken away.
V. Create in us clean hearts, O God;
R. And sustain us by your Holy Spirit.

Suffrages B

That this evening may be holy, good, and peaceful,
We entreat you, O Lord.

That your holy angels may lead us in paths of peace and goodwill,
We entreat you, O Lord.

That we may be pardoned and forgiven for our sins and offenses,
We entreat you, O Lord.

That there may be peace to your Church and to the whole world,
We entreat you, O Lord.

That we may depart this life in your faith and fear, and not be condemned before the great judgment seat of Christ,
We entreat you, O Lord.

That we may be bound together by your Holy Spirit in the communion of [_____ and] all your saints, entrusting one another and all our life to Christ,
We entreat you, O Lord.

The Officiant then says one or more of the following Collects

The Collect of the Day

A Collect for Sundays

Lord God, whose Son our Savior Jesus Christ triumphed over the powers of death and prepared for us our place in the new Jerusalem: Grant that we, who have this day given thanks for his resurrection, may praise you in that City of which he is the light, and where he lives and reigns for ever and ever. *Amen.*

A Collect for Fridays

Lord Jesus Christ, by your death you took away the sting of death: Grant to us your servants so to follow in faith where you have led the way, that we may at length fall asleep peacefully in you and wake up in your likeness; for your tender mercies' sake. *Amen.*

A Collect for Saturdays

O God, the source of eternal light: Shed forth your unending day upon us who watch for you, that our lips may praise you, our lives may bless you, and our worship on the morrow give you glory; through Jesus Christ our Lord. *Amen.*

A Collect for Peace

Most holy God, the source of all good desires, all right judgments, and all just works: Give to us, your servants, that peace which the world cannot give, so that our minds may be fixed on the doing of your will, and that we, being delivered from the fear of all enemies, may live in peace and quietness; through the mercies of Christ Jesus our Savior. *Amen.*

A Collect for Aid against Perils

Be our light in the darkness, O Lord, and in your great mercy defend us from all perils and dangers of this night; for the love of your only Son, our Savior Jesus Christ. *Amen.*

A Collect for Protection

O God, the life of all who live, the light of the faithful, the strength of those who labor, and the repose of the dead: We thank you for the blessings of the day that is past, and humbly ask for your protection through the coming night. Bring us in safety to the morning hours; through him who died and rose again for us, your Son our Savior Jesus Christ. *Amen.*

A Collect for the Presence of Christ

Lord Jesus, stay with us, for evening is at hand and the day is past; be our companion in the way, kindle our hearts, and awaken hope, that we may know you as you are revealed in Scripture and the breaking of bread. Grant this for the sake of your love. *Amen.*

Then, unless the Eucharist or a form of general intercession is to follow, one of these prayers for mission is added

O God and Father of all, whom the whole heavens adore: Let the whole earth also worship you, all nations obey you, all tongues confess and bless you, and men and women everywhere love you and serve you in peace; through Jesus Christ our Lord. *Amen.*

or this

Keep watch, dear Lord, with those who work, or watch, or weep this night, and give your angels charge over those who sleep. Tend the sick, Lord Christ; give rest to the weary, bless the dying, soothe the suffering, pity the afflicted, shield the joyous; and all for your love's sake. *Amen.*

or the following

O God, you manifest in your servants the signs of your presence: Send forth upon us the Spirit of love, that in companionship with one another your abounding grace may increase among us; through Jesus Christ our Lord. *Amen.*

Here may be sung a hymn or anthem.

Authorized intercessions and thanksgivings may follow.

Before the close of the Office one or both of the following may be used

The General Thanksgiving

Officiant and People

Almighty God, Father of all mercies, we your unworthy servants give you humble thanks for all your goodness and loving-kindness to us and to all whom you have made. We bless you for our creation, preservation, and all the blessings of this life; but above all for your immeasurable love in the redemption of the world by our Lord Jesus Christ; for the means of grace, and for the hope of glory. And, we pray, give us such an awareness of your mercies, that with truly thankful hearts we may show forth your praise, not only with our lips, but in our lives, by giving up our selves to your service, and by walking before you in holiness and righteousness all our days; through Jesus Christ our Lord, to whom, with you and the Holy Spirit, be honor and glory throughout all ages. *Amen.*

A Prayer of St. Chrysostom

Almighty God, you have given us grace at this time with one accord to make our common supplication to you; and you have promised through your well-beloved Son that when two or three are gathered together in his Name you will be in the midst of them: Fulfill now, O Lord, our desires and petitions as may be best for us; granting us in this world knowledge of your truth, and in the age to come life everlasting. *Amen.*

Then may be said

Let us bless the Lord.
Thanks be to God.

From Easter Day through the Day of Pentecost "Alleluia, alleluia" may be added to the preceding versicle and response.

The Officiant may then conclude with one of the following

The grace of our Lord Jesus Christ, and the love of God, and the fellowship of the Holy Spirit, be with us all evermore. *Amen.*
 2 Corinthians 13:14

May the God of hope fill us with all joy and peace in believing through the power of the Holy Spirit. *Amen.*
 Romans 15:13

Glory to God whose power, working in us, can do infinitely more than we can ask or imagine: Glory to him from generation to generation in the Church, and in Christ Jesus for ever and ever. *Amen.*
 Ephesians 3:20,21

An Order for Compline

The Officiant begins

The Lord Almighty grant us a peaceful night and a perfect end. *Amen.*

Officiant	Our help is in the Name of the Lord;
People	The maker of heaven and earth.

The Officiant may then say
Let us confess our sins to God.

Silence may be kept

Officiant and People

Almighty God, our heavenly Father: We have sinned against you, through our own fault, in thought, and word, and deed, and in what we have left undone. For the sake of your Son our Lord Jesus Christ, forgive us all our offenses; and grant that we may serve you in newness of life, to the glory of your Name. Amen.

Officiant

May the Almighty God grant us forgiveness of all our sins, and the grace and comfort of the Holy Spirit. *Amen.*

The Officiant then says

	O God, make speed to save us.
People	O Lord, make haste to help us.

Officiant and People

Glory be to the Father, and to the Son, and to the Holy Spirit: *
as it was in the beginning, is now, and ever shall be, world
without end. Amen..

Except in Lent, add   Alleluia.

*One or more of the following Psalms are sung or said. Other
suitable selections may be substituted.*

Psalm 4 *Cum invocarem*

1 Answer me when I call, O God, defender of my
     cause; *
   you set me free when I am hard-pressed;
   have mercy on me and hear my prayer.

2 "You mortals, how long will you dishonor my
     glory? *
   how long will you worship dumb idols
   and run after false gods?"

3 Know that the LORD does wonders for the faithful; *
   when I call upon the LORD, he will hear me.

4 Tremble, then, and do not sin; *
   speak to your heart in silence upon your bed.

5 Offer the appointed sacrifices *
   and put your trust in the LORD.

6 Many are saying, "Oh, that we might see better
     times!" *
   Lift up the light of your countenance upon us, O
   LORD.

7 You have put gladness in my heart, *
  more than when grain and wine and oil increase.

8 I lie down in peace; at once I fall asleep; *
  for only you, LORD, make me dwell in safety.

Psalm 31 *In te, Domine, speravi*

1 In you, O LORD, have I taken refuge;
  let me never be put to shame: *
  deliver me in your righteousness.

2 Incline your ear to me; *
  make haste to deliver me.

3 Be my strong rock, a castle to keep me safe,
  for you are my crag and my stronghold; *
  for the sake of your Name, lead me and guide me.

4 Take me out of the net that they have secretly set for
  me, *
  for you are my tower of strength.

5 Into your hands I commend my spirit, *
  for you have redeemed me,
  O LORD, O God of truth.

Psalm 91 *Qui habitat*

1 He who dwells in the shelter of the Most High *
  abides under the shadow of the Almighty.

2 He shall say to the LORD,
  "You are my refuge and my stronghold, *
  my God in whom I put my trust."

3   He shall deliver you from the snare of the hunter *
    and from the deadly pestilence.

4   He shall cover you with his pinions,
    and you shall find refuge under his wings; *
    his faithfulness shall be a shield and buckler.

5   You shall not be afraid of any terror by night, *
    nor of the arrow that flies by day;

6   Of the plague that stalks in the darkness, *
    nor of the sickness that lays waste at mid-day.

7   A thousand shall fall at your side
    and ten thousand at your right hand, *
    but it shall not come near you.

8   Your eyes have only to behold *
    to see the reward of the wicked.

9   Because you have made the LORD your refuge, *
    and the Most High your habitation,

10 There shall no evil happen to you, *
    neither shall any plague come near your dwelling.

11 For he shall give his angels charge over you, *
    to keep you in all your ways.

12 They shall bear you in their hands, *
    lest you dash your foot against a stone.

13 You shall tread upon the lion and adder; *
    you shall trample the young lion and the serpent
    under your feet.

14 Because he is bound to me in love,
    therefore will I deliver him; *
    I will protect him, because he knows my Name.

15 He shall call upon me, and I will answer him; *
    I am with him in trouble;
    I will rescue him and bring him to honor.
16 With long life will I satisfy him, *
    and show him my salvation.

Psalm 134 *Ecce nunc*

1 Behold now, bless the LORD, all you servants of the
   LORD, *
   you that stand by night in the house of the LORD.

2 Lift up your hands in the holy place and bless the
   LORD; *
   the LORD who made heaven and earth bless you
   out of Zion.

At the end of the Psalms is sung or said

Glory be to the Father, and to the Son, and to the Holy Spirit: *
as it was in the beginning, is now, and ever shall be, world
without end. Amen.

*One of the following, or some other suitable passage of
Scripture, is read*

Lord, you are in the midst of us, and we are called by
your Name: Do not forsake us, O Lord our God.
Jeremiah 14:9,22

People Thanks be to God.

or this

Come to me, all who labor and are heavy-laden, and I will give you rest. Take my yoke upon you, and learn from me; for I am gentle and lowly in heart, and you will find rest for your souls. For my yoke is easy, and my burden is light. *Matthew 11:28-30*

People Thanks be to God.

> *or the following*

May the God of peace, who brought again from the dead our Lord Jesus, the great shepherd of the sheep, by the blood of the eternal covenant, equip you with everything good that you may do his will, working in you that which is pleasing in his sight, through Jesus Christ; to whom be glory for ever and ever. *Hebrews 13:20-21*

People Thanks be to God.

> *or this*

Be sober, be watchful. Your adversary the devil prowls around like a roaring lion, seeking someone to devour. Resist him, firm in your faith. *I Peter 5:8-9a*

People Thanks be to God.

A hymn suitable for the evening may be sung.

Then follows

V. Into your hands, O Lord, I commend my spirit;
R. For you have redeemed me, O Lord, O God of truth.
V. Keep us, O Lord, as the apple of your eye;
R. Hide us under the shadow of your wings.

Lord, have mercy.
Christ, have mercy.
Lord, have mercy.

Officiant and People

Our Father, who art in heaven, hallowed be thy Name, thy kingdom come, thy will be done, on earth as it is in heaven. Give us this day our daily bread. And forgive us our trespasses, as we forgive those who trespass against us. And lead us not into temptation, but deliver us from evil. For thine is the kingdom, and the power, and the glory, for ever and ever. Amen.

Or this

Our Father in heaven, hallowed be your Name, your kingdom come, your will be done, on earth as in heaven. Give us today our daily bread. Forgive us our sins as we forgive those who sin against us. Save us from the time of trial, and deliver us from evil. For the kingdom, the power, and the glory are yours, now and for ever. Amen.

Officiant	Lord, hear our prayer;
People	And let our cry come to you.
Officiant	Let us pray.

The Officiant then says one of the following Collects

Be our light in the darkness, O Lord, and in your great mercy defend us from all perils and dangers of this night; for the love of your only Son, our Savior Jesus Christ. *Amen.*

Be present, O merciful God, and protect us through the hours of this night, so that we who are wearied by the changes and chances of this life may rest in your eternal changelessness; through Jesus Christ our Lord. *Amen.*

Look down, O Lord, from your heavenly throne, and illumine this night with your celestial brightness; that by night as by day your people may glorify your holy Name; through Jesus Christ our Lord. *Amen.*

Visit this place, O Lord, and drive far from it all snares of the enemy; let your holy angels dwell with us to preserve us in peace; and let your blessing be upon us always; through Jesus Christ our Lord. *Amen.*

A Collect for Saturdays

We give you thanks, O God, for revealing your Son Jesus Christ to us by the light of his resurrection: Grant that as we sing your glory at the close of this day, our joy may abound in the morning as we celebrate the Paschal mystery; through Jesus Christ our Lord. *Amen.*

One of the following prayers may be added

Keep watch, dear Lord, with those who work, or watch, or weep this night, and give your angels charge over those who sleep. Tend the sick, Lord Christ; give rest to the weary, bless the dying, soothe the suffering, pity the afflicted, shield the joyous; and all for your love's sake. *Amen.*

or this

O God, your unfailing providence sustains the world we live in and the life we live: Watch over those, both night and day, who work while others sleep, and grant that we may never forget that our common life depends upon each other's toil; through Jesus Christ our Lord. *Amen.*

Silence may be kept, and free intercessions and thanksgivings may be offered.

The service concludes with the Song of Simeon with this Antiphon, which is sung or said by all

Guide us waking, O Lord, and guard us sleeping; that awake we may watch with Christ, and asleep we may rest in peace.

In Easter Season, add Alleluia, alleluia, alleluia.

Lord, you now have set your servant free *
   to go in peace as you have promised;

For these eyes of mine have seen the Savior, *
   whom you have prepared for all the world to see:

A Light to enlighten the nations, *
   and the glory of your people Israel.

Glory be to the Father, and to the Son, and to the Holy Spirit: *
as it was in the beginning, is now, and ever shall be, world without end. Amen.

All repeat the Antiphon

Guide us waking, O Lord, and guard us sleeping; that awake we may watch with Christ, and asleep we may rest in peace.

In Easter Season, add Alleluia, alleluia, alleluia.

Officiant	Let us bless the Lord.
People	Thanks be to God.

The Officiant concludes

The almighty and merciful Lord, Father, Son, and Holy Spirit, bless us and keep us. *Amen.*

Concerning the Rite of Reconciliation

The ministry of reconciliation, which has been committed by Christ to his Church, is exercised through the care each Christian has for others, through the common prayer of Christians assembled for public worship, and through the priesthood of the Church and its ministers declaring absolution.

The Reconciliation of a Penitent is available for all who desire it. It is not restricted to times of sickness. Confessions may be heard anytime and anywhere.

The absolution in these services may be pronounced only by a bishop or priest. Another Christian may be asked to hear a confession, but it must be made clear to the penitent that absolution will not be pronounced; instead, a declaration of forgiveness is provided.

When a confession is heard in a church building, the confessor may sit inside the altar rails or in a place set aside to give greater privacy, and the penitent kneels nearby. If preferred, the confessor and penitent may sit face to face for a spiritual conference leading to absolution or a declaration of forgiveness.

When the penitent has confessed all serious sins troubling the conscience and has given evidence of due contrition, the priest gives such counsel and encouragement as are needed and pronounces absolution. Before giving absolution, the priest may assign to the penitent a psalm, prayer, or hymn to be said, or something to be done, as a sign of penitence and act of thanksgiving.

The content of a confession is not normally a matter of subsequent discussion. The secrecy of a confession is morally absolute for the confessor, and must under no circumstances be broken.

The Reconciliation of a Penitent

The Penitent begins

Bless me [father], for I have sinned.

The Priest says

The Lord be in your heart and upon your lips that you
may truly and humbly confess your sins: In the Name
of the Father, and of the Son, and of the Holy Spirit.
Amen.

Penitent

I confess to Almighty God, to his Church, and to you,
that I have sinned by my own fault in thought, word,
and deed, in things done and left undone; especially
_____ . For these and all other sins which I
cannot now remember, I am truly sorry. I pray God to
have mercy on me. I firmly intend amendment of life,
and I humbly beg forgiveness of God and his Church,
and ask you for counsel, direction, and absolution.

*Here the Priest may offer counsel, direction, and
comfort.*

The Priest then pronounces this absolution

Our Lord Jesus Christ, who has left power to his
Church to absolve all sinners who truly repent and
believe in him, of his great mercy forgive you all your
offenses; and by his authority committed to me, I
absolve you from all your sins: In the Name of the
Father, and of the Son, and of the Holy Spirit. Amen.

   or this

Our Lord Jesus Christ, who offered himself to be
sacrificed for us to the Father, and who conferred
power on his Church to forgive sins, absolve you
through my ministry by the grace of the Holy Spirit,
and restore you in the perfect peace of the Church.
Amen.

The Priest adds

The Lord has put away all your sins.

Penitent   Thanks be to God.

The Priest concludes

Go (or abide) in peace, and pray for me, a sinner.

*Declaration of Forgiveness to be used by a Deacon or
Lay Person*

Our Lord Jesus Christ, who offered himself to be
sacrificed for us to the Father, forgives your sins by the
grace of the Holy Spirit. Amen.

An Exhortation

This Exhortation may be used, in whole or in part, either during the Liturgy or at other times. In the absence of a deacon or priest, this Exhortation may be read by a lay person. The people stand or sit.

Beloved in the Lord: Our Savior Christ, on the night before he suffered, instituted the Sacrament of his Body and Blood as a sign and pledge of his love, for the continual remembrance of the sacrifice of his death, and for a spiritual sharing in his risen life. For in these holy Mysteries we are made one with Christ, and Christ with us; we are made one body in him, and members one of another.

Having in mind, therefore, his great love for us, and in obedience to his command, his Church renders to Almighty God our heavenly Father never-ending thanks for the creation of the world, for his continual providence over us, for his love for all mankind, and for the redemption of the world by our Savior Christ, who took upon himself our flesh, and humbled himself even to death on the cross, that he might make us the children of God by the power of the Holy Spirit, and exalt us to everlasting life.

But if we are to share rightly in the celebration of those holy Mysteries, and be nourished by that spiritual Food, we must remember the dignity of that holy Sacrament. I therefore call upon you to consider how Saint Paul exhorts all persons to   prepare themselves carefully before eating of that Bread and drinking of that Cup.

For, as the benefit is great, if with penitent hearts and living faith we receive the holy Sacrament, so is the danger great, if we receive it improperly, not recognizing the Lord's Body. Judge yourselves, therefore, lest you be judged by the Lord. Examine your lives and conduct by the rule of God's commandments, that you may perceive wherein you have offended in what you have done or left undone, whether in thought, word, or deed. And acknowledge your sins before Almighty God, with full purpose of amendment of life, being   ready to make restitution for all injuries and wrongs done by you to others; and also being ready to forgive those who have offended you, in order that you yourselves may be forgiven. And then, being reconciled with one another, come to the banquet of that most heavenly Food.

And if, in your preparation, you need help and counsel, then go and open your grief to a discreet and understanding priest, and confess your sins, that you may receive the benefit of absolution, and spiritual counsel and advice; to the removal of scruple and doubt, the assurance of pardon, and the strengthening of your faith.

To Christ our Lord who loves us, and washed us in his own blood, and made us a kingdom of priests to serve his God and Father, to him be glory in the Church evermore. Through him let us offer continually the sacrifice of praise, which is our bounden duty and service, and, with faith in him, come boldly before the throne of grace [and humbly confess our sins to Almighty God].

See Matthew 18:15-20 and 1 Corinthians 11:27-29

The Decalogue: Traditional

God spake these words, and said:
I am the Lord thy God who brought thee out of the
land of Egypt, out of the house of bondage. Thou shalt
have none other gods but me.
   Lord, have mercy upon us,
   and incline our hearts to keep this law.

Thou shalt not make to thyself any graven image, nor
the likeness of any thing that is in heaven above, or in
the earth beneath, or in the water under the earth; thou
shalt not bow down to them, nor worship them.
   Lord, have mercy upon us,
   and incline our hearts to keep this law.

Thou shalt not take the Name of the Lord thy God in
vain.
   Lord, have mercy upon us,
   and incline our hearts to keep this law.

Remember that thou keep holy the Sabbath day.
   Lord, have mercy upon us,
   and incline our hearts to keep this law.

Honor thy father and thy mother.
   Lord, have mercy upon us,
   and incline our hearts to keep this law.

Thou shalt do no murder.
   Lord, have mercy upon us,
   and incline our hearts to keep this law.

Thou shalt not commit adultery.

Lord, have mercy upon us,
and incline our hearts to keep this law.

Thou shalt not steal.
Lord, have mercy upon us,
and incline our hearts to keep this law.

Thou shalt not bear false witness against thy neighbor.
Lord, have mercy upon us,
and incline our hearts to keep this law.

Thou shalt not covet.
Lord, have mercy upon us,
and write all these thy laws in our hearts,
we beseech thee.

A Penitential Order
Contemporary Rite

For use at the beginning of the Liturgy, or as a separate service.

A hymn, psalm, or anthem may be sung.

The people standing, the Celebrant says

Blessed be God: Father, Son, and Holy Spirit.

People And blessed be his kingdom, now and for ever. Amen.

In place of the above, from Easter Day through the Day of Pentecost

Celebrant Alleluia. Christ is risen.
People The Lord is risen indeed. Alleluia.

In Lent and on other penitential occasions

Celebrant Bless the Lord who forgives all our sins;
People His mercy endures for ever.

When used as a separate service, the Exhortation, page 63, may be read, or a homily preached.

The Decalogue may be said, the people kneeling.

The Celebrant may read one of the following sentences

Jesus said, "The first commandment is this: Hear, O Israel: The Lord our God is the only Lord. Love the Lord your   God with all your heart, with all your soul, with all your mind, and with all your strength. The second is this: Love your neighbor as yourself. There is no other commandment greater than these."
   Mark 12:29-31

If we say that we have no sin, we deceive ourselves, and the   truth is not in us. But if we confess our sins, God, who is   faithful and just, will forgive our sins and cleanse us from all   unrighteousness.   *1 John 1 8 9*

Since we have a great high priest who has passed through the heavens, Jesus, the Son of God, let us with confidence draw near to the throne of grace, that we may receive mercy and find grace to help in time of need. *Hebrews 4:14, 16*

The Deacon or Celebrant then says

Let us confess our sins against God and our neighbor.

Silence may be kept.

Minister and People

Most merciful God,
    we confess that we have sinned against you
    in thought, word, and deed,
    by what we have done,
    and by what we have left undone.
We have not loved you with our whole heart;
    we have not loved our neighbors as ourselves.
We are truly sorry and we humbly repent.
For the sake of your Son Jesus Christ,
    have mercy on us and forgive us;
    that we may delight in your will,
    and walk in your ways,
    to the glory of your Name. Amen.

The Bishop when present, or the Priest, stands and says

Almighty God have mercy on you, forgive you all your sins through our Lord Jesus Christ, strengthen you in all goodness, and by the power of the Holy Spirit keep you in eternal life. *Amen.*

A deacon or lay person using the preceding form substitutes "us" for "you" and "our" for "your."

When this Order is used at the beginning of the Liturgy, the service continues with the Gloria in excelsis, the Kyrie eleison, or the Trisagion.

When used separately, it concludes with suitable prayers, and the Grace or a blessing.

Disciplinary Rubrics

If the priest knows that a person who is living a notoriously evil life intends to come to Communion, the priest shall speak to that person privately, and tell him that he may not come to the Holy Table until he has given clear proof of repentance and amendment of life.

The priest shall follow the same procedure with those who have done wrong to their neighbors and are a scandal to the other members of the congregation, not allowing such persons to receive Communion until they have made restitution for the wrong they have done, or have at least promised to do so.

When the priest sees that there is hatred between members of the congregation, he shall speak privately to each of them, telling them that they may not receive Communion until they have forgiven each other. And if the person or persons on one side truly forgive the others and desire and promise to make up for their faults, but those on the other side refuse to forgive, the priest shall allow those who are penitent to come to Communion, but not those who are stubborn.

In all such cases, the priest is required to notify the bishop, within 14 days at the most, giving the reasons for refusing Communion.

The Holy Eucharist
Contemporary Rite

The Word of God

A hymn, psalm, or anthem may be sung.

The people standing, the Celebrant says
> Blessed be God: Father, Son, and Holy Spirit.

People   And blessed be his kingdom, now and for ever. Amen.

In place of the above, from Easter Day through the Day of Pentecost

Celebrant   Alleluia. Christ is risen.
People   The Lord is risen indeed. Alleluia.

In Lent and on other penitential occasions

Celebrant   Bless the Lord who forgives all our sins;
People   His mercy endures for ever.

The Celebrant may say

Almighty God, to you all hearts are open, all desires known, and from you no secrets are hid: Cleanse the thoughts of our hearts by the inspiration of your Holy Spirit, that we may perfectly love you, and worthily magnify your holy Name;through Christ our Lord. *Amen.*

The Summary of the Law (p. 67) and General Confession (p. 77) may be offered here rather than later.

When appointed, the following hymn or some other song of praise is sung or said, all standing

Glory to God in the highest,
and peace to his people on earth.

Lord God, heavenly King,
almighty God and Father,
we worship you, we give you thanks
we praise you for your glory.

Lord Jesus Christ, only Son of the Father,
Lord God, Lamb of God,
you take away the sin of the world:
have mercy on us;
you are seated at the right hand of the Father:
receive our prayer.

For you alone are the Holy One,
you alone are the Lord,
you alone are the Most High,
Jesus Christ,
with the Holy Spirit,
in the glory of God the Father. Amen.

On other occasions the following is used

Lord, have mercy.		Kyrie eleison.
Christ, have mercy.	*or*	*Christe eleison.*
Lord, have mercy.		Kyrie eleison.

or this

Holy God,
Holy and Mighty,
Holy Immortal One,
Have mercy upon us.

The Collect of the Day

The Celebrant says to the people

The Lord be with you.

People   And also with you.

Celebrant   Let us pray.

The Celebrant says the Collect.

People   Amen.

The Lessons

The people sit. One or two Lessons, as appointed, are read, the Reader first saying

A Reading (Lesson) from _____ .

A citation giving chapter and verse may be added.

After each Reading, the Reader may say

The Word of the Lord.

People   Thanks be to God.

or the Reader may say   Here ends the Reading (Epistle).

Silence may follow.

A Psalm, hymn, or anthem may follow each Reading.

Then, all standing, the Deacon or a Priest reads the Gospel, first saying

The Holy Gospel of our Lord Jesus Christ according to _____ .

People   Glory to you, Lord Christ.

After the Gospel, the Reader says

　　　　　The Gospel of the Lord.

People　　　Praise to you, Lord Christ.

The Sermon

On Sundays and other Major Feasts there follows, all standing

The Nicene Creed　*"I" may be used in place of "We"*

We believe in one God,
　　the Father, the Almighty,
　　maker of heaven and earth,
　　of all that is, seen and unseen.
We believe in one Lord, Jesus Christ,
　　the only Son of God,
　　eternally begotten of the Father,
　　God from God, Light from Light,
　　true God from true God,
　　begotten, not made,
　　of one Being with the Father.
Through him all things were made.
For us and for our salvation
　　he came down from heaven:
　　by the power of the Holy Spirit
　　he became incarnate from the Virgin Mary,
　　and was made man.
For our sake he was crucified under Pontius Pilate;
　　he suffered death and was buried.
On the third day he rose again
　　in accordance with the Scriptures;
　　he ascended into heaven
　　and is seated at the right hand of the Father.
He will come again in glory to judge the living and the
　　dead, and his kingdom will have no end.

We believe in the Holy Spirit, the Lord, the giver of life,
who proceeds from the Father and the Son.
With the Father and the Son he is worshiped and
glorified.
He has spoken through the Prophets.
We believe in one holy catholic and apostolic
Church.
We acknowledge one baptism for the forgiveness
of sins.
We look for the resurrection of the dead,
and the life of the world to come. Amen.

The Prayers of the People

Form III

The Leader and People pray responsively

Father, we pray for your holy Catholic Church;
That we all may be one.

Grant that every member of the Church may truly and
humbly serve you;
That your Name may be glorified by all people.

We pray for all bishops, priests, and deacons;
*That they may be faithful ministers of your Word and
Sacraments.*

We pray for all who govern and hold authority in the
nations of the world;
That there may be justice and peace on the earth.

Give us grace to do your will in all that we undertake;
That our works may find favor in your sight.

Have compassion on those who suffer from any grief
or trouble;
That they may be delivered from their distress.

Give to the departed eternal rest;
Let light perpetual shine upon them.

We praise you for your saints who have entered into joy;
May we also come to share in your heavenly kingdom.

Let us pray for our own needs and those of others.

Silence

The People may add their own petitions.

The Celebrant adds a concluding Collect. See page 114.

See additional forms beginning on page 101.

*If there is no celebration of the Communion, or if a priest is not
available, the service may continue with a hymn or anthem, and
the offerings of the people received. The service may then
conclude with the Lord's Prayer; and with either the Grace or a
blessing, or with the exchange of the Peace.*

Confession of Sin

*A Confession of Sin is said here if it has not been said earlier.
On occasion, the Confession may be omitted.*

*One of the sentences from the Penitential Order on page ## may
be said.*

The Deacon or Celebrant says

Let us confess our sins against God and our neighbor.

Silence may be kept.

Minister and People

Most merciful God,
we confess that we have sinned against you
in thought, word, and deed,
by what we have done,
and by what we have left undone.
We have not loved you with our whole heart;
we have not loved our neighbors as ourselves.
We are truly sorry and we humbly repent.
For the sake of your Son Jesus Christ,
have mercy on us and forgive us;
that we may delight in your will,
and walk in your ways,
to the glory of your Name. Amen.

The Bishop when present, or the Priest, stands and says

Almighty God have mercy on you, forgive you all
your sins through our Lord Jesus Christ, strengthen
you in all goodness, and by the power of the Holy
Spirit keep you in eternal life. Amen.

The Peace
All stand. The Celebrant says to the people
>The peace of the Lord be always with you.

People   And also with you.

*Then the Ministers and People may greet one another in the
name of the Lord.*

The Holy Communion

The Celebrant may begin the Offertory with one of the following sentences, or with some other sentence of Scripture.

Offertory Sentences

One of the following, or some other appropriate sentence of Scripture, may be used

Offer to God a sacrifice of thanksgiving, and make good your vows to the Most High. *Psalm 50:14*

Ascribe to the Lord the honor due his Name; bring offerings and come into his courts. *Psalm 96:8*

Walk in love, as Christ loved us and gave himself for us, an offering and sacrifice to God. *Ephesians 5:2*

I appeal to you, brethren, by the mercies of God, to present yourselves as a living sacrifice, holy and acceptable to God, which is your spiritual worship. *Romans 12:1*

If you are offering your gift at the altar, and there remember that your brother has something against you, leave your gift there before the altar and go; first be reconciled to your brother, and then come and offer your gift. *Matthew 5:23,24*

Through Christ let us continually offer to God the sacrifice of praise, that is, the fruit of lips that acknowledge his Name. But do not neglect to do good and to share what you have, for such sacrifices are pleasing to God.
Hebrews 13:15,16

O Lord our God, you are worthy to receive glory and honor and power; because you have created all things, and by your will they were created and have their being.
Revelation 4:11

Yours, O Lord, is the greatness, the power, the glory, the victory, and the majesty. For everything in heaven and on earth is yours. Yours, O Lord, is the kingdom, and you are exalted as head over all. *1 Chronicles 29:11*

or this bidding

Let us with gladness present the offerings and oblations of our life and labor to the Lord.

During the Offertory, a hymn, psalm, or anthem may be sung.

Representatives of the congregation bring the people's offerings of bread and wine, and money or other gifts, to the deacon or celebrant.

The people stand while the offerings are presented and placed on the Altar.

The Great Thanksgiving

Alternative forms will be found on page 88 and following.

Eucharistic Prayer A

The people remain standing. The Celebrant, whether bishop or priest, faces them and sings or says

	The Lord be with you.
People	And also with you.
Celebrant	Lift up your hearts.
People	We lift them to the Lord.
Celebrant	Let us give thanks to the Lord our God.
People	It is right to give him thanks and praise.

Then, facing the Holy Table, the Celebrant proceeds

It is right, and a good and joyful thing, always and every where to give thanks to you, Father Almighty, Creator of heaven and earth.

Here a Proper Preface is sung or said on all Sundays, and on other occasions as appointed. Seasonal Prefaces begin on page 97.

Preface of the Lord's Day

1. Of God the Father
For you are the source of light and life; you made us in your image, and called us to new life in Jesus Christ our Lord.

> *or this*

2. Of God the Son
Through Jesus Christ our Lord; who on the first day of the week overcame death and the grave, and by his glorious resurrection opened to us the way of everlasting life.

> *or the following*

3. Of God the Holy Spirit
For by water and the Holy Spirit you have made us a new people in Jesus Christ our Lord, to show forth your glory in all the world.

Therefore we praise you, joining our voices with Angels and Archangels and with all the company of heaven, who for ever sing this hymn to proclaim the glory of your Name:

Celebrant and People

Holy, holy, holy Lord, God of power and might,
heaven and earth are full of your glory.
    Hosanna in the highest.
Blessed is he who comes in the name of the Lord.
    Hosanna in the highest.

The people stand or kneel.

Then the Celebrant continues

Holy and gracious Father: In your infinite love you
made us for yourself; and, when we had fallen into sin
and become subject to evil and death, you, in your
mercy, sent Jesus Christ, your only and eternal Son, to
share our human nature, to live and die as one of us, to
reconcile us to you, the God and Father of all.

He stretched out his arms upon the cross, and offered
himself in obedience to your will, a perfect sacrifice
for the whole world.

*At the following words concerning the bread, the Celebrant is
to hold it or lay a hand upon it; and at the words concerning the
cup, to hold or place a hand upon the cup and any other vessel
containing wine to be consecrated.*

On the night he was handed over to suffering and
death, our Lord Jesus Christ took bread; and when he
had given thanks to you, he broke it, and gave it to his
disciples, and said, "Take, eat: This is my Body, which
is given for you. Do this for the remembrance of me."

After supper he took the cup of wine; and when he had given thanks, he gave it to them, and said, "Drink this, all of you: This is my Blood of the new Covenant, which is shed for you and for many for the forgiveness of sins. Whenever you drink it, do this for the remembrance of me."

Therefore we proclaim the mystery of faith:

Celebrant and People

Christ has died.
Christ is risen.
Christ will come again.

The Celebrant continues

We celebrate the memorial of our redemption, O Father, in this sacrifice of praise and thanksgiving. Recalling his death, resurrection, and ascension, we offer you these gifts.

Sanctify them by your Holy Spirit to be for your people the Body and Blood of your Son, the holy food and drink of new and unending life in him. Sanctify us also that we may faithfully receive this holy Sacrament, and serve you in unity, constancy, and peace; and at the last day bring us with all your saints into the joy of your eternal kingdom.

All this we ask through your Son Jesus Christ. By him, and with him, and in him, in the unity of the Holy Spirit all honor and glory is yours, Almighty Father, now and for ever. AMEN.

And now, as our Savior
Christ has taught us,
we are bold to say,

As our Savior Christ
has taught us,
we now pray,

People and Celebrant

Our Father, who art in heaven,
hallowed be thy Name,
thy kingdom come,
thy will be done,
on earth as it is in heaven.
Give us this day our daily
bread.
And forgive us our trespasses,
as we forgive those
who trespass against us.
And lead us not into,
temptation
but deliver us from evil.
For thine is the kingdom,
and the power, and the glory,
for ever and ever.
Amen.

Our Father in heaven,
hallowed be your Name,
your kingdom come,
your will be done,
on earth as in heaven.
Give us today our daily
bread.
Forgive us our sins
as we forgive those
who sin against us.
Save us from the time of
trial,
 and deliver us from evil.
For the kingdom, the
power, and the glory are
yours, now and for ever.
Amen.

The Breaking of the Bread

The Celebrant breaks the consecrated Bread.

A period of silence is kept.

Then may be sung or said

[Alleluia.] Christ our Passover is sacrificed for us;
Therefore let us keep the feast. [Alleluia.]

*In Lent, Alleluia is omitted, and may be omitted at other times
except during Easter Season.*

In place of, or in addition to, the preceding, some other suitable anthem may be used. The following anthem may be used at the Breaking of the Bread:

Lamb of God, you take away the sins of the world:
    have mercy on us.
Lamb of God, you take away the sins of the world:
    have mercy on us.
Lamb of God, you take away the sins of the world:
    grant us peace.

[Behold the Lamb of God. Behold Him who takes away the sins of the World.]

[Lord, I am not worthy that You should come under my roof, but speak the word only and my soul shall be healed.]

Facing the people, the Celebrant says the following Invitation

The Gifts of God for the People of God.

    and may add

Take them in remembrance that Christ died for you, and feed on him in your hearts by faith, with thanksgiving.

The ministers receive the Sacrament in both kinds, and then immediately deliver it to the people.

The Bread and the Cup are given to the communicants with these words

The Body (Blood) of our Lord Jesus Christ keep you in everlasting life. [Amen.]

    or with these words

The Body of Christ, the bread of heaven. [Amen.]
The Blood of Christ, the cup of salvation. [Amen.]

During the ministration of Communion, hymns, psalms, or anthems may be sung.

After Communion, the Celebrant says

Let us pray.

Celebrant and People

Eternal God, heavenly Father,
you have graciously accepted us as living members
of your Son our Savior Jesus Christ,
and you have fed us with spiritual food
in the Sacrament of his Body and Blood.
Send us now into the world in peace,
and grant us strength and courage
to love and serve you
with gladness and singleness of heart;
through Christ our Lord. Amen.

or the following

Almighty and everliving God,
we thank you for feeding us with the spiritual food
of the most precious Body and Blood
of your Son our Savior Jesus Christ;
and for assuring us in these holy mysteries
that we are living members of the Body of your Son,
and heirs of your eternal kingdom.
And now, Father, send us out
to do the work you have given us to do,
to love and serve you
as faithful witnesses of Christ our Lord.
To him, to you, and to the Holy Spirit,
be honor and glory, now and for ever. Amen.

The Bishop when present, or the Priest, may bless the people.

The peace of God, which passeth all understanding, keep your hearts and minds in the knowledge and love of God, and of his Son Jesus Christ our Lord; and the blessing of God Almighty, the Father, the Son, and the Holy Ghost, be amongst you, and remain with you always. Amen.

or this

The blessing of God Almighty, the Father, the Son, and the Holy Spirit, be upon you and remain with you for ever. Amen.

The Deacon, or the Celebrant, dismisses them with these words

	Let us go forth in the name of Christ.
People	Thanks be to God.

or this

Deacon	Go in peace to love and serve the Lord.
People	Thanks be to God.

or this

Deacon	Let us go forth into the world, rejoicing in the power of the Spirit.
People	Thanks be to God.

or this

Deacon	Let us bless the Lord.
People	Thanks be to God.

From the Easter Vigil through the Day of Pentecost "Alleluia, alleluia" may be added to any of the dismissals.

The People respond Thanks be to God. Alleluia, alleluia.

If the consecrated Bread or Wine does not suffice for the number of communicants, the celebrant is to return to the Holy Table, and consecrate more of either or both, by saying

Hear us, O heavenly Father, and with thy (your) Word and Holy Spirit bless and sanctify this bread (wine) that it, also, may be the Sacrament of the precious Body (Blood) of thy (your) Son Jesus Christ our Lord, who took bread (the cup) and said, "This is my Body (Blood)." Amen.

Alternative Forms of the Great Thanksgiving

Eucharistic Prayer B

The people remain standing. The Celebrant, whether bishop or priest, faces them and sings or says

	The Lord be with you.
People	And also with you.
Celebrant	Lift up your hearts.
People	We lift them to the Lord.
Celebrant	Let us give thanks to the Lord our God.
People	It is right to give him thanks and praise.

Then, facing the Holy Table, the Celebrant proceeds

It is right, and a good and joyful thing, always and every where to give thanks to you, Father Almighty, Creator of heaven and earth.

Here a Proper Preface is sung or said on all Sundays, and on other occasions as appointed. Seasonal Prefaces begin on page 82.

Preface of the Lord's Day

1. Of God the Father
For you are the source of light and life; you made us in your image, and called us to new life in Jesus Christ our Lord.

  or this

2. Of God the Son

Through Jesus Christ our Lord; who on the first day of the week overcame death and the grave, and by his glorious resurrection opened to us the way of everlasting life.

or the following

3. Of God the Holy Spirit

For by water and the Holy Spirit you have made us a new people in Jesus Christ our Lord, to show forth your glory in all the world.

Therefore we praise you, joining our voices with Angels and Archangels and with all the company of heaven, who for ever sing this hymn to proclaim the glory of your Name:

Celebrant and People

> Holy, holy, holy Lord, God of power and might,
> heaven and earth are full of your glory.
> Hosanna in the highest.
> Blessed is he who comes in the name of the Lord.
> Hosanna in the highest.

The people stand or kneel.

Then the Celebrant continues

We give thanks to you, O God, for the goodness and love which you have made known to us in creation; in the calling of Israel to be your people; in your Word spoken through the prophets; and above all in the Word made flesh, Jesus, your Son. For in these last days you sent him to be incarnate from the Virgin

Mary, to be the Savior and Redeemer of the world. In him, you have delivered us from evil, and made us worthy to stand before you. In him, you have brought us out of error into truth, out of sin into righteousness, out of death into life.

At the following words concerning the bread, the Celebrant is to hold it or lay a hand upon it; and at the words concerning the cup, to hold or place a hand upon the cup and any other vessel containing wine to be consecrated.

On the night before he died for us, our Lord Jesus Christ took bread; and when he had given thanks to you, he broke it, and gave it to his disciples, and said, "Take, eat: This is my Body, which is given for you. Do this for the remembrance of me."

After supper he took the cup of wine; and when he had given thanks, he gave it to them, and said, "Drink this, all of you: This is my Blood of the new Covenant, which is shed for you and for many for the forgiveness of sins. Whenever you drink it, do this for the remembrance of me."

Therefore, according to his command, O Father,
Celebrant and People

We remember his death,
We proclaim his resurrection,
We await his coming in glory;

The Celebrant continues

And we offer our sacrifice of praise and thanksgiving to you, O Lord of all; presenting to you, from your creation, this bread and this wine.

We pray you, gracious God, to send your Holy Spirit upon these gifts that they may be the Sacrament of the Body of Christ and his Blood of the new Covenant. Unite us to your Son in his sacrifice, that we may be acceptable through him, being sanctified by the Holy Spirit. In the fullness of time, put all things in subjection under your Christ, and bring us to that heavenly country where, with [_____ and] all your saints, we may enter the everlasting heritage of your sons and daughters; through Jesus Christ our Lord, the firstborn of all creation, the head of the Church, and the author of our salvation.

By him, and with him, and in him, in the unity of the Holy Spirit all honor and glory is yours, Almighty Father, now and for ever. AMEN.

| And now, as our Savior Christ has taught us, we are bold to say, | As our Savior Christ has taught us, we now pray, |

Continue with the Lord's Prayer on page 83.

Eucharistic Prayer D

The people remain standing. The Celebrant, whether bishop or priest, faces them and sings or says

	The Lord be with you.
People	And also with you.
Celebrant	Lift up your hearts.
People	We lift them to the Lord.
Celebrant	Let us give thanks to the Lord our God.
People	It is right to give him thanks and praise.

It is truly right to glorify you, Father, and to give you thanks; for you alone are God, living and true, dwelling in light inaccessible from before time and for ever.

Fountain of life and source of all goodness, you made all things and fill them with your blessing; you created them to rejoice in the splendor of your radiance.

Countless throngs of angels stand before you to serve you night and day; and, beholding the glory of your presence, they offer you unceasing praise. Joining with them, and giving voice to every creature under heaven, we acclaim you, and glorify your Name, as we sing (say),

Celebrant and People

Holy, holy, holy Lord, God of power and might,
heaven and earth are full of your glory.
Hosanna in the highest.
Blessed is he who comes in the name of the Lord.
Hosanna in the highest.

The people stand or kneel.

Then the Celebrant continues

We acclaim you, holy Lord, glorious in power. Your mighty works reveal your wisdom and love. You formed us in your own image, giving the whole world into our care, so that, in obedience to you, our Creator, we might rule and serve all your creatures. When our disobedience took us far from you, you did not abandon us to the power of death. In your mercy you came to our help, so that in seeking you we might find you. Again and again you called us into covenant with you, and through the prophets you taught us to hope for salvation.

Father, you loved the world so much that in the fullness of time you sent your only Son to be our Savior. Incarnate by the Holy Spirit, born of the Virgin Mary, he lived as one of us, yet without sin. To the poor he proclaimed the good news of salvation; to prisoners, freedom; to the sorrowful, joy. To fulfill your purpose he gave himself up to death; and, rising from the grave, destroyed death, and made the whole creation new.

And, that we might live no longer for ourselves, but for him who died and rose for us, he sent the Holy Spirit, his own first gift for those who believe, to complete his work in the world, and to bring to fulfillment the sanctification of all.

At the following words concerning the bread, the Celebrant is to hold it or lay a hand upon it; and at the words concerning the cup, to hold or place a hand upon the cup and any other vessel containing wine to be consecrated.

When the hour had come for him to be glorified by you, his heavenly Father, having loved his own who were in the world, he loved them to the end; at supper with them he took bread, and when he had given thanks to you, he broke it, and gave it to his disciples, and said, "Take, eat: This is my Body, which is given for you. Do this for the remembrance of me."

After supper he took the cup of wine; and when he had given thanks, he gave it to them, and said, "Drink this, all of you. This is my Blood of the new Covenant, which is shed for you and for many for the forgiveness of sins. Whenever you drink it, do this for the remembrance of me."

Father, we now celebrate this memorial of our redemption. Recalling Christ's death and his descent among the dead, proclaiming his resurrection and ascension to your right hand, awaiting his coming in glory; and offering to you, from the gifts you have given us, this bread and this cup, we praise you and we bless you.

Celebrant and People

We praise you, we bless you,
we give thanks to you,
and we pray to you, Lord our God.

The Celebrant continues

Lord, we pray that in your goodness and mercy your Holy Spirit may descend upon us, and upon these gifts, sanctifying them and showing them to be holy gifts for your holy people, the bread of life and the cup of salvation, the Body and Blood of your Son Jesus Christ.

Grant that all who share this bread and cup may become one body and one spirit, a living sacrifice in Christ, to the praise of your Name.

Remember, Lord, your one holy catholic and apostolic Church, redeemed by the blood of your Christ. Reveal its unity, guard its faith, and preserve it in peace.

[Remember (NN. and) all who minister in your Church.]
[Remember all your people, and those who seek your truth.]
[Remember _____.]
[Remember all who have died in the peace of Christ, and those whose faith is known to you alone; bring them into the place of eternal joy and light.]

And grant that we may find our inheritance with [the Blessed Virgin Mary, with patriarchs, prophets, apostles, and martyrs, (with _____) and] all the saints who have found favor with you in ages past. We praise you in union with them and give you glory through your Son Jesus Christ our Lord.

Through Christ, and with Christ, and in Christ, all honor and glory are yours, Almighty God and Father, in the unity of the Holy Spirit, for ever and ever. AMEN.

And now, as our Savior Christ has taught us, we are bold to say,	As our Savior Christ has taught us, we now pray,

Continue with the Lord's Prayer on page 83.

Offertory Sentences

One of the following, or some other appropriate sentence of Scripture, may be used

Offer to God a sacrifice of thanksgiving, and make good your vows to the Most High. *Psalm 50:14*

Ascribe to the Lord the honor due his Name; bring   offerings and come into his courts. *Psalm 96:8*

Walk in love, as Christ loved us and gave himself for us, an offering and sacrifice to God. *Ephesians 5:2*

I appeal to you, brethren, by the mercies of God, to present yourselves as a living sacrifice, holy and acceptable to God, which is your spiritual worship. *Romans 12:1*

If you are offering your gift at the altar, and there remember that your brother has something against you, leave your gift there before the altar and go; first be reconciled to your brother, and then come and offer your gift. *Matthew 5:23,24*

Through Christ let us continually offer to God the sacrifice of praise, that is, the fruit of lips that acknowledge his Name. But do not neglect to do good and to share what you have, for such sacrifices are pleasing to God. *Hebrews 13:15,16*

O Lord our God, you are worthy to receive glory and honor and power; because you have created all things, and by your will they were created and have their being. *Revelation 4:11*

Yours, O Lord, is the greatness, the power, the glory, the victory, and the majesty. For everything in heaven and on earth is yours. Yours, O Lord, is the kingdom, and you are exalted as head over all. *1 Chronicles 29:11*

> *or this bidding*

Let us with gladness present the offerings and oblations of our life and labor to the Lord.

Proper Prefaces

To be used on Sundays as appointed, but not on the succeeding weekdays

Preface of the Lord's Day

1. Of God the Father
For you are the source of light and life; you made us in your image, and called us to new life in Jesus Christ our Lord.

or this

2. Of God the Son
Through Jesus Christ our Lord; who on the first day of the week overcame death and the grave, and by his glorious resurrection opened to us the way of everlasting life.

or the following

3. Of God the Holy Spirit
For by water and the Holy Spirit you have made us a new people in Jesus Christ our Lord, to show forth your glory in all the world.

Prefaces for Seasons

To be used on Sundays and weekdays alike, except as otherwise appointed for Holy Days and Various Occasions

Advent
Because you sent your beloved Son to redeem us from sin and death, and to make us heirs in him of everlasting life; that when he shall come again in power and great triumph to judge the world, we may without shame or fear rejoice to behold his appearing.

Incarnation
Because you gave Jesus Christ, your only Son, to be born for us; who, by the mighty power of the Holy Spirit, was made perfect Man of the flesh of the Virgin Mary his mother; so that we might be delivered from the bondage of sin, and receive power to become your children.

Epiphany

Because in the mystery of the Word made flesh, you have caused a new light to shine in our hearts, to give the knowledge of your glory in the face of your Son Jesus Christ our Lord.

Lent

Through Jesus Christ our Lord, who was tempted in every way as we are, yet did not sin. By his grace we are able to triumph over every evil, and to live no longer for ourselves alone, but for him who died for us and rose again.

or this

You bid your faithful people cleanse their hearts, and prepare with joy for the Paschal feast; that, fervent in prayer and in works of mercy, and renewed by your Word and Sacraments, they may come to the fullness of grace which you have prepared for those who love you.

Holy Week

Through Jesus Christ our Lord. For our sins he was lifted high upon the cross, that he might draw the whole world to himself; and, by his suffering and death, he became the source of eternal salvation for all who put their trust in him.

Easter

But chiefly are we bound to praise you for the glorious resurrection of your Son Jesus Christ our Lord; for he is the true Paschal Lamb, who was sacrificed for us, and has taken away the sin of the world. By his death he has destroyed death, and by his rising to life again he has won for us everlasting life.

Ascension

Through your dearly beloved Son Jesus Christ our Lord. After his glorious resurrection he openly appeared to his disciples, and in their sight ascended into heaven, to prepare a place for us; that where he is, there we might also be, and reign with him in glory.

Pentecost

Through Jesus Christ our Lord. Tn fulfillment of his true promise, the Holy Spirit came down [on this day] from heaven, lighting upon the disciples, to teach them and to lead them into all truth; uniting peoples of many tongues in the confession of one faith, and giving to your Church the power to serve you as a royal priesthood, and to preach the Gospel to all nations.

Prefaces for Other Occasions

Trinity Sunday

For with your co-eternal Son and Holy Spirit, you are one God, one Lord, in Trinity of Persons and in Unity of Being: and we celebrate the one and equal glory of you, O Father, and of the Son, and of the Holy Spirit.

All Saints

For in the multitude of your saints, you have surrounded us with a great cloud of witnesses, that we might rejoice in their fellowship, and run with endurance the race that is set before us; and, together with them, receive the crown of glory that never fades away.

A Saint

For the wonderful grace and virtue declared in all your saints, who have been the chosen vessels of your grace, and the lights of the world in their generations.

or this

Because in the obedience of your saints you have given us an example of righteousness, and in their eternal joy a glorious pledge of the hope of our calling.

or this

Because you are greatly glorified in the assembly of your saints. All your creatures praise you, and your faithful servants bless you, confessing before the rulers of this world the great Name of your only Son.

Apostles and Ordinations

Through the great shepherd of your flock, Jesus Christ our Lord; who after his resurrection sent forth his apostles to preach the Gospel and to teach all nations; and promised to be with them always, even to the end of the ages.

Dedication of a Church

Through Jesus Christ our great High Priest, in whom we are built up as living stones of a holy temple, that we might offer before you a sacrifice of praise and prayer which is holy and pleasing in your sight.

Baptism

Because in Jesus Christ our Lord you have received us as your sons and daughters, made us citizens of your kingdom, and given us the Holy Spirit to guide us into all truth.

Marriage

Because in the love of wife and husband, you have given us an image of the heavenly Jerusalem, adorned as a bride for her bridegroom, your Son Jesus Christ our Lord; who loves her and gave himself for her, that he might make the whole creation new.

Commemoration of the Dead

Through Jesus Christ our Lord; who rose victorious from the dead, and comforts us with the blessed hope of everlasting life. For to your faithful people, O Lord, life is changed, not ended; and when our mortal body lies in death, there is prepared for us a dwelling place eternal in the heavens.

The Prayers of the People

Prayer is offered with intercession for

The Universal Church, its members, and its mission
The Nation and all in authority
The welfare of the world
The concerns of the local community
Those who suffer and those in any trouble
The departed (with commemoration of a saint when
appropriate)

Any of the forms which follow may be used.

Adaptations or insertions suitable to the occasion may be made.
Any of the forms may be conformed to the language of the Rite
being used. A bar in the margin indicates petitions which may
be omitted. The Celebrant may introduce the Prayers with a
sentence of invitation related to the occasion, or the season, or
the Proper of the Day.

Form I

Deacon or other leader

With all our heart and with all our mind, let us pray to
the Lord, saying, "Lord, have mercy."

For the peace from above, for the loving kindness of
God, and for the salvation of our souls, let us pray to
the Lord.
Lord, have mercy.

For the peace of the world, for the welfare of the holy
Church of God, and for the unity of all peoples, let us
pray to the Lord.
Lord, have mercy.

For our Bishop, and for all the clergy and people, let us pray to the Lord.
Lord, have mercy.

For our President, for the leaders of the nations, and for all in authority, let us pray to the Lord.
Lord, have mercy.

For this city (town, village, _____), for every city and community, and for those who live in them, let us pray to the Lord.
Lord, have mercy.

For seasonable weather, and for an abundance of the fruits of the earth, let us pray to the Lord.
Lord, have mercy.

For the good earth which God has given us, and for the wisdom and will to conserve it, let us pray to the Lord.
Lord, have mercy.

For those who travel on land, on water, or in the air [or through space], let us pray to the Lord.
Lord, have mercy.

For the aged and infirm, for the widowed and orphans, and for the sick and the suffering, let us pray to the Lord.
Lord, have mercy.

For _____ , let us pray to the Lord.
Lord, have mercy.

For the poor and the oppressed, for the unemployed and the destitute, for prisoners and captives, and for all who remember and care for them, let us pray to the Lord.
Lord, have mercy.

For all who have died in the hope of the resurrection, and for all the departed, let us pray to the Lord.
Lord, have mercy.

For deliverance from all danger, violence, oppression, and degradation, let us pray to the Lord.
Lord, have mercy.

For the absolution and remission of our sins and offenses, let us pray to the Lord.
Lord, have mercy.

That we may end our lives in faith and hope, without suffering and without reproach, let us pray to the Lord.
Lord, have mercy.

Defend us, deliver us, and in thy compassion protect us, O Lord, by thy grace.
Lord, have mercy.

In the communion of [_____ and of all the] saints, let us commend ourselves, and one another, and all our life, to Christ our God.
To thee, O Lord our God.

Silence

The Celebrant adds a concluding Collect.

Form II

In the course of the silence after each bidding, the People offer their own prayers, either silently or aloud.

I ask your prayers for God's people throughout the world; for our Bishop(s) _____ ; for this gathering; and for all ministers and people.

Pray for the Church.

Silence

I ask your prayers for peace; for goodwill among nations; and for the well-being of all people.

Pray for justice and peace.

Silence

I ask your prayers for the poor, the sick, the hungry, the oppressed, and those in prison.

Pray for those in any need or trouble.

Silence

I ask your prayers for all who seek God, or a deeper knowledge of him.

Pray that they may find and be found by him.

Silence

I ask your prayers for the departed [especially _____].

Pray for those who have died.

Silence

Members of the congregation may ask the prayers or the thanksgivings of those present

I ask your prayers for _____ .
I ask your thanksgiving for _____ .

Silence

Praise God for those in every generation in whom Christ has been honored [especially _____ whom we remember today].

Pray that we may have grace to glorify Christ in our own day.

Silence

The Celebrant adds a concluding Collect.

Form III

The Leader and People pray responsively

Father, we pray for your holy Catholic Church;
That we all may be one.

Grant that every member of the Church may truly and humbly serve you;
That your Name may be glorified by all people.

We pray for all bishops, priests, and deacons;
That they may be faithful ministers of your Word and Sacraments.

We pray for all who govern and hold authority in the nations of the world;
That there may be justice and peace on the earth.

Give us grace to do your will in all that we undertake;
That our works may find favor in your sight.

Have compassion on those who suffer from any grief or trouble;
That they may be delivered from their distress.

Give to the departed eternal rest;
Let light perpetual shine upon them.

We praise you for your saints who have entered into joy;
May we also come to share in your heavenly kingdom.

Let us pray for our own needs and those of others.

Silence

The People may add their own petitions.

The Celebrant adds a concluding Collect.

Form IV

Deacon or other leader

Let us pray for the Church and for the world.

Grant, Almighty God, that all who confess your Name may be united in your truth, live together in your love, and reveal your glory in the world.

Silence

Lord, in your mercy
Hear our prayer.

Guide the people of this land, and of all the nations, in the ways of justice and peace; that we may honor one another and serve the common good.

Silence

Lord, in your mercy
Hear our prayer.

Give us all a reverence for the earth as your own creation, that we may use its resources rightly in the service of others and to your honor and glory.

Silence

Lord, in your mercy
Hear our prayer.

Bless all whose lives are closely linked with ours, and grant that we may serve Christ in them, and love one another as he loves us.

Silence

Lord, in your mercy
Hear our prayer.

Comfort and heal all those who suffer in body, mind, or spirit; give them courage and hope in their troubles, and bring them the joy of your salvation.

Silence

Lord, in your mercy
Hear our prayer.

We commend to your mercy all who have died, that your will for them may be fulfilled; and we pray that we may share with all your saints in your eternal kingdom.

Silence

Lord, in your mercy
Hear our prayer.

The Celebrant adds a concluding Collect.

Form V

Deacon or other leader

In peace, let us pray to the Lord, saying, "Lord, have mercy" (or "Kyrie eleison").

For the holy Church of God, that it may be filled with truth and love, and be found without fault at the day of your coming, we pray to you, O Lord.

Here and after every petition the People respond

> Kyrie eleison.   *or*   Lord, have mercy.

For N. our Archbishop, for N. (N.) our own bishop(s), for all bishops and other ministers, and for all the holy people of God, we pray to you, O Lord.

For all who fear God and believe in you, Lord Christ, that our divisions may cease, and that all may be one as you and the Father are one, we pray to you, O Lord.

For the mission of the Church, that in faithful witness it may preach the Gospel to the ends of the earth, we pray to you, O Lord.

For those who do not yet believe, and for those who have lost their faith, that they may receive the light of the Gospel, we pray to you, O Lord.

For the peace of the world, that a spirit of respect and forbearance may grow among nations and peoples, we pray to you, O Lord.

For those in positions of public trust [especially _____], that they may serve justice, and promote the dignity and   freedom of every person, we pray to you, O Lord.

For all who live and work in this community [especially _____], we pray to you, O Lord.

For a blessing upon all human labor, and for the right use of the riches of creation, that the world may be freed from poverty, famine, and disaster, we pray to you, O Lord.

For the poor, the persecuted, the sick, and all who suffer; for refugees, prisoners, and all who are in danger; that they may be relieved and protected, we pray to you, O Lord.

For this congregation [for those who are present, and for those who are absent], that we may be delivered from hardness of heart, and show forth your glory in all that we do, we pray to you, O Lord.

For our enemies and those who wish us harm; and for all whom we have injured or offended, we pray to you, O Lord. For ourselves; for the forgiveness of our sins, and for the grace of the Holy Spirit to amend our lives, we pray to you, O Lord.

For all who have commended themselves to our prayers; for our families, friends, and neighbors; that being freed from anxiety, they may live in joy, peace, and health, we pray to you, O Lord.

For _____ , we pray to you, O Lord.

For all who have died in the communion of your Church, and those whose faith is known to you alone, that, with all the saints, they may have rest in that place where there is no pain or grief, but life eternal, we pray to you, O Lord.

Rejoicing in the fellowship of [the ever-blessed Virgin Mary, (blessed N.) and] all the saints, let us commend ourselves, and one another, and all our life to Christ our God.

To you, O Lord our God.

Silence

The Celebrant adds a concluding Collect, or the following Doxology

For yours is the majesty, O Father, Son, and Holy Spirit; yours is the kingdom and the power and the glory, now and for ever. *Amen.*

Form VI

The Leader and People pray responsively

In peace, we pray to you, Lord God.

Silence

For all people in their daily life and work;
For our families, friends, and neighbors, and for those who are alone.

For this community, the nation, and the world;
For all who work for justice, freedom, and peace.

For the just and proper use of your creation;
For the victims of hunger, fear, injustice, and oppression.

For all who are in danger, sorrow, or any kind of trouble;
For those who minister to the sick, the friendless, and the needy.

For the peace and unity of the Church of God;
For all who proclaim the Gospel, and all who seek the Truth.

For [N. our Archbishop, and N. (N.) our Bishop(s); and for] all bishops and other ministers;
For all who serve God in his Church.
For the special needs and concerns of this congregation.

Silence

The People may add their own petitions

Hear us, Lord;
For your mercy is great.

We thank you, Lord, for all the blessings of this life.

Silence

The People may add their own thanksgivings

We will exalt you, O God our King;
And praise your Name for ever and ever.

We pray for all who have died, that they may have a place in your eternal kingdom.

Silence

The People may add their own petitions

Lord, let your loving-kindness be upon them;
Who put their trust in you.

We pray to you also for the forgiveness of our sins.

Silence may be kept.

The following confession is optional

Leader and People

Have mercy upon us, most merciful Father;
in your compassion forgive us our sins,
known and unknown,
things done and left undone;
and so uphold us by your Spirit
that we may live and serve you in newness of life,
to the honor and glory of your Name;
through Jesus Christ our Lord. Amen.

The Celebrant concludes with an absolution or a suitable Collect.

The Collect at the Prayers

For the concluding Collect, the Celebrant selects

> *(a) a Collect appropriate to the Season or occasion being celebrated;*
>
> *(b) a Collect expressive of some special need in the life of the local congregation;*
>
> *(c) a Collect for the mission of the Church;*
>
> *(d) a general Collect such as the following:*

1. Lord, hear the prayers of thy people; and what we have asked faithfully, grant that we may obtain effectually, to the glory of thy Name; through Jesus Christ our Lord. *Amen.*

2. Heavenly Father, you have promised to hear what we ask in the Name of your Son: Accept and fulfill our petitions, we pray, not as we ask in our ignorance, nor as we deserve in our sinfulness, but as you know and love us in your Son Jesus Christ our Lord. *Amen.*

3. Almighty and eternal God, ruler of all things in heaven and earth: Mercifully accept the prayers of your people, and strengthen us to do your will; through Jesus Christ our Lord. *Amen.*

4. Almighty God, to whom our needs are known before we ask, help us to ask only what accords with your will; and those good things which we dare not, or in our blindness cannot ask, grant us for the sake of your Son Jesus Christ our Lord. *Amen.*

5. O Lord our God, accept the fervent prayers of your people; in the multitude of your mercies, look with compassion upon us and all who turn to you for help; for you are gracious, O lover of souls, and to you we give glory, Father, Son, and Holy Spirit, now and for ever. *Amen.*

6. Lord Jesus Christ, you said to your apostles, "Peace I give to you; my own peace I leave with you:" Regard not our sins, but the faith of your Church, and give to us the peace and unity of that heavenly City, where with the Father and the Holy Spirit, you live and reign, now and for ever. *Amen.*

7. Hasten, O Father, the coming of thy kingdom; and grant that we thy servants, who now live by faith, may with joy behold thy Son at his coming in glorious majesty; even Jesus Christ, our only Mediator and Advocate. *Amen.*

8. Almighty God, by your Holy Spirit you have made us one with your saints in heaven and on earth: Grant that in our earthly pilgrimage we may always be supported by this fellowship of love and prayer, and know ourselves to be surrounded by their witness to your power and mercy. We ask this for the sake of Jesus Christ, in whom all our intercessions are acceptable through the Spirit, and who lives and reigns for ever and ever. *Amen.*

Communion under Special Circumstances

This form is intended for use with those who for reasonable cause cannot be present at a public celebration of the Eucharist.

When persons are unable to be present for extended periods, it is desirable that the priest arrange to celebrate the Eucharist with them from time to time on a regular basis, using either the Proper of the Day or one of those appointed for Various Occasions. If it is necessary to shorten the service, the priest may begin the celebration at the Offertory, but it is desirable that a passage from the Gospel first be read.

At other times, or when desired, such persons may be communicated from the reserved Sacrament, using the following form.

It is desirable that fellow parishioners, relatives, and friends be present, when possible, to communicate with them.

The Celebrant, whether priest or deacon, reads a passage of Scripture appropriate to the day or occasion, or else one of the following

God so loved the world that he gave his only Son, that whoever believes in him should not perish, but have eternal life.   *John 3:16*

Jesus said," I am the bread of life; whoever comes to me shall not hunger, and whoever believes in me shall never thirst."   *John 6:35*

Jesus said," I am the living bread which came down from heaven; if anyone eats of this bread, he will live for ever; and the bread which I shall give for the life of the world is my flesh. For my flesh is food indeed, and my blood is drink indeed. Whoever eats my flesh and drinks my blood abides in me, and I in him." John 6:51,55-56

Jesus said, "Abide in me, as I in you. As the branch cannot bear fruit by itself, unless it abides in the vine, neither can you, unless you abide in me. I am the vine, you are the branches. By this my Father is glorified, that you bear much fruit, and so prove to be my disciples. As the Father has loved me, so have I loved you; abide in my love." *John 15:4-5a,8-9*

After the Reading, the Celebrant may comment on it briefly.

Suitable prayers may be offered, concluding with the following or some other Collect

Almighty Father, whose dear Son, on the night before he suffered, instituted the Sacrament of his Body and Blood: Mercifully grant that we may receive it thankfully in remembrance of Jesus Christ our Lord, who in these holy mysteries gives us a pledge of eternal life; and who lives and reigns for ever and ever. Amen.

A Confession of Sin may follow. The following or some other form is used

Most merciful God,
we confess that we have sinned against you
in thought, word, and deed,
by what we have done,

and by what we have left undone.
We have not loved you with our whole heart;
we have not loved our neighbors as ourselves.
We are truly sorry and we humbly repent.
For the sake of your Son Jesus Christ,
have mercy on us and forgive us;
that we may delight in your will,
and walk in your ways,
to the glory of your Name. Amen.

The Priest alone says

Almighty God have mercy on you, forgive you all
your sins through our Lord Jesus Christ, strengthen
you in all goodness, and by the power of the Holy
Spirit keep you in eternal life. *Amen.*

*A deacon using the preceding form substitutes "us" for "you"
and "our" for "your."*

The Peace may then be exchanged.

The Lord's Prayer is said, the Celebrant first saying

Let us pray in the words our Savior Christ has taught us.

Our Father, who art in heaven,	Our Father in heaven,
hallowed be thy Name,	hallowed be your Name,
thy kingdom come,	your kingdom come,
thy will be done,	your will be done,
on earth as it is in heaven.	on earth as in heaven.
Give us this day our daily bread.	Give us today our daily bread.
And forgive us our trespasses,	Forgive us our sins
as we forgive those	as we forgive those
who trespass against us.	who sin against us.
And lead us not into,	Save us from the time of

temptation	trial,
but deliver us from evil.	and deliver us from evil.
For thine is the kingdom,	For the kingdom, the and
the power, and the glory,	power,
for ever and ever. Amen.	and the glory are yours,
	now and for ever. Amen.

The Celebrant may say the following Invitation

The Gifts of God for the People of God.

and may add   Take them in remembrance that Christ died for you, and feed on him in your hearts by faith, with thanksgiving.

The Sacrament is administered with the following or other words

The Body (Blood) of our Lord Jesus Christ keep you in   everlasting life. [Amen.]

One of the usual postcommunion prayers is then said, or the following

Gracious Father, we give you praise and thanks for this Holy Communion of the Body and Blood of your beloved Son Jesus Christ, the pledge of our redemption; and we pray that it may bring us forgiveness of our sins, strength in our weakness, and everlasting salvation; through Jesus Christ our Lord. *Amen.*

The service concludes with a blessing or with a dismissal

Let us bless the Lord.
Thanks be to God.

Contemporary Collects

and

Private Devotions

Collects: Contemporary

First Sunday of Advent

Almighty God, give us grace to cast away the works of darkness, and put on the armor of light, now in the time of this mortal life in which your Son Jesus Christ came to visit us in great humility; that in the last day, when he shall come again in his glorious majesty to judge both the living and the dead, we may rise to the life immortal; through him who lives and reigns with you and the Holy Spirit, one God, now and for ever. *Amen.*

Preface of Advent

Second Sunday of Advent

Merciful God, who sent your messengers the prophets to preach repentance and prepare the way for our salvation: Give us grace to heed their warnings and forsake our sins, that we may greet with joy the coming of Jesus Christ our Redeemer; who lives and reigns with you and the Holy Spirit, one God, now and for ever. *Amen.*

Preface of Advent

Third Sunday of Advent

Stir up your power, O Lord, and with great might come among us; and, because we are sorely hindered by our sins, let your bountiful grace and mercy speedily help and deliver us; through Jesus Christ our Lord, to whom, with you and the Holy Spirit, be honor and glory, now and for ever. *Amen.*

Preface of Advent

Wednesday, Friday, and Saturday of this week are the traditional winter Ember Days.

Fourth Sunday of Advent

Purify our conscience, Almighty God, by your daily visitation, that your Son Jesus Christ, at his coming, may find in us a mansion prepared for himself; who lives and reigns with you, in the unity of the Holy Spirit, one God, now and for ever. *Amen.*

Preface of Advent

The Nativity of Our Lord: Christmas Day *December 25*

O God, you make us glad by the yearly festival of the birth of your only Son Jesus Christ: Grant that we, who joyfully receive him as our Redeemer, may with sure confidence behold him when he comes to be our Judge; who lives and reigns with you and the Holy Spirit, one God, now and for ever. *Amen.*

or this

O God, you have caused this holy night to shine with the brightness of the true Light: Grant that we, who have known the mystery of that Light on earth, may also enjoy him perfectly in heaven; where with you and the Holy Spirit he lives and reigns, one God, in glory everlasting. *Amen.*

or this

Almighty God, you have given your only-begotten Son to take our nature upon him, and to be born [this day] of a pure virgin: Grant that we, who have been born again and made your children by adoption and grace, may daily be renewed by your Holy Spirit; through our Lord Jesus Christ, to whom with you and the same Spirit be honor and glory, now and for ever. *Amen.*

Preface of the Incarnation

Collects   122

*The Collect immediately preceding and any of the sets of
Proper Lessons for Christmas Day serve for any weekdays
between Holy Innocents' Day and the First Sunday after
Christmas Day.*

First Sunday after Christmas Day

*This Sunday takes precedence over the three Holy Days
which follow Christmas Day. As necessary, the observance
of one, two, or all three of them, is postponed one day.*

Almighty God, you have poured upon us the new light of
your incarnate Word: Grant that this light, enkindled in our
hearts, may shine forth in our lives; through Jesus Christ
our Lord, who lives and reigns with you, in the unity of the
Holy Spirit, one God, now and for ever. *Amen.*

Preface of the Incarnation

The Holy Name *January 1*

Eternal Father, you gave to your incarnate Son the holy
name of Jesus to be the sign of our salvation: Plant in
every heart, we pray, the love of him who is the Savior of
the world, our Lord Jesus Christ; who lives and reigns with
you and the Holy Spirit, one God, in glory everlasting.
Amen.

Preface of the Incarnation

Second Sunday after Christmas Day

O God, who wonderfully created, and yet more
wonderfully restored, the dignity of human nature: Grant
that we may share the divine life of him who humbled
himself to share our humanity, your Son Jesus Christ; who
lives and reigns with you, in the unity of the Holy Spirit,
one God, for ever and ever. *Amen.*

Preface of the Incarnation

The Epiphany *January 6*

O God, by the leading of a star you manifested your only Son to the peoples of the earth: Lead us, who know you now by faith, to your presence, where we may see your glory face to face; through Jesus Christ our Lord, who lives and reigns with you and the Holy Spirit, one God, now and for ever. *Amen.*

Preface of the Epiphany

The preceding Collect, with the Psalm and Lessons for the Epiphany, or those for the Second Sunday after Christmas, serves for weekdays between the Epiphany and the following Sunday. The Preface of the Epiphany is used.

First Sunday after the Epiphany: The Baptism of our Lord

Father in heaven, who at the baptism of Jesus in the River Jordan proclaimed him your beloved Son and anointed him with the Holy Spirit: Grant that all who are baptized into his Name may keep the covenant they have made, and boldly confess him as Lord and Savior; who with you and the Holy Spirit lives and reigns, one God, in glory everlasting. *Amen.*

Preface of the Epiphany

Second Sunday after the Epiphany

Almighty God, whose Son our Savior Jesus Christ is the light of the world: Grant that your people, illumined by your Word and Sacraments, may shine with the radiance of Christ's glory, that he may be known, worshiped, and obeyed to the ends of the earth; through Jesus Christ our Lord, who with you and the Holy Spirit lives and reigns, one God, now and for ever. *Amen.*

Preface of the Epiphany, or of the Lord's Day

Third Sunday after the Epiphany

Give us grace, O Lord, to answer readily the call of our Savior Jesus Christ and proclaim to all people the Good News of his salvation, that we and the whole world may perceive the glory of his marvelous works; who lives and reigns with you and the Holy Spirit, one God, for ever and ever. *Amen.*

Preface of the Epiphany, or of the Lord's Day

Fourth Sunday after the Epiphany

Almighty and everlasting God, you govern all things both in heaven and on earth: Mercifully hear the supplications of your people, and in our time grant us your peace; through Jesus Christ our Lord, who lives and reigns with you and the Holy Spirit, one God, for ever and ever. *Amen.*

Preface of the Epiphany, or of the Lord's Day

Fifth Sunday after the Epiphany

Set us free, O God, from the bondage of our sins, and give us the liberty of that abundant life which you have made known to us in your Son our Savior Jesus Christ; who lives and reigns with you, in the unity of the Holy Spirit, one God, now and for ever. *Amen.*

Preface of the Epiphany, or of the Lord's Day

Sixth Sunday after the Epiphany

O God, the strength of all who put their trust in you: Mercifully accept our prayers; and because in our weakness we can do nothing good without you, give us the help of your grace, that in keeping your commandments we may please you both in will and deed; through Jesus Christ our Lord, who lives and reigns with you and the Holy Spirit, one God, for ever and ever. *Amen.*

Preface of the Epiphany, or of the Lord's Day

Seventh Sunday after the Epiphany

O Lord, you have taught us that without love whatever we do is worth nothing: Send your Holy Spirit and pour into our hearts your greatest gift, which is love, the true bond of peace and of all virtue, without which whoever lives is accounted dead before you. Grant this for the sake of your only Son Jesus Christ, who lives and reigns with you and the Holy Spirit, one God, now and for ever. *Amen.*

Preface of the Epiphany, or of the Lord's Day

Eighth Sunday after the Epiphany

Most loving Father, whose will it is for us to give thanks for all things, to fear nothing but the loss of you, and to cast all our care on you who care for us: Preserve us from faithless fears and worldly anxieties, that no clouds of this mortal life may hide from us the light of that love which is immortal, and which you have manifested to us in your Son Jesus Christ our Lord; who lives and reigns with you, in the unity of the Holy Spirit, one God, now and for ever. *Amen.*

Preface of the Epiphany, or of the Lord's Day

Last Sunday after the Epiphany

This Proper is always used on the Sunday before Ash Wednesday

O God, who before the passion of your only-begotten Son revealed his glory upon the holy mountain: Grant to us that we, beholding by faith the light of his countenance, may be strengthened to bear our cross, and be changed into his likeness from glory to glory; through Jesus Christ our Lord, who lives and reigns with you and the Holy Spirit, one God, for ever and ever. *Amen.*

Preface of the Epiphany

Ash Wednesday

The Proper Liturgy for this day is on page 264 of BCP

Almighty and everlasting God, you hate nothing you have made and forgive the sins of all who are penitent: Create and make in us new and contrite hearts, that we, worthily lamenting our sins and acknowledging our wretchedness, may obtain of you, the God of all mercy, perfect remission and forgiveness; through Jesus Christ our Lord, who lives and reigns with you and the Holy Spirit, one God, for ever and ever. *Amen.*

Preface of Lent

This Collect, with the corresponding Psalm and Lessons, also serves for the weekdays which follow, except as otherwise appointed.

First Sunday in Lent

Almighty God, whose blessed Son was led by the Spirit to be tempted by Satan: Come quickly to help us who are assaulted by many temptations; and, as you know the weaknesses of each of us, let each one find you mighty to save; through Jesus Christ your Son our Lord, who lives and reigns with you and the Holy Spirit, one God, now and for ever. *Amen.*

Preface of Lent

Wednesday, Friday, and Saturday of this week are the traditional spring Ember Days.

Second Sunday in Lent

O God, whose glory it is always to have mercy: Be gracious to all who have gone astray from your ways, and bring them again with penitent hearts and steadfast faith to embrace and hold fast the unchangeable truth of your Word, Jesus Christ your Son; who with you and the Holy Spirit lives and reigns, one God, for ever and ever. *Amen.*

Preface of Lent

Third Sunday in Lent

Almighty God, you know that we have no power in ourselves to help ourselves: Keep us both outwardly in our bodies and inwardly in our souls, that we may be defended from all adversities which may happen to the body, and from all evil thoughts which may assault and hurt the soul; through Jesus Christ our Lord, who lives and reigns with you and the Holy Spirit, one God, for ever and ever. *Amen.*

Preface of Lent

Fourth Sunday in Lent

Gracious Father, whose blessed Son Jesus Christ came down from heaven to be the true bread which gives life to the world: Evermore give us this bread, that he may live in us, and we in him; who lives and reigns with you and the Holy Spirit, one God, now and for ever. *Amen.*

Preface of Lent

Fifth Sunday in Lent

Almighty God, you alone can bring into order the unruly wills and affections of sinners: Grant your people grace to love what you command and desire what you promise; that, among the swift and varied changes of the world, our hearts may surely there be fixed where true joys are to be found; through Jesus Christ our Lord, who lives and reigns with you and the Holy Spirit, one God, now and for ever. *Amen.*

Preface of Lent

Sunday of the Passion: Palm Sunday

The Proper Liturgy for this day is on page 270 of BCP

Almighty and everliving God, in your tender love for the human race you sent your Son our Savior Jesus Christ to take upon him our nature, and to suffer death upon the cross, giving us the example of his great humility: Mercifully grant that we may walk in the way of his suffering, and also share in his resurrection; through Jesus Christ our Lord, who lives and reigns with you and the Holy Spirit, one God, for ever and ever. *Amen.*

Preface of Holy Week

Monday in Holy Week

Almighty God, whose most dear Son went not up to joy but first he suffered pain, and entered not into glory before he was crucified: Mercifully grant that we, walking in the way of the cross, may find it none other than the way of life and peace; through Jesus Christ your Son our Lord, who lives and reigns with you and the Holy Spirit, one God, for ever and ever. *Amen.*

Preface of Holy Week

Tuesday in Holy Week

O God, by the passion of your blessed Son you made an instrument of shameful death to be for us the means of life: Grant us so to glory in the cross of Christ, that we may gladly suffer shame and loss for the sake of your Son our Savior Jesus Christ; who lives and reigns with you and the Holy Spirit, one God, for ever and ever. *Amen.*

Preface of Holy Week

Wednesday in Holy Week

Lord God, whose blessed Son our Savior gave his body to be whipped and his face to be spit upon: Give us grace to accept joyfully the sufferings of the present time, confident of the glory that shall be revealed; through Jesus Christ your Son our Lord, who lives and reigns with you and the Holy Spirit, one God, for ever and ever. *Amen.*

Preface of Holy Week

Maundy Thursday

The Proper Liturgy for this day is on page 274.
Almighty Father, whose dear Son, on the night before he suffered, instituted the Sacrament of his Body and Blood: Mercifully grant that we may receive it thankfully in remembrance of Jesus Christ our Lord, who in these holy mysteries gives us a pledge of eternal life; and who now lives and reigns with you and the Holy Spirit, one God, for ever and ever. *Amen.*

Preface of Holy Week

Good Friday

The Proper Liturgy for this day is on page 276 of BCP
Almighty God, we pray you graciously to behold this your family, for whom our Lord Jesus Christ was willing to be betrayed, and given into the hands of sinners, and to suffer death upon the cross; who now lives and reigns with you and the Holy Spirit, one God, for ever and ever. *Amen.*

Holy Saturday

The Proper Liturgy for this day is on page 283 of BCP
O God, Creator of heaven and earth: Grant that, as the crucified body of your dear Son was laid in the tomb and rested on this holy Sabbath, so we may await with him the coming of the third day, and rise with him to newness of life; who now lives and reigns with you and the Holy Spirit, one God, for ever and ever. *Amen.*

Easter Day

The Liturgy of the Easter Vigil is on page 285.

O God, who for our redemption gave your only-begotten Son to the death of the cross, and by his glorious resurrection delivered us from the power of our enemy: Grant us so to die daily to sin, that we may evermore live with him in the joy of his resurrection; through Jesus Christ your Son our Lord, who lives and reigns with you and the Holy Spirit, one God, now and for ever. *Amen.*

or this

O God, who made this most holy night to shine with the glory of the Lord's resurrection: Stir up in your Church that Spirit of adoption which is given to us in Baptism, that we, being renewed both in body and mind, may worship you in sincerity and truth; through Jesus Christ our Lord, who lives and reigns with you, in the unity of the Holy Spirit, one God, now and for ever. *Amen.*

or this

Almighty God, who through your only-begotten Son Jesus Christ overcame death and opened to us the gate of everlasting life: Grant that we, who celebrate with joy the day of the Lord's resurrection, may be raised from the death of sin by your life-giving Spirit; through Jesus Christ our Lord, who lives and reigns with you and the Holy Spirit, one God, now and for ever. *Amen.*

Preface of Easter

Monday in Easter Week

Grant, we pray, Almighty God, that we who celebrate with awe the Paschal feast may be found worthy to attain to everlasting joys; through Jesus Christ our Lord, who lives and reigns with you and the Holy Spirit, one God, now and for ever. *Amen.*

Preface of Easter

Tuesday in Easter Week

O God, who by the glorious resurrection of your Son Jesus Christ destroyed death and brought life and immortality to light: Grant that we, who have been raised with him, may abide in his presence and rejoice in the hope of eternal glory; through Jesus Christ our Lord, to whom, with you and the Holy Spirit, be dominion and praise for ever and ever. *Amen.*

Preface of Easter

Wednesday in Easter Week

O God, whose blessed Son made himself known to his disciples in the breaking of bread: Open the eyes of our faith, that we may behold him in all his redeeming work; who lives and reigns with you, in the unity of the Holy Spirit, one God, now and for ever. *Amen.*

Preface of Easter

Thursday in Easter Week

Almighty and everlasting God, who in the Paschal mystery established the new covenant of reconciliation: Grant that all who have been reborn into the fellowship of Christ's Body may show forth in their lives what they profess by their faith; through Jesus Christ our Lord, who lives and reigns with you and the Holy Spirit, one God, for ever and ever. *Amen.*

Preface of Easter

Friday in Easter Week

Almighty Father, who gave your only Son to die for our sins and to rise for our justification: Give us grace so to put away the leaven of malice and wickedness, that we may always serve you in pureness of living and truth; through Jesus Christ your Son our Lord, who lives and reigns with you and the Holy Spirit, one God, now and for ever. *Amen.*

Preface of Easter

Saturday in Easter Week

We thank you, heavenly Father, that you have delivered us from the dominion of sin and death and brought us into the kingdom of your Son; and we pray that, as by his death he has recalled us to life, so by his love he may raise us to eternal joys; who lives and reigns with you, in the unity of the Holy Spirit, one God, now and for ever. *Amen.*

Preface of Easter

Second Sunday of Easter

Almighty and everlasting God, who in the Paschal mystery established the new covenant of reconciliation: Grant that all who have been reborn into the fellowship of Christ's Body may show forth in their lives what they profess by their faith; through Jesus Christ our Lord, who lives and reigns with you and the Holy Spirit, one God, for ever and ever. *Amen.*

Preface of Easter

Third Sunday of Easter

O God, whose blessed Son made himself known to his disciples in the breaking of bread: Open the eyes of our faith, that we may behold him in all his redeeming work; who lives and reigns with you, in the unity of the Holy Spirit, one God, now and for ever. *Amen.*

Preface of Easter

Fourth Sunday of Easter

O God, whose Son Jesus is the good shepherd of your people: Grant that when we hear his voice we may know him who calls us each by name, and follow where he leads; who, with you and the Holy Spirit, lives and reigns, one God, for ever and ever. *Amen.*

Preface of Easter

Fifth Sunday of Easter

Almighty God, whom truly to know is everlasting life: Grant us so perfectly to know your Son Jesus Christ to be the way, the truth, and the life, that we may steadfastly follow his steps in the way that leads to eternal life; through Jesus Christ your Son our Lord, who lives and reigns with you, in the unity of the Holy Spirit, one God, for ever and ever. *Amen.*

Preface of Easter

Sixth Sunday of Easter

O God, you have prepared for those who love you such good things as surpass our understanding: Pour into our hearts such love towards you, that we, loving you in all things and above all things, may obtain your promises, which exceed all that we can desire; through Jesus Christ our Lord, who lives and reigns with you and the Holy Spirit, one God, for ever and ever. *Amen.*

Preface of Easter

Monday, Tuesday, and Wednesday of this week are the traditional Rogation Days.

Ascension Day

Almighty God, whose blessed Son our Savior Jesus Christ ascended far above all heavens that he might fill all things: Mercifully give us faith to perceive that, according to his promise, he abides with his Church on earth, even to the end of the ages; through Jesus Christ our Lord, who lives and reigns with you and the Holy Spirit, one God, in glory everlasting. *Amen.*

or this

Grant, we pray, Almighty God, that as we believe your
only-begotten Son our Lord Jesus Christ to have ascended
into heaven, so we may also in heart and mind there
ascend, and with him continually dwell; who lives and
reigns with you and the Holy Spirit, one God, for ever and
ever. *Amen.*

Preface of the Ascension

*Either of the preceding Collects, with the proper Psalm and
Lessons for Ascension Day, serves for the following
weekdays, except as otherwise appointed .*

Seventh Sunday of Easter: The Sunday after Ascension Day
O God, the King of glory, you have exalted your only Son
Jesus Christ with great triumph to your kingdom in heaven:
Do not leave us comfortless, but send us your Holy Spirit
to strengthen us, and exalt us to that place where our
Savior Christ has gone before; who lives and reigns with
you and the Holy Spirit, one God, in glory everlasting.
Amen.

Preface of the Ascension

The Day of Pentecost: Whitsunday
*When a Vigil of Pentecost is observed, it begins with the
Service of Light, page 109 of BCP (substituting, if desired,
the Gloria in excelsis for the Phos hilaron), and continues
with the Salutation and Collect of the Day. Three or more
of the appointed Lessons are read before the Gospel, each
followed by a Psalm, Canticle, or hymn. Holy Baptism or
Confirmation (beginning with the Presentation of the
Candidates), or the Renewal of Baptismal Vows, page 292
of BCP, follows the Sermon.*

Almighty God, on this day you opened the way of eternal life to every race and nation by the promised gift of your Holy Spirit: Shed abroad this gift throughout the world by the preaching of the Gospel, that it may reach to the ends of the earth; through Jesus Christ our Lord, who lives and reigns with you, in the unity of the Holy Spirit, one God, for ever and ever. *Amen.*

or this

O God, who on this day taught the hearts of your faithful people by sending to them the light of your Holy Spirit: Grant us by the same Spirit to have a right judgment in all things, and evermore to rejoice in his holy comfort; through Jesus Christ your Son our Lord, who lives and reigns with you, in the unity of the Holy Spirit, one God, for ever and ever. *Amen.*

Preface of Pentecost

On the weekdays which follow, the numbered Proper which corresponds most closely to the date of Pentecost in that year is used. See page 158. Wednesday, Friday, and Saturday of this week are the traditional summer Ember Days.

First Sunday after Pentecost: Trinity Sunday

Almighty and everlasting God, you have given to us your servants grace, by the confession of a true faith, to acknowledge the glory of the eternal Trinity, and in the power of your divine Majesty to worship the Unity: Keep us steadfast in this faith and worship, and bring us at last to see you in your one and eternal glory, O Father; who with the Son and the Holy Spirit live and reign, one God, for ever and ever. *Amen.*

Preface of Trinity Sunday

On the weekdays which follow, the numbered Proper which corresponds most closely to the date of Trinity Sunday in that year is used.

The Season after Pentecost

Proper 1 *Week of the Sunday closest to May 11*
Remember, O Lord, what you have wrought in us and not what we deserve; and, as you have called us to your service, make us worthy of our calling; through Jesus Christ our Lord, who lives and reigns with you and the Holy Spirit, one God, now and for ever. *Amen.*

No Proper Preface is used.

Proper 2 *Week of the Sunday closest to May 18*
Almighty and merciful God, in your goodness keep us, we pray, from all things that may hurt us, that we, being ready both in mind and body, may accomplish with free hearts those things which belong to your purpose; through Jesus Christ our Lord, who lives and reigns with you and the Holy Spirit, one God, now and for ever; *Amen.*

No Proper Preface is used.

Proper 3 *The Sunday closest to May 25*
Grant, O Lord, that the course of this world may be peaceably governed by your providence; and that your Church may joyfully serve you in confidence and serenity; through Jesus Christ our Lord, who lives and reigns with you and the Holy Spirit, one God, for ever and ever. *Amen.*

Preface of the Lord's Day

Proper 4 *The Sunday closest to June 1*
O God, your never-failing providence sets in order all things both in heaven and earth: Put away from us, we entreat you, all hurtful things, and give us those things which are profitable for us; through Jesus Christ our Lord, who lives and reigns with you and the Holy Spirit, one God, for ever and ever. *Amen.*

Preface of the Lord's Day

Proper 5 *The Sunday closest to June 8*
O God, from whom all good proceeds: Grant that by your
inspiration we may think those things that are right, and by
your merciful guiding may do them; through Jesus Christ
our Lord, who lives and reigns with you and the Holy
Spirit, one God, for ever and ever. *Amen.*

Preface of the Lord's Day

Proper 6 *The Sunday closest to June 15*
Keep, O Lord, your household the Church in your steadfast
faith and love, that through your grace we may proclaim
your truth with boldness, and minister your justice with
compassion; for the sake of our Savior Jesus Christ, who
lives and reigns with you and the Holy Spirit, one God,
now and for ever. *Amen.*

Preface of the Lord's Day

Proper 7 *The Sunday closest to June 22*
O Lord, make us have perpetual love and reverence for
your holy Name, for you never fail to help and govern
those whom you have set upon the sure foundation of your
loving-kindness; through Jesus Christ our Lord, who lives
and reigns with you and the Holy Spirit, one God, for ever
and ever. *Amen.*

Preface of the Lord's Day

Proper 8 *The Sunday closest to June 29*
Almighty God, you have built your Church upon the
foundation of the apostles and prophets, Jesus Christ
himself being the chief cornerstone: Grant us so to be
joined together in unity of spirit by their teaching, that we
may be made a holy temple acceptable to you; through
Jesus Christ our Lord, who lives and reigns with you and
the Holy Spirit, one God, for ever and ever. *Amen.*

Preface of the Lord's Day

Proper 9 *The Sunday closest to July 6*
O God, you have taught us to keep all your commandments
by loving you and our neighbor: Grant us the grace of your
Holy Spirit, that we may be devoted to you with our whole
heart, and united to one another with pure affection;
through Jesus Christ our Lord, who lives and reigns with
you and the Holy Spirit, one God, for ever and ever. *Amen.*

Preface of the Lord's Day

Proper 10 *The Sunday closest to July 13*
O Lord, mercifully receive the prayers of your people who
call upon you, and grant that they may know and
understand what things they ought to do, and also may
have grace and power faithfully to accomplish them;
through Jesus Christ our Lord, who lives and reigns with
you and the Holy Spirit, one God, now and for ever. *Amen.*

Preface of the Lord's Day

Proper 11 *The Sunday closest to July 20*
Almighty God, the fountain of all wisdom, you know our
necessities before we ask and our ignorance in asking:
Have compassion on our weakness, and mercifully give us
those things which for our unworthiness we dare not, and
for our blindness we cannot ask; through the worthiness of
your Son Jesus Christ our Lord, who lives and reigns with
you and the Holy Spirit, one God, now and for ever. *Amen.*

Preface of the Lord's Day

Proper 12 *The Sunday closest to July 27*
O God, the protector of all who trust in you, without whom
nothing is strong, nothing is holy: Increase and multiply
upon us your mercy; that, with you as our ruler and guide,
we may so pass through things temporal, that we lose not
the things eternal; through Jesus Christ our Lord, who lives
and reigns with you and the Holy Spirit, one God, for ever
and ever. *Amen.*

Preface of the Lord's Day

Proper 13 *The Sunday closest to August 3*
Let your continual mercy, O Lord, cleanse and defend your
Church; and, because it cannot continue in safety without
your help, protect and govern it always by your goodness;
through Jesus Christ our Lord, who lives and reigns with
you and the Holy Spirit, one God, for ever and ever. *Amen.*

Preface of the Lord's Day

Proper 14 *The Sunday closest to August 10*
Grant to us, Lord, we pray, the spirit to think and do
always those things that are right, that we, who cannot
exist without you, may by you be enabled to live according
to your will; through Jesus Christ our Lord, who lives and
reigns with you and the Holy Spirit, one God, for ever and
ever. *Amen.*

Preface of the Lord's Day

Proper 15 *The Sunday closest to August 17*
Almighty God, you have given your only Son to be for us a
sacrifice for sin, and also an example of godly life: Give us
grace to receive thankfully the fruits of his redeeming
work, and to follow daily in the blessed steps of his most
holy life; through Jesus Christ your Son our Lord, who
lives and reigns with you and the Holy Spirit, one God,
now and for ever. *Amen.*

Preface of the Lord's Day

Proper 16 *The Sunday closest to August 24*
Grant, O merciful God, that your Church, being gathered
together in unity by your Holy Spirit, may show forth your
power among all peoples, to the glory of your Name;
through Jesus Christ our Lord, who lives and reigns with
you and the Holy Spirit, one God, for ever and ever. *Amen.*

Preface of the Lord's Day

Proper 17 *The Sunday closest to August 31*
Lord of all power and might, the author and giver of all
good things: Graft in our hearts the love of your Name;
increase in us true religion; nourish us with all goodness;
and bring forth in us the fruit of good works; through Jesus
Christ our Lord, who lives and reigns with you and the
Holy Spirit, one God for ever and ever. *Amen.*

Preface of the Lord's Day

Proper 18 *The Sunday closest to September 7*
Grant us, O Lord, to trust in you with all our hearts; for, as
you always resist the proud who confide in their own
strength, so you never forsake those who make their boast
of your mercy; through Jesus Christ our Lord, who lives
and reigns with you and the Holy Spirit, one God, now and
for ever. *Amen.*

Preface of the Lord's Day

Proper 19 *The Sunday closest to September 14*
O God, because without you we are not able to please you,
mercifully grant that your Holy Spirit may in all things
direct and rule our hearts; through Jesus Christ our Lord,
who lives and reigns with you and the Holy Spirit, one
God, now and for ever. *Amen.*

Preface of the Lord's Day
The Wednesday, Friday, and Saturday after September 14
are the traditional autumnal Ember Days..

Proper 20 *The Sunday closest to September 21*
Grant us, Lord, not to be anxious about earthly things, but
to love things heavenly; and even now, while we are placed
among things that are passing away, to hold fast to those
that shall endure; through Jesus Christ our Lord, who lives
and reigns with you and the Holy Spirit, one God, for ever
and ever. *Amen.*

Preface of the Lord's Day

Proper 21 *The Sunday closest to September 28*
O God, you declare your almighty power chiefly in
showing mercy and pity: Grant us the fullness of your
grace, that we, running to obtain your promises, may
become partakers of your heavenly treasure; through Jesus
Christ our Lord, who lives and reigns with you and the
Holy Spirit, one God, for ever and ever. *Amen.*

Preface of the Lord's Day

Proper 22 *The Sunday closest to October 5*
Almighty and everlasting God, you are always more ready
to hear than we to pray, and to give more than we either
desire or deserve: Pour upon us the abundance of your
mercy, forgiving us those things of which our conscience is
afraid, and giving us those good things for which we are
not worthy to ask, except through the merits and mediation
of Jesus Christ our Savior; who lives and reigns with you
and the Holy Spirit, one God, for ever and ever. *Amen.*

Preface of the Lord's Day

Proper 23 *The Sunday closest to October 12*
Lord, we pray that your grace may always precede and
follow us, that we may continually be given to good works;
through Jesus Christ our Lord, who lives and reigns with
you and the Holy Spirit, one God, now and for ever. *Amen.*

Preface of the Lord's Day

Proper 24 *The Sunday closest to October 19*
Almighty and everlasting God, in Christ you have revealed
your glory among the nations: Preserve the works of your
mercy, that your Church throughout the world may
persevere with steadfast faith in the confession of your
Name; through Jesus Christ our Lord, who lives and reigns
with you and the Holy Spirit, one God, for ever and ever.
Amen.

Preface of the Lord's Day

Proper 25 *The Sunday closest to October 26*
Almighty and everlasting God, increase in us the gifts of
faith, hope, and charity; and, that we may obtain what you
promise, make us love what you command; through Jesus
Christ our Lord, who lives and reigns with you and the
Holy Spirit, one God, for ever and ever. *Amen.*

Preface of the Lord's Day

Proper 26 *The Sunday closest to November 2*
Almighty and merciful God, it is only by your gift that
your faithful people offer you true and laudable service:
Grant that we may run without stumbling to obtain your
heavenly promises; through Jesus Christ our Lord, who
lives and reigns with you and the Holy Spirit, one God,
now and for ever. *Amen.*

Preface of the Lord's Day

Proper 27 *The Sunday closest to November 9*
O God, whose blessed Son came into the world that he
might destroy the works of the devil and make us children
of God and heirs of eternal life: Grant that, having this
hope, we may purify ourselves as he is pure; that, when he
comes again with power and great glory, we may be made
like him in his eternal and glorious kingdom; where he
lives and reigns with you and the Holy Spirit, one God, for
ever and ever. *Amen.*

Preface of the Lord's Day

Proper 28 *The Sunday closest to November 16*
Blessed Lord, who caused all holy Scriptures to be written
for our learning: Grant us so to hear them, read, mark,
learn, and inwardly digest them, that we may embrace and
ever hold fast the blessed hope of everlasting life, which
you have given us in our Savior Jesus Christ; who lives
and reigns with you and the Holy Spirit, one God, for ever
and ever. *Amen.*

Preface of the Lord's Day

Proper 29 *The Sunday closest to November 23*
Almighty and everlasting God, whose will it is to restore
all things in your well-beloved Son, the King of kings and
Lord of lords: Mercifully grant that the peoples of the
earth, divided and enslaved by sin, may be freed and
brought together under his most gracious rule; who lives
and reigns with you and the Holy Spirit, one God, now and
for ever. *Amen.*

Preface of the Lord's Day, or of Baptism

Holy Days

Saint Andrew *November 30*
Almighty God, who gave such grace to your apostle
Andrew that he readily obeyed the call of your Son Jesus
Christ, and brought his brother with him: Give us, who are
called by your Holy Word, grace to follow him without
delay, and to bring those near to us into his gracious
presence; who lives and reigns with you and the Holy
Spirit, one God, now and for ever. *Amen.*

Preface of Apostles

Saint Thomas *December 21*
Everliving God, who strengthened your apostle Thomas
with firm and certain faith in your Son's resurrection:
Grant us so perfectly and without doubt to believe in Jesus
Christ, our Lord and our God, that our faith may never be
found wanting in your sight; through him who lives and
reigns with you and the Holy Spirit, one God, now and for
ever. *Amen.*

Preface of Apostles

Saint Stephen *December 26*

We give you thanks, O Lord of glory, for the example of the first martyr Stephen, who looked up to heaven and prayed for his persecutors to your Son Jesus Christ, who stands at your right hand; where he lives and reigns with you and the Holy Spirit, one God, in glory everlasting. *Amen.*

Preface of the Incarnation

Saint John *December 27*

Shed upon your Church, O Lord, the brightness of your light, that we, being illumined by the teaching of your apostle and evangelist John, may so walk in the light of your truth, that at length we may attain to the fullness of eternal life; through Jesus Christ our Lord, who lives and reigns with you and the Holy Spirit, one God, for ever and ever. *Amen.*

Preface of the Incarnation

The Holy Innocents *December 28*

We remember today, O God, the slaughter of the holy innocents of Bethlehem by King Herod. Receive, we pray, into the arms of your mercy all innocent victims; and by your great might frustrate the designs of evil tyrants and establish your rule of justice, love, and peace; through Jesus Christ our Lord, who lives and reigns with you, in the unity of the Holy Spirit, one God, for ever and ever. *Amen.*

Preface of the Incarnation

Confession of Saint Peter *January 18*

Almighty Father, who inspired Simon Peter, first among the apostles, to confess Jesus as Messiah and Son of the living God: Keep your Church steadfast upon the rock of this faith, so that in unity and peace we may proclaim the one truth and follow the one Lord, our Savior Jesus Christ; who lives and reigns with you and the Holy Spirit, one God, now and for ever. *Amen.*

Preface of Apostles

Conversion of Saint Paul *January 25*

O God, by the preaching of your apostle Paul you have caused the light of the Gospel to shine throughout the world: Grant, we pray, that we, having his wonderful conversion in remembrance, may show ourselves thankful to you by following his holy teaching; through Jesus Christ our Lord, who lives and reigns with you, in the unity of the Holy Spirit, one God, now and for ever. *Amen.*

Preface of Apostles

The Presentation *February 2*

Almighty and everliving God, we humbly pray that, as your only-begotten Son was this day presented in the temple, so we may be presented to you with pure and clean hearts by Jesus Christ our Lord; who lives and reigns with you and the Holy Spirit, one God, now and for ever. *Amen.*

Preface of the Epiphany

Saint Matthias *February 24*

Almighty God, who in the place of Judas chose your faithful servant Matthias to be numbered among the Twelve: Grant that your Church, being delivered from false apostles, may always be guided and governed by faithful and true pastors; through Jesus Christ our Lord, who lives and reigns with you, in the unity of the Holy Spirit, one God, now and for ever. *Amen.*

Preface of Apostles

Saint Joseph *March 19*

O God, who from the family of your servant David raised up Joseph to be the guardian of your incarnate Son and the spouse of his virgin mother: Give us grace to imitate his uprightness of life and his obedience to your commands; through Jesus Christ our Lord, who lives and reigns with you and the Holy Spirit, one God, for ever and ever. *Amen.*

Preface of the Epiphany

The Annunciation *March 25*

Pour your grace into our hearts, O Lord, that we who have known the incarnation of your Son Jesus Christ, announced by an angel to the Virgin Mary, may by his cross and passion be brought to the glory of his resurrection; who lives and reigns with you, in the unity of the Holy Spirit, one God, now and for ever. *Amen.*

Preface of the Epiphany

Saint Mark *April 25*

Almighty God, by the hand of Mark the evangelist you have given to your Church the Gospel of Jesus Christ the Son of God: We thank you for this witness, and pray that we may be firmly grounded in its truth; through Jesus Christ our Lord, who lives and reigns with you and the Holy Spirit, one God, for ever and ever. *Amen.*

Preface of All Saints

Saint Philip and Saint James *May 1*

Almighty God, who gave to your apostles Philip and James grace and strength to bear witness to the truth: Grant that we, being mindful of their victory of faith, may glorify in life and death the Name of our Lord Jesus Christ; who lives and reigns with you and the Holy Spirit, one God, now and for ever. *Amen.*

Preface of Apostles

Collects 147

The Visitation *May 31*
Father in heaven, by your grace the virgin mother of your incarnate Son was blessed in bearing him, but still more blessed in keeping your word: Grant us who honor the exaltation of her lowliness to follow the example of her devotion to your will; through Jesus Christ our Lord, who lives and reigns with you and the Holy Spirit, one God, for ever and ever. *Amen.*

Preface of the Epiphany

Saint Barnabas *June 11*
Grant, O God, that we may follow the example of your faithful servant Barnabas, who, seeking not his own renown but the well-being of your Church, gave generously of his life and substance for the relief of the poor and the spread of the Gospel; through Jesus Christ our Lord, who lives and reigns with you and the Holy Spirit, one God, for ever and ever. *Amen.*

Preface of Apostles

The Nativity of Saint John the Baptist *June 24*
Almighty God, by whose providence your servant John the Baptist was wonderfully born, and sent to prepare the way of your Son our Savior by preaching repentance: Make us so to follow his teaching and holy life, that we may truly repent according to his preaching; and, following his example, constantly speak the truth, boldly rebuke vice, and patiently suffer for the truth's sake; through Jesus Christ your Son our Lord, who lives and reigns with you and the Holy Spirit, one God, for ever and ever. *Amen.*

Preface of Advent

Saint Peter and Saint Paul *June 29*

Almighty God, whose blessed apostles Peter and Paul glorified you by their martyrdom: Grant that your Church, instructed by their teaching and example, and knit together in unity by your Spirit, may ever stand firm upon the one foundation, which is Jesus Christ our Lord; who lives and reigns with you, in the unity of the Holy Spirit, one God, now and for ever. *Amen.*

Preface of Apostles

Independence Day *July 4*

Lord God Almighty, in whose Name the founders of this country won liberty for themselves and for us, and lit the torch of freedom for nations then unborn: Grant that we and all the people of this land may have grace to maintain our liberties in righteousness and peace; through Jesus Christ our Lord, who lives and reigns with you and the Holy Spirit, one God, for ever and ever. *Amen.*

The Collect "For the Nation," page 162, may be used instead.

Preface of Trinity Sunday

Saint Mary Magdalene *July 22*

Almighty God, whose blessed Son restored Mary Magdalene to health of body and of mind, and called her to be a witness of his resurrection: Mercifully grant that by your grace we may be healed from all our infirmities and know you in the power of his unending life; who with you and the Holy Spirit lives and reigns, one God, now and for ever. *Amen.*

Preface of All Saints

Saint James *July 25*

O gracious God, we remember before you today your servant and apostle James, first among the Twelve to suffer martyrdom for the Name of Jesus Christ; and we pray that you will pour out upon the leaders of your Church that spirit of self-denying service by which alone they may have true authority among your people; through Jesus Christ our Lord, who lives and reigns with you and the Holy Spirit, one God, now and for ever. *Amen.*

Preface of Apostles

The Transfiguration *August 6*

O God, who on the holy mount revealed to chosen witnesses your well-beloved Son, wonderfully transfigured, in raiment white and glistening: Mercifully grant that we, being delivered from the disquietude of this world, may by faith behold the King in his beauty; who with you, O Father, and you, O Holy Spirit, lives and reigns, one God, for ever and ever. *Amen.*

Preface of the Epiphany

Saint Mary the Virgin *August 15*

O God, you have taken to yourself the blessed Virgin Mary, mother of your incarnate Son: Grant that we, who have been redeemed by his blood, may share with her the glory of your eternal kingdom; through Jesus Christ our Lord, who lives and reigns with you, in the unity of the Holy Spirit, one God, now and for ever. *Amen.*

Preface of the Incarnation

Saint Bartholomew *August 24*

Almighty and everlasting God, who gave to your apostle Bartholomew grace truly to believe and to preach your Word: Grant that your Church may love what he believed and preach what he taught; through Jesus Christ our Lord, who lives and reigns with you and the Holy Spirit, one God, for ever and ever. *Amen.*

Preface of Apostles

Holy Cross Day *September 14*

Almighty God, whose Son our Savior Jesus Christ was lifted high upon the cross that he might draw the whole world to himself: Mercifully grant that we, who glory in the mystery of our redemption, may have grace to take up our cross and follow him; who lives and reigns with you and the Holy Spirit, one God, in glory everlasting. *Amen.*

Preface of Holy Week

Saint Matthew *September 21*

We thank you, heavenly Father, for the witness of your apostle and evangelist Matthew to the Gospel of your Son our Savior; and we pray that, after his example, we may with ready wills and hearts obey the calling of our Lord to follow him; through Jesus Christ our Lord, who lives and reigns with you and the Holy Spirit, one God, now and for ever. *Amen.*

Preface of Apostles

Saint Michael and All Angels *September 29*

Everlasting God, you have ordained and constituted in a wonderful order the ministries of angels and mortals: Mercifully grant that, as your holy angels always serve and worship you in heaven, so by your appointment they may help and defend us here on earth; through Jesus Christ our Lord, who lives and reigns with you and the Holy Spirit, one God, for ever and ever. *Amen.*

Preface of Trinity Sunday

Saint Luke *October 18*
Almighty God, who inspired your servant Luke the
physician to set forth in the Gospel the love and healing
power of your Son: Graciously continue in your Church
this love and power to heal, to the praise and glory of your
Name; through Jesus Christ our Lord, who lives and reigns
with you, in the unity of the Holy Spirit, one God, now and
for ever. *Amen.*

Preface of All Saints

Saint James of Jerusalem *October 23*
Grant, O God, that, following the example of your servant
James the Just, brother of our Lord, your Church may give
itself continually to prayer and to the reconciliation of all
who are at variance and enmity; through Jesus Christ our
Lord, who lives and reigns with you and the Holy Spirit,
one God, now and for ever. *Amen.*

Preface of All Saints

Saint Simon and Saint Jude *October 28*
O God, we thank you for the glorious company of the
apostles, and especially on this day for Simon and Jude;
and we pray that, as they were faithful and zealous in their
mission, so we may with ardent devotion make known the
love and mercy of our Lord and Savior Jesus Christ; who
lives and reigns with you and the Holy Spirit, one God, for
ever and ever. *Amen.*

Preface of Apostles

All Saints' Day *November 1*
Almighty God, you have knit together your elect in one
communion and fellowship in the mystical body of your
Son Christ our Lord: Give us grace so to follow your
blessed saints in all virtuous and godly living, that we may
come to those ineffable joys that you have prepared for
those who truly love you; through Jesus Christ our Lord,
who with you and the Holy Spirit lives and reigns, one
God, in glory everlasting. *Amen.*

Preface of All Saints

Thanksgiving Day
Almighty and gracious Father, we give you thanks for the
fruits of the earth in their season and for the labors of those
who harvest them. Make us, we pray, faithful stewards of
your great bounty, for the provision of our necessities and
the relief of all who are in need, to the glory of your Name;
through Jesus Christ our Lord, who lives and reigns with
you and the Holy Spirit, one God, now and for ever. *Amen.*
*For the Prayers of the People, the Litany of Thanksgiving
on page 836 of BCP may be used.*

Preface of Trinity Sunday

The Common of Saints

The festival of a saint is observed in accordance with the rules of precedence set forth in the Calendar of the Church Year. At the discretion of the Celebrant, and as appropriate, any of the following Collects, with one of the corresponding sets of Psalms and Lessons, may be used

a) at the commemoration of a saint listed in the Calendar for which no Proper is provided in this Book

b) at the patronal festival or commemoration of a saint not listed in the Calendar.

Of a Martyr
Almighty God, who gave to your servant *N.* boldness to confess the Name of our Savior Jesus Christ before the rulers of this world, and courage to die for this faith: Grant that we may always be ready to give a reason for the hope that is in us, and to suffer gladly for the sake of our Lord Jesus Christ; who lives and reigns with you and the Holy Spirit, one God, for ever and ever. *Amen.*

or this

Almighty God, by whose grace and power your holy martyr N. triumphed over suffering and was faithful even to death: Grant us, who now remember *him* in thanksgiving, to be so faithful in our witness to you in this world, that we may receive with *him* the crown of life; through Jesus Christ our Lord, who lives and reigns with you and the Holy Spirit, one God, for ever and ever. *Amen.*

or this

Almighty and everlasting God, who kindled the flame of your love in the heart of your holy martyr *N.*: Grant to us, your humble servants, a like faith and power of love, that we who rejoice in *her* triumph may profit by *her* example; through Jesus Christ our Lord, who lives and reigns with you and the Holy Spirit, one God, for ever and ever. *Amen.*

Preface of a Saint

Of a Missionary
Almighty and everlasting God, we thank you for your servant *N.*, whom you called to preach the Gospel to the people of_____ (*or* to the_____ people). Raise up in this and every land evangelists and heralds of your kingdom, that your Church may proclaim the unsearchable riches of our Savior Jesus Christ; who lives and reigns with you and the Holy Spirit, one God, now and for ever. *Amen.*

or the following

Almighty God, whose will it is to be glorified in your saints, and who raised up your servant *N.* to be a light in the world: Shine, we pray, in our hearts, that we also in our generation may show forth your praise, who called us out of darkness into your marvelous light; through Jesus Christ our Lord, who lives and reigns with you and the Holy Spirit, one God, now and for ever. *Amen.*

Preface of Pentecost

Of a Pastor
Heavenly Father, Shepherd of your people, we thank you for your servant *N.*, who was faithful in the care and nurture of your flock; and we pray that, following *his* example and the teaching of *his* holy life, we may by your grace grow into the stature of the fullness of our Lord and Savior Jesus Christ; who lives and reigns with you and the Holy Spirit, one God, for ever and ever. *Amen.*

or this

O God, our heavenly Father, who raised up your faithful servant *N.*, to be a [bishop and] pastor in your Church and to feed your flock: Give abundantly to all pastors the gifts of your Holy Spirit, that they may minister in your household as true servants of Christ and stewards of your divine mysteries; through Jesus Christ our Lord, who lives and reigns with you and the Holy Spirit, one God, for ever and ever. *Amen.*

Preface of a Saint

Of a Theologian and Teacher

O God, by your Holy Spirit you give to some the word of wisdom, to others the word of knowledge, and to others the word of faith: We praise your Name for the gifts of grace manifested in your servant *N.*, and we pray that your Church may never be destitute of such gifts; through Jesus Christ our Lord, who with you and the Holy Spirit lives and reigns, one God, for ever and ever. *Amen.*

or this

Almighty God, you gave to your servant *N.* special gifts of grace to understand and teach the truth as it is in Christ Jesus: Grant that by this teaching we may know you, the one true God, and Jesus Christ whom you have sent; who lives and reigns with you and the Holy Spirit, one God, for ever and ever. *Amen.*

Preface of a Saint, or of Trinity Sunday

Of a Monastic

O God, whose blessed Son became poor that we through his poverty might be rich: Deliver us from an inordinate love of this world, that we, inspired by the devotion of your servant N., may serve you with singleness of heart, and attain to the riches of the age to come; through Jesus Christ our Lord, who lives and reigns with you, in the unity of the Holy Spirit, one God, now and for ever. *Amen.*

or this

O God, by whose grace your servant *N.*, kindled with the flame of your love, became a burning and a shining light in your Church: Grant that we also may be aflame with the spirit of love and discipline, and walk before you as children of light; through Jesus Christ our Lord, who lives and reigns with you, in the unity of the Holy Spirit, one God, now and for ever. *Amen.*

Preface of a Saint

Of a Saint

Almighty God, you have surrounded us with a great cloud of witnesses: Grant that we, encouraged by the good example of your servant *N.*, may persevere in running the race that is set before us, until at last we may with *him* attain to your eternal joy; through Jesus Christ, the pioneer and perfecter of our faith, who lives and reigns with you and the Holy Spirit, one God, for ever and ever. *Amen.*

or this

O God, you have brought us near to an innumerable company of angels, and to the spirits of just men made perfect: Grant us during our earthly pilgrimage to abide in their fellowship, and in our heavenly country to become partakers of their joy; through Jesus Christ our Lord, who lives and reigns with you and the Holy Spirit, one God, now and for ever. *Amen.*

or this

Almighty God, by your Holy Spirit you have made us one with your saints in heaven and on earth: Grant that in our earthly pilgrimage we may always be supported by this fellowship of love and prayer, and know ourselves to be surrounded by their witness to your power and mercy. We ask this for the sake of Jesus Christ, in whom all our intercessions are acceptable through the Spirit, and who lives and reigns for ever and ever. *Amen.*

Preface of a Saint

Various Occasions

For optional use, when desired, subject to the rules set forth in the Calendar of the Church Year.

1. Of the Holy Trinity
Almighty God, you have revealed to your Church your eternal Being of glorious majesty and perfect love as one God in Trinity of Persons: Give us grace to continue steadfast in the confession of this faith, and constant in our worship of you, Father, Son, and Holy Spirit; for you live and reign, one God, now and for ever. *Amen.*

Preface of Trinity Sunday

2. Of the Holy Spirit
Almighty and most merciful God, grant that by the indwelling of your Holy Spirit we may be enlightened and strengthened for your service; through Jesus Christ our Lord, who lives and reigns with you, in the unity of the Holy Spirit, one God, now and for ever. *Amen.*

Preface of Pentecost

3. Of the Holy Angels
Everlasting God, you have ordained and constituted in a wonderful order the ministries of angels and mortals: Mercifully grant that, as your holy angels always serve and worship you in heaven, so by your appointment they may help and defend us here on earth; through Jesus Christ our Lord, who lives and reigns with you and the Holy Spirit, one God, for ever and ever. *Amen.*

Preface of Trinity Sunday

4. Of the Incarnation
O God, who wonderfully created, and yet more wonderfully restored, the dignity of human nature: Grant that we may share the divine life of him who humbled himself to share our humanity, your Son Jesus Christ; who lives and reigns with you, in the unity of the Holy Spirit, one God, for ever and ever. *Amen.*

Preface of the Epiphany

5. Of the Holy Eucharist
Especially suitable for Thursdays
God our Father, whose Son our Lord Jesus Christ in a wonderful Sacrament has left us a memorial of his passion: Grant us so to venerate the sacred mysteries of his Body and Blood, that we may ever perceive within ourselves the fruit of his redemption; who lives and reigns with you and the Holy Spirit, one God, for ever and ever. *Amen.*

Preface of the Epiphany

6. Of the Holy Cross
Especially suitable for Fridays
Almighty God, whose beloved Son willingly endured the agony and shame of the cross for our redemption: Give us courage to take up our cross and follow him; who lives and reigns with you and the Holy Spirit, one God, now and for ever. *Amen.*

Preface of Holy Week

7. For all Baptized Christians
Especially suitable for Saturdays

Grant, Lord God, to all who have been baptized into the death and resurrection of your Son Jesus Christ, that, as we have put away the old life of sin, so we may be renewed in the spirit of our minds, and live in righteousness and true holiness; through Jesus Christ our Lord, who lives and reigns with you, in the unity of the Holy Spirit, one God, now and for ever. *Amen.*

Preface of Baptism

8. For the Departed

Eternal Lord God, you hold all souls in life: Give to your whole Church in paradise and on earth your light and your peace; and grant that we, following the good examples of those who have served you here and are now at rest, may at the last enter with them into your unending joy; through Jesus Christ our Lord, who lives and reigns with you, in the unity of the Holy Spirit, one God, now and for ever. *Amen.*

or this

Almighty God, we remember before you today your faithful servant *N.*; and we pray that, having opened to *him* the gates of larger life, you will receive *him* more and more into your joyful service, that, with all who have faithfully served you in the past, *he* may share in the eternal victory of Jesus Christ our Lord; who lives and reigns with you, in the unity of the Holy Spirit, one God, for ever and ever. *Amen.*

Any of the Collects appointed for use at the Burial of the Dead may be used instead. For the Prayers of the People, one of the forms appointed for the Burial of the Dead may be used.

Preface of the Commemoration of the Dead

9. Of the Reign of Christ

Almighty and everlasting God, whose will it is to restore all things in your well-beloved Son, the King of kings and Lord of lords: Mercifully grant that the peoples of the earth, divided and enslaved by sin, may be freed and brought together under his most gracious rule; who lives and reigns with you and the Holy Spirit, one God, now and for ever. *Amen.*

Preface of the Ascension, or of Baptism

10. At Baptism

Almighty God, by our baptism into the death and resurrection of your Son Jesus Christ, you turn us from the old life of sin: Grant that we, being reborn to new life in him, may live in righteousness and holiness all our days; through Jesus Christ our Lord, who lives and reigns with you and the Holy Spirit, one God, now and for ever. *Amen.*

Preface of Baptism

11. At Confirmation

Grant, Almighty God, that we, who have been redeemed from the old life of sin by our baptism into the death and resurrection of your Son Jesus Christ, may be renewed in your Holy Spirit, and live in righteousness and true holiness; through Jesus Christ our Lord, who lives and reigns with you and the Holy Spirit, one God, now and for ever. *Amen.*

Preface of Baptism, or of Pentecost

12. On the Anniversary of the Dedication of a Church

Almighty God, to whose glory we celebrate the dedication of this house of prayer: We give you thanks for the fellowship of those who have worshiped in this place, and we pray that all who seek you here may find you, and be filled with your joy and peace; through Jesus Christ our Lord, who lives and reigns with you, in the unity of the Holy Spirit, one God, now and for ever. *Amen.*

The Litany of Thanksgiving for a Church, page 578 of BCP, may be used for the Prayers of the People.

Preface of the Dedication of a Church

13. For a Church Convention

Almighty and everlasting Father, you have given the Holy Spirit to abide with us for ever: Bless, we pray, with his grace and presence, the bishops and the other clergy and the laity here (or now, or soon to be) assembled in your Name, that your Church, being preserved in true faith and godly discipline, may fulfill all the mind of him who loved it and gave himself for it, your Son Jesus Christ our Savior; who lives and reigns with you, in the unity of the Holy Spirit, one God, now and for ever. *Amen.*

Preface of Pentecost, or of the Season

14. For the Unity of the Church

Almighty Father, whose blessed Son before his passion prayed for his disciples that they might be one, as you and he are one: Grant that your Church, being bound together in love and obedience to you, may be united in one body by the one Spirit, that the world may believe in him whom you have sent, your Son Jesus Christ our Lord; who lives and reigns with you, in the unity of the Holy Spirit, one God, now and for ever. *Amen.*

Preface of Baptism, or of Trinity Sunday

15. For the Ministry (Ember Days)
For use on the traditional days or at other times

I. For those to be ordained
Almighty God, the giver of all good gifts, in your divine
providence you have appointed various orders in your
Church: Give your grace, we humbly pray, to all who are
[now] called to any office and ministry for your people;
and so fill them with the truth of your doctrine and clothe
them with holiness of life, that they may faithfully serve
before you, to the glory of your great Name and for the
benefit of your holy Church; through Jesus Christ our
Lord, who lives and reigns with you, in the unity of the
Holy Spirit, one God, now and for ever. *Amen.*

Preface of Apostles

II. For the choice of fit persons for the ministry
O God, you led your holy apostles to ordain ministers in
every place: Grant that your Church, under the guidance of
the Holy Spirit, may choose suitable persons for the
ministry of Word and Sacrament, and may uphold them in
their work for the extension of your kingdom; through him
who is the Shepherd and Bishop of our souls, Jesus Christ
our Lord, who lives and reigns with you and the Holy
Spirit, one God, for ever and ever. *Amen.*

Preface of the Season

III. For all Christians in their vocation
Almighty and everlasting God, by whose Spirit the whole
body of your faithful people is governed and sanctified:
Receive our supplications and prayers, which we offer
before you for all members of your holy Church, that in
their vocation and ministry they may truly and devoutly
serve you; through our Lord and Savior Jesus Christ, who
lives and reigns with you, in the unity of the Holy Spirit,
one God, now and for ever. *Amen.*

Preface of Baptism, or of the Season

16. For the Mission of the Church

O God, you have made of one blood all the peoples of the earth, and sent your blessed Son to preach peace to those who are far off and to those who are near: Grant that people everywhere may seek after you and find you, bring the nations into your fold, pour out your Spirit upon all flesh, and hasten the coming of your kingdom; through Jesus Christ our Lord, who lives and reigns with you and the Holy Spirit, one God, now and for ever. *Amen.*

or this

O God of all the nations of the earth: Remember the multitudes who have been created in your image but have not known the redeeming work of our Savior Jesus Christ; and grant that, by the prayers and labors of your holy Church, they may be brought to know and worship you as you have been revealed in your Son; who lives and reigns with you and the Holy Spirit, one God, for ever and ever. *Amen.*

Preface of the Season, or of Pentecost

17. For the Nation

Lord God Almighty, you have made all the peoples of the earth for your glory, to serve you in freedom and in peace: Give to the people of our country a zeal for justice and the strength of forbearance, that we may use our liberty in accordance with your gracious will; through Jesus Christ our Lord, who lives and reigns with you and the Holy Spirit, one God, for ever and ever. *Amen.*

The Collect for Independence Day may be used instead.

Preface of Trinity Sunday

18. For Peace

Almighty God, kindle, we pray, in every heart the true love of peace, and guide with your wisdom those who take counsel for the nations of the earth, that in tranquillity your dominion may increase until the earth is filled with the knowledge of your love; through Jesus Christ our Lord, who lives and reigns with you, in the unity of the Holy Spirit, one God, now and for ever. *Amen.*

Preface of the Season

19. For Rogation Days
For use on the traditional days or at other times

I. For fruitful seasons

Almighty God, Lord of heaven and earth: We humbly pray that your gracious providence may give and preserve to our use the harvests of the land and of the seas, and may prosper all who labor to gather them, that we, who are constantly receiving good things from your hand, may always give you thanks; through Jesus Christ our Lord, who lives and reigns with you and the Holy Spirit, one God, for ever and ever. *Amen.*

Preface of the Season

II. For commerce and industry

Almighty God, whose Son Jesus Christ in his earthly life shared our toil and hallowed our labor: Be present with your people where they work; make those who carry on the industries and commerce of this land responsive to your will; and give to us all a pride in what we do, and a just return for our labor; through Jesus Christ our Lord, who lives and reigns with you, in the unity of the Holy Spirit, one God, now and for ever. *Amen.*

Preface of the Season

III. For stewardship of creation

O merciful Creator, your hand is open wide to satisfy the needs of every living creature: Make us always thankful for your loving providence; and grant that we, remembering the account that we must one day give, may be faithful stewards of your good gifts; through Jesus Christ our Lord, who with you and the Holy Spirit lives and reigns, one God, for ever and ever. *Amen.*

Preface of the Season

20. For the Sick

Heavenly Father, giver of life and health: Comfort and relieve your sick servants, and give your power of healing to those who minister to their needs, that those *(or N., or NN.)* for whom our prayers are offered may be strengthened in *their* weakness and have confidence in your loving care; through Jesus Christ our Lord, who lives and reigns with you and the Holy Spirit, one God, now and for ever. *Amen.*

Preface of the Season

The postcommunion prayer on page 457 of BCP may be used.

21. For Social Justice

Almighty God, who created us in your own image: Grant us grace fearlessly to contend against evil and to make no peace with oppression; and, that we may reverently use our freedom, help us to employ it in the maintenance of justice in our communities and among the nations, to the glory of your holy Name; through Jesus Christ our Lord, who lives and reigns with you and the Holy Spirit, one God, now and for ever. *Amen.*

Preface of the Season

22. For Social Service

Heavenly Father, whose blessed Son came not to be served but to serve: Bless all who, following in his steps, give themselves to the service of others; that with wisdom, patience, and courage, they may minister in his Name to the suffering, the friendless, and the needy- for the love of him who laid down his life for us, your Son our Savior Jesus Christ, who lives and reigns with you and the Holy Spirit, one God, for ever and ever. *Amen.*

Preface of the Season

23. For Education

Almighty God, the fountain of all wisdom: Enlighten by your Holy Spirit those who teach and those who learn, that, rejoicing in the knowledge of your truth, they may worship you and serve you from generation to generation; through Jesus Christ our Lord, who lives and reigns with you and the Holy Spirit, one God, for ever and ever. *Amen.*

Preface of the Season

24. For Vocation in Daily Work

Almighty God our heavenly Father, you declare your glory and show forth your handiwork in the heavens and in the earth: Deliver us in our various occupations from the service of self alone, that we may do the work you give us to do in truth and beauty and for the common good; for the sake of him who came among us as one who serves, your Son Jesus Christ our Lord, who lives and reigns with you and the Holy Spirit, one God, for ever and ever. *Amen.*

Preface of the Season

25. For Labor Day

Almighty God, you have so linked our lives one with another that all we do affects, for good or ill, all other lives: So guide us in the work we do, that we may do it not for self alone, but for the common good; and, as we seek a proper return for our own labor, make us mindful of the rightful aspirations of other workers, and arouse our concern for those who are out of work; through Jesus Christ our Lord, who lives and reigns with you and the Holy Spirit, one God, for ever and ever. *Amen.*

Preface of the Season

Prayers for the Sick

For a Sick Person

O Father of mercies and God of all comfort, our only help
in time of need: We humbly beseech thee to behold, visit,
and relieve thy sick servant N. for whom our prayers are
desired. Look upon him with the eyes of thy mercy;
comfort him with a sense of thy goodness; preserve him
from the temptations of the enemy; and give him patience
under his affliction. In thy good time, restore him to health,
and enable him to lead the residue of his life in thy fear,
and to thy glory; and grant that finally he may dwell with
thee in life everlasting; through Jesus Christ our Lord.
Amen.

For Recovery from Sickness

O God, the strength of the weak and the comfort of
sufferers: Mercifully accept our prayers, and grant to your
servant N. the help of your power, that his sickness may be
turned into health, and our sorrow into joy; through Jesus
Christ our Lord. *Amen.*

   or this

O God of heavenly powers, by the might of your command
you drive away from our bodies all sickness and all
infirmity: Be present in your goodness with your servant
N., that his weakness may be banished and his strength
restored; and that, his health being renewed, he may bless
your holy Name; through Jesus Christ our Lord. *Amen.*

For a Sick Child

Heavenly Father, watch with us over your child N., and
grant that he may be restored to that perfect health which it
is yours alone to give; through Jesus Christ our Lord.
Amen.

or this

Lord Jesus Christ, Good Shepherd of the sheep, you gather the lambs in your arms and carry them in your bosom: We commend to your loving care this child *N.* Relieve his pain, guard him from all danger, restore to him your gifts of gladness and strength, and raise him up to a life of service to you. Hear us, we pray, for your dear Name's sake. *Amen.*

Before an Operation

Almighty God our heavenly Father, graciously comfort your servant *N.* in his suffering, and bless the means made use of for his cure. Fill his heart with confidence that, though at times he may be afraid, he yet may put his trust in you; through Jesus Christ our Lord. *Amen.*

or this

Strengthen your servant *N.*, O God, to do what he has to do and bear what he has to bear; that, accepting your healing gifts through the skill of surgeons and nurses, he may be restored to usefulness in your world with a thankful heart; through Jesus Christ our Lord. *Amen.*

For Strength and Confidence

Heavenly Father, giver of life and health: Comfort and relieve your sick servant N., and give your power of healing to those who minister to his needs, that he may be strengthened in his weakness and have confidence in your loving care; through Jesus Christ our Lord. *Amen.*

For the Sanctification of Illness

Sanctify, O Lord, the sickness of your servant *N.*, that the sense of his weakness may add strength to his faith and seriousness to his repentance; and grant that he may live with you in everlasting life; through Jesus Christ our Lord. *Amen.*

For Health of Body and Soul

May God the Father bless you, God the Son heal you, God the Holy Spirit give you strength. May God the holy and undivided Trinity guard your body, save your soul, and bring you safely to his heavenly country; where he lives and reigns for ever and ever. *Amen.*

For Doctors and Nurses

Sanctify, O Lord, those whom you have called to the study and practice of the arts of healing, and to the prevention of disease and pain. Strengthen them by your life-giving Spirit, that by their ministries the health of the community may be promoted and your creation glorified; through Jesus Christ our Lord. *Amen.*

Thanksgiving for a Beginning of Recovery

O Lord, your compassions never fail and your mercies are new every morning: We give you thanks for giving our brother (sister) *N.* both relief from pain and hope of health renewed. Continue in him, we pray, the good work you have begun; that he, daily increasing in bodily strength, and rejoicing in your goodness, may so order his life and conduct that he may always think and do those things that please you; through Jesus Christ our Lord. *Amen.*

Prayers for use by a Sick Person

For Trust in God

O God, the source of all health: So fill my heart with faith in your love, that with calm expectancy I may make room for your power to possess me, and gracefully accept your healing; through Jesus Christ our Lord. *Amen.*

In Pain

Lord Jesus Christ, by your patience in suffering you hallowed earthly pain and gave us the example of obedience to your Father's will: Be near me in my time of weakness and pain; sustain me by your grace, that my strength and courage may not fail; heal me according to your will; and help me always to believe that what happens to me here is of little account if you hold me in eternal life, my Lord and my God. *Amen.*

For Sleep

O heavenly Father, you give your children sleep for the refreshing of soul and body: Grant me this gift, I pray; keep me in that perfect peace which you have promised to those whose minds are fixed on you; and give me such a sense of your presence, that in the hours of silence I may enjoy the blessed assurance of your love; through Jesus Christ our Savior. *Amen.*

In the Morning

This is another day, O Lord. I know not what it will bring forth, but make me ready, Lord, for whatever it may be. If I am to stand up, help me to stand bravely. If I am to sit still, help me to sit quietly. If I am to lie low, help me to do it patiently. And if I am to do nothing, let me do it gallantly. Make these words more than words, and give me the Spirit of Jesus. *Amen.*

Devotions

Let a person examine himself, then, and so eat of the bread and drink of the cup. For anyone who eats and drinks without discerning the body eats and drinks judgment on himself.
1 Corinthians 11:28, 29 [ESV]

Preparation for Holy Communion

It is a sad commentary on the way we order our priorities that we give so little attention to preparing our hearts for worship. It is a common understanding among the clergy that the number of people in the church will double from the time the processional (opening) hymn begins to the offering of the Collect for Purity (the first prayer). And, we are always happy for the increase! Even so, for those who regularly enter late, you are missing out on the opportunity to abide in Christ prior to worship [John 15.1-17].

Jesus refers to his disciples as friends [John 15.15]. Friends enjoy one another's company – they look forward to spending time together. But Jesus is more than just our friend, he is also our Lord and Savior. This means he deserves our respect and honor, along with our love. Ideally preparation for Holy Eucharist will begin Saturday evening with Evening Prayer or private devotions, and resume during the quiet moments of Sunday morning.

When available, you ought to give yourself the blessing of making a confession: All may; some should; none must. Unfortunately, some Anglican clergy have not emphasized the importance of regular private confession. That practice is viewed by many parishioners as "too Roman Catholic". However, it is a spiritually healthy, and comforting biblical practice [James 5.13-16]. And, one of the most valuable ways to prepare for Holy Eucharist.

Prayers for Private Devotions

What follows is a form of preparation for Holy Eucharist, with additional prayers. Many of the prayers listed here are not included in the Book of Common Prayer (or Common Worship) found in the pew, so I have included a number of prayers from other supplementary prayer books for your use.

Consider the counsel of Father Lasance,

"The following prayers are so arranged as to occupy your time usefully whenever you assist at Mass in preparation for holy communion. Remember, however, that you are not bound to say all these prayers; nor indeed any of them. In place of them, you may choose other prayers. If you can occupy a part or the whole of the time in meditating or reflecting on the Holy Eucharist in connection with the passion and death of Our Lord; on the Last Supper and the wonderful love and kindness of Jesus, our Savior, in instituting this marvelous sacrament; and in exciting in your heart holy desires and pious affections together with good resolutions, so much the better."

Rev. F.L. Lasance – My Prayer-Book

PREPARATION FOR HOLY COMMUNION

This first collection of prayers and guidelines comes from the 1950 edition of "The Practice of Religion – a Short Manual of Instructions and Devotions"

Anima Christi

Soul of Christ, sanctify me:
Body of Christ, save me:
Blood of Christ, refresh me:
Water from the side of Christ, wash me:
Passion of Christ, strengthen me:
O Good Jesu, hear me:
Within Thy wounds hide me:
Suffer me not to be separated from Thee:
From the malicious enemy defend me:
In the hour of my death call me,
And bid me come to Thee;
That with Thy Saints I may praise Thee
For all eternity. Amen.

Absolute Silence should be kept in the Nave and Sanctuary of the church for no less than 15 minutes prior to the processional hymn and the beginning of the Liturgy. This allows those who have come early to pray, to do so without distraction.

Ideally, preparation for Holy Communion also includes regular private confession.

It is well to be in Church a few minutes before the Service begins. Entering, genuflect if the Blessed Sacrament is there: if not, then bow to the Altar. Then kneel, sign the Cross and say silently:

In the Name of the Father and of the Son and of the Holy Ghost. Amen.

Antiphon.   I will go unto the Altar of God.

PSALM XLIII. *Judica me, Deus.*

1. Give sentence with me, O God, and defend my cause against the ungodly people; O deliver me from the deceitful and wicked man.

2. For Thou art the God of my strength, why hast Thou put me from Thee? And why go I so heavily, while the enemy oppresseth me?

3. O send out Thy light and Thy truth, that they may lead me, and bring me unto Thy holy hill, and to Thy dwelling;

4. And that I may go unto the Altar of God, even unto the God of my joy and gladness, and upon the harp will I give thanks unto Thee, O God, my God.

5. Why art thou so heavy, O my soul? And why art thou so disquieted within me?

6. O put thy trust in God, for I will yet give Him thanks, which is the help of my countenance, and my God.

Glory be to the Father, etc.

Antiphon. I will go unto the Altar of God, even unto the God of my joy and gladness.

Make me a clean heart, O Lord, and renew a right spirit within me. O grant me worthily to receive these Holy Mysteries and to love Thee with an everlasting love.

Before the Priest enters or while he is making his Preparation before the Altar, offer your Special Prayers and Thanksgivings, or your "Intentions" for the Mass, in your own words or as follows:

O Most Merciful Father, we humbly approach Thine Altar to offer and represent unto Thee the One, Pure, and Holy Sacrifice which Our Lord and Savior Jesus Christ made once upon the Cross and now ever pleads for us in Heaven and which He hath commanded us to show forth here on earth in this Memorial of His Death and Passion. Grant that this Offering may be acceptable at our hands, we beseech Thee, O God, and see us not as we are in ourselves but as we are in union with Our Savior Jesus Christ. We offer this Holy Eucharist unto Thee first for Thine Honour and Glory as the only Perfect Sacrifice which we can offer unto Thee. We also offer it in Thanksgiving for all Thy Blessings (especially...), for the forgiveness of all our sins, (especially...), for the increase of all graces and virtues (especially...), for Thy Holy Church, for our Parish and for the Clergy (especially...), for those near and dear to us (especially...), for the sick (especially...), for the dying (especially...), for the faithful departed (especially...), and with all other holy intentions (especially...) which Thou wouldst have us make. All of which we ask through the Merits and Mediation of Jesus Christ, Our Lord and Redeemer. Amen.

Take away from us all our iniquities we beseech Thee O Lord; that with pure hearts and minds we may go unto Thine Altar, through Jesus Christ, Our Lord. Amen.

ADDITIONAL DEVOTIONS

Before Communion

Almighty and Everlasting God, behold I approach the Sacrament of Thine Only begotten Son, Jesus Christ. As one sick I come to the Physician of life: as unclean to the Fountain of Mercy: as blind to the Light of eternal splendour: as needy to the Lord of Heaven and earth: as naked to the King of Glory: a lost sheep to the Good Shepherd: a fallen creature to its Creator: desolate to the kind Comforter: miserable to the Pitier: guilty to the Bestower of pardon: sinful to the Justifier: hardened to the Giver of Grace.

Collects 179

I implore therefore the abundance of Thy Infinite Bounty that Thou wouldst vouchsafe to heal my sickness, to wash my foulness, to enlighten my darkness, to enrich my poverty, and to clothe my nackedness; that I may receive the Bread of Angels, the King of Kings, the Lord of Lords, with such reverence and humility, with such love and contrition, with such faith and devotion as is good for the welfare of my soul. Grant me, I pray, not only to receive the Sacrament of the Lord's Body and Blood of Thy Son Jesus Christ, that I may be incorporated in His Mystical Body and washed from every stain of sin. And O Most Loving Father, grant me that Him, Whom I now purpose to receive beneath a veil, I may hereafter behold with unveiled face, even Thy Beloved Son, Who with Thee and the Holy Ghost liveth and reigneth ever One God, for ever and ever. Amen. *(Adapted from Saint Thomas Aquinas.)*

Be Thou Merciful to me, O Good Jesus, and grant unto me, Thy poor suppliant, sometimes at least to feel in Holy Communion the cordial affection of Thy love, that my faith may grow stronger, my hope increase, my love enkindle …. O Most Holy and Loving Lord, Whom I now desire to receive with devotion, Thou knowest my weakness and how often I am weighed down, tempted, troubled, and defiled. To Thee I come for remedy. To thee I pray for comfort and help. Behold, I stand before Thee, beseeching Thy grace and imploring Thy mercy. O cheer Thy famishing suppliant, inkindle my coldness with the fire of Thy love, enlighten my blindness with the brightness of Thy Presence, and raise my heart unto Thee…. With the greatest devotion and burning love, with all the affection and fervour of my heart I desire to receive Thee, O Lord. O deal with me in Thy mercy as Thou hast often dealt wonderfully with Thy saints of old, and prevent Thy servant in the blessing of Thy love, that I may worthily and devoutly approach and receive this Glorious Sacrament. Amen. *(Adapted from Saint Thomas 'a Kempis.)*

O Lord, we Thy servants bow down before Thy Holy Altar, waiting for the rich mercies which are from Thee. Send down upon us richly, we beseech Thee, Thy grace and benediction, and sanctify our souls and minds and bodies that we may worthily receive these Holy Mysteries, unto forgiveness of sins and everlasting life. For Thou, O God, with Thine Only-begotten Son and Thy Most Holy Spirit art to be worshiped and glorified now and for ever. *(Adapted from the Liturgy of Saint James.)*

O Lord, with this Holy Sacrifice we offer up our prayers and supplication unto Thee, asking for ourselves the peace from above, the Love of God, the Salvation of our Souls; for others that Thou wouldst be pleased to remember the poor, to help the suffering, to heal the sick, to comfort the broken-hearted, to watch over the traveler, to give peace to the Church, to grant prosperity to the world, bringing all people to love and confess Thee, the One and Only God. And especially do we pray for the heavenly and adorable gifts which are from Thee, and for the salvation of Thy priest who stands to offer them by Thy Divine Command. O Lord God, grant that our Oblations, hallowed by the Holy Ghost, may be well pleasing unto Thee, and accept them, we beseech Thee, for the forgiveness of our sins, the salvation of Thy people, and the repose of the faithful, that all at the Day of Judgment may find grace and mercy, through Jesus Christ Our Lord. *(Adapted from the Liturgy of Saint James.)*

Father, I have sinned against Heaven and before Thee, and am no more worthy to be called Thy son. I have ministered to my own desire and lusts, despising Thy Fatherly Love. I have dug for myself cisterns which hold no water, cisterns of earthly joys and vanities, leaving Thee the Fountain of many waters. I have sought pleasure in creatures which is only to be found Thee; and now behold all is vanity and vexation of spirit, for Thou hast made me for Thyself, and my heart findeth no true rest apart from Thee. Therefore I return to Thee, O Loving Father, Whose mercy is Infinite, Whose Goodness knoweth no end. Wherefore I cry, Father I have sinned against Heaven and before Thee and am no more worthy to be called Thy son; make me as one of Thine hired servants. O grant that henceforth I may walk in the straight path and narrow way that leadeth to Eternal Life, where with the Son and the Holy Spirit, Thou art unclouded Light and perfect Joy through Jesus Christ Our Lord. *(Adapted from Saint Augustine.)*

O Lord, Who dost bless those that bless Thee, and dost hallow those that put their trust in Thee, save Thy people and bless Thine inheritance. Guard, we beseech Thee, Thy Holy Church. Hallow those that love the beauty of Thine House. Forsake not us who put our trust in Thee. Give peace to the world, to the Church, to the Priesthood, to our Rulers, and to all Thy people; for every good gift and every perfect work is from above, coming from Thee, the Father of Lights, to Whom we ascribe, with the Son and the Holy Ghost, all glory, thanksgiving and worship now ever, unto the ages of ages. *(Adapted from the Liturgy of Saint Chrysostom.)*

O Lord, we offer unto Thee with this Holy Sacrifice ourselves and souls and bodies for Thee to accept for the sake of Thy Beloved Son, Jesus Christ, Our Lord. Grant, O God that hallowed by our union with Him, and cleansed in His Precious Blood, we may be an acceptable offering in Thy sight, and may evermore give our selves up in loving service and holy obedience to Thee; Who art to be praised and glorified, One God, for ever and ever.

O Lord, by this Most Sacred Mystery of Thy Body and Blood, grant us Thy manifold Gifts of Grace ... that we may receive this Blessed Sacrament to our health and comfort. For Thou hast said, "The Bread which I give is My Flesh for the life of the world. I am the Living Bread which came down from Heaven. If any man eat of this Bread, he shall live for ever." ... O Bread most sweet that ever refreshest and never failest, may we feed upon thee and may our inmost soul be filled with Thine Heavenly Peace. May we in our pilgrimage so receive Thee that we may not faint upon our way, but come in safety to the end of our journey. O Holy Bread, O Living Bread, O Adorable Bread, the very Body and Blood of Our Savior Christ, come unto us and cleanse us from all defilement of flesh and spirit. Drive away from us all our foes and so preserve us that we may come in safety to Thine Heavenly Kingdom, no longer to see Thee in Holy Mysteries, but then face to face. *(Taken from Prayers variously ascribed to Saints Anselm and Ambrose.)*

O Lord, as we receive Thy Precious Body and Blood, send forth Thine unseen Hand which is full of blessings and bountifully bless us all. Have mercy upon us and strengthen us by Thy Divine Power. Take away from us the sinful working of all fleshly lusts. Drive from before our eyes the encompassing gloom of sin and unite us with the blessed company of all faithful people, who have been well pleasing unto Thee. For through Thee and with Thee and in Thee, with the Father and Holy Ghost be all praise, honour, might, majesty, dominion and power, now and for ever, unto the ages of ages. Amen. *(Adapted from the Liturgy of Saint Mark.)*

We beseech Thee, O Lord, that this Holy Communion may be unto us a guide and provision for our journey unto the haven of everlasting Salvation. May it be to us comfort in sorrow, strength in trial, patience in difficulty, medicine in sickness, delight in prosperity, and love in all things. By these most Holy Mysteries, which we would receive, grant us right faith, firm hope, and perfect charity, purification of desire, gladness of mind, ardent love of Thee, and a due remembrance of the Passion of Thy Beloved Son, with grace to keep our lives full of faith and virtue. And in the hour of our departure grant that we may receive this great Mystery with true faith, sure hope, and sincere charity unto Everlasting Life. Amen. *(Adapted from Old Sarum Rite.)*

After Communion

Almighty and Everlasting God, Preserver of Souls and Redeemer of the world, most graciously regard me Thy servant prostrate before Thy Majesty; and this Sacrifice which in honour of Thy Name we have presented before Thee, for the Salvation of the faithful, whether living or departed and also for our sins and offences do Thou most mercifully regard. Take away from me Thy wrath, grant me Thy grace and mercy, open to me the door of Paradise, mightily rescue me from all evil and forgive whatever sin of my own guilt I have committed. And make me so to persevere in Thy Commandments in this world, that I may be made worthy to be united to the flock of the Elect, through Thy Bounty, O my God, Whose Blessed Name and Hour and Kingdom remaineth forever and ever. Amen. *(Adapted from Old Sarum Rite.)*

Almighty and Everlasting God, Jesus Christ my Lord, be Thou merciful to my sins, through the reception of Thy Body and Blood. For Thou, O Lord, hast said "Whoso eateth My Flesh and drinketh My Blood dwelleth in Me and I in Him." Wherefore I humbly beseech Thee, that Thou wouldst create in me a pure heart, and renew a right spirit within me; that Thou wouldst deign to stablish me with Thy Firm Spirit; and so deliver me from the snares of the devil and from all my sins, that I may attain to be a partaker of Thine heavenly joys; Who livest and reignest with the Father and the Holy Ghost, one God, for ever and ever. Amen. *(Adapted from Old Sarum Rite.)*

We yield Thee thanks, O Lord, Holy Father, Almighty, Everlasting God, Who not for any merit of ours, but of Thy mercy only, hast been pleased to feed us sinners, Thine unworthy servants, with the Precious Body and Blood of Thy Son, Our Lord, Jesus Christ. And we beseech Thee, that this Holy Communion may not accuse us unto condemnation but may be to us pardon and salvation. Let it be to us an armour of faith and a shield of good resolution. Let is be to us the riddance of all vices, the killing of all evil desires and longings, and the increase of love and patience, of humility and obedience, and of all virtues; a firm defense against all enemies visible and invisible, a constraining power to purity and holiness. Let it make us always cling closely to Thee, the One, True, and Only God, and end our earthy days in peace. And we pray Thee to bring us to that Heavenly Banquet, where Thou with Thy Son and the Holy Ghost art to Thy Saints true light, everlasting joy, and perfect happiness. Amen. *(Adapted from Old Sarum Rite.)*

May the performance of our bounden duty be pleasing unto Thee, O God, and grant that this Holy Sacrifice which we, though unworthy, have presented before Thy Divine Majesty, may be acceptable unto Thee and obtain mercy for us and for those for whom we pray, by Thy compassion, Who livest and reignest One God, world, without end. Amen. *(Adapted from Old Sarum Rite.)*

O Lord, we would remember in our prayers the Holy Catholic Church, that Thou mayst graciously vouchsafe to increase it in faith, hope and charity. We would remember the sick and suffering, the desolate and sorrowful, the poor and destitute, that Thou mayst heal, comfort and relieve them. We would remember the souls of the faithful departed, that they may rest in peace where their works do follow them. Mercifully perform this, we beseech Thee, O Eternal and Almighty Father, to Whom we offer this Holy Sacrifice. Amen. *(Adapted from the Mozarabic Liturgy.)*

Collects 185

Most Blessed Lord and Savior Jesus Christ the great High Priest, Who for us didst offer Thyself upon the Cross, a pure and spotless Victim, and didst ordain this Holy Mystery and give us Thy Flesh to eat and Thy Blood to drink, saying, Do this in remembrance of Me, I pray Thee to wash us from our sins, and teach us by Thy Holy Spirit to receive these Sacred Gifts with such reverence and honour, such devotion and love as is meet and fitting. Make us through Thy Grace, always to believe and think and speak of this great Mystery as shall please Thee and be good for our souls. Let Thy Holy Spirit enter into our hearts and speak and teach all truth. For these Sacred Mysteries are beyond man's understanding. In Thy Mercy grant us to receive this Holy Eucharist with a clean heart and pure mind. Drive away all vain, evil, impure and unholy thoughts. Defend us with the loving and faithful protection of the blessed angels, and keep us free from the spirit of pride and vanity, envy and blasphemy, doubt and distrust and fill us with boundless love of Thee. Amen. *(From Prayers ascribed to Saint Anselm or Saint Ambrose.)*

O Most Merciful Savior, look with compassion, we beseech Thee, upon us who have received the sacred gifts of Thy Body and Blood. Bless the lips which have praised Thee, the heart which has loved Thee, the body which has worshipped Thee, the soul which has adored Thee, that in the world to come they may be Thine for ever. Amen.

O God, Who art Holy and Wonderful and Mighty, Whose Power and Wisdom have no end, before Whom all things bow, and the heavens and earth declare Thy Glory, grant me to love Thee and to worship Thee for ever and ever. Guide me unto the perfect light, that, illumined by its radiance, all darkness may flee away. Let the holy flame of Thy love so burn in my heart that it may be made pure and holy, for none but the pure in heart can see and know an receive Thee, the King of Kings, Our Lord and God. Amen. *(Adapted from Saint Augustine.)*

May Our Lord and Savior, Jesus Christ, Who comes to us in the Blessed Sacrament of the Altar, be to us the Way to Everlasting life.

In the Peace of Christ let us depart.
In the Peace of Christ let us sing.

From Glory to Glory let us go forth, hymning in our hearts to Thee, the Savior of our souls. Glory be to the Father and to the Son and to the Holy Ghost. We praise Thee the Savior of our Souls.

From Strength to Strength advancing, we who have accomplished the Divine Ministration in Thy Temple, now pray unto Thee, O God. Vouchsafe to us Thy Mercy, guide our feet aright, root us firmly in Thy love, and at last count us worthy of Thine Heavenly Kingdom, through the Merits and Mediation of Thy Son, to Whom with Thee and the Holy Ghost be Glory, Honour, and Power unto the Ages of Ages. *(Adapted from the Liturgy of Saint James.)*

RECOMMENDED PSALTER & SCRIPTURE READINGS

In preparation for the Sacrament of Reconciliation, or Holy Eucharist, consider reading through a passage of Scripture for your devotions, and offering it as a prayer.

Here are some suggestions:

Psalm 51, 84, 85, 86, 116:10-16, 130

Genesis 22.1-19
Exodus 12.1-27
Leviticus 16
Hosea 6.6
Matthew 26.17-29
Mark 14.12-25
Luke 22.7-20, 24.13-35
John 1.36, 6.25-65
Acts 2.42
1 Corinthians 10:16-17; 11:23-32
Hebrews 6.19-20, and chapters 7, 8, 9 and 10.1-25
Revelation chapters 4 and 5

The Psalter

Book One

First Day: Morning Prayer

1 *Beatus vir qui non abiit*

1 Happy are they who have not walked in the counsel
of the wicked, *
nor lingered in the way of sinners,
nor sat in the seats of the scornful!
2 Their delight is in the law of the Lord, *
and they meditate on his law day and night.
3 They are like trees planted by streams of water,
bearing fruit in due season, with leaves that do not
wither; *
everything they do shall prosper.
4 It is not so with the wicked; *
they are like chaff which the wind blows away.
5 Therefore the wicked shall not stand upright when
judgment comes, *
nor the sinner in the council of the righteous.
6 For the Lord knows the way of the righteous, *
but the way of the wicked is doomed.

2 *Quare fremuerunt gentes?*

1 Why are the nations in an uproar? *
Why do the peoples mutter empty threats?
2 Why do the kings of the earth rise up in revolt,
and the princes plot together, *
against the Lord and against his Anointed?
3 "Let us break their yoke," they say; *
"let us cast off their bonds from us."
4 He whose throne is in heaven is laughing; *
the Lord has them in derision.

5 Then he speaks to them in his wrath, *
and his rage fills them with terror.
6 "I myself have set my king *
upon my holy hill of Zion."
7 Let me announce the decree of the Lord: *
he said to me, "You are my Son;
this day have I begotten you.
8 Ask of me, and I will give you the nations for
your inheritance *
and the ends of the earth for your possession.
9 You shall crush them with an iron rod *
and shatter them like a piece of pottery."
10 And now, you kings, be wise; *
be warned, you rulers of the earth.
11 Submit to the Lord with fear, *
and with trembling bow before him;
12 Lest he be angry and you perish; *
for his wrath is quickly kindled.
13 Happy are they all *
who take refuge in him!

3 *Domine, quid multiplicati*

1 Lord, how many adversaries I have! *
how many there are who rise up against me!
2 How many there are who say of me, *
"There is no help for him in his God."
3 But you, O Lord, are a shield about me; *
you are my glory, the one who lifts up my head.
4 I call aloud upon the Lord, *
and he answers me from his holy hill;
5 I lie down and go to sleep; *
I wake again, because the Lord sustains me.
6 I do not fear the multitudes of people *
who set themselves against me all around.

7 Rise up, O Lord; set me free, O my God; *
surely, you will strike all my enemies across the face,
you will break the teeth of the wicked.
8 Deliverance belongs to the Lord. *
Your blessing be upon your people!

4 *Cum invocarem*

1 Answer me when I call, O God, defender of my
cause; *
you set me free when I am hard-pressed;
have mercy on me and hear my prayer.
2 "You mortals, how long will you dishonor my glory; *
how long will you worship dumb idols
and run after false gods?"
3 Know that the Lord does wonders for the faithful; *
when I call upon the Lord, he will hear me.
4 Tremble, then, and do not sin; *
speak to your heart in silence upon your bed.
5 Offer the appointed sacrifices *
and put your trust in the Lord.
6 Many are saying,
"Oh, that we might see better times!" *
Lift up the light of your countenance upon us, O Lord.
7 You have put gladness in my heart, *
more than when grain and wine and oil increase.
8 I lie down in peace; at once I fall asleep; *
for only you, Lord, make me dwell in safety.

5 *Verba mea auribus*

1 Give ear to my words, O Lord; *
consider my meditation.
2 Hearken to my cry for help, my King and my God, *
for I make my prayer to you.

3 In the morning, Lord, you hear my voice; *
early in the morning I make my appeal and watch for
you.
4 For you are not a God who takes pleasure in
wickedness, *
and evil cannot dwell with you.
5 Braggarts cannot stand in your sight; *
you hate all those who work wickedness.
6 You destroy those who speak lies; *
the bloodthirsty and deceitful, O Lord, you abhor.
7 But as for me, through the greatness of your mercy I
will go into your house; *
I will bow down toward your holy temple in awe of
you.
8 Lead me, O Lord, in your righteousness,
because of those who lie in wait for me; *
make your way straight before me.
9 For there is no truth in their mouth; *
there is destruction in their heart;
10 Their throat is an open grave; *
they flatter with their tongue.
11 Declare them guilty, O God; *
let them fall, because of their schemes.
12 Because of their many transgressions cast them out, *
for they have rebelled against you.
13 But all who take refuge in you will be glad; *
they will sing out their joy for ever.
14 You will shelter them, *
so that those who love your Name may exult in you.
15 For you, O Lord, will bless the righteous; *
you will defend them with your favor as with a shield.

6 *Domine, ne in furore*

1 Lord, do not rebuke me in your anger; *
do not punish me in your wrath.
2 Have pity on me, Lord, for I am weak; *
heal me, Lord, for my bones are racked.
3 My spirit shakes with terror; *
how long, O Lord, how long?
4 Turn, O Lord, and deliver me; *
save me for your mercy's sake.
5 For in death no one remembers you; *
and who will give you thanks in the grave?
6 I grow weary because of my groaning; *
every night I drench my bed
and flood my couch with tears.
7 My eyes are wasted with grief *
and worn away because of all my enemies.
8 Depart from me, all evildoers, *
for the Lord has heard the sound of my weeping.
9 The Lord has heard my supplication; *
the Lord accepts my prayer.
10 All my enemies shall be confounded and quake with
fear; *
they shall turn back and suddenly be put to shame.

7 *Domine, Deus meus*

1 O Lord my God, I take refuge in you; *
save and deliver me from all who pursue me;
2 Lest like a lion they tear me in pieces *
and snatch me away with none to deliver me.
3 O Lord my God, if I have done these things: *
if there is any wickedness in my hands,

4 If I have repaid my friend with evil, *
or plundered him who without cause is my enemy;
5 Then let my enemy pursue and overtake me, *
trample my life into the ground,
and lay my honor in the dust.
6 Stand up, O Lord, in your wrath; *
rise up against the fury of my enemies.
7 Awake, O my God, decree justice; *
let the assembly of the peoples gather round you.
8 Be seated on your lofty throne, O Most High; *
O Lord, judge the nations.
9 Give judgment for me according to my
righteousness, O Lord, *
and according to my innocence, O Most High.
10 Let the malice of the wicked come to an end,
but establish the righteous; *
for you test the mind and heart, O righteous God.
11 God is my shield and defense; *
he is the savior of the true in heart.
12 God is a righteous judge; *
God sits in judgment every day.
13 If they will not repent, God will whet his sword; *
he will bend his bow and make it ready.
14 He has prepared his weapons of death; *
he makes his arrows shafts of fire.
15 Look at those who are in labor with wickedness, *
who conceive evil, and give birth to a lie.
16 They dig a pit and make it deep *
and fall into the hole that they have made.
17 Their malice turns back upon their own head; *
their violence falls on their own scalp.
18 I will bear witness that the Lord is righteous; *
I will praise the Name of the Lord Most High.

8 *Domine, Dominus noster*

1 O Lord our Governor, *
how exalted is your Name in all the world!
2 Out of the mouths of infants and children *
your majesty is praised above the heavens.
3 You have set up a stronghold against your
adversaries, *
to quell the enemy and the avenger.
4 When I consider your heavens, the work of your
fingers, *
the moon and the stars you have set in their courses,
5 What is man that you should be mindful of him? *
the son of man that you should seek him out?
6 You have made him but little lower than the angels; *
you adorn him with glory and honor;
7 You give him mastery over the works of your hands; *
you put all things under his feet:
8 All sheep and oxen, *
even the wild beasts of the field,
9 The birds of the air, the fish of the sea, *
and whatsoever walks in the paths of the sea.
10 O Lord our Governor, *
how exalted is your Name in all the world!

Second Day: Morning Prayer

9 *Confitebor tibi*

1 I will give thanks to you, O Lord, with my whole
heart; *
I will tell of all your marvelous works.
2 I will be glad and rejoice in you; *
I will sing to your Name, O Most High.

3 When my enemies are driven back, *
they will stumble and perish at your presence.
4 For you have maintained my right and my cause; *
you sit upon your throne judging right.
5 You have rebuked the ungodly and destroyed the
wicked; *
you have blotted out their name for ever and ever.
6 As for the enemy, they are finished, in perpetual ruin, *
their cities ploughed under, the memory of them
perished;
7 But the Lord is enthroned for ever; *
he has set up his throne for judgment.
8 It is he who rules the world with righteousness; *
he judges the peoples with equity.
9 The Lord will be a refuge for the oppressed, *
a refuge in time of trouble.
10 Those who know your Name will put their trust in
you, *
for you never forsake those who seek you, O Lord.
11 Sing praise to the Lord who dwells in Zion; *
proclaim to the peoples the things he has done.
12 The Avenger of blood will remember them; *
he will not forget the cry of the afflicted.
13 Have pity on me, O Lord; *
see the misery I suffer from those who hate me,
O you who lift me up from the gate of death;
14 So that I may tell of all your praises
and rejoice in your salvation *
in the gates of the city of Zion.
15 The ungodly have fallen into the pit they dug, *
and in the snare they set is their own foot caught.
16 The Lord is known by his acts of justice; *
the wicked are trapped in the works of their own
hands.

17 The wicked shall be given over to the grave, *
and also all the peoples that forget God.
18 For the needy shall not always be forgotten, *
and the hope of the poor shall not perish for ever.
19 Rise up, O Lord, let not the ungodly have the upper
hand; *
let them be judged before you.
20 Put fear upon them, O Lord; *
let the ungodly know they are but mortal.

10 *Ut quid, Domine?*

1 Why do you stand so far off, O Lord, *
and hide yourself in time of trouble?
2 The wicked arrogantly persecute the poor, *
but they are trapped in the schemes they have devised.
3 The wicked boast of their heart's desire; *
the covetous curse and revile the Lord.
4 The wicked are so proud that they care not for God; *
their only thought is, "God does not matter."
5 Their ways are devious at all times;
your judgments are far above out of their sight; *
they defy all their enemies.
6 They say in their heart, "I shall not be shaken; *
no harm shall happen to me ever."
7 Their mouth is full of cursing, deceit, and
oppression; *
under their tongue are mischief and wrong.
8 They lurk in ambush in public squares
and in secret places they murder the innocent; *
they spy out the helpless.
9 They lie in wait, like a lion in a covert;
they lie in wait to seize upon the lowly; *
they seize the lowly and drag them away in their net.

10 The innocent are broken and humbled before them; *
the helpless fall before their power.
11 They say in their heart, "God has forgotten; *
he hides his face; he will never notice."
12 Rise up, O Lord;
lift up your hand, O God; *
do not forget the afflicted.
13 Why should the wicked revile God? *
why should they say in their heart, "You do not care"?
14 Surely, you behold trouble and misery; *
you see it and take it into your own hand.
15 The helpless commit themselves to you, *
for you are the helper of orphans.
16 Break the power of the wicked and evil; *
search out their wickedness until you find none.
17 The Lord is King for ever and ever; *
the ungodly shall perish from his land.
18 The Lord will hear the desire of the humble; *
you will strengthen their heart and your ears shall hear;
19 To give justice to the orphan and oppressed, *
so that mere mortals may strike terror no more.

11 *In Domino confido*

1 In the Lord have I taken refuge; *
how then can you say to me,
"Fly away like a bird to the hilltop;
2 For see how the wicked bend the bow
and fit their arrows to the string, *
to shoot from ambush at the true of heart.
3 When the foundations are being destroyed, *
what can the righteous do?"
4 The Lord is in his holy temple; *
the Lord's throne is in heaven.

5 His eyes behold the inhabited world; *
his piercing eye weighs our worth.
6 The Lord weighs the righteous as well as the wicked, *
but those who delight in violence he abhors.
7 Upon the wicked he shall rain coals of fire and
burning sulphur; *
a scorching wind shall be their lot.
8 For the Lord is righteous;
he delights in righteous deeds; *
and the just shall see his face.

Second Day: Evening Prayer

12 *Salvum me fac*

1 Help me, Lord, for there is no godly one left; *
the faithful have vanished from among us.
2 Everyone speaks falsely with his neighbor; *
with a smooth tongue they speak from a double heart.
3 Oh, that the Lord would cut off all smooth tongues, *
and close the lips that utter proud boasts!
4 Those who say, "With our tongue will we prevail; *
our lips are our own; who is lord over us?"
5 "Because the needy are oppressed,
and the poor cry out in misery, *
I will rise up," says the Lord,
"and give them the help they long for."
6 The words of the Lord are pure words, *
like silver refined from ore
and purified seven times in the fire.
7 O Lord, watch over us *
and save us from this generation for ever.
8 The wicked prowl on every side, *
and that which is worthless is highly prized by
everyone.

13 *Usquequo, Domine?*

1 How long, O Lord?
will you forget me for ever? *
how long will you hide your face from me?
2 How long shall I have perplexity in my mind,
and grief in my heart, day after day? *
how long shall my enemy triumph over me?
3 Look upon me and answer me, O Lord my God; *
give light to my eyes, lest I sleep in death;
4 Lest my enemy say, "I have prevailed over him," *
and my foes rejoice that I have fallen.
5 But I put my trust in your mercy; *
my heart is joyful because of your saving help.
6 I will sing to the Lord, for he has dealt with me
richly; *
I will praise the Name of the Lord Most High.

14 *Dixit insipiens*

1 The fool has said in his heart, "There is no God." *
All are corrupt and commit abominable acts;
there is none who does any good.
2 The Lord looks down from heaven upon us all, *
to see if there is any who is wise,
if there is one who seeks after God.
3 Every one has proved faithless;
all alike have turned bad; *
there is none who does good; no, not one.
4 Have they no knowledge, all those evildoers *
who eat up my people like bread
and do not call upon the Lord?
5 See how they tremble with fear, *
because God is in the company of the righteous.

The Psalter 202

6 Their aim is to confound the plans of the afflicted, *
but the Lord is their refuge.
7 Oh, that Israel's deliverance would come out of Zion! *
when the Lord restores the fortunes of his people,
Jacob will rejoice and Israel be glad.

Third Day: Morning Prayer

15 *Domine, quis habitabit?*

1 Lord, who may dwell in your tabernacle? *
who may abide upon your holy hill?
2 Whoever leads a blameless life and does what is
right, *
who speaks the truth from his heart.
3 There is no guile upon his tongue;
he does no evil to his friend; *
he does not heap contempt upon his neighbor.
4 In his sight the wicked is rejected, *
but he honors those who fear the Lord.
5 He has sworn to do no wrong *
and does not take back his word.
6 He does not give his money in hope of gain, *
nor does he take a bribe against the innocent.
7 Whoever does these things *
shall never be overthrown.

16 *Conserva me, Domine*

1 Protect me, O God, for I take refuge in you; *
I have said to the Lord, "You are my Lord,
my good above all other."
2 All my delight is upon the godly that are in the land, *
upon those who are noble among the people.
3 But those who run after other gods *
shall have their troubles multiplied.

4 Their libations of blood I will not offer, *
nor take the names of their gods upon my lips.
5 O Lord, you are my portion and my cup; *
it is you who uphold my lot.
6 My boundaries enclose a pleasant land; *
indeed, I have a goodly heritage.
7 I will bless the Lord who gives me counsel; *
my heart teaches me, night after night.
8 I have set the Lord always before me; *
because he is at my right hand I shall not fall.
9 My heart, therefore, is glad, and my spirit rejoices; *
my body also shall rest in hope.
10 For you will not abandon me to the grave, *
nor let your holy one see the Pit.
11 You will show me the path of life; *
in your presence there is fullness of joy,
and in your right hand are pleasures for evermore.

17 *Exaudi, Domine*

1 Hear my plea of innocence, O Lord;
give heed to my cry; *
listen to my prayer, which does not come from lying lips.
2 Let my vindication come forth from your presence; *
let your eyes be fixed on justice.
3 Weigh my heart, summon me by night, *
melt me down; you will find no impurity in me.
4 I give no offense with my mouth as others do; *
I have heeded the words of your lips.
5 My footsteps hold fast to the ways of your law; *
in your paths my feet shall not stumble.
6 I call upon you, O God, for you will answer me; *
incline your ear to me and hear my words.
7 Show me your marvelous loving-kindness, *
O Savior of those who take refuge at your right hand
from those who rise up against them.

8 Keep me as the apple of your eye; *
hide me under the shadow of your wings,
9 From the wicked who assault me, *
from my deadly enemies who surround me.
10 They have closed their heart to pity, *
and their mouth speaks proud things.
11 They press me hard,
now they surround me, *
watching how they may cast me to the ground,
12 Like a lion, greedy for its prey, *
and like a young lion lurking in secret places.
13 Arise, O Lord; confront them and bring them down; *
deliver me from the wicked by your sword.
14 Deliver me, O Lord, by your hand *
from those whose portion in life is this world;
15 Whose bellies you fill with your treasure, *
who are well supplied with children
and leave their wealth to their little ones.
16 But at my vindication I shall see your face; *
when I awake, I shall be satisfied, beholding
your likeness.

Third Day: Evening Prayer

18

Part 1 *Diligam te, Domine.*
1 I love you, O Lord my strength, *
O Lord my stronghold, my crag, and my haven.
2 My God, my rock in whom I put my trust, *
my shield, the horn of my salvation, and my refuge;
you are worthy of praise.
3 I will call upon the Lord, *
and so shall I be saved from my enemies.

4 The breakers of death rolled over me, *
and the torrents of oblivion made me afraid.
5 The cords of hell entangled me, *
and the snares of death were set for me.
6 I called upon the Lord in my distress *
and cried out to my God for help.
7 He heard my voice from his heavenly dwelling; *
my cry of anguish came to his ears.
8 The earth reeled and rocked; *
the roots of the mountains shook;
they reeled because of his anger.
9 Smoke rose from his nostrils
and a consuming fire out of his mouth; *
hot burning coals blazed forth from him.
10 He parted the heavens and came down *
with a storm cloud under his feet.
11 He mounted on cherubim and flew; *
he swooped on the wings of the wind.
12 He wrapped darkness about him; *
he made dark waters and thick clouds his pavilion.
13 From the brightness of his presence, through the
clouds, *
burst hailstones and coals of fire.
14 The Lord thundered out of heaven; *
the Most High uttered his voice.
15 He loosed his arrows and scattered them; *
he hurled thunderbolts and routed them.
16 The beds of the seas were uncovered,
and the foundations of the world laid bare, *
at your battle cry, O Lord,
at the blast of the breath of your nostrils.
17 He reached down from on high and grasped me; *
he drew me out of great waters.

18 He delivered me from my strong enemies
and from those who hated me; *
for they were too mighty for me.
19 They confronted me in the day of my disaster; *
but the Lord was my support.
20 He brought me out into an open place; *
he rescued me because he delighted in me.

Psalm 18: Part II *Et retribuet mihi*
21 The Lord rewarded me because of my righteous
dealing; *
because my hands were clean he rewarded me;
22 For I have kept the ways of the Lord *
and have not offended against my God;
23 For all his judgments are before my eyes, *
and his decrees I have not put away from me;
24 For I have been blameless with him *
and have kept myself from iniquity;
25 Therefore the Lord rewarded me according to my
righteous dealing, *
because of the cleanness of my hands in his sight.
26 With the faithful you show yourself faithful, O God; *
with the forthright you show yourself forthright.
27 With the pure you show yourself pure, *
but with the crooked you are wily.
28 You will save a lowly people, *
but you will humble the haughty eyes.
29 You, O Lord, are my lamp; *
my God, you make my darkness bright.
30 With you I will break down an enclosure; *
with the help of my God I will scale any wall.
31 As for God, his ways are perfect;
the words of the Lord are tried in the fire; *
he is a shield to all who trust in him.

32 For who is God, but the Lord? *
who is the Rock, except our God?
33 It is God who girds me about with strength *
and makes my way secure.
34 He makes me sure-footed like a deer *
and lets me stand firm on the heights.
35 He trains my hands for battle *
and my arms for bending even a bow of bronze.
36 You have given me your shield of victory; *
your right hand also sustains me;
your loving care makes me great.
37 You lengthen my stride beneath me, *
and my ankles do not give way.
38 I pursue my enemies and overtake them; *
I will not turn back till I have destroyed them.
39 I strike them down, and they cannot rise; *
they fall defeated at my feet.
40 You have girded me with strength for the battle; *
you have cast down my adversaries beneath me;
you have put my enemies to flight.
41 I destroy those who hate me;
they cry out, but there is none to help them; *
they cry to the Lord, but he does not answer.
42 I beat them small like dust before the wind; *
I trample them like mud in the streets.
43 You deliver me from the strife of the peoples; *
you put me at the head of the nations.
44 A people I have not known shall serve me;
no sooner shall they hear than they shall obey me; *
strangers will cringe before me.
45 The foreign peoples will lose heart; *
they shall come trembling out of their strongholds.
46 The Lord lives! Blessed is my Rock! *
Exalted is the God of my salvation!

47 He is the God who gave me victory *
and cast down the peoples beneath me.
48 You rescued me from the fury of my enemies;
you exalted me above those who rose against me; *
you saved me from my deadly foe.
49 Therefore will I extol you among the nations, O
Lord, *
and sing praises to your Name.
50 He multiplies the victories of his king; *
he shows loving-kindness to his anointed,
to David and his descendants for ever.

Fourth Day: Morning Prayer

19 *Cæli enarrant*

1 The heavens declare the glory of God, *
and the firmament shows his handiwork.
2 One day tells its tale to another, *
and one night imparts knowledge to another.
3 Although they have no words or language, *
and their voices are not heard,
4 Their sound has gone out into all lands, *
and their message to the ends of the world.
5 In the deep has he set a pavilion for the sun; *
it comes forth like a bridegroom out of his chamber;
it rejoices like a champion to run its course.
6 It goes forth from the uttermost edge of the heavens
and runs about to the end of it again; *
nothing is hidden from its burning heat.
7 The law of the Lord is perfect
and revives the soul; *
the testimony of the Lord is sure
and gives wisdom to the innocent.

8 The statutes of the Lord are just
and rejoice the heart; *
the commandment of the Lord is clear
and gives light to the eyes.
9 The fear of the Lord is clean
and endures for ever; *
the judgments of the Lord are true
and righteous altogether.
10 More to be desired are they than gold,
more than much fine gold, *
sweeter far than honey,
than honey in the comb.
11 By them also is your servant enlightened, *
and in keeping them there is great reward.
12 Who can tell how often he offends? *
cleanse me from my secret faults.
13 Above all, keep your servant from presumptuous sins;
let them not get dominion over me; *
then shall I be whole and sound,
and innocent of a great offense.
14 Let the words of my mouth and the meditation of my
heart be acceptable in your sight, *
O Lord, my strength and my redeemer.

20 *Exaudiat te Dominus*

1 May the Lord answer you in the day of trouble, *
the Name of the God of Jacob defend you;
2 Send you help from his holy place *
and strengthen you out of Zion;
3 Remember all your offerings *
and accept your burnt sacrifice;
4 Grant you your heart's desire *
and prosper all your plans.

5 We will shout for joy at your victory
and triumph in the Name of our God; *
may the Lord grant all your requests.
6 Now I know that the Lord gives victory to his
anointed; *
he will answer him out of his holy heaven,
with the victorious strength of his right hand.
7 Some put their trust in chariots and some in horses, *
but we will call upon the Name of the Lord our God.
8 They collapse and fall down, *
but we will arise and stand upright.
9 O Lord, give victory to the king *
and answer us when we call.

21 *Domine, in virtute tua*

1 The king rejoices in your strength, O Lord; *
how greatly he exults in your victory!
2 You have given him his heart's desire; *
you have not denied him the request of his lips.
3 For you meet him with blessings of prosperity, *
and set a crown of fine gold upon his head.
4 He asked you for life, and you gave it to him: *
length of days, for ever and ever.
5 His honor is great, because of your victory; *
splendor and majesty have you bestowed upon him.
6 For you will give him everlasting felicity *
and will make him glad with the joy of your presence.
7 For the king puts his trust in the Lord; *
because of the loving-kindness of the Most High, he
will not fall.
8 Your hand will lay hold upon all your enemies; *
your right hand will seize all those who hate you.
9 You will make them like a fiery furnace *
at the time of your appearing, O Lord;

10 You will swallow them up in your wrath, *
and fire shall consume them.
11 You will destroy their offspring from the land *
and their descendants from among the peoples of the
earth.
12 Though they intend evil against you
and devise wicked schemes, *
yet they shall not prevail.
13 For you will put them to flight *
and aim your arrows at them.
14 Be exalted, O Lord, in your might; *
we will sing and praise your power.

Fourth Day: Evening Prayer

22 *Deus, Deus meus*

1 My God, my God, why have you forsaken me? *
and are so far from my cry
and from the words of my distress?
2 O my God, I cry in the daytime, but you do not
answer; *
by night as well, but I find no rest.
3 Yet you are the Holy One, *
enthroned upon the praises of Israel.
4 Our forefathers put their trust in you; *
they trusted, and you delivered them.
5 They cried out to you and were delivered; *
they trusted in you and were not put to shame.
6 But as for me, I am a worm and no man, *
scorned by all and despised by the people.
7 All who see me laugh me to scorn; *
they curl their lips and wag their heads, saying,

8 "He trusted in the Lord; let him deliver him; *
let him rescue him, if he delights in him."
9 Yet you are he who took me out of the womb, *
and kept me safe upon my mother's breast.
10 I have been entrusted to you ever since I was born; *
you were my God when I was still in my
mother's womb.
11 Be not far from me, for trouble is near, *
and there is none to help.
12 Many young bulls encircle me; *
strong bulls of Bashan surround me.
13 They open wide their jaws at me, *
like a ravening and a roaring lion.
14 I am poured out like water;
all my bones are out of joint; *
my heart within my breast is melting wax.
15 My mouth is dried out like a pot-sherd;
my tongue sticks to the roof of my mouth; *
and you have laid me in the dust of the grave.
16 Packs of dogs close me in,
and gangs of evildoers circle around me; *
they pierce my hands and my feet;
I can count all my bones.
17 They stare and gloat over me; *
they divide my garments among them;
they cast lots for my clothing.
18 Be not far away, O Lord; *
you are my strength; hasten to help me.
19 Save me from the sword, *
my life from the power of the dog.
20 Save me from the lion's mouth, *
my wretched body from the horns of wild bulls.
21 I will declare your Name to my brethren; *
in the midst of the congregation I will praise you.

22 Praise the Lord, you that fear him; *
stand in awe of him, O offspring of Israel;
all you of Jacob's line, give glory.
23 For he does not despise nor abhor the poor in their
poverty;
neither does he hide his face from them; *
but when they cry to him he hears them.
24 My praise is of him in the great assembly; *
I will perform my vows in the presence of those who
worship him.
25 The poor shall eat and be satisfied,
and those who seek the Lord shall praise him: *
"May your heart live for ever!"
26 All the ends of the earth shall remember and turn to
the Lord, *
and all the families of the nations shall bow before
him.
27 For kingship belongs to the Lord; *
he rules over the nations.
28 To him alone all who sleep in the earth bow down
in worship; *
all who go down to the dust fall before him.
29 My soul shall live for him;
my descendants shall serve him; *
they shall be known as the Lord's for ever.
30 They shall come and make known to a people yet
unborn *
the saving deeds that he has done.

23 *Dominus regit me*

1 The Lord is my shepherd; *
I shall not be in want.
2 He makes me lie down in green pastures *
and leads me beside still waters.

3 He revives my soul *
and guides me along right pathways for his Name's
sake.
4 Though I walk through the valley of the shadow of
death,
I shall fear no evil; *
for you are with me;
your rod and your staff, they comfort me.
5 You spread a table before me in the presence of those
who trouble me; *
you have anointed my head with oil,
and my cup is running over.
6 Surely your goodness and mercy shall follow me all
the days of my life, *
and I will dwell in the house of the Lord for ever.

Fifth Day: Morning Prayer

24 *Domini est terra*

1 The earth is the Lord's and all that is in it, *
the world and all who dwell therein.
2 For it is he who founded it upon the seas *
and made it firm upon the rivers of the deep.
3 "Who can ascend the hill of the Lord? *
and who can stand in his holy place?"
4 "Those who have clean hands and a pure heart, *
who have not pledged themselves to falsehood,
nor sworn by what is a fraud.
5 They shall receive a blessing from the Lord *
and a just reward from the God of their salvation."
6 Such is the generation of those who seek him, *
of those who seek your face, O God of Jacob.
7 Lift up your heads, O gates;
lift them high, O everlasting doors; *
and the King of glory shall come in.

8 "Who is this King of glory?" *
"The Lord, strong and mighty,
the Lord, mighty in battle."
9 Lift up your heads, O gates;
lift them high, O everlasting doors; *
and the King of glory shall come in.
10 "Who is he, this King of glory?"
"The Lord of hosts,
he is the King of glory."

25 *Ad te, Domine, levavi*

1 To you, O Lord, I lift up my soul;
my God, I put my trust in you; *
let me not be humiliated,
nor let my enemies triumph over me.
2 Let none who look to you be put to shame; *
let the treacherous be disappointed in their schemes.
3 Show me your ways, O Lord, *
and teach me your paths.
4 Lead me in your truth and teach me, *
for you are the God of my salvation;
in you have I trusted all the day long.
5 Remember, O Lord, your compassion and love, *
for they are from everlasting.
6 Remember not the sins of my youth and my
transgressions; *
remember me according to your love
and for the sake of your goodness, O Lord.
7 Gracious and upright is the Lord; *
therefore he teaches sinners in his way.
8 He guides the humble in doing right *
and teaches his way to the lowly.
9 All the paths of the Lord are love and faithfulness *
to those who keep his covenant and his testimonies.

10 For your Name's sake, O Lord, *
forgive my sin, for it is great.
11 Who are they who fear the Lord? *
he will teach them the way that they should choose.
12 They shall dwell in prosperity, *
and their offspring shall inherit the land.
13 The Lord is a friend to those who fear him *
and will show them his covenant.
14 My eyes are ever looking to the Lord, *
for he shall pluck my feet out of the net.
15 Turn to me and have pity on me, *
for I am left alone and in misery.
16 The sorrows of my heart have increased; *
bring me out of my troubles.
17 Look upon my adversity and misery *
and forgive me all my sin.
18 Look upon my enemies, for they are many, *
and they bear a violent hatred against me.
19 Protect my life and deliver me; *
let me not be put to shame, for I have trusted in you.
20 Let integrity and uprightness preserve me, *
for my hope has been in you.
21 Deliver Israel, O God, *
out of all his troubles.

26 *Judica me, Domine*

1 Give judgment for me, O Lord,
for I have lived with integrity; *
I have trusted in the Lord and have not faltered.
2 Test me, O Lord, and try me; *
examine my heart and my mind.
3 For your love is before my eyes; *
I have walked faithfully with you.

4 I have not sat with the worthless, *
nor do I consort with the deceitful.
5 I have hated the company of evildoers; *
I will not sit down with the wicked.
6 I will wash my hands in innocence, O Lord, *
that I may go in procession round your altar,
7 Singing aloud a song of thanksgiving *
and recounting all your wonderful deeds.
8 Lord, I love the house in which you dwell *
and the place where your glory abides.
9 Do not sweep me away with sinners, *
nor my life with those who thirst for blood,
10 Whose hands are full of evil plots, *
and their right hand full of bribes.
11 As for me, I will live with integrity; *
redeem me, O Lord, and have pity on me.
12 My foot stands on level ground; *
in the full assembly I will bless the Lord.

Fifth Day: Evening Prayer

27 *Dominus illuminatio*

1 The Lord is my light and my salvation;
whom then shall I fear? *
the Lord is the strength of my life;
of whom then shall I be afraid?
2 When evildoers came upon me to eat up my flesh, *
it was they, my foes and my adversaries, who
stumbled and fell.
3 Though an army should encamp against me, *
yet my heart shall not be afraid;
4 And though war should rise up against me, *
yet will I put my trust in him.

5 One thing have I asked of the Lord;
one thing I seek; *
that I may dwell in the house of the Lord all the days
of my life;
6 To behold the fair beauty of the Lord *
and to seek him in his temple.
7 For in the day of trouble he shall keep me safe
in his shelter; *
he shall hide me in the secrecy of his dwelling
and set me high upon a rock.
8 Even now he lifts up my head *
above my enemies round about me.
9 Therefore I will offer in his dwelling an oblation
with sounds of great gladness; *
I will sing and make music to the Lord.
10 Hearken to my voice, O Lord, when I call; *
have mercy on me and answer me.
11 You speak in my heart and say, "Seek my face." *
Your face, Lord, will I seek.
12 Hide not your face from me, *
nor turn away your servant in displeasure.
13 You have been my helper;
cast me not away; *
do not forsake me, O God of my salvation.
14 Though my father and my mother forsake me, *
the Lord will sustain me.
15 Show me your way, O Lord; *
lead me on a level path, because of my enemies.
16 Deliver me not into the hand of my adversaries, *
for false witnesses have risen up against me,
and also those who speak malice.
17 What if I had not believed
that I should see the goodness of the Lord *
in the land of the living!

18 O tarry and await the Lord's pleasure;
be strong, and he shall comfort your heart; *
wait patiently for the Lord.

28 *Ad te, Domine*

1 O Lord, I call to you;
my Rock, do not be deaf to my cry; *
lest, if you do not hear me,
I become like those who go down to the Pit.
2 Hear the voice of my prayer when I cry out to you, *
when I lift up my hands to your holy of holies.
3 Do not snatch me away with the wicked or with the
evildoers, *
who speak peaceably with their neighbors,
while strife is in their hearts.
4 Repay them according to their deeds, *
and according to the wickedness of their actions.
5 According to the work of their hands repay them, *
and give them their just deserts.
6 They have no understanding of the Lord's doings,
nor of the works of his hands; *
therefore he will break them down and not
build them up.
7 Blessed is the Lord! *
for he has heard the voice of my prayer.
8 The Lord is my strength and my shield; *
my heart trusts in him, and I have been helped;
9 Therefore my heart dances for joy, *
and in my song will I praise him..10 The Lord is the
strength of his people, *
a safe refuge for his anointed.
11 Save your people and bless your inheritance; *
shepherd them and carry them for ever.

29 *Afferte Domino*

1 Ascribe to the Lord, you gods, *
ascribe to the Lord glory and strength.
2 Ascribe to the Lord the glory due his Name; *
worship the Lord in the beauty of holiness.
3 The voice of the Lord is upon the waters;
the God of glory thunders; *
the Lord is upon the mighty waters.
4 The voice of the Lord is a powerful voice; *
the voice of the Lord is a voice of splendor.
5 The voice of the Lord breaks the cedar trees; *
the Lord breaks the cedars of Lebanon;
6 He makes Lebanon skip like a calf, *
and Mount Hermon like a young wild ox.
7 The voice of the Lord splits the flames of fire;
the voice of the Lord shakes the wilderness; *
the Lord shakes the wilderness of Kadesh.
8 The voice of the Lord makes the oak trees writhe *
and strips the forests bare.
9 And in the temple of the Lord *
all are crying, "Glory!"
10 The Lord sits enthroned above the flood; *
the Lord sits enthroned as King for evermore.
11 The Lord shall give strength to his people; *
the Lord shall give his people the blessing of peace.

Sixth Day: Morning Prayer

30 *Exaltabo te, Domine*

1 I will exalt you, O Lord,
because you have lifted me up *
and have not let my enemies triumph over me.

2 O Lord my God, I cried out to you, *
and you restored me to health.
3 You brought me up, O Lord, from the dead; *
you restored my life as I was going down to the grave.
4 Sing to the Lord, you servants of his; *
give thanks for the remembrance of his holiness.
5 For his wrath endures but the twinkling of an eye, *
his favor for a lifetime.
6 Weeping may spend the night, *
but joy comes in the morning.
7 While I felt secure, I said,
"I shall never be disturbed. *
You, Lord, with your favor, made me as strong as
the mountains."
8 Then you hid your face, *
and I was filled with fear.
9 I cried to you, O Lord; *
I pleaded with the Lord, saying,
10 "What profit is there in my blood, if I go down to
the Pit? *
will the dust praise you or declare your faithfulness?
11 Hear, O Lord, and have mercy upon me; *
O Lord, be my helper."
12 You have turned my wailing into dancing; *
you have put off my sack-cloth and clothed me with joy.
13 Therefore my heart sings to you without ceasing; *
O Lord my God, I will give you thanks for ever.

31 *In te, Domine, speravi*

1 In you, O Lord, have I taken refuge;
let me never be put to shame; *
deliver me in your righteousness.
2 Incline your ear to me; *
make haste to deliver me.

3 Be my strong rock, a castle to keep me safe,
for you are my crag and my stronghold; *
for the sake of your Name, lead me and guide me.
4 Take me out of the net that they have secretly set for me, *
for you are my tower of strength.
5 Into your hands I commend my spirit, *
for you have redeemed me,
O Lord, O God of truth.
6 I hate those who cling to worthless idols, *
and I put my trust in the Lord.
7 I will rejoice and be glad because of your mercy; *
for you have seen my affliction;
you know my distress.
8 You have not shut me up in the power of the enemy; *
you have set my feet in an open place.
9 Have mercy on me, O Lord, for I am in trouble; *
my eye is consumed with sorrow,
and also my throat and my belly.
10 For my life is wasted with grief,
and my years with sighing; *
my strength fails me because of affliction,
and my bones are consumed.
11 I have become a reproach to all my enemies and
even to my neighbors,
a dismay to those of my acquaintance; *
when they see me in the street they avoid me.
12 I am forgotten like a dead man, out of mind; *
I am as useless as a broken pot.
13 For I have heard the whispering of the crowd;
fear is all around; *
they put their heads together against me;
they plot to take my life.
14 But as for me, I have trusted in you, O Lord. *
I have said, "You are my God.

15 My times are in your hand; *
rescue me from the hand of my enemies,
and from those who persecute me.
16 Make your face to shine upon your servant, *
and in your loving-kindness save me."
17 Lord, let me not be ashamed for having called upon
you; *
rather, let the wicked be put to shame;
let them be silent in the grave.
18 Let the lying lips be silenced which speak against
the righteous, *
haughtily, disdainfully, and with contempt.
19 How great is your goodness, O Lord!
which you have laid up for those who fear you; *
which you have done in the sight of all
for those who put their trust in you.
20 You hide them in the covert of your presence from
those who slander them; *
you keep them in your shelter from the strife of
tongues.
21 Blessed be the Lord! *
for he has shown me the wonders of his love in a
besieged city.
22 Yet I said in my alarm,
"I have been cut off from the sight of your eyes." *
Nevertheless, you heard the sound of my entreaty
when I cried out to you.
23 Love the Lord, all you who worship him; *
the Lord protects the faithful,
but repays to the full those who act haughtily.
24 Be strong and let your heart take courage, *
all you who wait for the Lord.

32 *Beati quorum*

1 Happy are they whose transgressions are forgiven, *
and whose sin is put away!

2 Happy are they to whom the Lord imputes no guilt, *
and in whose spirit there is no guile!

3 While I held my tongue, my bones withered away, *
because of my groaning all day long.

4 For your hand was heavy upon me day and night; *
my moisture was dried up as in the heat of summer.

5 Then I acknowledged my sin to you, *
and did not conceal my guilt.

6 I said, "I will confess my transgressions to the Lord." *
Then you forgave me the guilt of my sin.

7 Therefore all the faithful will make their prayers to
you in time of trouble; *
when the great waters overflow, they shall not reach
them.

8 You are my hiding-place;
you preserve me from trouble; *
you surround me with shouts of deliverance.

9 "I will instruct you and teach you in the way that you
should go; *
I will guide you with my eye.

10 Do not be like horse or mule, which have no
understanding; *
who must be fitted with bit and bridle,
or else they will not stay near you."

11 Great are the tribulations of the wicked; *
but mercy embraces those who trust in the Lord.

12 Be glad, you righteous, and rejoice in the Lord; *
shout for joy, all who are true of heart.

33 *Exultate, justi*

1 Rejoice in the Lord, you righteous; *
it is good for the just to sing praises.
2 Praise the Lord with the harp; *
play to him upon the psaltery and lyre.
3 Sing for him a new song; *
sound a fanfare with all your skill upon the trumpet.
4 For the word of the Lord is right, *
and all his works are sure.
5 He loves righteousness and justice; *
the loving-kindness of the Lord fills the whole earth.
6 By the word of the Lord were the heavens made, *
by the breath of his mouth all the heavenly hosts.
7 He gathers up the waters of the ocean as in a water-skin *
and stores up the depths of the sea.
8 Let all the earth fear the Lord; *
let all who dwell in the world stand in awe of him.
9 For he spoke, and it came to pass; *
he commanded, and it stood fast.
10 The Lord brings the will of the nations to naught; *
he thwarts the designs of the peoples.
11 But the Lord's will stands fast for ever, *
and the designs of his heart from age to age.
12 Happy is the nation whose God is the Lord! *
happy the people he has chosen to be his own!
13 The Lord looks down from heaven, *
and beholds all the people in the world.
14 From where he sits enthroned he turns his gaze *
on all who dwell on the earth.
15 He fashions all the hearts of them *
and understands all their works.

16 There is no king that can be saved by a mighty army;
a strong man is not delivered by his great strength.
17 The horse is a vain hope for deliverance; *
for all its strength it cannot save.
18 Behold, the eye of the Lord is upon those who fear
him, *
on those who wait upon his love,
19 To pluck their lives from death, *
and to feed them in time of famine.
20 Our soul waits for the Lord; *
he is our help and our shield.
21 Indeed, our heart rejoices in him, *
for in his holy Name we put our trust.
22 Let your loving-kindness, O Lord, be upon us, *
as we have put our trust in you.

34 *Benedicam Dominum*

1 I will bless the Lord at all times; *
his praise shall ever be in my mouth.
2 I will glory in the Lord; *
let the humble hear and rejoice.
3 Proclaim with me the greatness of the Lord;
let us exalt his Name together.
4 I sought the Lord, and he answered me *
and delivered me out of all my terror.
5 Look upon him and be radiant, *
and let not your faces be ashamed.
6 I called in my affliction and the Lord heard me *
and saved me from all my troubles.
7 The angel of the Lord encompasses those who fear
him, *
and he will deliver them.
8 Taste and see that the Lord is good; *
happy are they who trust in him!

9 Fear the Lord, you that are his saints, *
for those who fear him lack nothing.
10 The young lions lack and suffer hunger, *
but those who seek the Lord lack nothing that is good.
11 Come, children, and listen to me; *
I will teach you the fear of the Lord.
12 Who among you loves life *
and desires long life to enjoy prosperity?
13 Keep your tongue from evil-speaking *
and your lips from lying words.
14 Turn from evil and do good; *
seek peace and pursue it.
15 The eyes of the Lord are upon the righteous, *
and his ears are open to their cry.
16 The face of the Lord is against those who do evil, *
to root out the remembrance of them from the earth.
17 The righteous cry, and the Lord hears them *
and delivers them from all their troubles.
18 The Lord is near to the brokenhearted *
and will save those whose spirits are crushed.
19 Many are the troubles of the righteous, *
but the Lord will deliver him out of them all.
20 He will keep safe all his bones; *
not one of them shall be broken.
21 Evil shall slay the wicked, *
and those who hate the righteous will be punished.
22 The Lord ransoms the life of his servants, *
and none will be punished who trust in him.

Seventh Day: Morning Prayer

35 *Judica, Domine*

1 Fight those who fight me, O Lord; *
attack those who are attacking me.

2 Take up shield and armor *
and rise up to help me.
3 Draw the sword and bar the way against those
who pursue me; *
say to my soul, "I am your salvation."
4 Let those who seek after my life be shamed and
humbled, *
let those who plot my ruin fall back and be dismayed.
5 Let them be like chaff before the wind, *
and let the angel of the Lord drive them away.
6 Let their way be dark and slippery, *
and let the angel of the Lord pursue them.
7 For they have secretly spread a net for me without a
cause; *
without a cause they have dug a pit to take me alive.
8 Let ruin come upon them unawares; *
let them be caught in the net they hid;
let them fall into the pit they dug.
9 Then I will be joyful in the Lord; *
I will glory in his victory.
10 My very bones will say, "Lord, who is like you? *
You deliver the poor from those who are too strong for
them, the poor and needy from those who rob them."
11 Malicious witnesses rise up against me; *
they charge me with matters I know nothing about.
12 They pay me evil in exchange for good; *
my soul is full of despair.
13 But when they were sick I dressed in sack-cloth *
and humbled myself by fasting;
14 I prayed with my whole heart,
as one would for a friend or a brother; *
I behaved like one who mourns for his mother,
bowed down and grieving.

15 But when I stumbled, they were glad and gathered
together;
they gathered against me; *
strangers whom I did not know tore me to pieces and
would not stop.
16 They put me to the test and mocked me; *
they gnashed at me with their teeth.
17 O Lord, how long will you look on? *
rescue me from the roaring beasts,
and my life from the young lions.
18 I will give you thanks in the great congregation; *
I will praise you in the mighty throng.
19 Do not let my treacherous foes rejoice over me, *
nor let those who hate me without a cause
wink at each other.
20 For they do not plan for peace, *
but invent deceitful schemes against the
quiet in the land.
21 They opened their mouths at me and said, *
"Aha! we saw it with our own eyes."
22 You saw it, O Lord; do not be silent; *
O Lord, be not far from me.
23 Awake, arise, to my cause! *
to my defense, my God and my Lord!
24 Give me justice, O Lord my God,
according to your righteousness; *
do not let them triumph over me.
25 Do not let them say in their hearts,
"Aha! just what we want!" *
Do not let them say, "We have swallowed him up."
26 Let all who rejoice at my ruin be ashamed and
disgraced; *
let those who boast against me be clothed with
dismay and shame.

27 Let those who favor my cause sing out with joy and
be glad; *
let them say always, "Great is the Lord,
who desires the prosperity of his servant."
28 And my tongue shall be talking of your
righteousness *
and of your praise all the day long.

36 *Dixit injustus*

1 There is a voice of rebellion deep in the heart of the
wicked; *
there is no fear of God before his eyes.
2 He flatters himself in his own eyes *
that his hateful sin will not be found out.
3 The words of his mouth are wicked and deceitful, *
he has left off acting wisely and doing good.
4 He thinks up wickedness upon his bed
and has set himself in no good way; *
he does not abhor that which is evil.
5 Your love, O Lord, reaches to the heavens, *
and your faithfulness to the clouds.
6 Your righteousness is like the strong mountains,
your justice like the great deep; *
you save both man and beast, O Lord.
7 How priceless is your love, O God! *
your people take refuge under the
shadow of your wings.
8 They feast upon the abundance of your house; *
you give them drink from the river of your delights.
9 For with you is the well of life, *
and in your light we see light.
10 Continue your loving-kindness to those who know
you, *
and your favor to those who are true of heart.

11 Let not the foot of the proud come near me, *
nor the hand of the wicked push me aside.
12 See how they are fallen, those who work
wickedness! *
they are cast down and shall not be able to rise.

Seventh Day: Evening Prayer

37

Part I *Noli æmulari*
1 Do not fret yourself because of evildoers; *
do not be jealous of those who do wrong.
2 For they shall soon wither like the grass, *
and like the green grass fade away.
3 Put your trust in the Lord and do good; *
dwell in the land and feed on its riches.
4 Take delight in the Lord, *
and he shall give you your heart's desire.
5 Commit your way to the Lord and put your trust in
him, *
and he will bring it to pass.
6 He will make your righteousness as clear as the light *
and your just dealing as the noonday.
7 Be still before the Lord *
and wait patiently for him.
8 Do not fret yourself over the one who prospers, *
the one who succeeds in evil schemes.
9 Refrain from anger, leave rage alone; *
do not fret yourself; it leads only to evil.
10 For evildoers shall be cut off, *
but those who wait upon the Lord shall possess the
land.
11 In a little while the wicked shall be no more; *
you shall search out their place, but they will not be there.

12 But the lowly shall possess the land; *
they will delight in abundance of peace.
13 The wicked plot against the righteous *
and gnash at them with their teeth.
14 The Lord laughs at the wicked, *
because he sees that their day will come.
15 The wicked draw their sword and bend their bow
to strike down the poor and needy, *
to slaughter those who are upright in their ways.
16 Their sword shall go through their own heart, *
and their bow shall be broken.
17 The little that the righteous has *
is better than great riches of the wicked.
18 For the power of the wicked shall be broken, *
but the Lord upholds the righteous.

Psalm 37: Part II *Novit Dominus*
19 The Lord cares for the lives of the godly, *
and their inheritance shall last for ever.
20 They shall not be ashamed in bad times, *
and in days of famine they shall have enough.
21 As for the wicked, they shall perish, *
and the enemies of the Lord, like the glory of
the meadows, shall vanish;
they shall vanish like smoke.
22 The wicked borrow and do not repay, *
but the righteous are generous in giving.
23 Those who are blessed by God shall possess the
land, *
but those who are cursed by him shall be destroyed.
24 Our steps are directed by the Lord; *
he strengthens those in whose way he delights.
25 If they stumble, they shall not fall headlong, *
for the Lord holds them by the hand.

26 I have been young and now I am old, *
but never have I seen the righteous forsaken,
or their children begging bread.
27 The righteous are always generous in their lending, *
and their children shall be a blessing.
28 Turn from evil, and do good, *
and dwell in the land for ever.
29 For the Lord loves justice; *
he does not forsake his faithful ones.
30 They shall be kept safe for ever, *
but the offspring of the wicked shall be destroyed.
31 The righteous shall possess the land *
and dwell in it for ever.
32 The mouth of the righteous utters wisdom, *
and their tongue speaks what is right.
33 The law of their God is in their heart, *
and their footsteps shall not falter.
34 The wicked spy on the righteous *
and seek occasion to kill them.
35 The Lord will not abandon them to their hand, *
nor let them be found guilty when brought to trial.
36 Wait upon the Lord and keep his way; *
he will raise you up to possess the land,
and when the wicked are cut off, you will see it.
37 I have seen the wicked in their arrogance, *
flourishing like a tree in full leaf.
38 I went by, and behold, they were not there; *
I searched for them, but they could not be found.
39 Mark those who are honest;
observe the upright; *
for there is a future for the peaceable.
40 Transgressors shall be destroyed, one and all; *
the future of the wicked is cut off.

41 But the deliverance of the righteous comes from the Lord; *

he is their stronghold in time of trouble.

42 The Lord will help them and rescue them; *

he will rescue them from the wicked and deliver them, because they seek refuge in him.

Eighth Day: Morning Prayer

38 *Domine, ne in furore*

1 O Lord, do not rebuke me in your anger; *

do not punish me in your wrath.

2 For your arrows have already pierced me, *

and your hand presses hard upon me.

3 There is no health in my flesh,

because of your indignation; *

there is no soundness in my body, because of my sin.

4 For my iniquities overwhelm me; *

like a heavy burden they are too much for me to bear.

5 My wounds stink and fester *

by reason of my foolishness.

6 I am utterly bowed down and prostrate; *

I go about in mourning all the day long.

7 My loins are filled with searing pain; *

there is no health in my body.

8 I am utterly numb and crushed; *

I wail, because of the groaning of my heart.

9 O Lord, you know all my desires, *

and my sighing is not hidden from you.

10 My heart is pounding, my strength has failed me, *

and the brightness of my eyes is gone from me.

11 My friends and companions draw back from my affliction; *

my neighbors stand afar off.

12 Those who seek after my life lay snares for me; *
those who strive to hurt me speak of my ruin
and plot treachery all the day long.
13 But I am like the deaf who do not hear, *
like those who are mute and do not open their mouth.
14 I have become like one who does not hear *
and from whose mouth comes no defense.
15 For in you, O Lord, have I fixed my hope; *
you will answer me, O Lord my God.
16 For I said, "Do not let them rejoice at my expense, *
those who gloat over me when my foot slips."
17 Truly, I am on the verge of falling, *
and my pain is always with me.
18 I will confess my iniquity *
and be sorry for my sin.
19 Those who are my enemies without cause are
mighty, *
and many in number are those who wrongfully hate me.
20 Those who repay evil for good slander me, *
because I follow the course that is right.
21 O Lord, do not forsake me; *
be not far from me, O my God.
22 Make haste to help me, *
O Lord of my salvation.

39 *Dixi, Custodiam*

1 I said, "I will keep watch upon my ways, *
so that I do not offend with my tongue.
2 I will put a muzzle on my mouth *
while the wicked are in my presence."
3 So I held my tongue and said nothing; *
I refrained from rash words;
but my pain became unbearable.

4 My heart was hot within me;
while I pondered, the fire burst into flame; *
I spoke out with my tongue:
5 Lord, let me know my end and the number of my
days, *
so that I may know how short my life is.
6 You have given me a mere handful of days,
and my lifetime is as nothing in your sight; *
truly, even those who stand erect are but a puff of wind.
7 We walk about like a shadow,
and in vain we are in turmoil; *
we heap up riches and cannot tell who will gather them.
8 And now, what is my hope? *
O Lord, my hope is in you.
9 Deliver me from all my transgressions *
and do not make me the taunt of the fool.
10 I fell silent and did not open my mouth, *
for surely it was you that did it.
11 Take your affliction from me; *
I am worn down by the blows of your hand.
12 With rebukes for sin you punish us;
like a moth you eat away all that is dear to us; *
truly, everyone is but a puff of wind.
13 Hear my prayer, O Lord,
and give ear to my cry; *
hold not your peace at my tears.
14 For I am but a sojourner with you, *
a wayfarer, as all my forebears were.
15 Turn your gaze from me, that I may be glad again, *
before I go my way and am no more.

40 *Expectans, expectavi*

1 I waited patiently upon the Lord; *
he stooped to me and heard my cry.

2 He lifted me out of the desolate pit, out of the mire and clay; *
he set my feet upon a high cliff and made my footing sure.
3 He put a new song in my mouth,
a song of praise to our God; *
many shall see, and stand in awe,
and put their trust in the Lord.
4 Happy are they who trust in the Lord! *
they do not resort to evil spirits or turn to false gods.
5 Great things are they that you have done, O Lord my God!
how great your wonders and your plans for us! *
there is none who can be compared with you.
6 Oh, that I could make them known and tell them! *
but they are more than I can count.
7 In sacrifice and offering you take no pleasure *
(you have given me ears to hear you);
8 Burnt-offering and sin-offering you have not required, *
and so I said, "Behold, I come.
9 In the roll of the book it is written concerning me: *
'I love to do your will, O my God;
your law is deep in my heart.'"
10 I proclaimed righteousness in the great congregation; *
behold, I did not restrain my lips;
and that, O Lord, you know.
11 Your righteousness have I not hidden in my heart;
I have spoken of your faithfulness and your deliverance; *
I have not concealed your love and faithfulness from the great congregation.

12 You are the Lord;
do not withhold your compassion from me; *
let your love and your faithfulness keep me safe for
ever,
13 For innumerable troubles have crowded upon me;
my sins have overtaken me, and I cannot see; *
they are more in number than the hairs of my head,
and my heart fails me.
14 Be pleased, O Lord, to deliver me; *
O Lord, make haste to help me.
15 Let them be ashamed and altogether dismayed
who seek after my life to destroy it; *
let them draw back and be disgraced
who take pleasure in my misfortune.
16 Let those who say "Aha!" and gloat over me be
confounded,
because they are ashamed.
17 Let all who seek you rejoice in you and be glad; *
let those who love your salvation continually say,
"Great is the Lord!"
18 Though I am poor and afflicted, *
the Lord will have regard for me.
19 You are my helper and my deliverer; *
do not tarry, O my God.

Eighth Day: Evening Prayer

41 *Beatus qui intelligit*

1 Happy are they who consider the poor and needy! *
the Lord will deliver them in the time of trouble.
2 The Lord preserves them and keeps them alive,
so that they may be happy in the land; *
he does not hand them over to the will of their
enemies.

3 The Lord sustains them on their sickbed *
and ministers to them in their illness.
4 I said, "Lord, be merciful to me; *
heal me, for I have sinned against you."
5 My enemies are saying wicked things about me: *
"When will he die, and his name perish?"
6 Even if they come to see me, they speak empty
words; *
their heart collects false rumors;
they go outside and spread them.
7 All my enemies whisper together about me *
and devise evil against me.
8 "A deadly thing," they say, "has fastened on him; *
he has taken to his bed and will never get up again."
9 Even my best friend, whom I trusted,
who broke bread with me, *
has lifted up his heel and turned against me.
10 But you, O Lord, be merciful to me and raise me up, *
and I shall repay them.
11 By this I know you are pleased with me, *
that my enemy does not triumph over me.
12 In my integrity you hold me fast, *
and shall set me before your face for ever.
13 Blessed be the Lord God of Israel, *
from age to age. Amen. Amen.

Book Two

42 *Quemadmodum*

1 As the deer longs for the water-brooks, *
so longs my soul for you, O God.
2 My soul is athirst for God, athirst for the living God; *
when shall I come to appear before the presence of
God?

3 My tears have been my food day and night, *
while all day long they say to me,
"Where now is your God?"
4 I pour out my soul when I think on these things: *
how I went with the multitude and led them into the
house of God,
5 With the voice of praise and thanksgiving, *
among those who keep holy-day.
6 Why are you so full of heaviness, O my soul? *
and why are you so disquieted within me?
7 Put your trust in God; *
for I will yet give thanks to him,
who is the help of my countenance, and my God.
8 My soul is heavy within me; *
therefore I will remember you from the land of Jordan,
and from the peak of Mizar among the heights of
Hermon.
9 One deep calls to another in the noise of your
cataracts; *
all your rapids and floods have gone over me.
10 The Lord grants his loving-kindness in the daytime; *
in the night season his song is with me,
a prayer to the God of my life.
11 I will say to the God of my strength,
"Why have you forgotten me? *
and why do I go so heavily while the enemy
oppresses me?"
12 While my bones are being broken, *
my enemies mock me to my face;
13 All day long they mock me *
and say to me, "Where now is your God?"
14 Why are you so full of heaviness, O my soul? *
and why are you so disquieted within me?

15 Put your trust in God; *

for I will yet give thanks to him,

who is the help of my countenance, and my God.

43 *Judica me, Deus*

1 Give judgment for me, O God,

and defend my cause against an ungodly people; *

deliver me from the deceitful and the wicked.

2 For you are the God of my strength;

why have you put me from you? *

and why do I go so heavily while the enemy

oppresses me?

3 Send out your light and your truth, that they may lead

me, *

and bring me to your holy hill and to your dwelling;

4 That I may go to the altar of God,

to the God of my joy and gladness; *

and on the harp I will give thanks to you, O God my God.

5 Why are you so full of heaviness, O my soul? *

and why are you so disquieted within me?

6 Put your trust in God; *

for I will yet give thanks to him,

who is the help of my countenance, and my God.

Ninth Day: Morning Prayer

44 *Deus, auribus*

1 We have heard with our ears, O God,

our forefathers have told us, *

the deeds you did in their days, in the days of old.

2 How with your hand you drove the peoples out

and planted our forefathers in the land; *

how you destroyed nations and made your people

flourish.

3 For they did not take the land by their sword,
nor did their arm win the victory for them; *
but your right hand, your arm, and the
light of your countenance,
because you favored them.
4 You are my King and my God; *
you command victories for Jacob.
5 Through you we pushed back our adversaries; *
through your Name we trampled on those who
rose up against us.
6 For I do not rely on my bow, *
and my sword does not give me the victory.
7 Surely, you gave us victory over our adversaries *
and put those who hate us to shame.
8 Every day we gloried in God, *
and we will praise your Name for ever.
9 Nevertheless, you have rejected and humbled us *
and do not go forth with our armies.
10 You have made us fall back before our adversary, *
and our enemies have plundered us.
11 You have made us like sheep to be eaten *
and have scattered us among the nations.
12 You are selling your people for a trifle *
and are making no profit on the sale of them.
13 You have made us the scorn of our neighbors, *
a mockery and derision to those around us.
14 You have made us a byword among the nations, *
a laughing-stock among the peoples.
15 My humiliation is daily before me, *
and shame has covered my face;
16 Because of the taunts of the mockers and
blasphemers, *
because of the enemy and avenger.

17 All this has come upon us; *
yet we have not forgotten you,
nor have we betrayed your covenant.
18 Our heart never turned back, *
nor did our footsteps stray from your path;
19 Though you thrust us down into a place of misery, *
and covered us over with deep darkness.
20 If we have forgotten the Name of our God, *
or stretched out our hands to some strange god,
21 Will not God find it out? *
for he knows the secrets of the heart.
22 Indeed, for your sake we are killed all the day long; *
we are accounted as sheep for the slaughter.
23 Awake, O Lord! why are you sleeping? *
Arise! do not reject us for ever.
24 Why have you hidden your face *
and forgotten our affliction and oppression?
25 We sink down into the dust; *
our body cleaves to the ground.
26 Rise up, and help us, *
and save us, for the sake of your steadfast love.

45 *Eructavit cor meum*

1 My heart is stirring with a noble song;
let me recite what I have fashioned for the king; *
my tongue shall be the pen of a skilled writer.
2 You are the fairest of men; *
grace flows from your lips,
because God has blessed you for ever.
3 Strap your sword upon your thigh, O mighty warrior, *
in your pride and in your majesty.
4 Ride out and conquer in the cause of truth *
and for the sake of justice.

5 Your right hand will show you marvelous things; *
your arrows are very sharp, O mighty warrior.
6 The peoples are falling at your feet, *
and the king's enemies are losing heart.
7 Your throne, O God, endures for ever and ever, *
a scepter of righteousness is the scepter of your
kingdom;
you love righteousness and hate iniquity.
8 Therefore God, your God, has anointed you *
with the oil of gladness above your fellows.
9 All your garments are fragrant with myrrh, aloes, and
cassia, *
and the music of strings from ivory palaces makes you glad.
10 Kings' daughters stand among the ladies of the
court; *
on your right hand is the queen,
adorned with the gold of Ophir.
11 "Hear, O daughter; consider and listen closely; *
forget your people and your father's house.
12 The king will have pleasure in your beauty; *
he is your master; therefore do him honor.
13 The people of Tyre are here with a gift; *
the rich among the people seek your favor."
14 All glorious is the princess as she enters; *
her gown is cloth-of-gold.
15 In embroidered apparel she is brought to the king; *
after her the bridesmaids follow in procession.
16 With joy and gladness they are brought, *
and enter into the palace of the king.
17 "In place of fathers, O king, you shall have sons; *
you shall make them princes over all the earth.
18 I will make your name to be remembered
from one generation to another; *
therefore nations will praise you for ever and ever."

46 *Deus noster refugium*

1 God is our refuge and strength, *
a very present help in trouble.
2 Therefore we will not fear, though the earth be
moved, *
and though the mountains be toppled into the
depths of the sea;
3 Though its waters rage and foam, *
and though the mountains tremble at its tumult.
4 The Lord of hosts is with us; *
the God of Jacob is our stronghold.
5 There is a river whose streams make glad the city of
God, *
the holy habitation of the Most High.
6 God is in the midst of her;
she shall not be overthrown; *
God shall help her at the break of day.
7 The nations make much ado, and the kingdoms are
shaken; *
God has spoken, and the earth shall melt away.
8 The Lord of hosts is with us; *
the God of Jacob is our stronghold.
9 Come now and look upon the works of the Lord, *
what awesome things he has done on earth.
10 It is he who makes war to cease in all the world; *
he breaks the bow, and shatters the spear,
and burns the shields with fire.
11 "Be still, then, and know that I am God; *
I will be exalted among the nations;
I will be exalted in the earth."
12 The Lord of hosts is with us; *
the God of Jacob is our stronghold.

47 *Omnes gentes, plaudite*

1 Clap your hands, all you peoples; *
shout to God with a cry of joy.
2 For the Lord Most High is to be feared; *
he is the great King over all the earth.
3 He subdues the peoples under us, *
and the nations under our feet.
4 He chooses our inheritance for us, *
the pride of Jacob whom he loves.
5 God has gone up with a shout, *
the Lord with the sound of the ram's-horn.
6 Sing praises to God, sing praises; *
sing praises to our King, sing praises.
7 For God is King of all the earth; *
sing praises with all your skill.
8 God reigns over the nations; *
God sits upon his holy throne.
9 The nobles of the peoples have gathered together *
with the people of the God of Abraham.
10 The rulers of the earth belong to God, *
and he is highly exalted.

48 *Magnus Dominus*

1 Great is the Lord, and highly to be praised; *
in the city of our God is his holy hill.
2 Beautiful and lofty, the joy of all the earth, is the
hill of Zion, *
the very center of the world and the city of the great
King.
3 God is in her citadels; *
he is known to be her sure refuge.

4 Behold, the kings of the earth assembled *
and marched forward together.
5 They looked and were astounded; *
they retreated and fled in terror.
6 Trembling seized them there; *
they writhed like a woman in childbirth,
like ships of the sea when the east wind shatters them.
7 As we have heard, so have we seen,
in the city of the Lord of hosts, in the city of our God; *
God has established her for ever.
8 We have waited in silence on your loving-kindness,
O God, *
in the midst of your temple.
9 Your praise, like your Name, O God, reaches to
the world's end; *
your right hand is full of justice.
10 Let Mount Zion be glad
and the cities of Judah rejoice, *
because of your judgments.
11 Make the circuit of Zion;
walk round about her; *
count the number of her towers.
12 Consider well her bulwarks;
examine her strongholds; *
that you may tell those who come after.
13 This God is our God for ever and ever; *
he shall be our guide for evermore.

49 *Audite hæc, omnes*

1 Hear this, all you peoples;
hearken, all you who dwell in the world, *
you of high degree and low, rich and poor together.
2 My mouth shall speak of wisdom, *
and my heart shall meditate on understanding.

3 I will incline my ear to a proverb *
and set forth my riddle upon the harp.
4 Why should I be afraid in evil days, *
when the wickedness of those at my heels surrounds me,
5 The wickedness of those who put their trust in their goods, *
and boast of their great riches?
6 We can never ransom ourselves, *
or deliver to God the price of our life;
7 For the ransom of our life is so great, *
that we should never have enough to pay it,
8 In order to live for ever and ever, *
and never see the grave.
9 For we see that the wise die also;
like the dull and stupid they perish *
and leave their wealth to those who come after them.
10 Their graves shall be their homes for ever,
their dwelling places from generation to generation, *
though they call the lands after their own names.
11 Even though honored, they cannot live for ever; *
they are like the beasts that perish.
12 Such is the way of those who foolishly trust in themselves, *
and the end of those who delight in their own words.
13 Like a flock of sheep they are destined to die;
Death is their shepherd; *
they go down straightway to the grave.
14 Their form shall waste away, *
and the land of the dead shall be their home.
15 But God will ransom my life; *
he will snatch me from the grasp of death.
16 Do not be envious when some become rich, *
or when the grandeur of their house increases;

17 For they will carry nothing away at their death, *
nor will their grandeur follow them.

18 Though they thought highly of themselves while
they lived, *
and were praised for their success,

19 They shall join the company of their forebears, *
who will never see the light again.

20 Those who are honored, but have no understanding, *
are like the beasts that perish.

Tenth Day: Morning Prayer

50 *Deus deorum*

1 The Lord, the God of gods, has spoken; *
he has called the earth from the rising of the sun to
its setting.

2 Out of Zion, perfect in its beauty, *
God reveals himself in glory.

3 Our God will come and will not keep silence; *
before him there is a consuming flame,
and round about him a raging storm.

4 He calls the heavens and the earth from above *
to witness the judgment of his people.

5 "Gather before me my loyal followers, *
those who have made a covenant with me
and sealed it with sacrifice."

6 Let the heavens declare the rightness of his cause; *
for God himself is judge.

7 Hear, O my people, and I will speak:
"O Israel, I will bear witness against you; *
for I am God, your God.

8 I do not accuse you because of your sacrifices; *
your offerings are always before me.

9 I will take no bull-calf from your stalls, *
nor he-goats out of your pens;

10 For all the beasts of the forest are mine, *
the herds in their thousands upon the hills.
11 I know every bird in the sky, *
and the creatures of the fields are in my sight.
12 If I were hungry, I would not tell you, *
for the whole world is mine and all that is in it.
13 Do you think I eat the flesh of bulls, *
or drink the blood of goats?
14 Offer to God a sacrifice of thanksgiving *
and make good your vows to the Most High.
15 Call upon me in the day of trouble; *
I will deliver you, and you shall honor me."
16 But to the wicked God says: *
"Why do you recite my statutes,
and take my covenant upon your lips;
17 Since you refuse discipline, *
and toss my words behind your back?
18 When you see a thief, you make him your friend, *
and you cast in your lot with adulterers.
19 You have loosed your lips for evil, *
and harnessed your tongue to a lie.
20 You are always speaking evil of your brother *
and slandering your own mother's son.
21 These things you have done, and I kept still, *
and you thought that I am like you."
22 "I have made my accusation; *
I have put my case in order before your eyes.
23 Consider this well, you who forget God, *
lest I rend you and there be none to deliver you.
24 Whoever offers me the sacrifice of thanksgiving
honors me; *
but to those who keep in my way will I show
the salvation of God."

51 *Miserere mei, Deus*

1 Have mercy on me, O God, according to your
loving-kindness; *
in your great compassion blot out my offenses.
2 Wash me through and through from my wickedness *
and cleanse me from my sin.
3 For I know my transgressions, *
and my sin is ever before me.
4 Against you only have I sinned *
and done what is evil in your sight.
5 And so you are justified when you speak *
and upright in your judgment.
6 Indeed, I have been wicked from my birth, *
a sinner from my mother's womb.
7 For behold, you look for truth deep within me, *
and will make me understand wisdom secretly.
8 Purge me from my sin, and I shall be pure; *
wash me, and I shall be clean indeed.
9 Make me hear of joy and gladness, *
that the body you have broken may rejoice.
10 Hide your face from my sins *
and blot out all my iniquities.
11 Create in me a clean heart, O God, *
and renew a right spirit within me.
12 Cast me not away from your presence *
and take not your holy Spirit from me.
13 Give me the joy of your saving help again *
and sustain me with your bountiful Spirit.
14 I shall teach your ways to the wicked, *
and sinners shall return to you.
15 Deliver me from death, O God, *
and my tongue shall sing of your righteousness,
O God of my salvation.

16 Open my lips, O Lord, *
and my mouth shall proclaim your praise.
17 Had you desired it, I would have offered sacrifice, *
but you take no delight in burnt-offerings.
18 The sacrifice of God is a troubled spirit; *
a broken and contrite heart, O God, you will not
despise.
19 Be favorable and gracious to Zion, *
and rebuild the walls of Jerusalem.
20 Then you will be pleased with the appointed
sacrifices,
with burnt-offerings and oblations; *
then shall they offer young bullocks upon your altar.

52 *Quid gloriaris?*

1 You tyrant, why do you boast of wickedness *
against the godly all day long?
2 You plot ruin;
your tongue is like a sharpened razor, *
O worker of deception.
3 You love evil more than good *
and lying more than speaking the truth.
4 You love all words that hurt, *
O you deceitful tongue.
5 Oh, that God would demolish you utterly, *
topple you, and snatch you from your dwelling,
and root you out of the land of the living!
6 The righteous shall see and tremble, *
and they shall laugh at him, saying,
7 "This is the one who did not take God for a refuge, *
but trusted in great wealth
and relied upon wickedness."
8 But I am like a green olive tree in the house of God; *
I trust in the mercy of God for ever and ever.

9 I will give you thanks for what you have done *
and declare the goodness of your Name in the presence
of the godly.

Tenth Day: Evening Prayer

53 *Dixit insipiens*

1 The fool has said in his heart, "There is no God." *
All are corrupt and commit abominable acts;
there is none who does any good.
2 God looks down from heaven upon us all, *
to see if there is any who is wise,
if there is one who seeks after God.
3 Every one has proved faithless;
all alike have turned bad; *
there is none who does good; no, not one.
4 Have they no knowledge, those evildoers *
who eat up my people like bread
and do not call upon God?
5 See how greatly they tremble,
such trembling as never was; *
for God has scattered the bones of the enemy;
they are put to shame, because God has rejected them.
6 Oh, that Israel's deliverance would come out of Zion! *
when God restores the fortunes of his people
Jacob will rejoice and Israel be glad.

54 *Deus, in nomine*

1 Save me, O God, by your Name; *
in your might, defend my cause.
2 Hear my prayer, O God; *
give ear to the words of my mouth.

3 For the arrogant have risen up against me,
and the ruthless have sought my life, *
those who have no regard for God.
4 Behold, God is my helper; *
it is the Lord who sustains my life.
5 Render evil to those who spy on me; *
in your faithfulness, destroy them.
6 I will offer you a freewill sacrifice *
and praise your Name, O Lord, for it is good.
7 For you have rescued me from every trouble, *
and my eye has seen the ruin of my foes.

55 *Exaudi, Deus*

1 Hear my prayer, O God; *
do not hide yourself from my petition.
2 Listen to me and answer me; *
I have no peace, because of my cares.
3 I am shaken by the noise of the enemy *
and by the pressure of the wicked;
4 For they have cast an evil spell upon me *
and are set against me in fury.
5 My heart quakes within me, *
and the terrors of death have fallen upon me.
6 Fear and trembling have come over me, *
and horror overwhelms me.
7 And I said, "Oh, that I had wings like a dove! *
I would fly away and be at rest.
8 I would flee to a far-off place *
and make my lodging in the wilderness.
9 I would hasten to escape *
from the stormy wind and tempest."
10 Swallow them up, O Lord;
confound their speech; *
for I have seen violence and strife in the city.

11 Day and night the watchmen make their rounds upon her walls, *

but trouble and misery are in the midst of her.

12 There is corruption at her heart; *

her streets are never free of oppression and deceit.

13 For had it been an adversary who taunted me, then I could have borne it; *

or had it been an enemy who vaunted himself against me, then I could have hidden from him.

14 But it was you, a man after my own heart, *

my companion, my own familiar friend.

15 We took sweet counsel together, *

and walked with the throng in the house of God.

16 Let death come upon them suddenly;

let them go down alive into the grave; *

for wickedness is in their dwellings, in their very midst.

17 But I will call upon God, *

and the Lord will deliver me.

18 In the evening, in the morning, and at noonday,

I will complain and lament, *

and he will hear my voice.

19 He will bring me safely back from the battle waged against me; *

for there are many who fight me.

20 God, who is enthroned of old, will hear me and bring them down; *

they never change; they do not fear God.

21 My companion stretched forth his hand against his comrade; *

he has broken his covenant.

22 His speech is softer than butter, *

but war is in his heart.

23 His words are smoother than oil, *

but they are drawn swords.

24 Cast your burden upon the Lord,
and he will sustain you; *
he will never let the righteous stumble.
25 For you will bring the bloodthirsty and deceitful *
down to the pit of destruction, O God.
26 They shall not live out half their days, *
but I will put my trust in you.

Eleventh Day: Morning Prayer

56 *Miserere mei, Deus*

1 Have mercy on me, O God,
for my enemies are hounding me; *
all day long they assault and oppress me.
2 They hound me all the day long; *
truly there are many who fight against me, O Most High.
3 Whenever I am afraid, *
I will put my trust in you.
4 In God, whose word I praise,
in God I trust and will not be afraid, *
for what can flesh do to me?
5 All day long they damage my cause; *
their only thought is to do me evil.
6 They band together; they lie in wait; *
they spy upon my footsteps;
because they seek my life.
7 Shall they escape despite their wickedness? *
O God, in your anger, cast down the peoples.
8 You have noted my lamentation;
put my tears into your bottle; *
are they not recorded in your book?
9 Whenever I call upon you, my enemies will be put to
flight; *
this I know, for God is on my side.

10 In God the Lord, whose word I praise,
in God I trust and will not be afraid, *
for what can mortals do to me?
11 I am bound by the vow I made to you, O God; *
I will present to you thank-offerings;
12 For you have rescued my soul from death and my
feet from stumbling, *
that I may walk before God in the light of the living.

57 *Miserere mei, Deus*

1 Be merciful to me, O God, be merciful,
for I have taken refuge in you; *
in the shadow of your wings will I take refuge
until this time of trouble has gone by.
2 I will call upon the Most High God, *
the God who maintains my cause.
3 He will send from heaven and save me;
he will confound those who trample upon me; *
God will send forth his love and his faithfulness.
4 I lie in the midst of lions that devour the people; *
their teeth are spears and arrows,
their tongue a sharp sword.
5 They have laid a net for my feet,
and I am bowed low; *
they have dug a pit before me,
but have fallen into it themselves.
6 Exalt yourself above the heavens, O God, *
and your glory over all the earth.
7 My heart is firmly fixed, O God, my heart is fixed; *
I will sing and make melody.
8 Wake up, my spirit;
awake, lute and harp; *
I myself will waken the dawn.

9 I will confess you among the peoples, O Lord; *
I will sing praise to you among the nations.
10 For your loving-kindness is greater than the heavens, *
and your faithfulness reaches to the clouds.
11 Exalt yourself above the heavens, O God, *
and your glory over all the earth.

58 *Si vere utique*

1 Do you indeed decree righteousness, you rulers? *
do you judge the peoples with equity?
2 No; you devise evil in your hearts, *
and your hands deal out violence in the land.
3 The wicked are perverse from the womb; *
liars go astray from their birth.
4 They are as venomous as a serpent, *
they are like the deaf adder which stops its ears,
5 Which does not heed the voice of the charmer, *
no matter how skillful his charming.
6 O God, break their teeth in their mouths; *
pull the fangs of the young lions, O Lord.
7 Let them vanish like water that runs off; *
let them wither like trodden grass.
8 Let them be like the snail that melts away, *
like a stillborn child that never sees the sun.
9 Before they bear fruit, let them be cut down like a brier; *
like thorns and thistles let them be swept away.
10 The righteous will be glad when they see the vengeance; *
they will bathe their feet in the blood of the wicked.
11 And they will say,
"Surely, there is a reward for the righteous; *
surely, there is a God who rules in the earth."

Eleventh Day: Evening Prayer

59 *Eripe me de inimicis*

1 Rescue me from my enemies, O God; *
protect me from those who rise up against me.

2 Rescue me from evildoers *
and save me from those who thirst for my blood.

3 See how they lie in wait for my life,
how the mighty gather together against me; *
not for any offense or fault of mine, O Lord.

4 Not because of any guilt of mine *
they run and prepare themselves for battle.

5 Rouse yourself, come to my side, and see; *
for you, Lord God of hosts, are Israel's God.

6 Awake, and punish all the ungodly; *
show no mercy to those who are faithless and evil.

7 They go to and fro in the evening; *
they snarl like dogs and run about the city.

8 Behold, they boast with their mouths,
and taunts are on their lips; *
"For who," they say, "will hear us?"

9 But you, O Lord, you laugh at them; *
you laugh all the ungodly to scorn.

10 My eyes are fixed on you, O my Strength; *
for you, O God, are my stronghold.

11 My merciful God comes to meet me; *
God will let me look in triumph on my enemies.

12 Slay them, O God, lest my people forget; *
send them reeling by your might
and put them down, O Lord our shield.

13 For the sins of their mouths, for the words of their lips,
for the cursing and lies that they utter, *
let them be caught in their pride.

14 Make an end of them in your wrath; *
make an end of them, and they shall be no more.
15 Let everyone know that God rules in Jacob, *
and to the ends of the earth.
16 They go to and fro in the evening; *
they snarl like dogs and run about the city.
17 They forage for food, *
and if they are not filled, they howl.
18 For my part, I will sing of your strength; *
I will celebrate your love in the morning;
19 For you have become my stronghold, *
a refuge in the day of my trouble.
20 To you, O my Strength, will I sing; *
for you, O God, are my stronghold and my merciful
God.

60 *Deus, repulisti nos*

1 O God, you have cast us off and broken us; *
you have been angry; oh, take us back to you again.
2 You have shaken the earth and split it open; *
repair the cracks in it, for it totters.
3 You have made your people know hardship; *
you have given us wine that makes us stagger.
4 You have set up a banner for those who fear you, *
to be a refuge from the power of the bow.
5 Save us by your right hand and answer us, *
that those who are dear to you may be delivered.
6 God spoke from his holy place and said: *
"I will exult and parcel out Shechem;
I will divide the valley of Succoth.
7 Gilead is mine and Manasseh is mine; *
Ephraim is my helmet and Judah my scepter.

8 Moab is my wash-basin,
on Edom I throw down my sandal to claim it, *
and over Philistia will I shout in triumph."
9 Who will lead me into the strong city? *
who will bring me into Edom?
10 Have you not cast us off, O God? *
you no longer go out, O God, with our armies.
11 Grant us your help against the enemy, *
for vain is the help of man.
12 With God we will do valiant deeds, *
and he shall tread our enemies under foot.

61 *Exaudi, Deus*

1 Hear my cry, O God, *
and listen to my prayer.
2 I call upon you from the ends of the earth
with heaviness in my heart; *
set me upon the rock that is higher than I.
3 For you have been my refuge, *
a strong tower against the enemy.
4 I will dwell in your house for ever; *
I will take refuge under the cover of your wings.
5 For you, O God, have heard my vows; *
you have granted me the heritage of those
who fear your Name.
6 Add length of days to the king's life; *
let his years extend over many generations.
7 Let him sit enthroned before God for ever; *
bid love and faithfulness watch over him.
8 So will I always sing the praise of your Name, *
and day by day I will fulfill my vows.

62 *Nonne Deo?*

1 For God alone my soul in silence waits; *
from him comes my salvation.
2 He alone is my rock and my salvation, *
my stronghold, so that I shall not be greatly shaken.
3 How long will you assail me to crush me,
all of you together, *
as if you were a leaning fence, a toppling wall?
4 They seek only to bring me down from my place of
honor; *
lies are their chief delight.
5 They bless with their lips, *
but in their hearts they curse.
6 For God alone my soul in silence waits; *
truly, my hope is in him.
7 He alone is my rock and my salvation, *
my stronghold, so that I shall not be shaken.
8 In God is my safety and my honor; *
God is my strong rock and my refuge.
9 Put your trust in him always, O people, *
pour out your hearts before him, for God is our refuge.
10 Those of high degree are but a fleeting breath, *
even those of low estate cannot be trusted.
11 On the scales they are lighter than a breath, *
all of them together.
12 Put no trust in extortion;
in robbery take no empty pride; *
though wealth increase, set not your heart upon it.
13 God has spoken once, twice have I heard it, *
that power belongs to God.
14 Steadfast love is yours, O Lord, *
for you repay everyone according to his deeds.

63 *Deus, Deus meus*

1 O God, you are my God; eagerly I seek you; *
my soul thirsts for you, my flesh faints for you,
as in a barren and dry land where there is no water.
2 Therefore I have gazed upon you in your holy place, *
that I might behold your power and your glory.
3 For your loving-kindness is better than life itself; *
my lips shall give you praise.
4 So will I bless you as long as I live *
and lift up my hands in your Name.
5 My soul is content, as with marrow and fatness, *
and my mouth praises you with joyful lips,
6 When I remember you upon my bed, *
and meditate on you in the night watches.
7 For you have been my helper, *
and under the shadow of your wings I will rejoice.
8 My soul clings to you; *
your right hand holds me fast.
9 May those who seek my life to destroy it *
go down into the depths of the earth;
10 Let them fall upon the edge of the sword, *
and let them be food for jackals.
11 But the king will rejoice in God;
all those who swear by him will be glad; *
for the mouth of those who speak lies shall be stopped.

64 *Exaudi, Deus*

1 Hear my voice, O God, when I complain; *
protect my life from fear of the enemy.
2 Hide me from the conspiracy of the wicked, *
from the mob of evildoers.
3 They sharpen their tongue like a sword, *
and aim their bitter words like arrows,

4 That they may shoot down the blameless from
ambush; *
they shoot without warning and are not afraid.
5 They hold fast to their evil course; *
they plan how they may hide their snares.
6 They say, "Who will see us?
who will find out our crimes? *
we have thought out a perfect plot."
7 The human mind and heart are a mystery; *
but God will loose an arrow at them,
and suddenly they will be wounded.
8 He will make them trip over their tongues, *
and all who see them will shake their heads.
9 Everyone will stand in awe and declare God's deeds; *
they will recognize his works.
10 The righteous will rejoice in the Lord and put their
trust in him, *
and all who are true of heart will glory.

Twelfth Day: Evening Prayer

65 *Te decet hymnus*

1 You are to be praised, O God, in Zion; *
to you shall vows be performed in Jerusalem.
2 To you that hear prayer shall all flesh come, *
because of their transgressions.
3 Our sins are stronger than we are, *
but you will blot them out.
4 Happy are they whom you choose
and draw to your courts to dwell there! *
they will be satisfied by the beauty of your house,
by the holiness of your temple.

5 Awesome things will you show us in your
righteousness, O God of our salvation, *
O Hope of all the ends of the earth
and of the seas that are far away.
6 You make fast the mountains by your power; *
they are girded about with might.
7 You still the roaring of the seas, *
the roaring of their waves,
and the clamor of the peoples.
8 Those who dwell at the ends of the earth will tremble
at your marvelous signs; *
you make the dawn and the dusk to sing for joy.
9 You visit the earth and water it abundantly;
you make it very plenteous; *
the river of God is full of water.
10 You prepare the grain, *
for so you provide for the earth.
11 I You drench the furrows and smooth out the ridges; *
with heavy rain you soften the ground and bless its
increase.
12 You crown the year with your goodness, *
and your paths overflow with plenty.
13 May the fields of the wilderness be rich for grazing, *
and the hills be clothed with joy.
14 May the meadows cover themselves with flocks,
and the valleys cloak themselves with grain; *
let them shout for joy and sing.

66 *Jubilate Deo*

1 Be joyful in God, all you lands; *
sing the glory of his Name;
sing the glory of his praise.

2 Say to God, "How awesome are your deeds! *
because of your great strength your enemies
cringe before you.
3 All the earth bows down before you, *
sings to you, sings out your Name."
4 Come now and see the works of God, *
how wonderful he is in his doing toward all people.
5 He turned the sea into dry land,
so that they went through the water on foot, *
and there we rejoiced in him.
6 In his might he rules for ever;
his eyes keep watch over the nations; *
let no rebel rise up against him.
7 Bless our God, you peoples; *
make the voice of his praise to be heard;
8 Who holds our souls in life, *
and will not allow our feet to slip.
9 For you, O God, have proved us; *
you have tried us just as silver is tried.
10 You brought us into the snare; *
you laid heavy burdens upon our backs.
11 You let enemies ride over our heads;
we went through fire and water; *
but you brought us out into a place of refreshment.
12 I will enter your house with burnt-offerings
and will pay you my vows, *
which I promised with my lips
and spoke with my mouth when I was in trouble.
13 I will offer you sacrifices of fat beasts
with the smoke of rams; *
I will give you oxen and goats.
14 Come and listen, all you who fear God, *
and I will tell you what he has done for me.

15 I called out to him with my mouth, *
and his praise was on my tongue.
16 If I had found evil in my heart, *
the Lord would not have heard me;
17 But in truth God has heard me; *
he has attended to the voice of my prayer.
18 Blessed be God, who has not rejected my prayer, *
nor withheld his love from me.

67 *Deus misereatur*

1 May God be merciful to us and bless us, *
show us the light of his countenance and come to us.
2 Let your ways be known upon earth, *
your saving health among all nations.
3 Let the peoples praise you, O God; *
let all the peoples praise you.
4 Let the nations be glad and sing for joy, *
for you judge the peoples with equity
and guide all the nations upon earth.
5 Let the peoples praise you, O God; *
let all the peoples praise you.
6 The earth has brought forth her increase; *
may God, our own God, give us his blessing.
7 May God give us his blessing, *
and may all the ends of the earth stand in awe of him.

Thirteenth Day: Morning Prayer

68 *Exsurgat Deus*

1 Let God arise, and let his enemies be scattered; *
let those who hate him flee before him.
2 Let them vanish like smoke when the wind drives it
away; *
as the wax melts at the fire, so let the wicked perish at
the presence of God.

3 But let the righteous be glad and rejoice before God; *
let them also be merry and joyful.
4 Sing to God, sing praises to his Name;
exalt him who rides upon the heavens; *
Yahweh is his Name, rejoice before him!
5 Father of orphans, defender of widows, *
God in his holy habitation!
6 God gives the solitary a home and brings forth
prisoners into freedom; *
but the rebels shall live in dry places.
7 O God, when you went forth before your people, *
when you marched through the wilderness,
8 The earth shook, and the skies poured down rain,
at the presence of God, the God of Sinai, *
at the presence of God, the God of Israel.
9 You sent a gracious rain, O God, upon your
inheritance; *
you refreshed the land when it was weary.
10 Your people found their home in it; *
in your goodness, O God, you have made provision
for the poor.
11 The Lord gave the word; *
great was the company of women who bore the
tidings:
12 "Kings with their armies are fleeing away; *
the women at home are dividing the spoils."
13 Though you lingered among the sheepfolds, *
you shall be like a dove whose wings are covered with
silver, whose feathers are like green gold.
14 When the Almighty scattered kings, *
it was like snow falling in Zalmon.
15 O mighty mountain, O hill of Bashan! *
O rugged mountain, O hill of Bashan!

16 Why do you look with envy, O rugged mountain,
at the hill which God chose for his resting place? *
truly, the Lord will dwell there for ever.
17 The chariots of God are twenty thousand,
even thousands of thousands; *
the Lord comes in holiness from Sinai.
18 You have gone up on high and led captivity captive;
you have received gifts even from your enemies, *
that the Lord God might dwell among them.
19 Blessed be the Lord day by day, *
the God of our salvation, who bears our burdens.
20 He is our God, the God of our salvation; *
God is the Lord, by whom we escape death.
21 God shall crush the heads of his enemies, *
and the hairy scalp of those who go on still in their
wickedness.
22 The Lord has said, "I will bring them back from
Bashan; *
I will bring them back from the depths of the sea;
23 That your foot may be dipped in blood, *
the tongues of your dogs in the blood of your enemies."
24 They see your procession, O God, *
your procession into the sanctuary, my God and my King.
25 The singers go before, musicians follow after, *
in the midst of maidens playing upon the hand-drums.
26 Bless God in the congregation; *
bless the Lord, you that are of the fountain of Israel.
27 There is Benjamin, least of the tribes, at the head;
the princes of Judah in a company; *
and the princes of Zebulon and Naphtali.
28 Send forth your strength, O God; *
establish, O God, what you have wrought for us.
29 Kings shall bring gifts to you, *
for your temple's sake at Jerusalem.

30 Rebuke the wild beast of the reeds, *
and the peoples, a herd of wild bulls with its calves.
31 Trample down those who lust after silver; *
scatter the peoples that delight in war.
32 Let tribute be brought out of Egypt; *
let Ethiopia stretch out her hands to God.
33 Sing to God, O kingdoms of the earth; *
sing praises to the Lord.
34 He rides in the heavens, the ancient heavens; *
he sends forth his voice, his mighty voice.
35 Ascribe power to God; *
his majesty is over Israel;
his strength is in the skies.
36 How wonderful is God in his holy places! *
the God of Israel giving strength and power to his people!
Blessed be God!

Thirteenth Day: Evening Prayer

69 *Salvum me fac*

1 Save me, O God, *
for the waters have risen up to my neck.
2 I am sinking in deep mire, *
and there is no firm ground for my feet.
3 I have come into deep waters, *
and the torrent washes over me.
4 I have grown weary with my crying;
my throat is inflamed; *
my eyes have failed from looking for my God.
5 Those who hate me without a cause are more than
the hairs of my head;
my lying foes who would destroy me are mighty. *
Must I then give back what I never stole?

6 O God, you know my foolishness, *
and my faults are not hidden from you.
7 Let not those who hope in you be put to shame
through me, Lord God of hosts; *
let not those who seek you be disgraced because of
me, O God of Israel.
8 Surely, for your sake have I suffered reproach, *
and shame has covered my face.
9 I have become a stranger to my own kindred, *
an alien to my mother's children.
10 Zeal for your house has eaten me up; *
the scorn of those who scorn you has fallen upon me.
11 I humbled myself with fasting, *
but that was turned to my reproach.
12 I put on sack-cloth also, *
and became a byword among them.
13 Those who sit at the gate murmur against me, *
and the drunkards make songs about me.
14 But as for me, this is my prayer to you, *
at the time you have set, O Lord:
15 "In your great mercy, O God, *
answer me with your unfailing help.
16 Save me from the mire; do not let me sink; *
let me be rescued from those who hate me
and out of the deep waters.
17 Let not the torrent of waters wash over me,
neither let the deep swallow me up; *
do not let the Pit shut its mouth upon me.
18 Answer me, O Lord, for your love is kind; *
in your great compassion, turn to me.'
19 "Hide not your face from your servant; *
be swift and answer me, for I am in distress.
20 Draw near to me and redeem me; *
because of my enemies deliver me.

21 You know my reproach, my shame, and my dishonor; *
my adversaries are all in your sight."
22 Reproach has broken my heart, and it cannot be healed; *
I looked for sympathy, but there was none,
for comforters, but I could find no one.
23 They gave me gall to eat, *
and when I was thirsty, they gave me vinegar to drink.
24 Let the table before them be a trap *
and their sacred feasts a snare.
25 Let their eyes be darkened, that they may not see, *
and give them continual trembling in their loins.
26 Pour out your indignation upon them, *
and let the fierceness of your anger overtake them.
27 Let their camp be desolate, *
and let there be none to dwell in their tents.
28 For they persecute him whom you have stricken *
and add to the pain of those whom you have pierced.
29 Lay to their charge guilt upon guilt, *
and let them not receive your vindication.
30 Let them be wiped out of the book of the living *
and not be written among the righteous.
31 As for me, I am afflicted and in pain; *
your help, O God, will lift me up on high.
32 I will praise the Name of God in song; *
I will proclaim his greatness with thanksgiving.
33 This will please the Lord more than an offering of oxen, *
more than bullocks with horns and hoofs.
34 The afflicted shall see and be glad; *
you who seek God, your heart shall live.
35 For the Lord listens to the needy, *
and his prisoners he does not despise.

36 Let the heavens and the earth praise him, *
the seas and all that moves in them;
37 For God will save Zion and rebuild the cities of
Judah; *
they shall live there and have it in possession.
38 The children of his servants will inherit it, *
and those who love his Name will dwell therein.

70 *Deus, in adjutorium*

1 Be pleased, O God, to deliver me; *
O Lord, make haste to help me.
2 Let those who seek my life be ashamed
and altogether dismayed; *
let those who take pleasure in my misfortune
draw back and be disgraced.
3 Let those who say to me "Aha!" and gloat over me
turn back, *
because they are ashamed.
4 Let all who seek you rejoice and be glad in you; *
let those who love your salvation say for ever,
"Great is the Lord!"
5 But as for me, I am poor and needy; *
come to me speedily, O God.
6 You are my helper and my deliverer; *
O Lord, do not tarry.

Fourteenth Day: Morning Prayer

71 *In te, Domine, speravi*

1 In you, O Lord, have I taken refuge; *
let me never be ashamed.
2 In your righteousness, deliver me and set me free; *
incline your ear to me and save me.

3 Be my strong rock, a castle to keep me safe; *
you are my crag and my stronghold.
4 Deliver me, my God, from the hand of the wicked, *
from the clutches of the evildoer and the oppressor.
5 For you are my hope, O Lord God, *
my confidence since I was young.
6 I have been sustained by you ever since I was born;
from my mother's womb you have been my strength; *
my praise shall be always of you.
7 I have become a portent to many; *
but you are my refuge and my strength.
8 Let my mouth be full of your praise *
and your glory all the day long.
9 Do not cast me off in my old age; *
forsake me not when my strength fails.
10 For my enemies are talking against me, *
and those who lie in wait for my life take counsel
together.
11 They say, "God has forsaken him;
go after him and seize him; *
because there is none who will save."
12 O God, be not far from me; *
come quickly to help me, O my God.
13 Let those who set themselves against me be put to
shame and be disgraced; *
let those who seek to do me evil be covered with scorn
and reproach.
14 But I shall always wait in patience, *
and shall praise you more and more.
15 My mouth shall recount your mighty acts
and saving deeds all day long; *
though I cannot know the number of them.
16 I will begin with the mighty works of the Lord God *
I will recall your righteousness, yours alone.

17 O God, you have taught me since I was young, *
and to this day I tell of your wonderful works.
18 And now that I am old and gray-headed, O God, do
not forsake me, *
till I make known your strength to this generation
and your power to all who are to come.
19 Your righteousness, O God, reaches to the heavens; *
you have done great things;
who is like you, O God?
20 You have showed me great troubles and adversities, *
but you will restore my life and bring me up again
from the deep places of the earth.
21 You strengthen me more and more;
you enfold and comfort me,
22 Therefore I will praise you upon the lyre for your
faithfulness, O my God; *
I will sing to you with the harp, O Holy One of Israel.
23 My lips will sing with joy when I play to you, *
and so will my soul, which you have redeemed.
24 My tongue will proclaim your righteousness all day
long, *
for they are ashamed and disgraced who sought to do
me harm.

72 *Deus, judicium*

1 Give the King your justice, O God, *
and your righteousness to the King's Son;
2 That he may rule your people righteously *
and the poor with justice;
3 That the mountains may bring prosperity to the
people, *
and the little hills bring righteousness.
4 He shall defend the needy among the people; *
he shall rescue the poor and crush the oppressor.

5 He shall live as long as the sun and moon endure, *
from one generation to another.
6 He shall come down like rain upon the mown field, *
like showers that water the earth.
7 In his time shall the righteous flourish; *
there shall be abundance of peace till the moon shall
be no more.
8 He shall rule from sea to sea, *
and from the River to the ends of the earth.
9 His foes shall bow down before him, *
and his enemies lick the dust.
10 The kings of Tarshish and of the isles shall pay
tribute, *
and the kings of Arabia and Saba offer gifts.
11 All kings shall bow down before him, *
and all the nations do him service.
12 For he shall deliver the poor who cries out in
distress, *
and the oppressed who has no helper.
13 He shall have pity on the lowly and poor; *
he shall preserve the lives of the needy.
14 He shall redeem their lives from oppression and
violence, *
and dear shall their blood be in his sight.
15 Long may he live!
and may there be given to him gold from Arabia; *
may prayer be made for him always,
and may they bless him all the day long.
16 May there be abundance of grain on the earth,
growing thick even on the hilltops; *
may its fruit flourish like Lebanon,
and its grain like grass upon the earth.

17 May his Name remain for ever
and be established as long as the sun endures; *
may all the nations bless themselves in him and
call him blessed.
18 Blessed be the Lord God, the God of Israel, *
who alone does wondrous deeds!
19 And blessed be his glorious Name for ever! *
and may all the earth be filled with his glory.
Amen. Amen.

Book Three
Fourteenth Day: Evening Prayer

73 *Quam bonus Israel!*

1 Truly, God is good to Israel, *
to those who are pure in heart.
2 But as for me, my feet had nearly slipped; *
I had almost tripped and fallen;
3 Because I envied the proud *
and saw the prosperity of the wicked:
4 For they suffer no pain, *
and their bodies are sleek and sound;
5 In the misfortunes of others they have no share; *
they are not afflicted as others are;
6 Therefore they wear their pride like a necklace *
and wrap their violence about them like a cloak.
7 Their iniquity comes from gross minds, *
and their hearts overflow with wicked thoughts.
8 They scoff and speak maliciously; *
out of their haughtiness they plan oppression.
9 They set their mouths against the heavens, *
and their evil speech runs through the world.
10 And so the people turn to them *
and find in them no fault.

11 They say, "How should God know? *
is there knowledge in the Most High?"
12 So then, these are the wicked; *
always at ease, they increase their wealth.
13 In vain have I kept my heart clean, *
and washed my hands in innocence.
14 I have been afflicted all day long, *
and punished every morning.
15 Had I gone on speaking this way, *
I should have betrayed the generation of your children.
16 When I tried to understand these things, *
it was too hard for me;
17 Until I entered the sanctuary of God *
and discerned the end of the wicked.
18 Surely, you set them in slippery places; *
you cast them down in ruin.
19 Oh, how suddenly do they come to destruction, *
come to an end, and perish from terror!
20 Like a dream when one awakens, O Lord, *
when you arise you will make their image vanish.
21 When my mind became embittered, *
I was sorely wounded in my heart.
22 I was stupid and had no understanding; *
I was like a brute beast in your presence.
23 Yet I am always with you; *
you hold me by my right hand.
24 You will guide me by your counsel, *
and afterwards receive me with glory.
25 Whom have I in heaven but you? *
and having you I desire nothing upon earth.
26 Though my flesh and my heart should waste away, *
God is the strength of my heart and my portion for
ever.

27 Truly, those who forsake you will perish; *
you destroy all who are unfaithful.
28 But it is good for me to be near God; *
I have made the Lord God my refuge.
29 I will speak of all your works *
in the gates of the city of Zion.

74 *Ut quid, Deus?*

1 O God, why have you utterly cast us off? *
why is your wrath so hot against the sheep of your
pasture?
2 Remember your congregation that you purchased
long ago, *
the tribe you redeemed to be your inheritance,
and Mount Zion where you dwell.
3 Turn your steps toward the endless ruins; *
the enemy has laid waste everything in your sanctuary.
4 Your adversaries roared in your holy place; *
they set up their banners as tokens of victory.
5 They were like men coming up with axes to a grove
of trees; *
they broke down all your carved work with hatchets
and hammers.
6 They set fire to your holy place; *
they defiled the dwelling-place of your Name
and razed it to the ground.
7 They said to themselves, "Let us destroy them
altogether." *
They burned down all the meeting-places of God
in the land.
8 There are no signs for us to see;
there is no prophet left; *
there is not one among us who knows how long.

9 How long, O God, will the adversary scoff? *
will the enemy blaspheme your Name for ever?
10 Why do you draw back your hand? *
why is your right hand hidden in your bosom?
11 Yet God is my King from ancient times, *
victorious in the midst of the earth.
12 You divided the sea by your might *
and shattered the heads of the dragons upon the
waters;
13 You crushed the heads of Leviathan *
and gave him to the people of the desert for food.
14 You split open spring and torrent; *
you dried up ever-flowing rivers.
15 Yours is the day, yours also the night; *
you established the moon and the sun.
16 You fixed all the boundaries of the earth; *
you made both summer and winter.
17 Remember, O Lord, how the enemy scoffed, *
how a foolish people despised your Name.
18 Do not hand over the life of your dove to wild
beasts; *
never forget the lives of your poor.
19 Look upon your covenant; *
the dark places of the earth are haunts of violence.
20 Let not the oppressed turn away ashamed; *
let the poor and needy praise your Name.
21 Arise, O God, maintain your cause; *
remember how fools revile you all day long.
22 Forget not the clamor of your adversaries, *
the unending tumult of those who rise up against you.

75 *Confitebimur tibi*

1 We give you thanks, O God, we give you thanks, *
calling upon your Name and declaring all your
wonderful deeds.
2 "I will appoint a time," says God; *
"I will judge with equity.
3 Though the earth and all its inhabitants are quaking, *
I will make its pillars fast.
4 I will say to the boasters, 'Boast no more,' *
and to the wicked, 'Do not toss your horns;
5 Do not toss your horns so high, *
nor speak with a proud neck.'"
6 For judgment is neither from the east nor from the
west, *
nor yet from the wilderness or the mountains.
7 It is God who judges; *
he puts down one and lifts up another.
8 For in the Lord's hand there is a cup,
full of spiced and foaming wine, which he pours out, *
and all the wicked of the earth shall drink and
drain the dregs.
9 But I will rejoice for ever; *
I will sing praises to the God of Jacob.
10 He shall break off all the horns of the wicked; *
but the horns of the righteous shall be exalted.

76 *Notus in Judæa*

1 In Judah is God known; *
his Name is great in Israel.
2 At Salem is his tabernacle, *
and his dwelling is in Zion.

3 There he broke the flashing arrows, *
the shield, the sword, and the weapons of battle.
4 How glorious you are! *
more splendid than the everlasting mountains!
5 The strong of heart have been despoiled;
they sink into sleep; *
none of the warriors can lift a hand.
6 At your rebuke, O God of Jacob, *
both horse and rider lie stunned.
7 What terror you inspire! *
who can stand before you when you are angry?
8 From heaven you pronounced judgment; *
the earth was afraid and was still;
9 When God rose up to judgment *
and to save all the oppressed of the earth.
10 Truly, wrathful Edom will give you thanks, *
and the remnant of Hamath will keep your feasts.
11 Make a vow to the Lord your God and keep it; *
let all around him bring gifts to him who is worthy
to be feared.
12 He breaks the spirit of princes, *
and strikes terror in the kings of the earth.

77 *Voce mea ad Dominum*

1 I will cry aloud to God; *
I will cry aloud, and he will hear me.
2 In the day of my trouble I sought the Lord; *
my hands were stretched out by night and did not tire;
I refused to be comforted.
3 I think of God, I am restless, *
I ponder, and my spirit faints.
4 You will not let my eyelids close; *
I am troubled and I cannot speak.

5 I consider the days of old; *
I remember the years long past;
6 I commune with my heart in the night; *
I ponder and search my mind.
7 Will the Lord cast me off for ever? *
will he no more show his favor?
8 Has his loving-kindness come to an end for ever? *
has his promise failed for evermore?
9 Has God forgotten to be gracious? *
has he, in his anger, withheld his compassion?
10 And I said, "My grief is this: *
the right hand of the Most High has lost its power."
11 I will remember the works of the Lord, *
and call to mind your wonders of old time.
12 I will meditate on all your acts *
and ponder your mighty deeds.
13 Your way, O God, is holy; *
who is so great a god as our God?
14 You are the God who works wonders *
and have declared your power among the peoples.
15 By your strength you have redeemed your people, *
the children of Jacob and Joseph.
16 The waters saw you, O God;
the waters saw you and trembled; *
the very depths were shaken.
17 The clouds poured out water;
the skies thundered; *
your arrows flashed to and fro;
18 The sound of your thunder was in the whirlwind;
your lightnings lit up the world; *
the earth trembled and shook.
19 Your way was in the sea,
and your paths in the great waters, *
yet your footsteps were not seen.

20 You led your people like a flock *
by the hand of Moses and Aaron.

Fifteenth Day: Evening Prayer

78

Part I *Attendite, popule*
1 Hear my teaching, O my people; *
incline your ears to the words of my mouth.
2 I will open my mouth in a parable; *
I will declare the mysteries of ancient times.
3 That which we have heard and known,
and what our forefathers have told us, *
we will not hide from their children.
4 We will recount to generations to come
the praiseworthy deeds and the power of the Lord, *
and the wonderful works he has done.
5 He gave his decrees to Jacob
and established a law for Israel, *
which he commanded them to teach their children;
6 That the generations to come might know,
and the children yet unborn; *
that they in their turn might tell it to their children;
7 So that they might put their trust in God, *
and not forget the deeds of God,
but keep his commandments;
8 And not be like their forefathers,
a stubborn and rebellious generation, *
a generation whose heart was not steadfast,
and whose spirit was not faithful to God.
9 The people of Ephraim, armed with the bow, *
turned back in the day of battle;
10 They did not keep the covenant of God, *
and refused to walk in his law;

11 They forgot what he had done, *
and the wonders he had shown them.
12 He worked marvels in the sight of their forefathers, *
in the land of Egypt, in the field of Zoan.
13 He split open the sea and let them pass through; *
he made the waters stand up like walls.
14 He led them with a cloud by day, *
and all the night through with a glow of fire.
15 He split the hard rocks in the wilderness *
and gave them drink as from the great deep.
16 He brought streams out of the cliff, *
and the waters gushed out like rivers.
17 But they went on sinning against him, *
rebelling in the desert against the Most High.
18 They tested God in their hearts, *
demanding food for their craving.
19 They railed against God and said, *
"Can God set a table in the wilderness?
20 True, he struck the rock, the waters gushed out, and
the gullies overflowed; *
but is he able to give bread
or to provide meat for his people?"
21 When the Lord heard this, he was full of wrath; *
a fire was kindled against Jacob,
and his anger mounted against Israel;
22 For they had no faith in God, *
nor did they put their trust in his saving power.
23 So he commanded the clouds above *
and opened the doors of heaven.
24 He rained down manna upon them to eat *
and gave them grain from heaven.
25 So mortals ate the bread of angels; *
he provided for them food enough.

26 He caused the east wind to blow in the heavens *
and led out the south wind by his might.
27 He rained down flesh upon them like dust *
and wingèd birds like the sand of the sea.
28 He let it fall in the midst of their camp *
and round about their dwellings.
29 So they ate and were well filled, *
for he gave them what they craved.
30 But they did not stop their craving, *
though the food was still in their mouths.
31 So God's anger mounted against them; *
he slew their strongest men
and laid low the youth of Israel.
32 In spite of all this, they went on sinning *
and had no faith in his wonderful works.
33 So he brought their days to an end like a breath *
and their years in sudden terror.
34 Whenever he slew them, they would seek him, *
and repent, and diligently search for God.
35 They would remember that God was their rock, *
and the Most High God their redeemer.
36 But they flattered him with their mouths *
and lied to him with their tongues.
37 Their heart was not steadfast toward him, *
and they were not faithful to his covenant.
38 But he was so merciful that he forgave their sins
and did not destroy them; *
many times he held back his anger
and did not permit his wrath to be roused.
39 For he remembered that they were but flesh, *
a breath that goes forth and does not return.

Psalm 78: Part II *Quoties exacerbaverunt*

40 How often the people disobeyed him in the
wilderness *

and offended him in the desert!

41 Again and again they tempted God *

and provoked the Holy One of Israel.

42 They did not remember his power *

in the day when he ransomed them from the enemy;

43 How he wrought his signs in Egypt *

and his omens in the field of Zoan.

44 He turned their rivers into blood, *

so that they could not drink of their streams.

45 He sent swarms of flies among them, which ate
them up, *

and frogs, which destroyed them.

46 He gave their crops to the caterpillar, *

the fruit of their toil to the locust.

47 He killed their vines with hail *

and their sycamores with frost.

48 He delivered their cattle to hailstones *

and their livestock to hot thunderbolts.

49 He poured out upon them his blazing anger: *

fury, indignation, and distress,

a troop of destroying angels.

50 He gave full rein to his anger;

he did not spare their souls from death; *

but delivered their lives to the plague.

51 He struck down all the firstborn of Egypt, *

the flower of manhood in the dwellings of Ham.

52 He led out his people like sheep *

and guided them in the wilderness like a flock.

53 He led them to safety, and they were not afraid; *

but the sea overwhelmed their enemies.

54 He brought them to his holy land, *
the mountain his right hand had won.
55 He drove out the Canaanites before them
and apportioned an inheritance to them by lot; *
he made the tribes of Israel to dwell in their tents.
56 But they tested the Most High God, and defied him, *
and did not keep his commandments.
57 They turned away and were disloyal like their
fathers; *
they were undependable like a warped bow.
58 They grieved him with their hill-altars *
and provoked his displeasure with their idols.
59 When God heard this, he was angry *
and utterly rejected Israel.
60 He forsook the shrine at Shiloh, *
the tabernacle where he had lived among his people.
61 He delivered the ark into captivity, *
his glory into the adversary's hand.
62 He gave his people to the sword *
and was angered against his inheritance.
63 The fire consumed their young men; *
there were no wedding songs for their maidens.
64 Their priests fell by the sword, *
and their widows made no lamentation.
65 Then the Lord woke as though from sleep, *
like a warrior refreshed with wine.
66 He struck his enemies on the backside *
and put them to perpetual shame.
67 He rejected the tent of Joseph *
and did not choose the tribe of Ephraim;
68 He chose instead the tribe of Judah *
and Mount Zion, which he loved.
69 He built his sanctuary like the heights of heaven, *
like the earth which he founded for ever.

70 He chose David his servant, *
and took him away from the sheepfolds.
71 He brought him from following the ewes, *
to be a shepherd over Jacob his people
and over Israel his inheritance.
72 So he shepherded them with a faithful and true heart *
and guided them with the skillfulness of his hands.

Sixteenth Day: Morning Prayer

79 *Deus, venerunt*

1 O God, the heathen have come into your inheritance;
they have profaned your holy temple; *
they have made Jerusalem a heap of rubble.
2 They have given the bodies of your servants as food
for the birds of the air, *
and the flesh of your faithful ones to the beasts of the
field.
3 They have shed their blood like water on every side
of Jerusalem, *
and there was no one to bury them.
4 We have become a reproach to our neighbors, *
an object of scorn and derision to those around us.
5 How long will you be angry, O Lord? *
will your fury blaze like fire for ever?
6 Pour out your wrath upon the heathen who have not
known you *
and upon the kingdoms that have not called upon
your Name.
7 For they have devoured Jacob *
and made his dwelling a ruin.
8 Remember not our past sins;
let your compassion be swift to meet us; *
for we have been brought very low.

9 Help us, O God our Savior, for the glory of your Name; *

deliver us and forgive us our sins, for your Name's sake.

10 Why should the heathen say, "Where is their God?" *

Let it be known among the heathen and in our sight
that you avenge the shedding of your servants' blood.

11 Let the sorrowful sighing of the prisoners come before you, *

and by your great might spare those who are condemned to die.

12 May the revilings with which they reviled you, O Lord, *

return seven-fold into their bosoms.

13 For we are your people and the sheep of your pasture; *

we will give you thanks for ever
and show forth your praise from age to age.

80 *Qui regis Israel*

1 Hear, O Shepherd of Israel, leading Joseph like a flock; *

shine forth, you that are enthroned upon the cherubim.

2 In the presence of Ephraim, Benjamin, and Manasseh, *

stir up your strength and come to help us.

3 Restore us, O God of hosts; *

show the light of your countenance, and we shall be saved.

4 O Lord God of hosts, *

how long will you be angered
despite the prayers of your people?

5 You have fed them with the bread of tears; *

you have given them bowls of tears to drink.

6 You have made us the derision of our neighbors, *
and our enemies laugh us to scorn.
7 Restore us, O God of hosts; *
show the light of your countenance, and we shall be
saved.
8 You have brought a vine out of Egypt; *
you cast out the nations and planted it.
9 You prepared the ground for it; *
it took root and filled the land.
10 The mountains were covered by its shadow *
and the towering cedar trees by its boughs.
11 You stretched out its tendrils to the Sea *
and its branches to the River.
12 Why have you broken down its wall, *
so that all who pass by pluck off its grapes?
13 The wild boar of the forest has ravaged it, *
and the beasts of the field have grazed upon it.
14 Turn now, O God of hosts, look down from heaven;
behold and tend this vine; *
preserve what your right hand has planted.
15 They burn it with fire like rubbish; *
at the rebuke of your countenance let them perish.
16 Let your hand be upon the man of your right hand, *
the son of man you have made so strong for yourself.
17 And so will we never turn away from you; *
give us life, that we may call upon your Name.
18 Restore us, O Lord God of hosts; *
show the light of your countenance, and we shall be
saved.

81 *Exultate Deo*

1 Sing with joy to God our strength *
and raise a loud shout to the God of Jacob.

2 Raise a song and sound the timbrel, *
the merry harp, and the lyre.
3 Blow the ram's-horn at the new moon, *
and at the full moon, the day of our feast.
4 For this is a statute for Israel, *
a law of the God of Jacob.
5 He laid it as a solemn charge upon Joseph, *
when he came out of the land of Egypt.
6 I heard an unfamiliar voice saying *
"I eased his shoulder from the burden;
his hands were set free from bearing the load."
7 You called on me in trouble, and I saved you; *
I answered you from the secret place of thunder
and tested you at the waters of Meribah.
8 Hear, O my people, and I will admonish you: *
O Israel, if you would but listen to me!
9 There shall be no strange god among you; *
you shall not worship a foreign god.
10 I am the Lord your God,
who brought you out of the land of Egypt and said, *
"Open your mouth wide, and I will fill it."
11 And yet my people did not hear my voice, *
and Israel would not obey me.
12 So I gave them over to the stubbornness of their
hearts, *
to follow their own devices.
13 Oh, that my people would listen to me! *
that Israel would walk in my ways!
14 I should soon subdue their enemies *
and turn my hand against their foes.
15 Those who hate the Lord would cringe before him, *
and their punishment would last for ever.
16 But Israel would I feed with the finest wheat *
and satisfy him with honey from the rock.

82 *Deus stetit*

1 God takes his stand in the council of heaven; *
he gives judgment in the midst of the gods:
2 "How long will you judge unjustly, *
and show favor to the wicked?
3 Save the weak and the orphan; *
defend the humble and needy;
4 Rescue the weak and the poor; *
deliver them from the power of the wicked.
5 They do not know, neither do they understand;
they go about in darkness; *
all the foundations of the earth are shaken.
6 Now I say to you, 'You are gods, *
and all of you children of the Most High;
7 Nevertheless, you shall die like mortals, *
and fall like any prince.'"
8 Arise, O God, and rule the earth, *
for you shall take all nations for your own.

83 *Deus, quis similis?*

1 O God, do not be silent; *
do not keep still nor hold your peace, O God;
2 For your enemies are in tumult, *
and those who hate you have lifted up their heads.
3 They take secret counsel against your people *
and plot against those whom you protect.
4 They have said, "Come, let us wipe them out from
among the nations; *
let the name of Israel be remembered no more."
5 They have conspired together; *
they have made an alliance against you:

6 The tents of Edom and the Ishmaelites; *
the Moabites and the Hagarenes;
7 Gebal, and Ammon, and Amalek; *
the Philistines and those who dwell in Tyre.
8 The Assyrians also have joined them, *
and have come to help the people of Lot.
9 Do to them as you did to Midian, *
to Sisera, and to Jabin at the river of Kishon:
10 They were destroyed at Endor; *
they became like dung upon the ground.
11 Make their leaders like Oreb and Zeëb, *
and all their commanders like Zebah and Zalmunna,
12 Who said, "Let us take for ourselves *
the fields of God as our possession."
13 O my God, make them like whirling dust *
and like chaff before the wind;
14 Like fire that burns down a forest, *
like the flame that sets mountains ablaze.
15 Drive them with your tempest *
and terrify them with your storm;
16 Cover their faces with shame, O Lord,
that they may seek your Name.
17 Let them be disgraced and terrified for ever;
let them be put to confusion and perish.
18 Let them know that you, whose Name is Yahweh, *
you alone are the Most High over all the earth.

84 *Quam dilecta!*

1 How dear to me is your dwelling, O Lord of hosts! *
My soul has a desire and longing for the courts of
the Lord;
my heart and my flesh rejoice in the living God.

2 The sparrow has found her a house
and the swallow a nest where she may lay her young; *
by the side of your altars, O Lord of hosts,
my King and my God.
3 Happy are they who dwell in your house! *
they will always be praising you.
4 Happy are the people whose strength is in you! *
whose hearts are set on the pilgrims' way.
5 Those who go through the desolate valley will find
it a place of springs, *
for the early rains have covered it with pools of water.
6 They will climb from height to height, *
and the God of gods will reveal himself in Zion.
7 Lord God of hosts, hear my prayer; *
hearken, O God of Jacob.
8 Behold our defender, O God; *
and look upon the face of your Anointed.
9 For one day in your courts is better than
a thousand in my own room, *
and to stand at the threshold of the house of my God
than to dwell in the tents of the wicked.
10 For the Lord God is both sun and shield; *
he will give grace and glory;
11 No good thing will the Lord withhold *
from those who walk with integrity.
12 O Lord of hosts, *
happy are they who put their trust in you!

85 *Benedixisti, Domine*

1 You have been gracious to your land, O Lord, *
you have restored the good fortune of Jacob.
2 You have forgiven the iniquity of your people *
and blotted out all their sins.

3 You have withdrawn all your fury *
and turned yourself from your wrathful indignation.
4 Restore us then, O God our Savior; *
let your anger depart from us.
5 Will you be displeased with us for ever? *
will you prolong your anger from age to age?
6 Will you not give us life again, *
that your people may rejoice in you?
7 Show us your mercy, O Lord, *
and grant us your salvation.
8 I will listen to what the Lord God is saying, *
for he is speaking peace to his faithful people
and to those who turn their hearts to him.
9 Truly, his salvation is very near to those who fear
him, *
that his glory may dwell in our land.
10 Mercy and truth have met together; *
righteousness and peace have kissed each other.
11 Truth shall spring up from the earth, *
and righteousness shall look down from heaven.
12 The Lord will indeed grant prosperity, *
and our land will yield its increase.
13 Righteousness shall go before him, *
and peace shall be a pathway for his feet.

Seventeenth Day: Morning Prayer

86 *Inclina, Domine*

1 Bow down your ear, O Lord, and answer me, *
for I am poor and in misery.
2 Keep watch over my life, for I am faithful; *
save your servant who puts his trust in you.
3 Be merciful to me, O Lord, for you are my God; *
I call upon you all the day long.

4 Gladden the soul of your servant, *
for to you, O Lord, I lift up my soul.
5 For you, O Lord, are good and forgiving, *
and great is your love toward all who call upon you.
6 Give ear, O Lord, to my prayer, *
and attend to the voice of my supplications.
7 In the time of my trouble I will call upon you, *
for you will answer me.
8 Among the gods there is none like you, O Lord, *
nor anything like your works.
9 All nations you have made will come and
worship you, O Lord, *
and glorify your Name.
10 For you are great;
you do wondrous things; *
and you alone are God.
11 Teach me your way, O Lord,
and I will walk in your truth; *
knit my heart to you that I may fear your Name.
12 I will thank you, O Lord my God, with all my heart, *
and glorify your Name for evermore.
13 For great is your love toward me; *
you have delivered me from the nethermost Pit.
14 The arrogant rise up against me, O God,
and a band of violent men seeks my life; *
they have not set you before their eyes.
15 But you, O Lord, are gracious and full of
compassion, *
slow to anger, and full of kindness and truth.
16 Turn to me and have mercy upon me; *
give your strength to your servant;
and save the child of your handmaid.

17 Show me a sign of your favor,
so that those who hate me may see it and be ashamed; *
because you, O Lord, have helped me and comforted
me.

87 *Fundamenta ejus*

1 On the holy mountain stands the city he has founded; *
the Lord loves the gates of Zion
more than all the dwellings of Jacob.
2 Glorious things are spoken of you, *
O city of our God.
3 I count Egypt and Babylon among those who know
me; *
behold Philistia, Tyre, and Ethiopia:
in Zion were they born.
4 Of Zion it shall be said, "Everyone was born in her, *
and the Most High himself shall sustain her."
5 The Lord will record as he enrolls the peoples, *
"These also were born there."
6 The singers and the dancers will say, *
"All my fresh springs are in you."

88 *Domine, Deus*

1 O Lord, my God, my Savior, *
by day and night I cry to you.
2 Let my prayer enter into your presence; *
incline your ear to my lamentation.
3 For I am full of trouble; *
my life is at the brink of the grave.
4 I am counted among those who go down to the Pit; *
I have become like one who has no strength;
5 Lost among the dead, *
like the slain who lie in the grave,

6 Whom you remember no more, *
for they are cut off from your hand.
7 You have laid me in the depths of the Pit, *
in dark places, and in the abyss.
8 Your anger weighs upon me heavily, *
and all your great waves overwhelm me.
9 You have put my friends far from me;
you have made me to be abhorred by them; *
I am in prison and cannot get free.
10 My sight has failed me because of trouble; *
Lord, I have called upon you daily;
I have stretched out my hands to you.
11 Do you work wonders for the dead? *
will those who have died stand up and give you
thanks?
12 Will your loving-kindness be declared in the grave? *
your faithfulness in the land of destruction?
13 Will your wonders be known in the dark? *
or your righteousness in the country where all
is forgotten?
14 But as for me, O Lord, I cry to you for help; *
in the morning my prayer comes before you.
15 Lord, why have you rejected me? *
why have you hidden your face from me?
16 Ever since my youth, I have been wretched and at
the point of death; *
I have borne your terrors with a troubled mind.
17 Your blazing anger has swept over me; *
your terrors have destroyed me;
18 They surround me all day long like a flood; *
they encompass me on every side.
19 My friend and my neighbor you have put away from
me, *
and darkness is my only companion.

89

Part I *Misericordias Domini*
1 Your love, O Lord, for ever will I sing; *
from age to age my mouth will proclaim your
faithfulness.
2 For I am persuaded that your love is established for
ever; *
you have set your faithfulness firmly in the heavens.
3 "I have made a covenant with my chosen one; *
I have sworn an oath to David my servant:
4 'I will establish your line for ever, *
and preserve your throne for all generations.'"
5 The heavens bear witness to your wonders, O Lord, *
and to your faithfulness in the assembly of the holy
ones;
6 For who in the skies can be compared to the Lord? *
who is like the Lord among the gods?
7 God is much to be feared in the council of the holy
ones, *
great and terrible to all those round about him.
8 Who is like you, Lord God of hosts? *
O mighty Lord, your faithfulness is all around you.
9 You rule the raging of the sea *
and still the surging of its waves.
10 You have crushed Rahab of the deep with a deadly
wound; *
you have scattered your enemies with your mighty arm.
11 Yours are the heavens; the earth also is yours; *
you laid the foundations of the world and all that is in it.
12 You have made the north and the south; *
Tabor and Hermon rejoice in your Name.

13 You have a mighty arm; *
strong is your hand and high is your right hand.
14 Righteousness and justice are the foundations of
your throne; *
love and truth go before your face.
15 Happy are the people who know the festal shout! *
they walk, O Lord, in the light of your presence.
16 They rejoice daily in your Name; *
they are jubilant in your righteousness.
17 For you are the glory of their strength, *
and by your favor our might is exalted.
18 Truly, the Lord is our ruler; *
the Holy One of Israel is our King.

Psalm 89: Part II *Tunc locutus es*
19 You spoke once in a vision and said to your faithful
people: *
"I have set the crown upon a warrior
and have exalted one chosen out of the people.
20 I have found David my servant; *
with my holy oil have I anointed him.
21 My hand will hold him fast *
and my arm will make him strong.
22 No enemy shall deceive him, *
nor any wicked man bring him down.
23 I will crush his foes before him *
and strike down those who hate him.
24 My faithfulness and love shall be with him, *
and he shall be victorious through my Name.
25 I shall make his dominion extend *
from the Great Sea to the River.
26 He will say to me, 'You are my Father, *
my God, and the rock of my salvation.'

27 I will make him my firstborn *
and higher than the kings of the earth.
28 I will keep my love for him for ever, *
and my covenant will stand firm for him.
29 I will establish his line for ever *
and his throne as the days of heaven."
30 "If his children forsake my law *
and do not walk according to my judgments;
31 If they break my statutes *
and do not keep my commandments;
32 I will punish their transgressions with a rod *
and their iniquities with the lash;
33 But I will not take my love from him, *
nor let my faithfulness prove false.
34 I will not break my covenant, *
nor change what has gone out of my lips.
35 Once for all I have sworn by my holiness: *
'I will not lie to David.
36 His line shall endure for ever *
and his throne as the sun before me;
37 It shall stand fast for evermore like the moon, *
the abiding witness in the sky.'"
38 But you have cast off and rejected your anointed; *
you have become enraged at him.
39 You have broken your covenant with your servant, *
defiled his crown, and hurled it to the ground.
40 You have breached all his walls *
and laid his strongholds in ruins.
41 All who pass by despoil him; *
he has become the scorn of his neighbors.
42 You have exalted the right hand of his foes *
and made all his enemies rejoice.
43 You have turned back the edge of his sword *
and have not sustained him in battle.

44 You have put an end to his splendor *
and cast his throne to the ground.
45 You have cut short the days of his youth *
and have covered him with shame.
46 How long will you hide yourself, O Lord?
will you hide yourself for ever? *
how long will your anger burn like fire?
47 Remember, Lord, how short life is, *
how frail you have made all flesh.
48 Who can live and not see death? *
who can save himself from the power of the grave?
49 Where, Lord, are your loving-kindnesses of old, *
which you promised David in your faithfulness?
50 Remember, Lord, how your servant is mocked, *
how I carry in my bosom the taunts of many peoples,
51 The taunts your enemies have hurled, O Lord, *
which they hurled at the heels of your anointed.
52 Blessed be the Lord for evermore! *
Amen, I say, Amen.

Book Four
Eighteenth Day: Morning Prayer

90 *Domine, refugium*

1 Lord, you have been our refuge *
from one generation to another.
2 Before the mountains were brought forth,
or the land and the earth were born, *
from age to age you are God.
3 You turn us back to the dust and say, *
"Go back, O child of earth."
4 For a thousand years in your sight are like yesterday
when it is past *
and like a watch in the night.

5 You sweep us away like a dream; *
we fade away suddenly like the grass.
6 In the morning it is green and flourishes; *
in the evening it is dried up and withered.
7 For we consume away in your displeasure; *
we are afraid because of your wrathful indignation.
8 Our iniquities you have set before you, *
and our secret sins in the light of your countenance.
9 When you are angry, all our days are gone; *
we bring our years to an end like a sigh.
10 The span of our life is seventy years,
perhaps in strength even eighty; *
yet the sum of them is but labor and sorrow,
for they pass away quickly and we are gone.
11 Who regards the power of your wrath? *
who rightly fears your indignation?
12 So teach us to number our days *
that we may apply our hearts to wisdom.
13 Return, O Lord; how long will you tarry? *
be gracious to your servants.
14 Satisfy us by your loving-kindness in the morning; *
so shall we rejoice and be glad all the days of our life.
15 Make us glad by the measure of the days that you
afflicted us *
and the years in which we suffered adversity.
16 Show your servants your works *
and your splendor to their children.
17 May the graciousness of the Lord our God be upon
us; *
prosper the work of our hands; prosper our handiwork.

91 *Qui habitat*

1 He who dwells in the shelter of the Most High, *
abides under the shadow of the Almighty.

2 He shall say to the Lord,
"You are my refuge and my stronghold, *
my God in whom I put my trust."
3 He shall deliver you from the snare of the hunter *
and from the deadly pestilence.
4 He shall cover you with his pinions,
and you shall find refuge under his wings; *
his faithfulness shall be a shield and buckler.
5 You shall not be afraid of any terror by night, *
nor of the arrow that flies by day;
6 Of the plague that stalks in the darkness, *
nor of the sickness that lays waste at mid-day.
7 A thousand shall fall at your side
and ten thousand at your right hand, *
but it shall not come near you.
8 Your eyes have only to behold *
to see the reward of the wicked.
9 Because you have made the Lord your refuge, *
and the Most High your habitation,
10 There shall no evil happen to you, *
neither shall any plague come near your dwelling.
11 For he shall give his angels charge over you, *
to keep you in all your ways.
12 They shall bear you in their hands, *
lest you dash your foot against a stone.
13 You shall tread upon the lion and adder; *
you shall trample the young lion and the serpent
under your feet.
14 Because he is bound to me in love,
therefore will I deliver him; *
I will protect him, because he knows my Name.
15 He shall call upon me, and I will answer him; *
I am with him in trouble;
I will rescue him and bring him to honor.

16 With long life will I satisfy him, *
and show him my salvation.

92 *Bonum est confiteri*

1 It is a good thing to give thanks to the Lord, *
and to sing praises to your Name, O Most High;
2 To tell of your loving-kindness early in the morning *
and of your faithfulness in the night season;
3 On the psaltery, and on the lyre, *
and to the melody of the harp.
4 For you have made me glad by your acts, O Lord; *
and I shout for joy because of the works of your hands.
5 Lord, how great are your works! *
your thoughts are very deep.
6 The dullard does not know,
nor does the fool understand, *
that though the wicked grow like weeds,
and all the workers of iniquity flourish,
7 They flourish only to be destroyed for ever; *
but you, O Lord, are exalted for evermore.
8 For lo, your enemies, O Lord,
lo, your enemies shall perish, *
and all the workers of iniquity shall be scattered.
9 But my horn you have exalted like the horns of wild
bulls; *
I am anointed with fresh oil.
10 My eyes also gloat over my enemies, *
and my ears rejoice to hear the doom of the wicked
who rise up against me.
11 The righteous shall flourish like a palm tree, *
and shall spread abroad like a cedar of Lebanon.
12 Those who are planted in the house of the Lord *
shall flourish in the courts of our God;

13 They shall still bear fruit in old age; *
they shall be green and succulent;
14 That they may show how upright the Lord is, *
my Rock, in whom there is no fault.

Eighteenth Day: Evening Prayer

93 *Dominus regnavit*

1 The Lord is King;
he has put on splendid apparel; *
the Lord has put on his apparel
and girded himself with strength.
2 He has made the whole world so sure *
that it cannot be moved;
3 Ever since the world began, your throne has been
established; *
you are from everlasting.
4 The waters have lifted up, O Lord,
the waters have lifted up their voice; *
the waters have lifted up their pounding waves.
5 Mightier than the sound of many waters,
mightier than the breakers of the sea, *
mightier is the Lord who dwells on high.
6 Your testimonies are very sure, *
and holiness adorns your house, O Lord,
for ever and for evermore.

94 *Deus ultionum*

1 O Lord God of vengeance, *
O God of vengeance, show yourself
2 Rise up, O Judge of the world; *
give the arrogant their just deserts.
3 How long shall the wicked, O Lord, *
how long shall the wicked triumph?

4 They bluster in their insolence; *
all evildoers are full of boasting.
5 They crush your people, O Lord, *
and afflict your chosen nation.
6 They murder the widow and the stranger *
and put the orphans to death.
7 Yet they say, "The Lord does not see, *
the God of Jacob takes no notice."
8 Consider well, you dullards among the people; *
when will you fools understand?
9 He that planted the ear, does he not hear? *
he that formed the eye, does he not see?
10 He who admonishes the nations, will he not punish? *
he who teaches all the world, has he no knowledge?
11 The Lord knows our human thoughts; *
how like a puff of wind they are.
12 Happy are they whom you instruct, O Lord! *
whom you teach out of your law;
13 To give them rest in evil days, *
until a pit is dug for the wicked.
14 For the Lord will not abandon his people, *
nor will he forsake his own.
15 For judgment will again be just, *
and all the true of heart will follow it.
16 Who rose up for me against the wicked? *
who took my part against the evildoers?
17 If the Lord had not come to my help, *
I should soon have dwelt in the land of silence.
18 As often as I said, "My foot has slipped," *
your love, O Lord, upheld me.
19 When many cares fill my mind, *
your consolations cheer my soul.
20 Can a corrupt tribunal have any part with you, *
one which frames evil into law?

21 They conspire against the life of the just *
and condemn the innocent to death.
22 But the Lord has become my stronghold, *
and my God the rock of my trust.
23 He will turn their wickedness back upon them
and destroy them in their own malice; *
the Lord our God will destroy them.

Nineteenth Day: Morning Prayer

95 *Venite, exultemus*

1 Come, let us sing to the Lord; *
let us shout for joy to the Rock of our salvation.
2 Let us come before his presence with thanksgiving *
and raise a loud shout to him with psalms.
3 For the Lord is a great God, *
and a great King above all gods.
4 In his hand are the caverns of the earth, *
and the heights of the hills are his also.
5 The sea is his, for he made it, *
and his hands have molded the dry land.
6 Come, let us bow down, and bend the knee, *
and kneel before the Lord our Maker.
7 For he is our God,
and we are the people of his pasture and the sheep of
his hand. *
Oh, that today you would hearken to his voice!
8 Harden not your hearts,
as your forebears did in the wilderness, *
at Meribah, and on that day at Massah,
when they tempted me.
9 They put me to the test, *
though they had seen my works.

10 Forty years long I detested that generation and said, *
"This people are wayward in their hearts;
they do not know my ways."
11 So I swore in my wrath, *
"They shall not enter into my rest."

96 *Cantate Domino*

1 Sing to the Lord a new song; *
sing to the Lord, all the whole earth.
2 Sing to the Lord and bless his Name; *
proclaim the good news of his salvation from day to day.
3 Declare his glory among the nations *
and his wonders among all peoples.
4 For great is the Lord and greatly to be praised; *
he is more to be feared than all gods.
5 As for all the gods of the nations, they are but idols; *
but it is the Lord who made the heavens.
6 Oh, the majesty and magnificence of his presence! *
Oh, the power and the splendor of his sanctuary!
7 Ascribe to the Lord, you families of the peoples; *
ascribe to the Lord honor and power.
8 Ascribe to the Lord the honor due his Name; *
bring offerings and come into his courts.
9 Worship the Lord in the beauty of holiness; *
let the whole earth tremble before him.
10 Tell it out among the nations: "The Lord is King! *
he has made the world so firm that it cannot be moved;
he will judge the peoples with equity."
11 Let the heavens rejoice, and let the earth be glad;
let the sea thunder and all that is in it; *
let the field be joyful and all that is therein.
12 Then shall all the trees of the wood shout for joy
before the Lord when he comes, *
when he comes to judge the earth.

13 He will judge the world with righteousness *
and the peoples with his truth.

97 *Dominus regnavit*

1 The Lord is King; let the earth rejoice; *
let the multitude of the isles be glad.
2 Clouds and darkness are round about him, *
righteousness and justice are the foundations of his throne.
3 A fire goes before him *
and burns up his enemies on every side.
4 His lightnings light up the world; *
the earth sees it and is afraid.
5 The mountains melt like wax at the presence of the Lord, *
at the presence of the Lord of the whole earth.
6 The heavens declare his righteousness, *
and all the peoples see his glory.
7 Confounded be all who worship carved images
and delight in false gods! *
Bow down before him, all you gods.
8 Zion hears and is glad, and the cities of Judah rejoice, *
because of your judgments, O Lord.
9 For you are the Lord,
most high over all the earth; *
you are exalted far above all gods.
10 The Lord loves those who hate evil; *
he preserves the lives of his saints
and delivers them from the hand of the wicked.
11 Light has sprung up for the righteous, *
and joyful gladness for those who are truehearted.
12 Rejoice in the Lord, you righteous, *
and give thanks to his holy Name.

98 *Cantate Domino*

1 Sing to the Lord a new song, *
for he has done marvelous things.
2 With his right hand and his holy arm *
has he won for himself the victory.
3 The Lord has made known his victory; *
his righteousness has he openly shown in
the sight of the nations.
4 He remembers his mercy and faithfulness to
the house of Israel, *
and all the ends of the earth have seen the
victory of our God.
5 Shout with joy to the Lord, all you lands; *
lift up your voice, rejoice, and sing.
6 Sing to the Lord with the harp, *
with the harp and the voice of song.
7 With trumpets and the sound of the horn *
shout with joy before the King, the Lord.
8 Let the sea make a noise and all that is in it, *
the lands and those who dwell therein.
9 Let the rivers clap their hands, *
and let the hills ring out with joy before the Lord,
when he comes to judge the earth.
10 In righteousness shall he judge the world *
and the peoples with equity.

99 *Dominus regnavit*

1 The Lord is King;
let the people tremble; *
he is enthroned upon the cherubim;
let the earth shake.

2 The Lord is great in Zion; *
he is high above all peoples.
3 Let them confess his Name, which is great and
awesome; *
he is the Holy One.
4 "O mighty King, lover of justice,
you have established equity; *
you have executed justice and righteousness in Jacob."
5 Proclaim the greatness of the Lord our God
and fall down before his footstool; *
he is the Holy One.
6 Moses and Aaron among his priests,
and Samuel among those who call upon his Name, *
they called upon the Lord, and he answered them.
7 He spoke to them out of the pillar of cloud; *
they kept his testimonies and the decree that he gave
them.
8 "O Lord our God, you answered them indeed; *
you were a God who forgave them,
yet punished them for their evil deeds."
9 Proclaim the greatness of the Lord our God
and worship him upon his holy hill; *
for the Lord our God is the Holy One.

100 *Jubilate Deo*

1 Be joyful in the Lord, all you lands; *
serve the Lord with gladness
and come before his presence with a song.
2 Know this: The Lord himself is God; *
he himself has made us, and we are his;
we are his people and the sheep of his pasture.
3 Enter his gates with thanksgiving;
go into his courts with praise; *
give thanks to him and call upon his Name.

4 For the Lord is good;
his mercy is everlasting; *
and his faithfulness endures from age to age.

101 *Misericordiam et judicium*

1 I will sing of mercy and justice; *
to you, O Lord, will I sing praises.
2 I will strive to follow a blameless course;
oh, when will you come to me? *
I will walk with sincerity of heart within my house.
3 I will set no worthless thing before my eyes; *
I hate the doers of evil deeds;
they shall not remain with me.
4 A crooked heart shall be far from me; *
I will not know evil.
5 Those who in secret slander their neighbors I will
destroy; *
those who have a haughty look and a proud
heart I cannot abide.
6 My eyes are upon the faithful in the land, that they
may dwell with me, *
and only those who lead a blameless life shall
be my servants.
7 Those who act deceitfully shall not dwell in my
house, *
and those who tell lies shall not continue in my sight.
8 I will soon destroy all the wicked in the land, *
that I may root out all evildoers from the city of the
Lord.

102 *Domine, exaudi*

1 Lord, hear my prayer, and let my cry come before you; *

hide not your face from me in the day of my trouble.

2 Incline your ear to me; *

when I call, make haste to answer me,

3 For my days drift away like smoke, *

and my bones are hot as burning coals.

4 My heart is smitten like grass and withered, *

so that I forget to eat my bread.

5 Because of the voice of my groaning *

I am but skin and bones.

6 I have become like a vulture in the wilderness, *

like an owl among the ruins.

7 I lie awake and groan; *

I am like a sparrow, lonely on a house-top.

8 My enemies revile me all day long, *

and those who scoff at me have taken an oath against me.

9 For I have eaten ashes for bread *

and mingled my drink with weeping.

10 Because of your indignation and wrath *

you have lifted me up and thrown me away.

11 My days pass away like a shadow, *

and I wither like the grass.

12 But you, O Lord, endure for ever, *

and your Name from age to age.

13 You will arise and have compassion on Zion,

for it is time to have mercy upon her; *

indeed, the appointed time has come.

14 For your servants love her very rubble, *

and are moved to pity even for her dust.

15 The nations shall fear your Name, O Lord, *
and all the kings of the earth your glory.
16 For the Lord will build up Zion, *
and his glory will appear.
17 He will look with favor on the prayer of the
homeless; *
he will not despise their plea.
18 Let this be written for a future generation, *
so that a people yet unborn may praise the Lord.
19 For the Lord looked down from his holy place on high; *
from the heavens he beheld the earth;
20 That he might hear the groan of the captive *
and set free those condemned to die;
21 That they may declare in Zion the Name of the
Lord, *
and his praise in Jerusalem;
22 When the peoples are gathered together, *
and the kingdoms also, to serve the Lord.
23 He has brought down my strength before my time; *
he has shortened the number of my days;
24 And I said, "O my God,
do not take me away in the midst of my days; *
your years endure throughout all generations.
25 In the beginning, O Lord, you laid the foundations
of the earth, *
and the heavens are the work of your hands;
26 They shall perish, but you will endure;
they all shall wear out like a garment; *
as clothing you will change them,
and they shall be changed;
27 But you are always the same, *
and your years will never end.
28 The children of your servants shall continue, *
and their offspring shall stand fast in your sight."

103 *Benedic, anima mea*

1 Bless the Lord, O my soul, *
and all that is within me, bless his holy Name.
2 Bless the Lord, O my soul, *
and forget not all his benefits.
3 He forgives all your sins *
and heals all your infirmities;
4 He redeems your life from the grave *
and crowns you with mercy and loving-kindness;
5 He satisfies you with good things, *
and your youth is renewed like an eagle's.
6 The Lord executes righteousness *
and judgment for all who are oppressed.
7 He made his ways known to Moses *
and his works to the children of Israel.
8 The Lord is full of compassion and mercy, *
slow to anger and of great kindness.
9 He will not always accuse us, *
nor will he keep his anger for ever.
10 He has not dealt with us according to our sins, *
nor rewarded us according to our wickedness.
11 For as the heavens are high above the earth, *
so is his mercy great upon those who fear him.
12 As far as the east is from the west, *
so far has he removed our sins from us.
13 As a father cares for his children, *
so does the Lord care for those who fear him.
14 For he himself knows whereof we are made; *
he remembers that we are but dust.
15 Our days are like the grass; *
we flourish like a flower of the field;
16 When the wind goes over it, it is gone, *
and its place shall know it no more.

17 But the merciful goodness of the Lord endures for
ever on those who fear him, *
and his righteousness on children's children;
18 On those who keep his covenant *
and remember his commandments and do them.
19 The Lord has set his throne in heaven, *
and his kingship has dominion over all.
20 Bless the Lord, you angels of his,
you mighty ones who do his bidding, *
and hearken to the voice of his word.
21 Bless the Lord, all you his hosts, *
you ministers of his who do his will.
22 Bless the Lord, all you works of his,
in all places of his dominion; *
bless the Lord, O my soul.

Twentieth Day: Evening Prayer

104 *Benedic, anima mea*

1 Bless the Lord, O my soul; *
O Lord my God, how excellent is your greatness!
you are clothed with majesty and splendor.
2 You wrap yourself with light as with a cloak *
and spread out the heavens like a curtain.
3 You lay the beams of your chambers in the waters
above; *
you make the clouds your chariot;
you ride on the wings of the wind.
4 You make the winds your messengers *
and flames of fire your servants.
5 You have set the earth upon its foundations, *
so that it never shall move at any time.
6 You covered it with the Deep as with a mantle; *
the waters stood higher than the mountains.

7 At your rebuke they fled; *
at the voice of your thunder they hastened away.
8 They went up into the hills and down to the valleys beneath, *
to the places you had appointed for them.
9 You set the limits that they should not pass; *
they shall not again cover the earth.
10 You send the springs into the valleys; *
they flow between the mountains.
11 All the beasts of the field drink their fill from them, *
and the wild asses quench their thirst.
12 Beside them the birds of the air make their nests *
and sing among the branches.
13 You water the mountains from your dwelling on high; *
the earth is fully satisfied by the fruit of your works.
14 You make grass grow for flocks and herds *
and plants to serve mankind;
15 That they may bring forth food from the earth, *
and wine to gladden our hearts,
16 Oil to make a cheerful countenance, *
and bread to strengthen the heart.
17 The trees of the Lord are full of sap, *
the cedars of Lebanon which he planted,
18 In which the birds build their nests, *
and in whose tops the stork makes his dwelling.
19 The high hills are a refuge for the mountain goats, *
and the stony cliffs for the rock badgers.
20 You appointed the moon to mark the seasons, *
and the sun knows the time of its setting.
21 You make darkness that it may be night, *
in which all the beasts of the forest prowl.
22 The lions roar after their prey *
and seek their food from God.

23 The sun rises, and they slip away *
and lay themselves down in their dens.
24 Man goes forth to his work *
and to his labor until the evening.
25 O Lord, how manifold are your works! *
in wisdom you have made them all;
the earth is full of your creatures.
26 Yonder is the great and wide sea
with its living things too many to number, *
creatures both small and great.
27 There move the ships,
and there is that Leviathan, *
which you have made for the sport of it.
28 All of them look to you *
to give them their food in due season.
29 You give it to them; they gather it; *
you open your hand, and they are filled with good things.
30 You hide your face, and they are terrified; *
you take away their breath,
and they die and return to their dust.
31 You send forth your Spirit, and they are created; *
and so you renew the face of the earth.
32 May the glory of the Lord endure for ever; *
may the Lord rejoice in all his works.
33 He looks at the earth and it trembles; *
he touches the mountains and they smoke.
34 I will sing to the Lord as long as I live; *
I will praise my God while I have my being.
35 May these words of mine please him; *
I will rejoice in the Lord.
36 Let sinners be consumed out of the earth, *
and the wicked be no more.
37 Bless the Lord, O my soul. *
Hallelujah!

105

Part I *Confitemini Domino*

1 Give thanks to the Lord and call upon his Name; *
make known his deeds among the peoples.

2 Sing to him, sing praises to him, *
and speak of all his marvelous works.

3 Glory in his holy Name; *
let the hearts of those who seek the Lord rejoice.

4 Search for the Lord and his strength; *
continually seek his face.

5 Remember the marvels he has done, *
his wonders and the judgments of his mouth,

6 O offspring of Abraham his servant, *
O children of Jacob his chosen.

7 He is the Lord our God; *
his judgments prevail in all the world.

8 He has always been mindful of his covenant, *
the promise he made for a thousand generations:

9 The covenant he made with Abraham, *
the oath that he swore to Isaac,

10 Which he established as a statute for Jacob, *
an everlasting covenant for Israel,

11 Saying, "To you will I give the land of Canaan *
to be your allotted inheritance."

12 When they were few in number, *
of little account, and sojourners in the land,

13 Wandering from nation to nation *
and from one kingdom to another,

14 He let no one oppress them *
and rebuked kings for their sake,

15 Saying, "Do not touch my anointed *
and do my prophets no harm."
16 Then he called for a famine in the land *
and destroyed the supply of bread.
17 He sent a man before them, *
Joseph, who was sold as a slave.
18 They bruised his feet in fetters; *
his neck they put in an iron collar.
19 Until his prediction came to pass, *
the word of the Lord tested him.
20 The king sent and released him; *
the ruler of the peoples set him free.
21 He set him as a master over his household,
as a ruler over all his possessions,
22 To instruct his princes according to his will
and to teach his elders wisdom.

Psalm 105: Part II *Et intravit Israel*
23 Israel came into Egypt, *
and Jacob became a sojourner in the land of Ham.
24 The Lord made his people exceedingly fruitful; *
he made them stronger than their enemies;
25 Whose heart he turned, so that they hated his
people, *
and dealt unjustly with his servants.
26 He sent Moses his servant, *
and Aaron whom he had chosen.
27 They worked his signs among them, *
and portents in the land of Ham.
28 He sent darkness, and it grew dark; *
but the Egyptians rebelled against his words.
29 He turned their waters into blood *
and caused their fish to die.

30 Their land was overrun by frogs, *
in the very chambers of their kings.
31 He spoke, and there came swarms of insects *
and gnats within all their borders.
32 He gave them hailstones instead of rain, *
and flames of fire throughout their land.
33 He blasted their vines and their fig trees *
and shattered every tree in their country.
34 He spoke, and the locust came, *
and young locusts without number,
35 Which ate up all the green plants in their land *
and devoured the fruit of their soil.
36 He struck down the firstborn of their land, *
the first fruits of all their strength.
37 He led out his people with silver and gold; *
in all their tribes there was not one that stumbled.
38 Egypt was glad of their going, *
because they were afraid of them.
39 He spread out a cloud for a covering *
and a fire to give light in the night season.
40 They asked, and quails appeared, *
and he satisfied them with bread from heaven.
41 He opened the rock, and water flowed, *
so the river ran in the dry places.
42 For God remembered his holy word *
and Abraham his servant.
43 So he led forth his people with gladness, *
his chosen with shouts of joy.
44 He gave his people the lands of the nations, *
and they took the fruit of others' toil,
45 That they might keep his statutes *
and observe his laws.
Hallelujah!

106

Part I *Confitemini Domino*

1 Hallelujah!
Give thanks to the Lord, for he is good, *
for his mercy endures for ever.

2 Who can declare the mighty acts of the Lord *
or show forth all his praise?

3 Happy are those who act with justice *
and always do what is right!

4 Remember me, O Lord, with the favor you have
for your people, *
and visit me with your saving help;

5 That I may see the prosperity of your elect
and be glad with the gladness of your people, *
that I may glory with your inheritance.

6 We have sinned as our forebears did; *
we have done wrong and dealt wickedly.

7 In Egypt they did not consider your marvelous
works,
nor remember the abundance of your love; *
they defied the Most High at the Red Sea.

8 But he saved them for his Name's sake, *
to make his power known.

9 He rebuked the Red Sea, and it dried up, *
and he led them through the deep as through a desert.

10 He saved them from the hand of those who hated
them *
and redeemed them from the hand of the enemy.

11 The waters covered their oppressors; *
not one of them was left.

12 Then they believed his words *
and sang him songs of praise.

13 But they soon forgot his deeds *
and did not wait for his counsel.
14 A craving seized them in the wilderness, *
and they put God to the test in the desert.
15 He gave them what they asked, *
but sent leanness into their soul.
16 They envied Moses in the camp, *
and Aaron, the holy one of the Lord.
17 The earth opened and swallowed Dathan *
and covered the company of Abiram.
18 Fire blazed up against their company, *
and flames devoured the wicked.

Psalm 106: Part II *Et fecerunt vitulum*
19 Israel made a bull-calf at Horeb *
and worshiped a molten image;
20 And so they exchanged their Glory *
for the image of an ox that feeds on grass.
21 They forgot God their Savior, *
who had done great things in Egypt,
22 Wonderful deeds in the land of Ham, *
and fearful things at the Red Sea.
23 So he would have destroyed them,
had not Moses his chosen stood before him in the
breach, *
to turn away his wrath from consuming them.
24 They refused the pleasant land *
and would not believe his promise.
25 They grumbled in their tents *
and would not listen to the voice of the Lord.
26 So he lifted his hand against them, *
to overthrow them in the wilderness,
27 To cast out their seed among the nations, *
and to scatter them throughout the lands.

28 They joined themselves to Baal-Peor *
and ate sacrifices offered to the dead.
29 They provoked him to anger with their actions, *
and a plague broke out among them.
30 Then Phinehas stood up and interceded, *
and the plague came to an end.
31 This was reckoned to him as righteousness *
throughout all generations for ever.
32 Again they provoked his anger at the waters of Meribah, *
so that he punished Moses because of them;
33 For they so embittered his spirit *
that he spoke rash words with his lips.
34 They did not destroy the peoples *
as the Lord had commanded them.
35 They intermingled with the heathen *
and learned their pagan ways,
36 So that they worshiped their idols, *
which became a snare to them.
37 They sacrificed their sons *
and their daughters to evil spirits.
38 They shed innocent blood,
the blood of their sons and daughters, *
which they offered to the idols of Canaan,
and the land was defiled with blood.
39 Thus they were polluted by their actions *
and went whoring in their evil deeds.
40 Therefore the wrath of the Lord was kindled against his people *
and he abhorred his inheritance.
41 He gave them over to the hand of the heathen, *
and those who hated them ruled over them.
42 Their enemies oppressed them, *
and they were humbled under their hand.

43 Many a time did he deliver them,
but they rebelled through their own devices, *
and were brought down in their iniquity.
44 Nevertheless, he saw their distress, *
when he heard their lamentation.
45 He remembered his covenant with them *
and relented in accordance with his great mercy.
46 He caused them to be pitied *
by those who held them captive.
47 Save us, O Lord our God,
and gather us from among the nations, *
that we may give thanks to your holy Name
and glory in your praise.
48 Blessed be the Lord, the God of Israel,
from everlasting and to everlasting; *
and let all the people say, "Amen!"
Hallelujah!

Book Five
Twenty-second Day: Morning Prayer

107

Part I *Confitemini Domino*
1 Give thanks to the Lord, for he is good, *
and his mercy endures for ever.
2 Let all those whom the Lord has redeemed proclaim *
that he redeemed them from the hand of the foe.
3 He gathered them out of the lands; *
from the east and from the west,
from the north and from the south.
4 Some wandered in desert wastes; *
they found no way to a city where they might dwell.
5 They were hungry and thirsty; *
their spirits languished within them.

6 Then they cried to the Lord in their trouble, *
and he delivered them from their distress.
7 He put their feet on a straight path *
to go to a city where they might dwell.
8 Let them give thanks to the Lord for his mercy *
and the wonders he does for his children.
9 For he satisfies the thirsty *
and fills the hungry with good things.
10 Some sat in darkness and deep gloom, *
bound fast in misery and iron;
11 Because they rebelled against the words of God *
and despised the counsel of the Most High.
12 So he humbled their spirits with hard labor; *
they stumbled, and there was none to help.
13 Then they cried to the Lord in their trouble, *
and he delivered them from their distress.
14 He led them out of darkness and deep gloom *
and broke their bonds asunder.
15 Let them give thanks to the Lord for his mercy *
and the wonders he does for his children.
16 For he shatters the doors of bronze *
and breaks in two the iron bars.
17 Some were fools and took to rebellious ways; *
they were afflicted because of their sins.
18 They abhorred all manner of food *
and drew near to death's door.
19 Then they cried to the Lord in their trouble, *
and he delivered them from their distress.
20 He sent forth his word and healed them *
and saved them from the grave.
21 Let them give thanks to the Lord for his mercy *
and the wonders he does for his children.
22 Let them offer a sacrifice of thanksgiving *
and tell of his acts with shouts of joy.

23 Some went down to the sea in ships *
and plied their trade in deep waters;
24 They beheld the works of the Lord *
and his wonders in the deep.
25 Then he spoke, and a stormy wind arose, *
which tossed high the waves of the sea.
26 They mounted up to the heavens and fell back to the depths; *
their hearts melted because of their peril.
27 They reeled and staggered like drunkards *
and were at their wits' end.
28 Then they cried to the Lord in their trouble,
and he delivered them from their distress.
29 He stilled the storm to a whisper *
and quieted the waves of the sea.
30 Then were they glad because of the calm, *
and he brought them to the harbor they were bound for.
31 Let them give thanks to the Lord for his mercy *
and the wonders he does for his children.
32 Let them exalt him in the congregation of the people *
and praise him in the council of the elders.

Psalm 107: Part II *Posuit flumina*
33 The Lord changed rivers into deserts, *
and water-springs into thirsty ground,
34 A fruitful land into salt flats, *
because of the wickedness of those who dwell there.
35 He changed deserts into pools of water *
and dry land into water-springs.
36 He settled the hungry there, *
and they founded a city to dwell in.
37 They sowed fields, and planted vineyards, *
and brought in a fruitful harvest.

38 He blessed them, so that they increased greatly; *
he did not let their herds decrease.
39 Yet when they were diminished and brought low, *
through stress of adversity and sorrow,
40 (He pours contempt on princes *
and makes them wander in trackless wastes)
41 He lifted up the poor out of misery *
and multiplied their families like flocks of sheep.
42 The upright will see this and rejoice, *
but all wickedness will shut its mouth.
43 Whoever is wise will ponder these things, *
and consider well the mercies of the Lord.

Twenty-second Day: Evening Prayer

108 *Paratum cor meum*

1 My heart is firmly fixed, O God, my heart is fixed; *
I will sing and make melody.
2 Wake up, my spirit;
awake, lute and harp; *
I myself will waken the dawn.
3 I will confess you among the peoples, O Lord; *
I will sing praises to you among the nations.
4 For your loving-kindness is greater than the heavens, *
and your faithfulness reaches to the clouds.
5 Exalt yourself above the heavens, O God, *
and your glory over all the earth.
6 So that those who are dear to you may be delivered, *
save with your right hand and answer me.
7 God spoke from his holy place and said, *
"I will exult and parcel out Shechem;
I will divide the valley of Succoth.
8 Gilead is mine and Manasseh is mine; *
Ephraim is my helmet and Judah my scepter.

9 Moab is my washbasin,
on Edom I throw down my sandal to claim it, *
and over Philistia will I shout in triumph."
10 Who will lead me into the strong city? *
who will bring me into Edom?
11 Have you not cast us off, O God? *
you no longer go out, O God, with our armies.
12 Grant us your help against the enemy, *
for vain is the help of man.
13 With God we will do valiant deeds, *
and he shall tread our enemies under foot.

109 *Deus, laudem*

1 Hold not your tongue, O God of my praise; *
for the mouth of the wicked,
the mouth of the deceitful, is opened against me.
2 They speak to me with a lying tongue; *
they encompass me with hateful words
and fight against me without a cause.
3 Despite my love, they accuse me; *
but as for me, I pray for them.
4 They repay evil for good, *
and hatred for my love.
5 Set a wicked man against him, *
and let an accuser stand at his right hand.
6 When he is judged, let him be found guilty, *
and let his appeal be in vain.
7 Let his days be few, *
and let another take his office.
8 Let his children be fatherless, *
and his wife become a widow.
9 Let his children be waifs and beggars; *
let them be driven from the ruins of their homes.

10 Let the creditor seize everything he has; *
let strangers plunder his gains.
11 Let there be no one to show him kindness, *
and none to pity his fatherless children.
12 Let his descendants be destroyed, *
and his name be blotted out in the next generation.
13 Let the wickedness of his fathers be remembered
before the Lord, *
and his mother's sin not be blotted out;
14 Let their sin be always before the Lord; *
but let him root out their names from the earth;
15 Because he did not remember to show mercy, *
but persecuted the poor and needy
and sought to kill the brokenhearted.
16 He loved cursing,
let it come upon him; *
he took no delight in blessing,
let it depart from him.
17 He put on cursing like a garment, *
let it soak into his body like water
and into his bones like oil;
18 Let it be to him like the cloak which he
wraps around himself, *
and like the belt that he wears continually.
19 Let this be the recompense from the Lord to my
accusers, *
and to those who speak evil against me.
20 But you, O Lord my God,
oh, deal with me according to your Name; *
for your tender mercy's sake, deliver me.
21 For I am poor and needy, *
and my heart is wounded within me.
22 I have faded away like a shadow when it lengthens; *
I am shaken off like a locust.

23 My knees are weak through fasting, *
and my flesh is wasted and gaunt.
24 I have become a reproach to them; *
they see and shake their heads.
25 Help me, O Lord my God; *
save me for your mercy's sake.
26 Let them know that this is your hand, *
that you, O Lord, have done it.
27 They may curse, but you will bless; *
let those who rise up against me be put to shame,
and your servant will rejoice.
28 Let my accusers be clothed with disgrace *
and wrap themselves in their shame as in a cloak.
29 I will give great thanks to the Lord with my mouth; *
in the midst of the multitude will I praise him;
30 Because he stands at the right hand of the needy, *
to save his life from those who would condemn him.

Twenty-third Day: Morning Prayer

110 *Dixit Dominus*

1 The Lord said to my Lord, "Sit at my right hand, *
until I make your enemies your footstool."
2 The Lord will send the scepter of your power out of
Zion, *
saying, "Rule over your enemies round about you.
3 Princely state has been yours from the day of your
birth; *
in the beauty of holiness have I begotten you,
like dew from the womb of the morning."
4 The Lord has sworn and he will not recant: *
"You are a priest for ever after the order of
Melchizedek."

5 The Lord who is at your right hand
will smite kings in the day of his wrath; *
he will rule over the nations.
6 He will heap high the corpses; *
he will smash heads over the wide earth.
7 He will drink from the brook beside the road; *
therefore he will lift high his head.

111 *Confitebor tibi*

1 Hallelujah!
I will give thanks to the Lord with my whole heart, *
in the assembly of the upright, in the congregation.
2 Great are the deeds of the Lord! *
they are studied by all who delight in them.
3 His work is full of majesty and splendor, *
and his righteousness endures for ever.
4 He makes his marvelous works to be remembered; *
the Lord is gracious and full of compassion.
5 He gives food to those who fear him; *
he is ever mindful of his covenant.
6 He has shown his people the power of his works *
in giving them the lands of the nations.
7 The works of his hands are faithfulness and justice; *
all his commandments are sure.
8 They stand fast for ever and ever, *
because they are done in truth and equity.
9 He sent redemption to his people;
he commanded his covenant for ever; *
holy and awesome is his Name.
10 The fear of the Lord is the beginning of wisdom; *
those who act accordingly have a good understanding;
his praise endures for ever.

112 *Beatus vir*

1 Hallelujah!
Happy are they who fear the Lord *
and have great delight in his commandments!
2 Their descendants will be mighty in the land; *
the generation of the upright will be blessed.
3 Wealth and riches will be in their house, *
and their righteousness will last for ever.
4 Light shines in the darkness for the upright; *
the righteous are merciful and full of compassion.
5 It is good for them to be generous in lending *
and to manage their affairs with justice.
6 For they will never be shaken; *
the righteous will be kept in everlasting remembrance.
7 They will not be afraid of any evil rumors; *
their heart is right;
they put their trust in the Lord.
8 Their heart is established and will not shrink, *
until they see their desire upon their enemies.
9 They have given freely to the poor, *
and their righteousness stands fast for ever;
they will hold up their head with honor.
10 The wicked will see it and be angry;
they will gnash their teeth and pine away; *
the desires of the wicked will perish.

113 *Laudate, pueri*

1 Hallelujah!
Give praise, you servants of the Lord; *
praise the Name of the Lord.
2 Let the Name of the Lord be blessed, *
from this time forth for evermore.

3 From the rising of the sun to its going down *
let the Name of the Lord be praised.
4 The Lord is high above all nations, *
and his glory above the heavens.
5 Who is like the Lord our God, who sits enthroned on high *
but stoops to behold the heavens and the earth?
6 He takes up the weak out of the dust *
and lifts up the poor from the ashes.
7 He sets them with the princes, *
with the princes of his people.
8 He makes the woman of a childless house *
to be a joyful mother of children.

Twenty-third Day: Evening Prayer

114 *In exitu Israel*

1 Hallelujah!
When Israel came out of Egypt, *
the house of Jacob from a people of strange speech,
2 Judah became God's sanctuary *
and Israel his dominion.
3 The sea beheld it and fled; *
Jordan turned and went back.
4 The mountains skipped like rams, *
and the little hills like young sheep.
5 What ailed you, O sea, that you fled? *
O Jordan, that you turned back?
6 You mountains, that you skipped like rams? *
you little hills like young sheep?
7 Tremble, O earth, at the presence of the Lord, *
at the presence of the God of Jacob,
8 Who turned the hard rock into a pool of water *
and flint-stone into a flowing spring.

115 *Non nobis, Domine*

1 Not to us, O Lord, not to us,
but to your Name give glory; *
because of your love and because of your faithfulness.
2 Why should the heathen say, *
"Where then is their God?"
3 Our God is in heaven; *
whatever he wills to do he does.
4 Their idols are silver and gold, *
the work of human hands.
5 They have mouths, but they cannot speak; *
eyes have they, but they cannot see;
6 They have ears, but they cannot hear; *
noses, but they cannot smell;
7 They have hands, but they cannot feel;
feet, but they cannot walk; *
they make no sound with their throat.
8 Those who make them are like them, *
and so are all who put their trust in them.
9 O Israel, trust in the Lord; *
he is their help and their shield.
10 O house of Aaron, trust in the Lord; *
he is their help and their shield.
11 You who fear the Lord, trust in the Lord; *
he is their help and their shield.
12 The Lord has been mindful of us, and he will bless
us; *
he will bless the house of Israel;
he will bless the house of Aaron;
13 He will bless those who fear the Lord, *
both small and great together.
14 May the Lord increase you more and more, *
you and your children after you.

15 May you be blessed by the Lord, *
the maker of heaven and earth.
16 The heaven of heavens is the Lord's, *
but he entrusted the earth to its peoples.
17 The dead do not praise the Lord, *
nor all those who go down into silence;
18 But we will bless the Lord, *
from this time forth for evermore.
Hallelujah!

Twenty-fourth Day: Morning Prayer

116 *Dilexi, quoniam*

1 I love the Lord, because he has heard the voice of
my supplication, *
because he has inclined his ear to me whenever
I called upon him.
2 The cords of death entangled me;
the grip of the grave took hold of me; *
I came to grief and sorrow.
3 Then I called upon the Name of the Lord: *
"O Lord, I pray you, save my life."
4 Gracious is the Lord and righteous; *
our God is full of compassion.
5 The Lord watches over the innocent; *
I was brought very low, and he helped me.
6 Turn again to your rest, O my soul, *
for the Lord has treated you well.
7 For you have rescued my life from death, *
my eyes from tears, and my feet from stumbling.
8 I will walk in the presence of the Lord *
in the land of the living.
9 I believed, even when I said,
"I have been brought very low." *
In my distress I said, "No one can be trusted."

10 How shall I repay the Lord *
for all the good things he has done for me?
11 I will lift up the cup of salvation *
and call upon the Name of the Lord.
12 I will fulfill my vows to the Lord *
in the presence of all his people.
13 Precious in the sight of the Lord *
is the death of his servants.
14 O Lord, I am your servant; *
I am your servant and the child of your handmaid;
you have freed me from my bonds.
15 I will offer you the sacrifice of thanksgiving *
and call upon the Name of the Lord.
16 I will fulfill my vows to the Lord *
in the presence of all his people,
17 In the courts of the Lord's house, *
in the midst of you, O Jerusalem.
Hallelujah!

117 *Laudate Dominum*

1 Praise the Lord, all you nations; *
laud him, all you peoples.
2 For his loving-kindness toward us is great, *
and the faithfulness of the Lord endures for ever.
Hallelujah!

118 *Confitemini Domino*

1 Give thanks to the Lord, for he is good; *
his mercy endures for ever.
2 Let Israel now proclaim, *
"His mercy endures for ever."

3 Let the house of Aaron now proclaim, *
"His mercy endures for ever."
4 Let those who fear the Lord now proclaim, *
"His mercy endures for ever."
5 I called to the Lord in my distress; *
the Lord answered by setting me free.
6 The Lord is at my side, therefore I will not fear; *
what can anyone do to me?
7 The Lord is at my side to help me; *
I will triumph over those who hate me.
8 It is better to rely on the Lord *
than to put any trust in flesh.
9 It is better to rely on the Lord *
than to put any trust in rulers.
10 All the ungodly encompass me; *
in the name of the Lord I will repel them.
11 They hem me in, they hem me in on every side; *
in the name of the Lord I will repel them.
12 They swarm about me like bees;
they blaze like a fire of thorns; *
in the name of the Lord I will repel them.
13 I was pressed so hard that I almost fell, *
but the Lord came to my help.
14 The Lord is my strength and my song, *
and he has become my salvation.
15 There is a sound of exultation and victory *
in the tents of the righteous:
16 "The right hand of the Lord has triumphed! *
the right hand of the Lord is exalted!
the right hand of the Lord has triumphed!"
17 I shall not die, but live, *
and declare the works of the Lord.
18 The Lord has punished me sorely, *
but he did not hand me over to death.

19 Open for me the gates of righteousness; *
I will enter them;
I will offer thanks to the Lord.
20 "This is the gate of the Lord; *
he who is righteous may enter."
21 I will give thanks to you, for you answered me *
and have become my salvation.
22 The same stone which the builders rejected *
has become the chief cornerstone.
23 This is the Lord's doing, *
and it is marvelous in our eyes.
24 On this day the Lord has acted; *
we will rejoice and be glad in it.
25 Hosannah, Lord, hosannah! *
Lord, send us now success.
26 Blessed is he who comes in the name of the Lord; *
we bless you from the house of the Lord.
27 God is the Lord; he has shined upon us; *
form a procession with branches up to the horns of the
altar.
28 "You are my God, and I will thank you; *
you are my God, and I will exalt you."
29 Give thanks to the Lord, for he is good; *
his mercy endures for ever.

Twenty-fourth Day: Evening Prayer

119

Aleph *Beati immaculati*
1 Happy are they whose way is blameless, *
who walk in the law of the Lord!
2 Happy are they who observe his decrees *
and seek him with all their hearts!
3 Who never do any wrong, *
but always walk in his ways.

4 You laid down your commandments, *
that we should fully keep them.
5 Oh, that my ways were made so direct *
that I might keep your statutes!
6 Then I should not be put to shame, *
when I regard all your commandments.
7 I will thank you with an unfeigned heart, *
when I have learned your righteous judgments.
8 I will keep your statutes; *
do not utterly forsake me.

Beth *In quo corrigit?*
9 How shall a young man cleanse his way? *
By keeping to your words.
10 With my whole heart I seek you; *
let me not stray from your commandments.
11 I treasure your promise in my heart, *
that I may not sin against you.
12 Blessed are you, O Lord; *
instruct me in your statutes.
13 With my lips will I recite *
all the judgments of your mouth.
14 I have taken greater delight in the way of your
decrees *
than in all manner of riches.
15 I will meditate on your commandments *
and give attention to your ways.
16 My delight is in your statutes; *
I will not forget your word.

Gimel *Retribue servo tuo*
17 Deal bountifully with your servant, *
that I may live and keep your word.
18 Open my eyes, that I may see *
the wonders of your law.

19 I am a stranger here on earth; *
do not hide your commandments from me.
20 My soul is consumed at all times *
with longing for your judgments.
21 You have rebuked the insolent; *
cursed are they who stray from your commandments!
22 Turn from me shame and rebuke, *
for I have kept your decrees.
23 Even though rulers sit and plot against me, *
I will meditate on your statutes.
24 For your decrees are my delight, *
and they are my counselors.

Daleth *Adhæsit pavimento*
25 My soul cleaves to the dust; *
give me life according to your word.
26 I have confessed my ways, and you answered me; *
instruct me in your statutes.
27 Make me understand the way of your
commandments, *
that I may meditate on your marvelous works.
28 My soul melts away for sorrow; *
strengthen me according to your word.
29 Take from me the way of lying; *
let me find grace through your law.
30 I have chosen the way of faithfulness; *
I have set your judgments before me.
31 I hold fast to your decrees; *
O Lord, let me not be put to shame.
32 I will run the way of your commandments, *
for you have set my heart at liberty.

He *Legem pone*

33 Teach me, O Lord, the way of your statutes, *
and I shall keep it to the end.

34 Give me understanding, and I shall keep your law; *
I shall keep it with all my heart.

35 Make me go in the path of your commandments, *
for that is my desire.

36 Incline my heart to your decrees *
and not to unjust gain.

37 Turn my eyes from watching what is worthless; *
give me life in your ways.

38 Fulfill your promise to your servant, *
which you make to those who fear you.

39 Turn away the reproach which I dread, *
because your judgments are good.

40 Behold, I long for your commandments; *
in your righteousness preserve my life.

Waw *Et veniat super me*

41 Let your loving-kindness come to me, O Lord, *
and your salvation, according to your promise.

42 Then shall I have a word for those who taunt me, *
because I trust in your words.

43 Do not take the word of truth out of my mouth, *
for my hope is in your judgments.

44 I shall continue to keep your law; *
I shall keep it for ever and ever.

45 I will walk at liberty, *
because I study your commandments.

46 I will tell of your decrees before kings *
and will not be ashamed.

47 I delight in your commandments, *
which I have always loved.

48 I will lift up my hands to your commandments, *
and I will meditate on your statutes.

Zayin *Memor esto verbi tui*
49 Remember your word to your servant, *
because you have given me hope.
50 This is my comfort in my trouble, *
that your promise gives me life.
51 The proud have derided me cruelly, *
but I have not turned from your law.
52 When I remember your judgments of old, *
O Lord, I take great comfort.
53 I am filled with a burning rage, *
because of the wicked who forsake your law.
54 Your statutes have been like songs to me *
wherever I have lived as a stranger.
55 I remember your Name in the night, O Lord, *
and dwell upon your law.
56 This is how it has been with me, *
because I have kept your commandments.

Heth *Portio mea, Domine*
57 You only are my portion, O Lord; *
I have promised to keep your words.
58 I entreat you with all my heart, *
be merciful to me according to your promise.
59 I have considered my ways *
and turned my feet toward your decrees.
60 I hasten and do not tarry *
to keep your commandments.
61 Though the cords of the wicked entangle me, *
I do not forget your law.
62 At midnight I will rise to give you thanks, *
because of your righteous judgments.

63 I am a companion of all who fear you; *
and of those who keep your commandments.
64 The earth, O Lord, is full of your love; *
instruct me in your statutes.

Teth *Bonitatem fecisti*
65 O Lord, you have dealt graciously with your
servant, *
according to your word.
66 Teach me discernment and knowledge, *
for I have believed in your commandments.
67 Before I was afflicted I went astray, *
but now I keep your word.
68 You are good and you bring forth good; *
instruct me in your statutes.
69 The proud have smeared me with lies, *
but I will keep your commandments with my whole
heart.
70 Their heart is gross and fat, *
but my delight is in your law.
71 It is good for me that I have been afflicted, *
that I might learn your statutes.
72 The law of your mouth is dearer to me *
than thousands in gold and silver.

Twenty-fifth Day: Evening Prayer

Yodh *Manus tuæ fecerunt me*
73 Your hands have made me and fashioned me; *
give me understanding, that I may learn your
commandments.
74 Those who fear you will be glad when they see me, *
because I trust in your word.
75 I know, O Lord, that your judgments are right *
and that in faithfulness you have afflicted me.

The Psalter   347

76 Let your loving-kindness be my comfort, *
as you have promised to your servant.
77 Let your compassion come to me, that I may live, *
for your law is my delight.
78 Let the arrogant be put to shame, for they wrong me
with lies; *
but I will meditate on your commandments.
79 Let those who fear you turn to me, *
and also those who know your decrees.
80 Let my heart be sound in your statutes, *
that I may not be put to shame.

Kaph *Defecit in salutare*
81 My soul has longed for your salvation; *
I have put my hope in your word.
82 My eyes have failed from watching for your
promise, *
and I say, "When will you comfort me?"
83 I have become like a leather flask in the smoke, *
but I have not forgotten your statutes.
84 How much longer must I wait? *
when will you give judgment against those who
persecute me?
85 The proud have dug pits for me; *
they do not keep your law.
86 All your commandments are true; *
help me, for they persecute me with lies.
87 They had almost made an end of me on earth, *
but I have not forsaken your commandments.
88 In your loving-kindness, revive me, *
that I may keep the decrees of your mouth.

Lamedh *In æternum, Domine*
89 O Lord, your word is everlasting; *
it stands firm in the heavens.

90 Your faithfulness remains from one generation to another; *

you established the earth, and it abides.

91 By your decree these continue to this day, *

for all things are your servants.

92 If my delight had not been in your law, *

I should have perished in my affliction.

93 I will never forget your commandments, *

because by them you give me life.

94 I am yours; oh, that you would save me! *

for I study your commandments.

95 Though the wicked lie in wait for me to destroy me, *

I will apply my mind to your decrees.

96 I see that all things come to an end, *

but your commandment has no bounds.

Mem *Quomodo dilexi!*

97 Oh, how I love your law! *

all the day long it is in my mind.

98 Your commandment has made me wiser than my enemies, *

and it is always with me.

99 I have more understanding than all my teachers, *

for your decrees are my study.

100 I am wiser than the elders, *

because I observe your commandments.

101 I restrain my feet from every evil way, *

that I may keep your word.

102 I do not shrink from your judgments, *

because you yourself have taught me.

103 How sweet are your words to my taste! *

they are sweeter than honey to my mouth.

104 Through your commandments I gain understanding; *

therefore I hate every lying way.

Nun *Lucerna pedibus meis*
105 Your word is a lantern to my feet *
and a light upon my path.
106 I have sworn and am determined *
to keep your righteous judgments.
107 I am deeply troubled; *
preserve my life, O Lord, according to your word.
108 Accept, O Lord, the willing tribute of my lips, *
and teach me your judgments.
109 My life is always in my hand, *
yet I do not forget your law.
110 The wicked have set a trap for me, *
but I have not strayed from your commandments.
111 Your decrees are my inheritance for ever; *
truly, they are the joy of my heart.
112 I have applied my heart to fulfill your statutes *
for ever and to the end.

Samekh *Iniquos odio habui*
113 I hate those who have a divided heart, *
but your law do I love.
114 You are my refuge and shield; *
my hope is in your word.
115 Away from me, you wicked! *
I will keep the commandments of my God.
116 Sustain me according to your promise, that I may live, *
and let me not be disappointed in my hope.
117 Hold me up, and I shall be safe, *
and my delight shall be ever in your statutes.
118 You spurn all who stray from your statutes; *
their deceitfulness is in vain.

119 In your sight all the wicked of the earth are but dross; *

therefore I love your decrees.

120 My flesh trembles with dread of you; *

I am afraid of your judgments.

Ayin *Feci judicium*

121 I have done what is just and right; *

do not deliver me to my oppressors.

122 Be surety for your servant's good; *

let not the proud oppress me.

123 My eyes have failed from watching for your salvation *

and for your righteous promise.

124 Deal with your servant according to your loving-kindness *

and teach me your statutes.

125 I am your servant; grant me understanding, *

that I may know your decrees.

126 It is time for you to act, O Lord, *

for they have broken your law.

127 Truly, I love your commandments *

more than gold and precious stones.

128 I hold all your commandments to be right for me; *

all paths of falsehood I abhor.

Pe *Mirabilia*

129 Your decrees are wonderful; *

therefore I obey them with all my heart.

130 When your word goes forth it gives light; *

it gives understanding to the simple.

131 I open my mouth and pant; *

I long for your commandments.

132 Turn to me in mercy, *

as you always do to those who love your Name.

133 Steady my footsteps in your word; *
let no iniquity have dominion over me.
134 Rescue me from those who oppress me, *
and I will keep your commandments.
135 Let your countenance shine upon your servant *
and teach me your statutes.
136 My eyes shed streams of tears, *
because people do not keep your law.

Sadhe *Justus es, Domine*
137 You are righteous, O Lord, *
and upright are your judgments.
138 You have issued your decrees *
with justice and in perfect faithfulness.
139 My indignation has consumed me, *
because my enemies forget your words.
140 Your word has been tested to the uttermost, *
and your servant holds it dear.
141 I am small and of little account, *
yet I do not forget your commandments.
142 Your justice is an everlasting justice *
and your law is the truth.
143 Trouble and distress have come upon me, *
yet your commandments are my delight.
144 The righteousness of your decrees is everlasting; *
grant me understanding, that I may live.

Twenty-sixth Day: Evening Prayer

Qoph *Clamavi in toto corde meo*
145 I call with my whole heart; *
answer me, O Lord, that I may keep your statutes.
146 I call to you;
oh, that you would save me! *
I will keep your decrees.

147 Early in the morning I cry out to you, *
for in your word is my trust.
148 My eyes are open in the night watches, *
that I may meditate upon your promise.
149 Hear my voice, O Lord, according to your loving-
kindness; *
according to your judgments, give me life.
150 They draw near who in malice persecute me; *
they are very far from your law.
151 You, O Lord, are near at hand, *
and all your commandments are true.
152 Long have I known from your decrees *
that you have established them for ever.

Resh *Vide humilitatem*
153 Behold my affliction and deliver me, *
for I do not forget your law.
154 Plead my cause and redeem me; *
according to your promise, give me life.
155 Deliverance is far from the wicked, *
for they do not study your statutes.
156 Great is your compassion, O Lord; *
preserve my life, according to your judgments.
157 There are many who persecute and oppress me, *
yet I have not swerved from your decrees.
158 I look with loathing at the faithless, *
for they have not kept your word.
159 See how I love your commandments! *
O Lord, in your mercy, preserve me.
160 The heart of your word is truth; *
all your righteous judgments endure for evermore.

Shin *Principes persecuti sunt*
161 Rulers have persecuted me without a cause, *
but my heart stands in awe of your word.

162 I am as glad because of your promise *
as one who finds great spoils.
163 As for lies, I hate and abhor them, *
but your law is my love.
164 Seven times a day do I praise you, *
because of your righteous judgments.
165 Great peace have they who love your law; *
for them there is no stumbling block.
166 I have hoped for your salvation, O Lord, *
and I have fulfilled your commandments.
167 I have kept your decrees *
and I have loved them deeply.
168 I have kept your commandments and decrees, *
for all my ways are before you.

Taw *Appropinquet deprecatio*
169 Let my cry come before you, O Lord; *
give me understanding, according to your word.
170 Let my supplication come before you; *
deliver me, according to your promise.
171 My lips shall pour forth your praise, *
when you teach me your statutes.
172 My tongue shall sing of your promise, *
for all your commandments are righteous.
173 Let your hand be ready to help me, *
for I have chosen your commandments.
174 I long for your salvation, O Lord, *
and your law is my delight.
175 Let me live, and I will praise you, *
and let your judgments help me.
176 I have gone astray like a sheep that is lost; *
search for your servant,
for I do not forget your commandments.

120 *Ad Dominum*

1 When I was in trouble, I called to the Lord; *
I called to the Lord, and he answered me.
2 Deliver me, O Lord, from lying lips *
and from the deceitful tongue.
3 What shall be done to you, and what more besides, *
O you deceitful tongue?
4 The sharpened arrows of a warrior, *
along with hot glowing coals.
5 How hateful it is that I must lodge in Meshech *
and dwell among the tents of Kedar!
6 Too long have I had to live; *
among the enemies of peace.
7 I am on the side of peace, *
but when I speak of it, they are for war.

121 *Levavi oculos*

1 I lift up my eyes to the hills; *
from where is my help to come?
2 My help comes from the Lord, *
the maker of heaven and earth.
3 He will not let your foot be moved *
and he who watches over you will not fall asleep.
4 Behold, he who keeps watch over Israel *
shall neither slumber nor sleep;
5 The Lord himself watches over you; *
the Lord is your shade at your right hand,
6 So that the sun shall not strike you by day, *
nor the moon by night.
7 The Lord shall preserve you from all evil; *
it is he who shall keep you safe.

8 The Lord shall watch over your going out and your coming in, *
from this time forth for evermore.

122 *Lætatus sum*

1 I was glad when they said to me, *
"Let us go to the house of the Lord."
2 Now our feet are standing *
within your gates, O Jerusalem.
3 Jerusalem is built as a city *
that is at unity with itself;
4 To which the tribes go up,
the tribes of the Lord, *
the assembly of Israel,
to praise the Name of the Lord.
5 For there are the thrones of judgment, *
the thrones of the house of David.
6 Pray for the peace of Jerusalem: *
"May they prosper who love you.
7 Peace be within your walls *
and quietness within your towers.
8 For my brethren and companions' sake, *
I pray for your prosperity.
9 Because of the house of the Lord our God, *
I will seek to do you good."

123 *Ad te levavi oculos meos*

1 To you I lift up my eyes, *
to you enthroned in the heavens.
2 As the eyes of servants look to the hand of their masters, *
and the eyes of a maid to the hand of her mistress,
3 So our eyes look to the Lord our God, *
until he show us his mercy.

4 Have mercy upon us, O Lord, have mercy, *
for we have had more than enough of contempt,
5 Too much of the scorn of the indolent rich, *
and of the derision of the proud.

124 *Nisi quia Dominus*

1 If the Lord had not been on our side, *
let Israel now say;
2 If the Lord had not been on our side, *
when enemies rose up against us;
3 Then would they have swallowed us up alive *
in their fierce anger toward us;
4 Then would the waters have overwhelmed us *
and the torrent gone over us;
5 Then would the raging waters *
have gone right over us.
6 Blessed be the Lord! *
he has not given us over to be a prey for their teeth.
7 We have escaped like a bird from the snare of the fowler; *
the snare is broken, and we have escaped.
8 Our help is in the Name of the Lord, *
the maker of heaven and earth.

125 *Qui confidunt*

1 Those who trust in the Lord are like Mount Zion, *
which cannot be moved, but stands fast for ever.
2 The hills stand about Jerusalem; *
so does the Lord stand round about his people,
from this time forth for evermore.
3 The scepter of the wicked shall not hold sway over
the land allotted to the just, *
so that the just shall not put their hands to evil.

4 Show your goodness, O Lord, to those who are good *
and to those who are true of heart.
5 As for those who turn aside to crooked ways,
the Lord will lead them away with the evildoers; *
but peace be upon Israel.

Twenty-seventh Day: Evening Prayer

126 *In convertendo*

1 When the Lord restored the fortunes of Zion, *
then were we like those who dream.
2 Then was our mouth filled with laughter, *
and our tongue with shouts of joy.
3 Then they said among the nations, *
"The Lord has done great things for them."
4 The Lord has done great things for us, *
and we are glad indeed.
5 Restore our fortunes, O Lord, *
like the watercourses of the Negev.
6 Those who sowed with tears *
will reap with songs of joy.
7 Those who go out weeping, carrying the seed, *
will come again with joy, shouldering their sheaves.

127 *Nisi Dominus*

1 Unless the Lord builds the house, *
their labor is in vain who build it.
2 Unless the Lord watches over the city, *
in vain the watchman keeps his vigil.
3 It is in vain that you rise so early and go to bed so late; *
vain, too, to eat the bread of toil,
for he gives to his beloved sleep.
4 Children are a heritage from the Lord, *
and the fruit of the womb is a gift.

5 Like arrows in the hand of a warrior *
are the children of one's youth.
6 Happy is the man who has his quiver full of them! *
he shall not be put to shame
when he contends with his enemies in the gate.

128 *Beati omnes*

1 Happy are they all who fear the Lord, *
and who follow in his ways!
2 You shall eat the fruit of your labor; *
happiness and prosperity shall be yours.
3 Your wife shall be like a fruitful vine within your
house, *
your children like olive shoots round about your table.
4 The man who fears the Lord *
shall thus indeed be blessed.
5 The Lord bless you from Zion, *
and may you see the prosperity of Jerusalem all the
days of your life.
6 May you live to see your children's children; *
may peace be upon Israel.

129 *Sæpe expugnaverunt*

1 "Greatly have they oppressed me since my youth," *
let Israel now say;
2 "Greatly have they oppressed me since my youth, *
but they have not prevailed against me."
3 The plowmen plowed upon my back *
and made their furrows long.
4 The Lord, the Righteous One, *
has cut the cords of the wicked.
5 Let them be put to shame and thrown back, *
all those who are enemies of Zion.

6 Let them be like grass upon the housetops, *
which withers before it can be plucked;
7 Which does not fill the hand of the reaper, *
nor the bosom of him who binds the sheaves;
8 So that those who go by say not so much as,
"The Lord prosper you. *
We wish you well in the Name of the Lord."

130 *De profundis*

1 Out of the depths have I called to you, O Lord;
Lord, hear my voice; *
let your ears consider well the voice of my
supplication.
2 If you, Lord, were to note what is done amiss, *
O Lord, who could stand?
3 For there is forgiveness with you; *
therefore you shall be feared.
4 I wait for the Lord; my soul waits for him; *
in his word is my hope.
5 My soul waits for the Lord,
more than watchmen for the morning, *
more than watchmen for the morning.
6 O Israel, wait for the Lord, *
for with the Lord there is mercy;
7 With him there is plenteous redemption, *
and he shall redeem Israel from all their sins.

131 *Domine, non est*

1 O Lord, I am not proud; *
I have no haughty looks.
2 I do not occupy myself with great matters, *
or with things that are too hard for me.

3 But I still my soul and make it quiet,
like a child upon its mother's breast; *
my soul is quieted within me.
4 O Israel, wait upon the Lord, *
from this time forth for evermore.

Twenty-eighth Day: Morning Prayer

132 *Memento, Domine*

1 Lord, remember David, *
and all the hardships he endured;
2 How he swore an oath to the Lord *
and vowed a vow to the Mighty One of Jacob:
3 "I will not come under the roof of my house," *
nor climb up into my bed;
4 I will not allow my eyes to sleep, *
nor let my eyelids slumber;
5 Until I find a place for the Lord, *
a dwelling for the Mighty One of Jacob."
6 "The ark! We heard it was in Ephratah; *
we found it in the fields of Jearim.
7 Let us go to God's dwelling place; *
let us fall upon our knees before his footstool."
8 Arise, O Lord, into your resting-place, *
you and the ark of your strength.
9 Let your priests be clothed with righteousness; *
let your faithful people sing with joy.
10 For your servant David's sake, *
do not turn away the face of your Anointed.
11 The Lord has sworn an oath to David; *
in truth, he will not break it:
12 "A son, the fruit of your body *
will I set upon your throne.

13 If your children keep my covenant
and my testimonies that I shall teach them, *
their children will sit upon your throne for evermore."
14 For the Lord has chosen Zion; *
he has desired her for his habitation:
15 "This shall be my resting-place for ever; *
here will I dwell, for I delight in her.
16 I will surely bless her provisions, *
and satisfy her poor with bread.
17 I will clothe her priests with salvation, *
and her faithful people will rejoice and sing.
18 There will I make the horn of David flourish; *
I have prepared a lamp for my Anointed.
19 As for his enemies, I will clothe them with shame; *
but as for him, his crown will shine."

133 *Ecce, quam bonum!*

1 Oh, how good and pleasant it is, *
when brethren live together in unity!
2 It is like fine oil upon the head *
that runs down upon the beard,
3 Upon the beard of Aaron, *
and runs down upon the collar of his robe.
4 It is like the dew of Hermon *
that falls upon the hills of Zion.
5 For there the Lord has ordained the blessing: *
life for evermore.

134 *Ecce nunc*

1 Behold now, bless the Lord, all you servants of the
Lord, *
you that stand by night in the house of the Lord.

2 Lift up your hands in the holy place and bless the Lord; *

the Lord who made heaven and earth bless you out of Zion.

135 *Laudate nomen*

1 Hallelujah !
Praise the Name of the Lord; *
give praise, you servants of the Lord,
2 You who stand in the house of the Lord, *
in the courts of the house of our God.
3 Praise the Lord, for the Lord is good; *
sing praises to his Name, for it is lovely.
4 For the Lord has chosen Jacob for himself *
and Israel for his own possession.
5 For I know that the Lord is great, *
and that our Lord is above all gods.
6 The Lord does whatever pleases him, in heaven and on earth, *
in the seas and all the deeps.
7 He brings up rain clouds from the ends of the earth; *
he sends out lightning with the rain,
and brings the winds out of his storehouse.
8 It was he who struck down the firstborn of Egypt, *
the firstborn both of man and beast.
9 He sent signs and wonders into the midst of you, O Egypt, *
against Pharaoh and all his servants.
10 He overthrew many nations *
and put mighty kings to death:
11 Sihon, king of the Amorites,
and Og, the king of Bashan, *
and all the kingdoms of Canaan.

12 He gave their land to be an inheritance, *
an inheritance for Israel his people.
13 O Lord, your Name is everlasting; *
your renown, O Lord, endures from age to age.
14 For the Lord gives his people justice *
and shows compassion to his servants.
15 The idols of the heathen are silver and gold, *
the work of human hands.
16 They have mouths, but they cannot speak; *
eyes have they, but they cannot see.
17 They have ears, but they cannot hear; *
neither is there any breath in their mouth.
18 Those who make them are like them, *
and so are all who put their trust in them.
19 Bless the Lord, O house of Israel; *
O house of Aaron, bless the Lord.
20 Bless the Lord, O house of Levi; *
you who fear the Lord, bless the Lord.
21 Blessed be the Lord out of Zion, *
who dwells in Jerusalem.
Hallelujah!

Twenty-eighth Day: Evening Prayer

136 *Confitemini*

1 Give thanks to the Lord, for he is good, *
for his mercy endures for ever.
2 Give thanks to the God of gods, *
for his mercy endures for ever.
3 Give thanks to the Lord of Lords, *
for his mercy endures for ever.
4 Who only does great wonders, *
for his mercy endures for ever;

5 Who by wisdom made the heavens, *
for his mercy endures for ever;
6 Who spread out the earth upon the waters, *
for his mercy endures for ever;
7 Who created great lights, *
for his mercy endures for ever;
8 The sun to rule the day, *
for his mercy endures for ever;
9 The moon and the stars to govern the night, *
for his mercy endures for ever.
10 Who struck down the firstborn of Egypt, *
for his mercy endures for ever;
11 And brought out Israel from among them, *
for his mercy endures for ever;
12 With a mighty hand and a stretched-out arm, *
for his mercy endures for ever;
13 Who divided the Red Sea in two, *
for his mercy endures for ever;
14 And made Israel to pass through the midst of it, *
for his mercy endures for ever;
15 But swept Pharaoh and his army into the Red Sea, *
for his mercy endures for ever;
16 Who led his people through the wilderness, *
for his mercy endures for ever.
17 Who struck down great kings, *
for his mercy endures for ever;
18 And slew mighty kings, *
for his mercy endures for ever;
19 Sihon, king of the Amorites, *
for his mercy endures for ever;
20 And Og, the king of Bashan, *
for his mercy endures for ever;
21 And gave away their lands for an inheritance, *
for his mercy endures for ever;

22 An inheritance for Israel his servant, *
for his mercy endures for ever.
23 Who remembered us in our low estate, *
for his mercy endures for ever;
24 And delivered us from our enemies, *
for his mercy endures for ever;
25 Who gives food to all creatures, *
for his mercy endures for ever.
26 Give thanks to the God of heaven, *
for his mercy endures for ever.

137 *Super flumina*

1 By the waters of Babylon we sat down and wept, *
when we remembered you, O Zion.
2 As for our harps, we hung them up *
on the trees in the midst of that land.
3 For those who led us away captive asked us for a
song, and our oppressors called for mirth: *
"Sing us one of the songs of Zion."
4 How shall we sing the Lord's song *
upon an alien soil?
5 If I forget you, O Jerusalem, *
let my right hand forget its skill.
6 Let my tongue cleave to the roof of my mouth
if I do not remember you, *
if I do not set Jerusalem above my highest joy.
7 Remember the day of Jerusalem, O Lord,
against the people of Edom, *
who said, "Down with it! down with it!
even to the ground!"
8 O Daughter of Babylon, doomed to destruction, *
happy the one who pays you back
for what you have done to us!

9 Happy shall he be who takes your little ones, *
and dashes them against the rock!

138 *Confitebor tibi*

1 I will give thanks to you, O Lord, with my whole
heart; *
before the gods I will sing your praise.
2 I will bow down toward your holy temple
and praise your Name, *
because of your love and faithfulness;
3 For you have glorified your Name *
and your word above all things.
4 When I called, you answered me; *
you increased my strength within me.
5 All the kings of the earth will praise you, O Lord, *
when they have heard the words of your mouth.
6 They will sing of the ways of the Lord, *
that great is the glory of the Lord.
7 Though the Lord be high, he cares for the lowly; *
he perceives the haughty from afar.
8 Though I walk in the midst of trouble, you keep me
safe; *
you stretch forth your hand against the fury of my
enemies; your right hand shall save me.
9 The Lord will make good his purpose for me; *
O Lord, your love endures for ever;
do not abandon the works of your hands.

Twenty-ninth Day: Morning Prayer

139 *Domine, probasti*

1 Lord, you have searched me out and known me; *
you know my sitting down and my rising up;
you discern my thoughts from afar.

2 You trace my journeys and my resting-places *
and are acquainted with all my ways.
3 Indeed, there is not a word on my lips, *
but you, O Lord, know it altogether.
4 You press upon me behind and before *
and lay your hand upon me.
5 Such knowledge is too wonderful for me; *
it is so high that I cannot attain to it.
6 Where can I go then from your Spirit? *
where can I flee from your presence?
7 If I climb up to heaven, you are there; *
if I make the grave my bed, you are there also.
8 If I take the wings of the morning *
and dwell in the uttermost parts of the sea,
9 Even there your hand will lead me *
and your right hand hold me fast.
10 If I say, "Surely the darkness will cover me, *
and the light around me turn to night,"
11 Darkness is not dark to you;
the night is as bright as the day; *
darkness and light to you are both alike.
12 For you yourself created my inmost parts; *
you knit me together in my mother's womb.
13 I will thank you because I am marvelously made; *
your works are wonderful, and I know it well.
14 My body was not hidden from you, *
while I was being made in secret
and woven in the depths of the earth.
15 Your eyes beheld my limbs, yet unfinished in the
womb; all of them were written in your book; *
they were fashioned day by day,
when as yet there was none of them.
16 How deep I find your thoughts, O God! *
how great is the sum of them!

17 If I were to count them, they would be more in
number than the sand; *

to count them all, my life span would need to
be like yours.

18 Oh, that you would slay the wicked, O God! *
You that thirst for blood, depart from me.

19 They speak despitefully against you; *
your enemies take your Name in vain.

20 Do I not hate those, O Lord, who hate you? *
and do I not loathe those who rise up against you?

21 I hate them with a perfect hatred; *
they have become my own enemies.

22 Search me out, O God, and know my heart; *
try me and know my restless thoughts.

23 Look well whether there be any wickedness in me *
and lead me in the way that is everlasting.

140 *Eripe me, Domine*

1 Deliver me, O Lord, from evildoers; *
protect me from the violent,

2 Who devise evil in their hearts *
and stir up strife all day long.

3 They have sharpened their tongues like a serpent; *
adder's poison is under their lips.

4 Keep me, O Lord, from the hands of the wicked; *
protect me from the violent,

who are determined to trip me up.

5 The proud have hidden a snare for me
and stretched out a net of cords; *

they have set traps for me along the path.

6 I have said to the Lord, "You are my God; *
listen, O Lord, to my supplication.

7 O Lord God, the strength of my salvation, *
you have covered my head in the day of battle.

8 Do not grant the desires of the wicked, O Lord, *
Nor let their evil plans prosper.
9 Let not those who surround me lift up their heads; *
let the evil of their lips overwhelm them.
10 Let hot burning coals fall upon them; *
let them be cast into the mire, never to rise up again."
11 A slanderer shall not be established on the earth, *
and evil shall hunt down the lawless.
12 I know that the Lord will maintain the cause of the
poor *
and render justice to the needy.
13 Surely, the righteous will give thanks to your Name, *
and the upright shall continue in your sight.

Twenty-ninth Day: Evening Prayer

141 *Domine, clamavi*

1 O Lord, I call to you; come to me quickly; *
hear my voice when I cry to you.
2 Let my prayer be set forth in your sight as incense, *
the lifting up of my hands as the evening sacrifice.
3 Set a watch before my mouth, O Lord,
and guard the door of my lips; *
let not my heart incline to any evil thing.
4 Let me not be occupied in wickedness with evildoers, *
nor eat of their choice foods.
5 Let the righteous smite me in friendly rebuke;
let not the oil of the unrighteous anoint my head; *
for my prayer is continually against their wicked
deeds.
6 Let their rulers be overthrown in stony places, *
that they may know my words are true.
7 As when a plowman turns over the earth in furrows, *
let their bones be scattered at the mouth of the grave.

8 But my eyes are turned to you, Lord God; *
in you I take refuge;
do not strip me of my life.
9 Protect me from the snare which they have laid for me *
and from the traps of the evildoers.
10 Let the wicked fall into their own nets, *
while I myself escape.

142 *Voce mea ad Dominum*

1 I cry to the Lord with my voice; *
to the Lord I make loud supplication.
2 I pour out my complaint before him *
and tell him all my trouble.
3 When my spirit languishes within me, you know my
path; *
in the way wherein I walk they have hidden a trap for me.
4 I look to my right hand and find no one who knows me; *
I have no place to flee to, and no one cares for me.
5 I cry out to you, O Lord; *
I say, "You are my refuge,
my portion in the land of the living."
6 Listen to my cry for help, for I have been brought
very low; *
save me from those who pursue me,
for they are too strong for me.
7 Bring me out of prison, that I may give thanks to
your Name; *
when you have dealt bountifully with me,
the righteous will gather around me.

143 *Domine, exaudi*

1 Lord, hear my prayer,
and in your faithfulness heed my supplications; *
answer me in your righteousness.

2 Enter not into judgment with your servant, *
for in your sight shall no one living be justified.

3 For my enemy has sought my life;
he has crushed me to the ground; *
he has made me live in dark places like those who
are long dead.

4 My spirit faints within me; *
my heart within me is desolate.

5 I remember the time past;
I muse upon all your deeds; *
I consider the works of your hands.

6 I spread out my hands to you; *
my soul gasps to you like a thirsty land.

7 O Lord, make haste to answer me; my spirit fails me; *
do not hide your face from me
or I shall be like those who go down to the Pit.

8 Let me hear of your loving-kindness in the morning,
for I put my trust in you; *
show me the road that I must walk,
for I lift up my soul to you.

9 Deliver me from my enemies, O Lord, *
for I flee to you for refuge.

10 Teach me to do what pleases you, for you are my God; *
let your good Spirit lead me on level ground.

11 Revive me, O Lord, for your Name's sake; *
for your righteousness' sake, bring me out of trouble.

12 Of your goodness, destroy my enemies
and bring all my foes to naught, *
for truly I am your servant.

144 *Benedictus Dominus*

1 Blessed be the Lord my rock! *
who trains my hands to fight and my fingers to battle;
2 My help and my fortress, my stronghold and my deliverer, *
my shield in whom I trust,
who subdues the peoples under me.
3 O Lord, what are we that you should care for us? *
mere mortals that you should think of us?
4 We are like a puff of wind; *
our days are like a passing shadow.
5 Bow your heavens, O Lord, and come down; *
touch the mountains, and they shall smoke.
6 Hurl the lightning and scatter them; *
shoot out your arrows and rout them.
7 Stretch out your hand from on high; *
rescue me and deliver me from the great waters,
from the hand of foreign peoples,
8 Whose mouths speak deceitfully *
and whose right hand is raised in falsehood.
9 O God, I will sing to you a new song; *
I will play to you on a ten-stringed lyre.
10 You give victory to kings *
and have rescued David your servant.
11 Rescue me from the hurtful sword *
and deliver me from the hand of foreign peoples,
12 Whose mouths speak deceitfully *
and whose right hand is raised in falsehood.
13 May our sons be like plants well nurtured from their youth, *
and our daughters like sculptured corners of a palace.

14 May our barns be filled to overflowing with all
manner of crops; *

may the flocks in our pastures increase by thousands
and tens of thousands;

may our cattle be fat and sleek.

15 May there be no breaching of the walls, no going
into exile, no wailing in the public squares.

16 Happy are the people of whom this is so! *

happy are the people whose God is the Lord!

145 *Exaltabo te, Deus*

1 I will exalt you, O God my King, *
and bless your Name for ever and ever.

2 Every day will I bless you *
and praise your Name for ever and ever.

3 Great is the Lord and greatly to be praised; *
there is no end to his greatness.

4 One generation shall praise your works to another *
and shall declare your power.

5 I will ponder the glorious splendor of your majesty *
and all your marvelous works.

6 They shall speak of the might of your wondrous acts, *
and I will tell of your greatness.

7 They shall publish the remembrance of your great
goodness; *

they shall sing of your righteous deeds.

8 The Lord is gracious and full of compassion, *
slow to anger and of great kindness.

9 The Lord is loving to everyone *
and his compassion is over all his works.

10 All your works praise you, O Lord, *
and your faithful servants bless you.

11 They make known the glory of your kingdom *
and speak of your power;

12 That the peoples may know of your power *
and the glorious splendor of your kingdom.
13 Your kingdom is an everlasting kingdom; *
your dominion endures throughout all ages.
14 The Lord is faithful in all his words *
and merciful in all his deeds.
15 The Lord upholds all those who fall; *
he lifts up those who are bowed down.
16 The eyes of all wait upon you, O Lord, *
and you give them their food in due season.
17 You open wide your hand *
and satisfy the needs of every living creature.
18 The Lord is righteous in all his ways *
and loving in all his works.
19 The Lord is near to those who call upon him, *
to all who call upon him faithfully.
20 He fulfills the desire of those who fear him; *
he hears their cry and helps them.
21 The Lord preserves all those who love him, *
but he destroys all the wicked.
22 My mouth shall speak the praise of the Lord; *
let all flesh bless his holy Name for ever and ever.

146 *Lauda, anima mea*

1 Hallelujah!
Praise the Lord, O my soul! *
I will praise the Lord as long as I live;
I will sing praises to my God while I have my being.
2 Put not your trust in rulers, nor in any child of earth, *
for there is no help in them.
3 When they breathe their last, they return to earth, *
and in that day their thoughts perish.

The Psalter   375

4 Happy are they who have the God of Jacob for their help! *
whose hope is in the Lord their God;
5 Who made heaven and earth, the seas, and all that is in them; *
who keeps his promise for ever;
6 Who gives justice to those who are oppressed, *
and food to those who hunger.
7 The Lord sets the prisoners free;
the Lord opens the eyes of the blind; *
the Lord lifts up those who are bowed down;
8 The Lord loves the righteous;
the Lord cares for the stranger; *
he sustains the orphan and widow,
but frustrates the way of the wicked.
9 The Lord shall reign for ever, *
your God, O Zion, throughout all generations.
Hallelujah!

Thirtieth Day: Evening Prayer

147 *Laudate Dominum*

1 Hallelujah!
How good it is to sing praises to our God! *
how pleasant it is to honor him with praise!
2 The Lord rebuilds Jerusalem; *
he gathers the exiles of Israel.
3 He heals the brokenhearted *
and binds up their wounds.
4 He counts the number of the stars *
and calls them all by their names.
5 Great is our Lord and mighty in power; *
there is no limit to his wisdom.

6 The Lord lifts up the lowly, *
but casts the wicked to the ground.
7 Sing to the Lord with thanksgiving; *
make music to our God upon the harp.
8 He covers the heavens with clouds *
and prepares rain for the earth;
9 He makes grass to grow upon the mountains *
and green plants to serve mankind.
10 He provides food for flocks and herds *
and for the young ravens when they cry.
11 He is not impressed by the might of a horse; *
he has no pleasure in the strength of a man;
12 But the Lord has pleasure in those who fear him, *
in those who await his gracious favor.
13 Worship the Lord, O Jerusalem; *
praise your God, O Zion;
14 For he has strengthened the bars of your gates; *
he has blessed your children within you.
15 He has established peace on your borders; *
he satisfies you with the finest wheat.
16 He sends out his command to the earth, *
and his word runs very swiftly.
17 He gives snow like wool; *
he scatters hoarfrost like ashes.
18 He scatters his hail like bread crumbs; *
who can stand against his cold?
19 He sends forth his word and melts them; *
he blows with his wind, and the waters flow.
20 He declares his word to Jacob, *
his statutes and his judgments to Israel.
21 He has not done so to any other nation; *
to them he has not revealed his judgments.
Hallelujah!

148 *Laudate Dominum*

1 Hallelujah!
Praise the Lord from the heavens; *
praise him in the heights.
2 Praise him, all you angels of his; *
praise him, all his host.
3 Praise him, sun and moon; *
praise him, all you shining stars.
4 Praise him, heaven of heavens, *
and you waters above the heavens.
5 Let them praise the Name of the Lord; *
for he commanded, and they were created.
6 He made them stand fast for ever and ever; *
he gave them a law which shall not pass away.
7 Praise the Lord from the earth, *
you sea-monsters and all deeps;
8 Fire and hail, snow and fog, *
tempestuous wind, doing his will;
9 Mountains and all hills, *
fruit trees and all cedars;
10 Wild beasts and all cattle, *
creeping things and winged birds;
11 Kings of the earth and all peoples, *
princes and all rulers of the world;
12 Young men and maidens, *
old and young together.
13 Let them praise the Name of the Lord, *
for his Name only is exalted,
his splendor is over earth and heaven.
14 He has raised up strength for his people
and praise for all his loyal servants, *
the children of Israel, a people who are near him.
Hallelujah!

149 *Cantate Domino*

1 Hallelujah!
Sing to the Lord a new song; *
sing his praise in the congregation of the faithful.
2 Let Israel rejoice in his Maker; *
let the children of Zion be joyful in their King.
3 Let them praise his Name in the dance; *
let them sing praise to him with timbrel and harp.
4 For the Lord takes pleasure in his people *
and adorns the poor with victory.
5 Let the faithful rejoice in triumph; *
let them be joyful on their beds.
6 Let the praises of God be in their throat *
and a two-edged sword in their hand;
7 To wreak vengeance on the nations *
and punishment on the peoples;
8 To bind their kings in chains *
and their nobles with links of iron;
9 To inflict on them the judgment decreed; *
this is glory for all his faithful people.
Hallelujah!

150 *Laudate Dominum*

1 Hallelujah!
Praise God in his holy temple; *
praise him in the firmament of his power.
2 Praise him for his mighty acts; *
praise him for his excellent greatness.
3 Praise him with the blast of the ram's-horn; *
praise him with lyre and harp.
4 Praise him with timbrel and dance; *
praise him with strings and pipe.

5 Praise him with resounding cymbals; *
praise him with loud-clanging cymbals.
6 Let everything that has breath *
praise the Lord.
Hallelujah!

Lectionary

Concerning the Lectionary

The Lectionary for Sundays is arranged in a three-year cycle, in which Year A always begins on the First Sunday of Advent in years evenly divisible by three. (For example, 1977 divided by 3 is 659 with no remainder. Year A, therefore, begins on Advent Sunday of that year.)

The Psalms and Lessons appointed for the Sundays and for other major Holy Days are intended for use at all public services on such days, except when the same congregation attends two or more services. Thus, the same Lessons are to be read at the principal morning service, whether the Liturgy of the Word takes the form given in the Holy Eucharist, or that of the Daily Office.

When the same congregation is present for Morning or Evening Prayer, in addition to the Eucharist, the Lessons at the Office may be selected from one of the other years of the three-year Sunday cycle, or from the Lectionary for the Daily Office. The Psalms at such Offices are normally those appointed in the Office Lectionary; but, when desired, the Psalm cited in the selected Sunday Proper may be used instead.

In this Lectionary, the selections from the Psalter are frequently cited in a longer and shorter version, usually from the same Psalm. The longer version is particularly appropriate for use at the Office, the shorter version when the Psalm is sung between the

Lessons at the Eucharist. The selections may be further lengthened or shortened at discretion.

When an alternative Lesson is cited, it is sometimes identical with a Lesson appointed for the same day in the Daily Office Lectionary.

In the opening verses of Lessons, the Reader should omit initial conjunctions which refer only to what has preceded, substitute nouns for pronouns when the referent is not otherwise clear, or else prefix to the Reading some such introduction as, "N. said (to N.)."

Any Reading may be lengthened at discretion. Suggested lengthenings are shown in parentheses.

Please note: the following Lectionary is from the 1979 edition of the Book of Common Prayer and does not include the Revised Common Lectionary (RCL).

The Lectionary

Year A

	Psalm	Lessons
First Sunday of Advent	122	Isaiah 2:1-5 Romans 13:8-14 Matthew 24:37-44
Second Sunday of Advent	72 or 72:1-8	Isaiah 11:1-10 Romans 15:4-13 Matthew 3:1-12
Third Sunday of Advent	146 or 146:4-9	Isaiah 35:1-10 James 5:7-10 Matthew 11:2-11
Fourth Sunday of Advent	24 or 24:1-7	Isaiah 7:10-17 Romans 1:1-7 Matthew 1:18-25
Christmas Day I	96 or 96:1-4,11-12	Isaiah 9:2-4,6-7 Titus 2:11-14 Luke 2:1-14(15-20)
Christmas Day II	97 or 97:1-4,11-12	Isaiah 62:6-7,10-12 Titus 3:4-7 Luke 2:(1-14)15-20

Lectionary A

	Psalm	Lessons
Christmas Day III	98 or 98:1 -6	Isaiah 52:7-10 Hebrews 1:1-12 John 1:1-14
First Sunday after Christmas	147 or 147:13-21	Isaiah 61:10-62:3 Galatians 3:23-25;4:4-7 John 1:1-18
Holy Name January 1	8	Exodus 34:1-8 Romans 1:1-7 or Philippians 2:9-13 Luke 2:15-21
Second Sunday after Christmas	84 or 84:1-8	Jeremiah 31:7-14 Ephesians 1:3-6,15-19a Matthew 2:13-15,19-23 or Luke 2:41-52 or Matthew 2:1-12
The Epiphany January 6	72 or 72:1-2,10-17	Isaiah 60:1-6,9 Ephesians 3:1-12 Matthew 2:1-12
First Sunday after Epiphany	89:1-29 or 89:20-29	Isaiah 42:1-9 Acts 10:34-38 Matthew 3:13-17
Second Sunday after Epiphany	40:1-10	Isaiah 49:1-7 1 Corinthians 1:1-9 John 1:29-41
Third Sunday after Epiphany	139:1-17 or 139:1-11	Amos 3:1-8 1 Corinthians 1:10-17 Matthew 4:12-23

Lectionary A

	Psalm	Lessons
Fourth Sunday after Epiphany	37:1-18 or 37:1-6	Micah 6:1-8 1 Corinthians 1:(18-25)26-31 Matthew 5:1-12
Fifth Sunday after Epiphany	27 or 27:1-7	Habakkuk 3:1-6,17-19 1 Corinthians 2:1-11 Matthew 5:13-20
Sixth Sunday after Epiphany	119:1-16 or 119:9-16	Ecclesiasticus 15:11-20 1 Corinthians 3:1-9 Matthew 5:21-24,27-30,33-37
Seventh Sunday after Epiphany	71 or 71:16-24	Leviticus 19:1-2,9-18 1 Corinthians 3:10-11,16-23 Matthew 5:38-48
Eighth Sunday after Epiphany	62 or 62:6-14	Isaiah 49:8-18 1 Corinthians 4:1-5(6-7)8-13 Matthew 6:24-34
Last Sunday after Epiphany	99	Exodus 24:12(13-14)15-18 Philippians 3:7-14 Matthew 17:1-9
Ash Wednesday	103 or 103:8-14	Joel 2:1-2,12-17 or Isaiah 58:1-12 2 Corinthians 5:20b-6:10 Matthew 6:1-6,16-21
First Sunday in Lent	51 or 51:1-13	Genesis 2:4b-9,15-17,25-3:7 Romans 5:12-19(20-21) Matthew 4:1-11
Second Sunday in Lent	33:12-22	Genesis 12:1-8 Romans 4:1-5(6-12)13-17 John 3:1-17

Lectionary A

	Psalm	Lessons
Third Sunday in Lent	95 or 95:6-11	Exodus 17:1-7 Romans 5:1-11 John 4:5-26(27-38)39-42
Fourth Sunday in Lent	23	1 Samuel 16:1-13 Ephesians 5:(1-7)8-14 John 9:1-13(14-27)28-38
Fifth Sunday in Lent	130	Ezekiel 37:1-3(4-10)11-14 Romans 6:16-23 John 11:(1-17)18-44

Palm Sunday

	Psalm	Lessons
Liturgy of the Palms	118:19-29	Matthew 21:1-11
Liturgy of the Word	22:1-21 or 22:1-11	Isaiah 45:21-25 or Isaiah 52:13-53:12 Philippians 2:5-11 Matthew (26:36-75) 　　　　27:1-54(55-66)
Monday in Holy Week	36:5-10	Isaiah 42:1-9 Hebrews 11:39-12:3 John 12:1-11 or Mark 14:3-9
Tuesday in Holy Week	71:1-12	Isaiah 49:1-6 1 Corinthians 1:18-31 John 12:.37-38,42-50 or Mark 11:15-19
Wednesday in Holy Week	69:7-15, 22-23	Isaiah 50:4-9a Hebrews 9:11-15,24-28 John 13:21-35 or Matthew 26:1-5,14-25

The Book of Common Prayer　387

Lectionary A

	Psalm	Lessons
Maundy Thursday	78:14-20,23-25	Exodus 12:1-14a 1 Corinthians 11:23-26(27-32) John 13:1-15 or Luke 22:14-30
Good Friday	22:1-21 or 22:1-11 or 40:1-14 or 69:1-23	Isaiah 52:13-53:12 or Genesis 22:1-18 or Wisdom 2:1,12-24 Hebrews 10:1-25 John (18:1-40) 19:1-37
Holy Saturday	130 or 31:1-5	Job 14:1-14 1 Peter 4:1-8 Matthew 27:57-66 or John 19:38-42

Easter Day

The Great Vigil	See pages 288-291 of BCP.
Early Service	Use one of the Old Testament Lessons from the Vigil with

	Psalm	Lessons
	114	Romans 6:3-11 Matthew 28:1-10

Principal Service	118:14-29
	or 118:14-17,
	  22-24
		Acts 10:34-43
		or Exodus 14:10-14,21-25;
		  15:20-21
		Colossians 3:1-4
		or Acts 10:34-43
		John 20:1-10(11-18)
		or Matthew 28:1-10

Evening Service	114 or 136 or 118:14-17, 22-24	Acts 5:29a,30-32 or Daniel 12:1-3 1 Corinthians 5:6b-8 or Acts 5:29a,30-32 Luke 24:13-35

	Psalm	Lessons
Monday in Easter Week	16:8-11 or 118:19-24	Acts 2:14,22-32 Matthew 28:9-15
Tuesday in Easter Week	33:18-22 or 118:19-24	Acts 2:36-41 John 20:11-18
Wednesday in Easter Week	105:1-8 or 118:19-24	Acts 3:1-10 Luke 24:13-35
Thursday in Easter Week	8 or 114 or 118:19-24	Acts 3:11-26 Luke 24:36b-48
Friday in Easter Week	116:1-8 or 118:19-24	Acts 4:1-12 John 21:1-14
Saturday in Easter Week	118:14-18 or 118:19-24	Acts 4:13-21 Mark 16:9-15,20
Second Sunday of Easter	111 or 118:19-24	Acts 2:14a,22-32 or Genesis 8:6-16; 9:8-16 1 Peter 1:3-9 or Acts 2:14a,22-32 John 20:19-31
Third Sunday of Easter	116 or 116:10-17	Acts 2:14a,36-47 or Isaiah 43:1-12 1 Peter 1:17-23 or Acts 2:14a,36-47 Luke 24:13-35

Lectionary A

	Psalm	Lessons
Fourth Sunday of Easter	23	Acts 6:1-9; 7:2a,51-60 or Nehemiah 9:6-15 1 Peter 2:19-25 or Acts 6:1-9; 7:2a,51-60 John 10:1-10
Fifth Sunday of Easter	66:1-11 or 66:1-8	Acts 17:1-15 or Deuteronomy 6:20-25 1 Peter 2:1-10 or Acts 17:1-15 John 14:1-14
Sixth Sunday of Easter	148 or 148:7-14	Acts 17:22-31 or Isaiah 41:17-20 1 Peter 3:8-18 or Acts 17:22-31 John 15:1-8
Ascension Day	47 or 110:1-5	Acts 1:1-11 or Daniel 7:9-14 Ephesians 1:15-23 or Acts 1:1-11 Luke 24:49-53 or Mark 16:9-15,19-20
Seventh Sunday of Easter	68:1-20 or 47	Acts 1:(1-7)8-14 or Ezekiel 39:21-29 1 Peter 4:12-19 Acts 1:(1-7)8-14 John 17:1-11

Lectionary A

	Psalm	Lessons

Day of Pentecost

| Early or
Vigil Service | 33:12-22
Canticle 2
or 13
130
Canticle 9
104:25-32 | Genesis 11:1-9
or Exodus 19:1-9,16-20a;
20:18-20
or Ezekiel 37:1-14
or Joel 2:28-32
Acts 2:1-11
or Romans 8:14-17,22-27
John 7:37-39a |
| Principal Service | 104:25-37
or 104:25-32
or 33:12-15,
18-22 | Acts 2:1-11
or Ezekiel 11:17-20
1 Corinthians 12:4-13
or Acts 2:1-11
John 20:19-23
or John 14:8-17 |

On the weekdays which follow, the numbered Proper which corresponds most closely to the date of Pentecost in that year is used.

| Trinity Sunday | 150
or Canticle 2
or 13 | Genesis 1:1-2:3
2 Corinthians 13:(5-10)11-14
Matthew 28:16-20 |

On the weekdays which follow, the numbered Proper which corresponds most closely to the date of Trinity Sunday in that year is used.

The Season after Pentecost

Directions for the use of the Propers which follow are on page 158 of BCP.

| Proper I
Closest to
May 11 | 119:1-16
or 119:9-16 | Ecclesiasticus 15:11-20
1 Corinthians 3:1-9
Matthew 5:21-24,27-30,33-37 |

The Book of Common Prayer　391

Lectionary A

	Psalm	Lessons
Proper 2 Closest to May 18	71 or 71:16-24	Leviticus 19:1-2,9-18 1 Corinthians 3:10-11,16-23 Matthew 5:38-48
Proper 3 Closest to May 25	62 or 62:6-14	Isaiah 49:8-18 1 Corinthians 4:1-5(6-7)8-13 Matthew 6:24-34
Proper 4 Closest to June 1	31 or 31:1-5,19-24	Deuteronomy 11:18-21,26-28 Romans 3:21-25a,28 Matthew 7:21-27
Proper 5 Closest to June 8	50 or 50:7-15	Hosea 5:15-6:6 Romans 4:13-18 Matthew 9:9-13
Proper 6 Closest to June 15	100	Exodus 19:2-8a Romans 5:6-11 Matthew 9:35-10:8(9-15)
Proper 7 Closest to June 22	69:1-18 or 69:7-10, 16-18	Jeremiah 20:7-13 Romans 5:15b-19 Matthew 10:(16-23)24-33
Proper 8 Closest to June 29	89:1-18 or 89:1-4,15-18	Isaiah 2:10-17 Romans 6:3-11 Matthew 10:34-42
Proper 9 Closest to July 6	145 or 145:8-14	Zechariah 9:9-12 Romans 7:21-8:6 Matthew 11:25-30
Proper 10 Closest to July 13	65 or 65:9-14	Isaiah 55:1-5,10-13 Romans 8:9-17 Matthew 13:1-9,18-23

	Psalm	Lessons
Proper 11 Closest to July 20	86 or 86:11-17	Wisdom 12:13,16-19 Romans 8:18-25 Matthew 13:24-30,36-43
Proper 12 Closest to July 27	119:121-136 or 119:129-136	1 Kings 3:5-12 Romans 8:26-34 Matthew 13:31-33,44-49a
Proper 13 Closest to August 8	78:1-29 or 78:14-20, 23-25	Nehemiah 9:16-20 Romans 8:35-39 Matthew 14:13-21
Proper 14 Closest to August 10	29	Jonah 2:1-9 Romans 9:1-5 Matthew 14:22-33
Proper 15 Closest to August 17	67	Isaiah 56:1(2-5)6-7 Romans 11:13-15,29-32 Matthew 15:21-28
Proper 16 Closest to August 24	138	Isaiah 51:1-6 Romans 11:33-36 Matthew 16:13-20
Proper 17 Closest to August 31	26 or 26:1-8	Jeremiah 15:15-21 Romans 12:1-8 Matthew 16:21-27
Proper 18 Closest to September 7	119:33-48 or 119:33-40	Ezekiel 33:(1-6)7-11 Romans 12:9-21 Matthew 18:15-20
Proper 19 Closest to September 14	103 or 103:8-13	Ecclesiasticus 27:30-28:7 Romans 14:5-12 Matthew 18:21-35

Lectionary A

	Psalm	Lessons
Proper 20 Closest to September 21	145 or 145:1-8	Jonah 3:10-4:11 Philippians 1:21-27 Matthew 20:1-16
Proper 21 Closest to September 28	25:1-14 or 25:3-9	Ezekiel 18:1-4,25-32 Philippians 2:1-13 Matthew 21:28-32
Proper 22 Closest to October 5	80 or 80:7-14	Isaiah 5:1-7 Philippians 3:14-21 Matthew 21:33-43
Proper 23 Closest to October 12	23	Isaiah 25:1-9 Philippians 4:4-13 Matthew 22:1-14
Proper 24 Closest to October 19	96 or 96:1-9	Isaiah 45:1-7 1 Thessalonians 1:1-10 Matthew 22:15-22
Proper 25 Closest to October 26	1	Exodus 22:21-27 1 Thessalonians 2:1-8 Matthew 22:34-46
Proper 26 Closest to November 2	43	Micah 3:5-12 1 Thess. 2:9-13,17-20 Matthew 23:1-12
Proper 27 Closest to November 9	70	Amos 5:18-24 1 Thessalonians 4:13-18 Matthew 25:1-13
Proper 28 Closest to November 16	90 or 90:1-8,12	Zephaniah 1:7,12-18 1 Thessalonians 5:1-10 Matthew 25:14-15,19-29
Proper 29 Closest to November 28	95:1-7	Ezekiel 34:11-17 1 Corinthians 15:20-28 Matthew 25:31-46

Year B

First Sunday of Advent	80 or 80:1-7	Isaiah 64:1-9a 1 Corinthians 1:1-9 Mark 13:(24-32)33-37
Second Sunday of Advent	85 or 85:7-13	Isaiah 40:1-11 2 Peter 3:8-15a,18 Mark 1:1-8
Third Sunday of Advent	126 or Canticle 3 or 15	Isaiah 65:17-25 1 Thess. 5:(12-15)16-28 John 1:6-8,19-28 or John 3:23-30
Fourth Sunday of Advent	132 or 132:8-15	2 Samuel 7:4,8-16 Romans 16:25-27 Luke 1:26-38
Christmas Day I	96 or 96:1-4,11-12	Isaiah 9:2-4,6-7 Titus 2:11-14 Luke 2:1-14(15-20)

Lectionary B

	Psalm	Lessons
Christmas Day II	97 or 97:1-4,11-12	Isaiah 62:6-7,10-12 Titus 3:4-7 Luke 2:(1-14)15-20
Christmas Day III	98 or 98:1-6	Isaiah 52:7-10 Hebrews 1:1-12 John 1:1-14
First Sunday after Christmas	147 or 147:13-21	Isaiah 61:10-62:3 Galatians 3:23-25;4:4-7 John 1:1-18
Holy Name January 1	8	Exodus 34:1-8 Romans 1:1-7 Luke 2:15-21
Second Sunday after Christmas	84 or 84:1-8	Jeremiah 31:7-14 Ephesians 1:3-6,15-19a Matthew 2:13-15,19-23 or Luke 2:41-52 or Matthew 2:1-12
The Epiphany January 6	72 or 72:1-2,10-17	Isaiah 60:1-6,9 Ephesians 3:1-12 Matthew 2:1-12
First Sunday after Epiphany	89:1-29 or 89:20-29	Isaiah 42:1-9 Acts 10:34-38 Mark 1:7-11
Second Sunday after Epiphany	63:1-8	1 Samuel 3:1-10(11-20) 1 Corinthians 6:11b-20 John 1:43-51
Third Sunday after Epiphany	130	Jeremiah 3:21-4:2 1 Corinthians 7:17-23 Mark 1:14-20

	Psalm	Lessons
Fourth Sunday after Epiphany	111	Deuteronomy 18:15-20 1 Corinthians 8:1b-13 Mark 1:21-28
Fifth Sunday after Epiphany	142	2 Kings 4:(8-17)18-21(22-31) 32-37 1 Corinthians 9:16-23 Mark 1:29-39
Sixth Sunday after Epiphany	42 or 42:1-7	2 Kings 5:1-15ab 1 Corinthians 9:24-27 Mark 1:40-45
Seventh Sunday after Epiphany	32 or 32:1-8	Isaiah 43:18-25 2 Corinthians 1:18-22 Mark 2:1-12
Eighth Sunday after Epiphany	103 or 103:1-6	Hosea 2:14-23 2 Corinthians 3:(4-11)17-4:2 Mark 2:18-22
Last Sunday after Epiphany	27 or 27:5-11	1 Kings 19:9-18 2 Peter 1:16-19(20-21) Mark 9:2-9
Ash Wednesday	103 or 103:8-14	Joel 2:1-2,12-17 or Isaiah 58:1-12 2 Corinthians 5:20b-6:10 Matthew 6:1-6,16-21
First Sunday in Lent	25 or 25:3-9	Genesis 9:8-17 1 Peter 3:18-22 Mark 1:9-13
Second Sunday in Lent	16 or 16:5-11	Genesis 22:1-14 Romans 8:31-39 Mark 8:31-38

Lectionary B

	Psalm	Lessons
Third Sunday in Lent	19:7-14	Exodus 20:1-17 Romans 7:13-25 John 2:13-22
Fourth Sunday in Lent	122	2 Chronicles 36:14-23 Ephesians 2:4-10 John 6:4-15
Fifth Sunday in Lent	51 or 51:11-16	Jeremiah 31:31-34 Hebrews 5:(1-4)5-10 John 12:20-33
Palm Sunday		
Liturgy of the Palms	118:19-29	Mark 11:1-11a
Liturgy of the Word	22:1-21 or 22:1-11	Isaiah 45:21-25 or Isaiah 52:13-53:12 Philippians 2:5-11 Mark (14:32-72) 15:1-39(40-47)
Monday in Holy Week	36:5-10	Isaiah 42:1-9 Hebrews 11:39-12:3 John 12:1-11 or Mark 14:3-9
Tuesday in Holy Week	71:1-12	Isaiah 49:1-6 1 Corinthians 1:18-31 John 12:37-38,42-50 or Mark 11:15-19
Wednesday in Holy Week	69:7-15,22-23	Isaiah 50:4-9a Hebrews 9:11-15,24-28 John 13:21-35 or Matthew 26:1-5,14-25

	Psalm	Lessons
Maundy Thursday	78:14-20,23-25	Exodus 12:1-14a 1 Corinthians 11:23-26(27-32) John 13:1-15 or Luke 22:14-30
Good Friday	22:1-21 or 22:1-11 or 40:1 -14 or 69:1-23	Isaiah 52:13--53:12 or Genesis 22:1-18 or Wisdom 2:1,12-24 Hebrews 10:1-25 John (18:1-40) 19:1-37
Holy Saturday	130 or 31:1-5	Job 14:1-14 1 Peter 4:1-8 Matthew 27:57-66 or John 19:38-42
Easter Day		
The Great Vigil	See pages 288-291 of BCP.	
Early Service	Use one of the Old Testament Lessons from the Vigil with	
	114	Romans 6:3-11 Matthew 28:1-10
Principal Service	118:14-29 or 118:14-17, 22-24	Acts 10:34-43 or Isaiah 25:6-9 Colossians 3:1-4 or Acts 10:34-43 Mark 16:1-8
Evening Service	114 or 136 or 118:14-17, 22-24	Acts 5:29a,30-32 or Daniel 12:1-3 1 Corinthians 5:6b-8 or Acts 5:29a,30-32 Luke 24:13-35

Lectionary B

	Psalm	Lessons
Monday in Easter Week	16:8-11 or 118:19-24	Acts 2:14,22-32 Matthew 28:9-15
Tuesday in Easter Week	33:18-22 or 118:19-24	Acts 2:36-41 John 20:11-18
Wednesday in Easter Week	105:1-8 or 118:19-24	Acts 3:1-10 Luke 24:13-35
Thursday in Easter Week	8 or 114 or 118:19-24	Acts 3:11-26 Luke 24:36b-48
Friday in Easter Week	116:1-8 or 118:19-24	Acts 4:1-12 John 21:1-14
Saturday in Easter Week	118:14-18 or 118:19-24	Acts 4:13-21 Mark 16:9-15,20
Second Sunday of Easter	111 or 118:19-24	Acts 3:12a,13-15,17-26 or Isaiah 26:2-9,19 1 John 5:1-6 or Acts 3:12a,13-15,17-26 John 20:19-31
Third Sunday of Easter	98 or 98:1-5	Acts 4:5-12 or Micah 4:1-5 1 John 1:1-2:2 or Acts 4:5-12 Luke 24:36b-48
Fourth Sunday of Easter	23 or 100	Acts 4:(23-31)32-37 or Ezekiel 34:1-10 1 John 3:1-8 or Acts 4:(23-31)32-37 John 10:11-16

	Psalm	Lessons
Fifth Sunday of Easter	66:1-11 or 66:1-8	Acts 8:26-40 or Deuteronomy 4:32-40 1 John 3:(14-17)18-24 or Acts 8:26-40 John 14:15-21
Sixth Sunday of Easter	33 or 33:1-8,18-22	Acts 11:19-30 or Isaiah 45:11-13,18-19 1 John 4:7-21 or Acts 11:19-30 John 15:9-17
Ascension Day	47 or 110:1-5	Acts 1:1-11 or Ezekiel 1:3-5a,15-22,26-28 Ephesians 1:15-23 or Acts 1:1-11 Luke 24:49-53 or Mark 16:9-15,19-20
Seventh Sunday of Easter	68:1-20 or 47	Acts 1:15-26 or Exodus 28:1-4,9-10,29-30 1 John 5:9-15 or Acts 1:15-26 John 17:11b-19

Day of Pentecost

	Psalm	Lessons
Early or Vigil Service	33:12-22 Canticle 2 or 3 130 Canticle 9 104:25-32	Genesis 11:1-9 or Exodus 19:1-9,16-20a; 20:18-20 or Ezekiel 37:1-14 or Joel 2:28-32 Acts 2:1-11 or Romans 8:14-17,22-27 John 7:37-39a

Lectionary B

	Psalm	Lessons
Principal Service	104:25-37	Acts 2:1-11
	or 104:25-32	or Isaiah 44: 1-8
	or 33:12-15,	1 Corinthians 12:4-13
	18-22	or Acts 2:1-11
		John 20:19-23
		or John 14:8-17

On the weekdays which follow, the numbered Proper which corresponds most closely to the date of Pentecost in that year is used. See page 158 of BCP.

Trinity Sunday	93	Exodus 3:1-6
	or Canticle 2	Romans 8:12-17
	or 13	John 3:1-16

On the weekdays which follow, the numbered Proper which corresponds most closely to the date of Trinity Sunday in that year is used.

The Season after Pentecost

Directions for the use of the Propers which follow are on page 158 of BCP.

Proper 1	42	2 Kings 5:1-15ab
Closest to	or 42:1-7	1 Corinthians 9:24-27
May 11		Mark 1:40-45
Proper 2	32	Isaiah 43:18-25
Closest to	or 32:1-8	2 Corinthians 1:18-22
May 18		Mark 2:1-12
Proper 3	103	Hosea 2:14-23
Closest to	or 103:1-6	2 Corinthians 3:(4-11)17-4:2
May 25		Mark 2:18-22

	Psalm	Lessons
Proper 4 Closest to June 1	81 or 81:1-10	Deuteronomy 5:6-21 2 Corinthians 4:5-12 Mark 2:23-28
Proper 5 Closest to June 8	130	Genesis 3:(1-7)8-21 2 Corinthians 4:13-18 Mark 3:20-35
Proper 6 Closest to June 15	92 or 92:1-4,11-14	Ezekiel 31:1-6,10-14 2 Corinthians 5:1-10 Mark 4:26-34
Proper 7 Closest to June 22	107:1-32 or 107:1-3, 23-32	Job 38:1-11,16-18 2 Corinthians 5:14-21 Mark 4:35-41;(5:1-20)
Proper 8 Closest to June 29	112	Deuteronomy 15:7-11 2 Corinthians 8:1-9,13-15 Mark 5:22-24,35b-43
Proper 9 Closest to July 6	123	Ezekiel 2:1-7 2 Corinthians 12:2-10 Mark 6:1-6
Proper 10 Closest to July 13	85 or 85:7-13	Amos 7:7-15 Ephesians 1:1-14 Mark 6: 7- 13
Proper 11 Closest to July 20	22:22-30	Isaiah 57:14b-21 Ephesians 2:11-22 Mark 6:30-44
Proper 12 Closest to July 27	114	2 Kings 2:1-15 Ephesians 4:1-7,11-16 Mark 6:45-52

Lectionary B

	Psalm	Lessons
Proper 13 Closest to August 3	78:1-25 or 78:14-20, 23-25	Exodus 16:2-4,9-15 Ephesians 4:17-25 John 6:24-35
Proper 14 Closest to August 10	34 or 34:1-8	Deuteronomy 8:1-10 Ephesians 4:(25-29)30-5:2 John 6:37-51
Proper 15 Closest to August 17	147 or 34:9-14	Proverbs 9:1-6 Ephesians 5:15-20 John 6:53-59
Proper 16 Closest to August 24	16 or 34:15-22	Joshua 24:1-2a,14-25 Ephesians 5:21-33 John 6:60-69
Proper 17 Closest to August 31	15	Deuteronomy 4:1-9 Ephesians 6:10-20 Mark 7:1-8,14-15,21-23
Proper 18 Closest to September 7	146 or 146:4-9	Isaiah 35:4-7a James 1:17-27 Mark 7:31-37
Proper 19 Closest to September 14	116 or 116:1-8	Isaiah 50:4-9 James 2:1-5,8-10,14-18 Mark 8:27-38 or Mark 9:14-29
Proper 20 Closest to September 21	54	Wisdom 1:16-2:1(6-11)12-22 James 3:16--4:6 Mark 9:30-37
Proper 21 Closest to September 28	19 or 19:7-14	Numbers 11:4-6,10-16,24-29 James 4:7-12(13-5:6) Mark 9:38-43,45,47-48

	Psalm	Lessons
Proper 22 Closest to October 5	8 or 128	Genesis 2:18-24 Hebrews 2:(1-8)9-18 Mark 10:2-9
Proper 23 Closest to October 12	90 or 90:1-8,12	Amos 5:6-7,10-15 Hebrews 3:1-6 Mark 10:17-27(28-31)
Proper 24 Closest to October 19	91 or 91:9-16	Isaiah 53:4-12 Hebrews 4.12-16 Mark 10:35-45
Proper 25 Closest to October 26	13	Isaiah 59:(1-4)9-19 Hebrews 5:12-6:1,9-12 Mark 10:46-52
Proper 26 Closest to November 2	119:1-16 or 119:1-8	Deuteronomy 6:1-9 Hebrews 7:23-28 Mark 12:28-34
Proper 27 Closest to November 9	146 or 146:4-9	1 Kings 17:8-16 Hebrews 9 24-28 Mark 12:38-44
Proper 28 Closest to November 16	16 or 16:5-11	Daniel 12:1-4a(5-13) Hebrews 10 31-39 Mark 13:14-23
Proper 29 Closest to November 23	93	Daniel 7:9-14 Revelation 1:1-8 John 18:33-37 or Mark 11

Year C

	Psalm	Lessons
First Sunday of Advent	50 or 50:1-6	Zechariah 14:4-9 1 Thessalonians 3:9-13 Luke 21:25-31
Second Sunday of Advent	126	Baruch 5:1-9 Philippians 1:1-11 Luke 3:1-6
Third Sunday of Advent	85 or 85:7-13 or Canticle 9	Zephaniah 3:14-20 Philippians 4:4-7(8-9) Luke 3:7-18
Fourth Sunday of Advent	80 or 80:1-7	Micah 5:2-4 Hebrews 10:5-10 Luke 1:39-49(50-56)
Christmas Day I	96 or 96:1-4,11-12	Isaiah 9:2-4,6-7 Titus 2:11-14 Luke 2:1-14(15-20)
Christmas Day II	97 or 97:1-4,11-12	Isaiah 62:6-7,10-12 Titus 3:4-7 Luke 2:(1-14)15-20
Christmas Day III	98 or 98:1-6	Isaiah 52:7-10 Hebrews 1:1-12 John 1:1-14
First Sunday after Christmas	147 or 147:13-21	Isaiah 61:10-62:3 Galatians 3:23-25; 4:4-7 John 1:1-18

	Psalm	Lessons
Holy Name January 1	8	Exodus 34:1-8 Romans 1:1-7 Luke 2:15-21
Second Sunday after Christmas	84 or 84:1-8	Jeremiah 31:7-14 Ephesians 1:3-6,15-19a Matthew 2:13-15,19-23 or Luke 2:41-52 or Matthew 2:1-12
The Epiphany January 6	72 or 72:1-2,10-17	Isaiah 60:1-6,9 Ephesians 3:1-12 Matthew 2:1-12
First Sunday after Epiphany	89:1-29 or 89:20-29	Isaiah 42:1-9 Acts 10:34-38 Luke 3:15-16,21-22
Second Sunday after Epiphany	96 or 96:1-10	Isaiah 62:1-5 1 Corinthians 12:1-11 John 2:1-11
Third Sunday after Epiphany	113	Nehemiah 8:2-10 1 Corinthians 12:12-27 Luke 4:14-21
Fourth Sunday after Epiphany	71:1-17 or 71:1-6,15-17	Jeremiah 1:4-10 1 Corinthians 14:12b-20 Luke 4:21-32
Fifth Sunday after Epiphany	85 or 85:7-13	Judges 6:11-24a 1 Corinthians 15:1-11 Luke 5:1-11
Sixth Sunday after Epiphany	1	Jeremiah 17:5-10 1 Corinthians 15:12-20 Luke 6:17-26

Lectionary C

	Psalm	Lessons
Seventh Sunday after Epiphany	37:1-18 or 37:3-10	Genesis 45:3-11,21-28 1 Corinthians 15:35-38,42-50 Luke 6:27-38
Eighth Sunday after Epiphany	92 or 92:1-5,11-14	Jeremiah 7:1-7(8-15) 1 Corinthians 15:50-58 Luke 6:39-49
Last Sunday after Epiphany	99	Exodus 34:29-35 1 Corinthians 12:27-13:13 Luke 9:28-36
Ash Wednesday	103 or 103:8-14	Joel 2:1-2,12-17 or Isaiah 58:1-12 2 Corinthians 5:20b-6:10 Matthew 6:1-6,16-21
First Sunday in Lent	91 or 91:9-15	Deuteronomy 26:(1-4)5-11 Romans 10:(5-8a)8b-13 Luke 4:1-13
Second Sunday in Lent	27 or 27:10-18	Genesis 15:1-12,17-18 Philippians 3:17-4:1 Luke 13:(22-30)31-35
Third Sunday in Lent	103 or 103:1-11	Exodus 3:1-15 1 Corinthians 10:1-13 Luke 13:1-9
Fourth Sunday in Lent	34 or 34:1-8	Joshua (4:19-24);5:9-12 2 Corinthians 5:17-21 Luke 15:11-32
Fifth Sunday in Lent	126	Isaiah 43:16-21 Philippians 3:8-14 Luke 20:9-19

Lectionary C

	Psalm	Lessons
Palm Sunday		
Liturgy of the Palms	118:19-29	Luke 19:29-40
Liturgy of the Word	22:1-21 or 22:1-11	Isaiah 45:21-25 or Isaiah 52:13-53:12 Philippians 2:5-11 Luke (22:39-71) 23:1-49(50-56)
Monday in Holy Week	36:5-10	Isaiah 42:1-9 Hebrews 11:39-12:3 John 12:1-11 or Mark 14:3-9
Tuesday in Holy Week	71:1-12	Isaiah 49:1-6 1 Corinthians 1:18-31 John 12:37-38,42-50 or Mark 11:15-19
Wednesday in Holy Week	69:7-15,22-23	Isaiah 50:4-9a Hebrews 9:11-15,24-28 John 13:21-35 or Matthew 26:1-5,14-25
Maundy Thursday	78:14-20,23-25	Exodus 12:1-14a 1 Corinthians 11:23-26(27-32) John 13:1-15 or Luke 22:14-30
Good Friday	22:1-21 or 22:1-11 or 40:1-14 or 69:1-23	Isaiah 52:13-53:12 or Genesis 22:1-18 or Wisdom 2:1,12-24 Hebrews 10:1-25 John (18:1-40) 19:1-37

Lectionary C

	Psalm	Lessons
Holy Saturday	130 or 31:1-5	Job 14:1-14 1 Peter 4:1-8 Matthew 27:57-66 or John 19:38-42

Easter Day

The Great Vigil	See pages 288-291.

Early Service	Use one of the Old Testament Lessons from the Vigil with

	114	Romans 6:3-11 Matthew 28:1-10
Principal Service	118:14-29 or 118:14-17, 22-24	Acts 10:34-43 or Isaiah 51:9-11 Colossians 3:1-4 or Acts 10:34-43 Luke 24:1-10
Evening Service	114 or 136 or 118:14-17, 22-24	Acts 5:29a,30-32 or Daniel 12:1-3 1 Corinthians 5:6b-8 or Acts 5:29a,30-32 Luke 24:13-35
Monday in Easter Week	16:8-11 or 118:19-24	Acts 2:14,22-32 Matthew 28:9-15
Tuesday in Easter Week	33:18-22 or 118:19-24	Acts 2:36-41 John 20:11-18
Wednesday in Easter Week	105:1-8 or 118:19-24	Acts 3:1-10 Luke 24:13-35
Thursday in Easter Week	8 or 114 or 118:19-24	Acts 3:11-26 Luke 24:36b-48

Lectionary C

	Psalm	Lessons
Friday in Easter Week	116:1-8 or 118:19-24	Acts 4:1-12 John 21:1-14
Saturday in Easter Week	118:14-18 or 118:19-24	Acts 4:13-21 Mark 16:9-15,20
Second Sunday of Easter	111 or 118:19-24	Acts 5:12a, 17-22,25-29 or Job 42:1-6 Revelation 1:(1-8)9-19 or Acts 5:12a,17-22,25-29 John 20:19-31
Third Sunday of Easter	33 or 33:1-11	Acts 9:1-19a or Jeremiah 32:36-41 Revelation 5:6-14 or Acts 9:1-19a John 21:1-14
Fourth Sunday of Easter	100	Acts 13:15-16,26-33(34-39) or Numbers 27:12-23 Revelation 7:9-17 or Acts 13:15-16,26-33(34-39) John 10:22-30
Fifth Sunday of Easter	145 or 145:1-9	Acts 13:44-52 or Leviticus 19:1-2,9-18 Revelation 19:1,4-9 or Acts 13:44-52 John 13:31-35
Sixth Sunday of Easter	67	Acts 14:8-18 or Joel 2:21-27 Revelation 21:22-22:5 or Acts 14:8-18 John 14:23-29

Lectionary C

	Psalm	Lessons
Ascension Day	47 or 110:1-5	Acts 1:1-11 or 2 Kings 2:1-15 Ephesians 1:15-23 or Acts 1:1-11 Luke 24:49-53 or Mark 16:9-15,19-20
Seventh Sunday of Easter	68:1-20 or 47	Acts 16:16-34 or 1 Samuel 12:19-24 Revelation 22:12-14,16-17,20 or Acts 16:16-34 John 17:20-26
Day of Pentecost		

Early or
Vigil Service
	33:12-22
	Canticle 2
	  or 13
	130
	Canticle 9
	104:25-32
		Genesis 11:1-9
		or Exodus 19:1-9,16-20a;
		        20:18-20
		or Ezekiel 37:1-14
		or Joel 2:28-32
		Acts 2:1-11
		or Romans 8:14-17,22-27
		John 7:37-39a

Principal Service	104:25-37 or 104:25-32 or 33:12-15, 18-22	Acts 2:1-11 or Joel 2:28-32 1 Corinthians 12:4-13 or Acts 2:1-11 John 20:19-23 or John 14:8-17

On the weekdays which follow, the numbered Proper which corresponds most closely to the date of Pentecost in that year is used. See page 158 of BCP.

Lectionary C

	Psalms	Lessons
Trinity Sunday	29 or Canticle 2 or 13	Isaiah 6:1-8 Revelation 4:1-11 John 16:(5-11)12-15

On the weekdays which follow, the numbered Proper which corresponds most closely to the date of Trinity Sunday in that year is used.

The Season after Pentecost

Directions for the use of the Propers which follow are on page 158 of BCP.

Proper I Closest to May 11	1	Jeremiah 17:5-10 I Corinthians 15:12-20 Luke 6:17-26
Proper 2 Closest to May 18	37:1-18 or 37:3-10	Genesis 45:3-11,21-28 1 Corinthians 15:35-38,42-50 Luke 6:27-38
Proper 3 Closest to May 25	92 or 92:1-5, 11-14	Jeremiah 7:1-7(8-15) 1 Corinthians 15:50-58 Luke 6:39-49
Proper 4 Closest to June 1	96 or 96:1-9	1 Kings 8:22-23,27-30,41-43 Galatians 1:1-10 Luke 7:1-10
Proper 5 Closest to June 8	30 or 30:1-6,12-13	1 Kings 17:17-24 Galatians 1:11-24 Luke 7:11-17
Proper 6 Closest to June 15	32 or 32:1-8	2 Samuel 11:26-12:10,13-15 Galatians 2:11-21 Luke 7:36-50

Lectionary C

	Psalm	Lessons
Proper 7 Closest to June 22	63:1-8	Zechariah 12:8-10;13:1 Galatians 3:23-29 Luke 9:18-24
Proper 8 Closest to June 29	16 or 16:5-11	1 Kings 19:15-16,19-21 Galatians 5:1,13-25 Luke 9:51-62
Proper 9 Closest to July 6	66 or 66:1-8	Isaiah 66:10-16 Galatians 6:(1-10)14-18 Luke 10:1-12,16-20
Proper 10 Closest to July 13	25 or 25:3-9	Deuteronomy 30:9-14 Colossians 1:1-14 Luke 10:25-37
Proper 11 Closest to July 20	15	Genesis 18:1-10a(10b-14) Colossians 1:21-29 Luke 10:38-42
Proper 12 Closest to July 27	138	Genesis 18:20-33 Colossians 2:6-15 Luke 11:1-13
Proper 13 Closest to August 3	49 or 49:1-11	Ecclesiastes 1:12-14; 2:(1-7,11)18-23 Colossians 3:(5-11)12-17 Luke 12:13-21
Proper 14 Closest to August 10	33 or 33:12-15, 18-22	Genesis 15:1-6 Hebrews 11:1-3(4-7)8-16 Luke 12:32-40
Proper 15 Closest to August 17	82	Jeremiah 23:23-29 Hebrews 12:1-7(8-10)11-14 Luke 12:49-56

Lectionary C

	Psalm	Lessons
Proper 16 Closest to August 24	46	Isaiah 28:14-22 Hebrews 12:18-19,22-29 Luke 13:22-30
Proper 17 Closest to August 31	112	Ecclesiasticus 10:(7-11)12-18 Hebrews 13:1-8 Luke 14:1,7-14
Proper 18 Closest to September 7	1	Deuteronomy 30:15-20 Philemon 1-20 Luke 14:25-33
Proper 19 Closest to September 14	51:1-18 or 51:1-11	Exodus 32:1,7-14 1 Timothy 1:12-17 Luke 15:1-10
Proper 20 Closest to September 21	138	Amos 8:4-7(8-12) 1 Timothy 2:1-8 Luke 16:1-13
Proper 21 Closest to September 28	146 or 146:4-9	Amos 6:1-7 1 Timothy 6:11-19 Luke 16:19-31
Proper 22 Closest to October 5	37:1-18 or 37:3-10	Habakkuk 1:1-6(7-11)12-13; 2:1-4 2 Timothy 1:(1-5)6-14 Luke 17:5-10
Proper 23 Closest to October 12	113	Ruth 1:(1-7)8-19a 2 Timothy 2:(3-7)8-15 Luke 17:11-19
Proper 24 Closest to October 19	121	Genesis 32:3-8,22-30 2 Timothy 3:14-4:5 Luke 18:1-8a

Lectionary C

	Psalm	Lessons
Proper 25 Closest to October 26	84 or 84:1-6	Jeremiah 14:(1-6) 7-10, 19-22 2 Timothy 4:6-8,16-18 Luke 18:9-14
Proper 26 Closest to November 2	32 or 32:1-8	Isaiah 1:10-20 2 Thessalonians 1:1-5(6-10)11-12 Luke 19:1-10
Proper 27 Closest to November 9	17 or 17:1-8	Job 19:23-27a 2 Thessalonians 2:13-3:5 Luke 20:27(28-33)34-38
Proper 28 Closest to November 16	98 or 98:5-10	Malachi 3:13-4:2a,5-6 2 Thessalonians 3:6-13 Luke 21:5-19
Proper 29 Closest to November 23	46	Jeremiah 23:1-6 Colossians 1:11-20 Luke 23:35-43 or Luke 19:29-38

Holy Days

	Psalm	Lessons
St. Andrew November 30	19 or 19:1-6	Deuteronomy 30:11-14 Romans 10:8b-18 Matthew 4:18-22
St. Thomas December 21	126	Habakkuk 2:1-4 Hebrews 10:35 John 20:24-29

Holy Days

	Psalm	Lessons
St. Stephen December 26	31 or 31:1-5	Jeremiah 26:1-9,12-15 Acts 6:8-7:2a,51c-60 Matthew 23:34-39
St. John December 27	92 or 92:1-4,11-14	Exodus 33:18-23 1 John 1:1-9 John 21:19b-24
Holy Innocents December 28	124	Jeremiah 31:15-17 Revelation 21:1-7 Matthew 2:13-18
Confession of St. Peter January 18	23	Acts 4: 8-13 1 Peter 5:1-4 Matthew 16:13-19
Conversion of St. Paul January 25	67	Acts 26:9-21 Galatians 1:11-24 Matthew 10:16-22
The Presentation February 2	84 or 84:1-6	Malachi 3:1-4 Hebrews 2:14-18 Luke 2:22-40
St. Matthias February 24	15	Acts 1:15-26 Philippians 3:13-21 John 15:1,6-16
St. Joseph March 19	89:1-29 or 89:1-4, 26-29	2 Samuel 7:4,8-16 Romans 4:13-18 Luke 2:41-52
The Annunciation March 25	40:1-11 or 40:5-10 or Canticle 3 or 15	Isaiah 7:10-14 Hebrews 10:5-10 Luke 1:26-38

Holy Days

	Psalm	Lessons
St. Mark April 25	2 or 2:7-10	Isaiah 52:7-10 Ephesians 4:7-8,11-16 Mark 1:1-15 or Mark 16:15-20
St. Philip & St. James May 1	119:33-40	Isaiah 30:18-21 2 Corinthians 4:1-6 John 14:6-14
The Visitation May 31	113 or Canticle 9	Zephaniah 3:14-18a Colossians 3:12-17 Luke 1:39-49
St. Barnabas June 11	112	Isaiah 42:5-12 Acts 11:19-30;13:1-3 Matthew 10:7-16
Nativity of St. John the Baptist June 24	85 or 85:7-13	Isaiah 40:1-11 Acts 13:14b-26 Luke 1:57-80
St. Peter & St. Paul June 29	87	Ezekiel 34:11-16 2 Timothy 4:1-8 John 21:15-19
Independence Day July 4	145 or 145:1-9	Deuteronomy 10:17-21 Hebrews 11:8-16 Matthew 5:43-48

The Psalm and Lessons "For the Nation," page 930 of BCP, may he used instead.

	Psalm	Lessons
St. Mary Magdalene July 22	42:1-7	Judith 9:1,11-14 2 Corinthians 5:14-18 John 20:11-18

	Psalm	Lessons
St. James July 25	7:1-10	Jeremiah 45:1-5 Acts 11:27-12:3 Matthew 20:20-28
The Transfiguration August 6	99 or 99:5-9	Exodus 34:29-35 2 Peter 1:13-21 Luke 9:28-36
St. Mary the Virgin August 15	34 or 34:1-9	Isaiah 61:10-11 Galatians 4:4-7 Luke 1:46-55
St. Bartholomew August 24	91 or 91:1-4	Deuteronomy 18:15-18 1 Corinthians 4:9-15 Luke 22:24-30
Holy Cross Day September 14	98 or 98:1-4	Isaiah 45:21-25 Philippians 2:5-11 or Galatians 6:14-18 John 12:31-36a
St. Matthew September 21	119:33-40	Proverbs 3:1-6 2 Timothy 3:14-17 Matthew 9:9-13
St. Michael & All Angels September 29	103 or 103:19-22	Genesis 28:10-17 Revelation 12:7-12 John 1:47-51
St. Luke October 18	147 or 147:1-7	Ecclesiasticus 38:1-4,6-10,12-14 2 Timothy 4:5-13 Luke 4:14-21
St. James of Jerusalem October 23	1	Acts 15:12-22a 1 Corinthians 15:1-11 Matthew 13:54-58

Holy Days

	Psalm	Lessons
St. Simon & St. Jude October 28	119:89-96	Deuteronomy 32:1-4 Ephesians 2:13-22 John 15:17-27
All Saints' Day November 1	149	Ecclesiasticus 44:1-10,13-14 Revelation 7:2-4,9-17 Matthew 5:1-12
or this	149	Ecclesiasticus 2:(1-6), 7-11 Ephesians 1:(11-14), 15-23 Luke 6:20-26(27-36)
Thanksgiving Day	65 or 65:9-14	Deuteronomy 8:1-3, 6-10,(17-20) James 1:17-18,21-27 Matthew 6:25-33

The Common of Saints

	Psalm	Lessons
Of a Martyr I	126 or 121	2 Esdras 2:42-48 1 Peter 3:14-18,22 Matthew 10:16-22
Of a Martyr II	116 or 116:1-8	Ecclesiasticus 51:1-12 Revelation 7:13-17 Luke 12:2-12
Of a Martyr III	124 or 31:1-5	Jeremiah 15:15-21 1 Peter 4:12-19 Mark 8:34-38
Of a Missionary I	96 or 96:1-7	Isaiah 52:7-10 Acts 1:1-9 Luke 10:1-9

	Psalm	Lessons
Of a Missionary II	98 or 98:1-4	Isaiah 49:1-6 Acts 17:22-31 Matthew 28:16-20
Of a Pastor I	23	Ezekiel 34:11-16 1 Peter 5:1-4 John 21:15-17
Of a Pastor II	84 or 84:7-11	Acts 20:17-35 Ephesians 3:14-21 Matthew 24:42-47
Of a Theologian and Teacher I	119:97-104	Wisdom 7:7-14 1 Corinthians 2:6-10,13-16 John 17:18-23
Of a Theologian and Teacher II	119:89-96	Proverbs 3:1-7 1 Corinthians 3:5-11 Matthew 13:47-52
Of a Monastic I	34 or 34:1-8	Song of Songs 8:6-7 Philippians 3:7-15 Luke 12:33-37 or Luke 9:57-62
Of a Monastic II	133 or 119:161-168	Acts 2:42-47a 2 Corinthians 6:1-10 Matthew 6:24-33
Of a Saint I	15	Micah 6:6-8 Hebrews 12:1-2 Matthew 25:31-40
Of a Saint II	34 or 34:15-22	Wisdom 3:1-9 Philippians 4:4-9 Luke 6:17-23

The Common of Saints

	Psalm	Lessons
Of a Saint III	1	Ecclesiasticus 2:7-11 1 Corinthians 1:26-31 Matthew 25:1-13

Various Occasions

		Psalm	Lessons
1.	Of the Holy Trinity	29	Exodus 3:11-15 Romans 11:33-36 Matthew 28:18-20
2.	Of the Holy Spirit	139:1-17 or 139:1-9	Isaiah 61:1-3 1 Corinthians 12:4-14 Luke 11:9-13
3.	Of the Holy Angels	148 or 103:19-22	Daniel 7:9-10a or 2 Kings 6:8-17 Revelation 5:11-14 John 1:47-51
4.	Of the Incarnation	111 or 132:11-19	Isaiah 11:1-10 or Genesis 17:1-8 1 John 4:1-11 or 1 Timothy 3:14-16 Luke 1:26-33(34-38) or Luke 11:27-28
5.	Of the Holy Eucharist	34 or 116:10-17	Deuteronomy 8:2-3 Revelation 19:1-2a,4-9 or 1 Corinthians 10:1-4,16-17 or 1 Corinthians 11:23-29 John 6:47-58

	Psalm	Lessons

6. Of the   40:1-11   Isaiah 52:13-15; 53:10-12
    Holy Cross   or 40:5-11   1 Corinthians 1:18-24
                                  John 12:23-33

7. For All   16:5-11   Jeremiah 17:7-8
    Baptized   or Ezekiel 36:24-28
    Christians   Romans 6:3-11
                                  Mark 10:35-45

8. For the   116   Isaiah 25: 6-9
    Departed   or 103:13-22   or Wisdom 3:1-9
                   or 130   1 Corinthians 15:50-58
                                  John 5:24-27
                                  or John 6:37-40
                                  or John 11:21-27

Any of the Psalms and Lessons appointed at the Burial of the Dead may be used instead.

9. Of the   93   Daniel 7:9-14
    Reign of   or Canticle 18 Colossians 1:11-20
    Christ   John 18:33-37

Any of the Psalms and Lessons appointed in Proper 29 may be used instead.

10. At Baptism   15   Ezekiel 36:24-28 *
                   or 23   Romans 6:3-5
                   or 27   or Romans 8:14-17
                   or 42:1-7   or 2 Corinthians 5:17-20
                   or 84   Mark 1:9-11
                   or Canticle 9 or Mark 10:13-16
                                  or John 3:1-6

* Any of the other Old Testament Lessons for the Easter Vigil may be substituted.

Various Occasions

	Psalm	Lessons
11. At Confirmation	1	Isaiah 61:1-9 or 139:1-9 or Jeremiah 31:31-34 or Ezekiel 37:1-10 Romans 8:18-27 or Romans 12:1-8 or Galatians 5:16-25 or Ephesians 4:7,11-16 Matthew 5:1-12 or Matthew 16:24-27 or Luke 4:16-22 or John 14:15-21
12. Anniversary of the Dedication of a Church	84 or 84:1-6	1 Kings 8:22-30 or Genesis 28:10-17 1 Peter 2:1-5,9-10 Matthew 21:12-16
13. For a Church Convention	19:7-14	Isaiah 55:1-13 2 Corinthians 4:1-10 John 15:1-11
14. For the Unity of the Church	122	Isaiah 35:1-10 Ephesians 4:1-6 John 17:6a,15-23
15. For the Ministry I	99 or 27:1-9	Numbers 11:16-17,24-29 1 Corinthians 3:5-11 John 4:31-38
15. For the Ministry II	63:1-8	1 Samuel 3:1-10 Ephesians 4:11-16 Matthew 9:35-38
15. For the Ministry III	15	Exodus 19:3-8 1 Peter 4:7-11 Matthew 16:24-27

	Psalm	Lessons
16. For the Mission of the Church I	96 or 96:1-7	Isaiah 2:2-4 Ephesians 2:13-22 Luke 10:1-9
16. For the Mission of the Church II	67	Isaiah 49:5-13 Ephesians 3:1-12 Matthew 28:16-20
17. For the Nation	47	Isaiah 26:1-8 Romans 13:1-10 Mark 12:13-17

The Psalm and any of the Lessons appointed for Independence Day may be used instead.

	Psalm	Lessons
18. For Peace	85:7-13	Micah 4:1-5 Ephesians 2:13-18 or Colossians 3:12-15 John 16:23-33 or Matthew 5:43-48
19. For Rogation Days I	147 or 147:1-13	Deuteronomy 11:10-15 or Ezekiel 47:6-12 or Jeremiah 14:1-9 Romans 8:18-25 Mark 4:26-32
19. For Rogation Days II	107:1-9	Ecclesiasticus 38:27-32 1 Corinthians 3:10-14 Matthew 6:19-24
19. For Rogation Days III	104:25-37 or 104:1,13-15, 25-32	Job 38:1-11,16-18 1 Timothy 6:7-10,17-19 Luke 12:13-21

Various Occasions

	Psalm	Lessons
20. For the Sick	13 or 86:1-7	2 Kings 20:1-5 James 5:13-16 Mark 2:1-12

Any of the Psalms and Lessons appointed at the Ministration to the Sick may be used instead.

21. For Social Justice	72 or 72:1-4,12-14	Isaiah 42:1-7 James 2:5-9,12-17 Matthew 10:32-42
22. For Social Service	146 or 22:22-27	Zechariah 8:3-12,16-17 1 Peter 4:7-11 Mark 10:42-52
23. For Education	78:1-7	Deuteronomy 6:4-9,20-25 2 Timothy 3:14-4:5 Matthew 11:25-30
24. For Vocation in Daily Work	8	Ecclesiastes 3:1,9-13 1 Peter 2:11-17 Matthew 6:19-24
25. For Labor Day	107:1-9 or 90:1-2,16-17	Ecclesiasticus 38:27-32 1 Corinthians 3:10-14 Matthew 6:19-24

Daily Office
Lectionary

Concerning the Daily Office Lectionary

The Daily Office Lectionary is arranged in a two-year cycle. Year One begins on the First Sunday of Advent preceding odd-numbered years, and Year Two begins on the First Sunday of Advent preceding even-numbered years. (Thus, on the First Sunday of Advent, 1976, the Lectionary for Year One is begun.)

Three Readings are provided for each Sunday and weekday in each of the two years. Two of the Readings may be used in the morning and one in the evening; or, if the Office is read only once in the day, all three Readings may be used. When the Office is read twice in the day, it is suggested that the Gospel Reading be used in the evening in Year One, and in the morning in Year Two. If two Readings are desired at both Offices, the Old Testament Reading for the alternate year is used as the First Reading at Evening Prayer.

When more than one Reading is used at an Office, the first is always from the Old Testament (or the Apocrypha).

When a Major Feast interrupts the sequence of Readings, they may be re-ordered by lengthening, combining, or omitting some of them, to secure continuity or avoid repetition.

Any Reading may be lengthened at discretion. Suggested lengthenings are shown in parentheses.

In this Lectionary (except in the weeks from 4 Advent to 1 Epiphany, and Palm Sunday to 2 Easter), the Psalms are arranged in a seven-week pattern which recurs throughout the year, except for appropriate variations in Lent and Easter Season.

In the citation of the Psalms, those for the morning are given first, and then those for the evening. At the discretion of the officiant, however, any of the Psalms appointed for a given day may be used in the morning or in the evening. Likewise, Psalms appointed for any day may be used on any other day in the same week, except on major Holy Days.

Brackets and parentheses are used (brackets in the case of whole Psalms, parentheses in the case of verses) to indicate Psalms and verses of Psalms which may be omitted. In some instances, the entire portion of the Psalter assigned to a given Office has been bracketed, and alternative Psalmody provided. Those who desire to recite the Psalter in its entirety should, in each instance, use the bracketed Psalms rather than the alternatives.

Antiphons drawn from the Psalms themselves, or from the opening sentences given in the Offices, or from other passages of Scripture, may be used with the Psalms and biblical Canticles. The antiphons may be sung or said at the beginning and end of each Psalm or Canticle, or may be used as refrains after each verse or group of verses.

On Special Occasions, the officiant may select suitable Psalms and Readings.

Week of 1 Advent

Sunday	146, 147	-:-	111, 112, 113
	Isa. 1:1-9	2 Pet. 3:1-10	Matt. 25:1-18

Monday	1, 2, 3	-:-	4, 7
	Isa. 1:10-20	1 Thess. 1:1-10	Luke 20:1-8

Tuesday	5, 6	-:-	10, 11
	Isa. 1:21-31	1 Thess. 2:1-12	Luke 20:9-18

Wednesday	119:1-24	-:-	12, 13, 14
	Isa. 2:1-11	1 Thess. 2:13-20	Luke 20:19-26

Thursday	18:1-20	-:-	18:21-50
	Isa. 2:12-22	1 Thess. 3:1-13	Luke 20:27-40

Friday	16, 17	-:-	22
	Isa. 3:8-15	I Thess. 4:1-12	Luke 20:41-21:4

Saturday	20, 21:1-7(8-13)	-:-	110:5(6-7), 116, 117
	Isa. 4:2-6	1 Thess. 4:13-18	Luke 21:5-19

Week of 2 Advent

Sunday	148, 149, 150	-:-	114, 115
	Isa. 5:1-7	2 Pet. 3:11-18	Luke 7:28-35

Monday	25	-:-	9, 15
	Isa. 5:8-12, 18-23	1 Thess. 5:1-11	Luke 21:20-28

Tuesday	26, 28	-:-	36, 39
	Isa. 5:18-17, 24-25	1 Thess. 5:12-28	Luke 21:29-38

Wednesday	38	-:-	119:25-48
	Isa. 6:1-13	2 Thess. 1:1-12	John 7:53-8:11

Thursday	37:1-18	-:-	37:19-42
	Isa. 7:1-9	2 Thess. 2:1-12	Luke 22:1-13

Friday	31	-:-	35
	Isa. 7:10-25	2 Thess. 2:13-3:5	Luke 22:14-30

Saturday	30, 32	-:-	42, 43
	Isa. 8:1-15	2 Thess. 3:6-18	Luke 22:31-38

Daily Office Year One

Week of 1 Advent

Sunday	146, 147	-:- 111, 112, 113	
	Amos 1:1-5,13-2:8	1 Thess. 5:1-11	Luke 21:5-19

Monday	1, 2, 3	-:- 4, 7	
	Amos 2:6-16	2 Pet. 1:1-11	Matt. 21:1-11

Tuesday	5, 6	-:- 10, 11	
	Amos 3:1-11	2 Pet. 1:12-21	Matt. 21:12-22

Wednesday	119:1-24	-:- 12, 13, 14	
	Amos 3:12--4:5	2 Pet. 3:1-10	Matt. 21:23-32

Thursday	18:1-20	-:- 18:21-50	
	Amos 4:6-13	2 Pet. 3:11-18	Matt. 21:33-46

Friday	16, 17	-:- 22	
	Amos 5:1-17	Jude 1-16	Matt. 22:1-14

Saturday	20,21:1-7(8-13)	-:- 110:1-5(6-7), 116, 117	
	Amos 5:18-27	Jude 17-25	Matt. 22:15-22

Week of 2 Advent

Sunday	148, 149, 150	-:- 114, 115	
	Amos 6:1-14	2 Thess. 1:5-12	Luke 1:57-68

Monday	25	-:- 9, 15	
	Amos 7:1-9	Rev. 1:1-8	Matt. 22:23-33

Tuesday	26, 28	-:- 36, 39	
	Amos 7:10-17	Rev. 1:9-16	Matt. 22:34-46

Wednesday	38	-:- 119:25-48	
	Amos 8:1-14	Rev. 1:17-2:7	Matt. 23:1-12

Thursday	37:1-18	-:- 37:19-42	
	Amos 9:1-10	Rev. 2:8-17	Matt. 23:13-26

Friday	31	-:- 35	
	Haggai 1:1-15	Rev. 2:18-29	Matt. 23:27-39

Saturday	30, 32	-:- 42, 43	
	Haggai 2:1-9	Rev. 3:1-6	Matt. 24:1-14

Daily Office Year Two

Week of 3 Advent

Sunday	63:1-8(9-11),98	-:-	103
	Isa. 13:6-13	Heb. 12:18-29	John 3:22-30
Monday	41, 52	-:-	44
	Isa. 8:16-9:1	2 Pet. 1:1-11	Luke 22:39-53
Tuesday	45	-:-	47, 48
	Isa. 9:1-7	2 Pet. 1:12-21	Luke 22:54-69
Wednesday	119:49-72	-:-	49, [53]
	Isa. 9:8-17	2 Pet. 2:1-10a	Mark 1:1-8
Thursday	50	-:-	[59, 60] or 33
	Isa. 9:18-10:4	2 Pet. 2:10b-16	Matt. 3:1-12
Friday	40, 54	-:-	51
	Isa. 10:5-19	2 Pet. 2:17-22	Matt. 11:2-15
Saturday	55	-:-	138, 139:1-17(18-23)
	Isa. 10:20-27	Jude 17-25	Luke 3:1-9

Week of 4 Advent

Sunday	24, 29	-:-	8, 84
	Isa. 42:1-12	Eph. 6:10-20	John 3:16-21
Monday	61, 62	-:-	112, 115
	Isa. 11:1-9	Rev. 20:1-10	John 5:30-47
Tuesday	66, 67	-:-	116, 117
	Isa. 11:10-16	Rev. 20:11-21:8	Luke 1:5-25
Wednesday	72	-:-	111, 113
	Isa. 28:9-22	Rev. 21:9-21	Luke 1:26-38
Thursday	80	-:-	146, 147
	Isa. 29:13-24	Rev. 21:22--22:5	Luke 1:39- 48a
			(48b-56)
Friday	93, 96	-:-	148, 150
	Isa. 33:17-22	Rev. 22:6-11, 18-20	Luke 1:57-66
Dec. 24	45, 46	-:-	------
	Isa. 35:1-10	Rev. 22:12-17, 21	Luke 1:67-80
Christmas	--------	-:-	89:1-29
Eve	Isa. 59:15b-21	Phil. 2:5-11	

Daily Office Year One

Week of 3 Advent

Sunday	63:1-8(9-11), 98	-:-	103
	Amos 9:11-15	2 Thess. 2:1-3,13-17	John 5:30-47
Monday	41, 52	-:-	44
	Zech. 1:7-17	Rev. 3:7-13	Matt. 24:15-31
Tuesday	45	-:-	47, 48
	Zech. 2:1-13	Rev. 3:14-22	Matt. 24:32-44
Wednesday	119:49-72	-:-	49, [53]
	Zech. 3:1-10	Rev. 4:1-8	Matt. 24:45-51
Thursday	50	-:-	[59, 60] or 33
	Zech. 4:1-14	Rev. 4:9--5:5	Matt. 25:1-13
Friday	40, 54	-:-	51
	Zech. 7:8--8:8	Rev. 5:6-14	Matt. 25:14-30
Saturday	55	-:-	138,139:1-17(18-23)
	Zech. 8:9-17	Rev. 6:1-17	Matt. 25:31-46

Week of 4 Advent

Sunday	24, 29	-:-	8, 84
	Gen. 3:8-15	Rev. 12:1-10	John 3:16-21
Monday	61, 62	-:-	112, 115
	Zeph. 3:14-20	Titus 1:1-16	Luke 1:1-25
Tuesday	66, 67	-:-	116, 117
	1 Samuel 2:1b-10	Titus 2:1-10	Luke 1:26-38
Wednesday	72	-:-	111, 113
	2 Samuel 7:1-17	Titus 2:11-3:8a	Luke 1:39-48a, (48b-56)
Thursday	80	-:-	146, 147
	2 Samuel 7:18-29	Gal. 3:1-14	Luke 1:57-66
Friday	93, 96	-:-	148,150
	Baruch 4:21-29	Gal. 3:15-22	Luke 1:67-80 or Matt. 1:1-17
Dec. 24	45, 46	-:-	---------
	Baruch 4:36-5:9	Gal. 3:23--4:7	Matt. 1:18-25
Christmas Eve	-------	-:-	89:1-29
	Isa. 59:15b-21	Phil. 2:5-11	

Daily Office Year Two

Christmas Day and Following

Christmas	2, 85	-:-	110:1-5(6-7),132
Day	Zech. 2:10-13	1 John 4:7-16	John 3:31-36

First Sunday after Christmas	93, 96 -:-	34
	Isa. 62:6-7,10-12	Heb. 2:10-18	Matt. 1:18-25

Dec. 29	18:1-20	-:-	18:21-50 *
	Isa. 12:1-6	Rev. 1:1-8	John 7:37-52

Dec. 30	20,21:1-7(8-13)	-:-	23,27
	Isa. 25:1-9	Rev. 1:9-20	John 7:53--8:11

Dec. 31	46, 48	-:-	---------
	Isa. 26:1-9	2 Cor. 5:16--6:2	John 8:12-19

Eve of Holy Name	---------	-:-	90
	Isa. 65:15b-25	Rev. 21:1-6	

Holy Name	103	-:-	148
	Gen. 17:1-12a, 15-16	Col. 2:6-12	John 16:23b-30

Second Sunday after Christmas	66, 67 -:-	145
	Ecclus. 3:3-9, 14-17	1 John 2:12-17	John 6:41-47

Jan. 2	34	-:-	33
	Gen. 12:1-7	Heb. 11:1-12	John 6:35-42, 48-51

Jan. 3	68	-:-	72 **
	Gen.28:10-22	Heb. 11:13-22	John 10:7-17

Jan. 4	85, 8 7	-:-	89:1-29
	Exod. 3:1-12	Heb. 11:23-31	John 14:6-14

Jan. 5	2, 110:1-5(6-7)	ù:-	---------
	Joshua 1:1-9	Heb. 11:32--12:2	John 15:1-16

Eve of Epiphany	------	-:-	29, 98
	Isa. 66:18-23	Rom. 15:7-13	

* If today is Saturday, use Psalms 23 and 27 at Evening Prayer.
** If today is Saturday, use Psalm 136 at Evening Prayer.

Daily Office Year One

Christmas Day and Following

Christmas Day   2, 85   -:-   110:1-5(6-7),132
          Micah 4:1-5; 5:2-4   1 John 4:7-16   John 3:31-36

First Sunday after Christmas   93, 96   -:-   34
          1 Samuel 1:1-2, 7b-28   Col. 1:9-20   Luke 2:22-40

Dec. 29   18:1-20   -:-   18:21-50 *
          2 Samuel 23:13-17b   2 John 1-13   John 2:1-11

Dec. 30   20,21:1-7(8-13)   -:-   23,27
          1 Kings 17:17-24   3 John 1-15   John 4:46-54

Dec. 31   46, 48   -:-   ---------
          1 Kings 3:5-14   James 4:13-17; 5:7-11   John 5:1-15

Eve of Holy Name ---------   -:-   90
          Isa. 65:15b-25   Rev. 21:1-6

Holy Name   103   -:-   148
          Isa. 62:1-5,10-12   Rev. 19:11-16   Matt. 1:18-25

Second Sunday after Christmas   66, 67   -:-   145
          Wisdom 7:3-14   Col. 3:12-17   John 6:41-47

Jan. 2   34   -:-   33
          1 Kings 19:1-8   Eph. 4:1-16   John 6:1-14

Jan. 3   68   -:-   72 **
          1 Kings 19:9-18   Eph. 4:17-32   John 6:15-27

Jan. 4   85, 87   -:-   89:1-29 **
          Joshua 3:14 4:7   Eph. 5:1-20   John 9:1-12, 35-38

Jan. 5   2,110:1-5(6-7)   -:-   ----------
          Jonah 2:2-9   Eph. 6:10-20   John 11:17-27,38-44

Eve of Epiphany --------   -:-   29, 98
          Isa. 66:18-23   Rom. 15:7-13

* If today is Saturday, use Psalms 23 and 27 at Evening Prayer.
** If today is Saturday, use Psalm 136 at Evening Prayer.

Daily Office Year Two

The Epiphany and Following

```
Epiphany      46, 97               -:-           96, 100
              Isa. 52:7-10   Rev. 21:22-27   Matt. 12:14-21

Jan. 7 *      103                  -:-           114,115
              Isa. 52:3-6    Rev. 2:1-7      John 2:1-11

Jan. 8        117, 118             -:-           112, 113
              Isa. 59:15-21  Rev. 2:8-17     John 4:46-54

Jan. 9        121,122, 123         -:-           131, 132
              Isa. 63:1-5    Rev. 2:18-29    John 5:1-15

Jan. 10       138,139:1-17(18-23)  -:-           147
              Isa. 65:1-9    Rev. 3:1-6      John 6:1-14

Jan. 11       148,150              -:-           91, 92
              Isa. 65:13-16  Rev. 3:7-13     John 6:15-27

Jan. 12       98, 99, [100]        -:-           --------
              Isa. 66:1-2, 22-23  Rev. 3:14-22  John 9:1-12, 35-38

Eve of 1 Epiphany  ---------       -:-           104
              Isa. 61:1-9    Gal. 3:23-29; 4:4-7
```

Week of 1 Epiphany

```
Sunday        146,147              -:-           111, 112, 113
              Isa. 40:1-11   Heb. 1:1-12    John 1:1-7, 19-20, 29-34

Monday        1, 2, 3              -:-           4, 7
              Isa. 40:12-23  Eph. 1:1-14    Mark 1:1-13

Tuesday       5, 6                 -:-           10,11
              Isa. 40:25-31  Eph. 1:15-23   Mark 1:14-28

Wednesday     119:1-24             -:-           12,13,14
              Isa. 41:1-16   Eph. 2:1-10    Mark 1:29-45

Thursday      18:1-20              -:-           18:21-50
              Isa. 41:17-29  Eph. 2:11-22   Mark 2:1-12

Friday        16, 17               -:-           22
              Isa. 42:(1-9)10-17   Eph. 3:1-13  Mark 2:13-22

Saturday      20,21:1-7(8-13)      -:-           110:1-5(6-7),116,117
              Isa. 43:1-13   Eph. 3:14-21   Mark 2:23-3:6
```

* The Psalms and Readings for the dated days after the Epiphany
are used only until the following Saturday evening.

Daily Office Year One

The Epiphany and Following

Epiphany	46, 97	-:-	96, 100
	Isa. 49:1-7	Rev. 21:22-27	Matt. 12:14-21
Jan. 7 *	103	-:-	114, 115
	Deut. 8:1-3	Col. 1:1-14	John 6:30-33, 48-51
Jan. 8	117, 118	-:-	112, 113
	Exod. 17:1-7	Col. 1:15-23	John 7:37-52
Jan. 9	121, 122, 123	-:-	131,132
	Isa. 45:14-19	Col. 1:24--2:7	John 8:12-19
Jan. 10	138, 139:1-17(18-23) -:-		147
	Jer. 23:1-8	Col. 2:8-23	John 10:7-17
Jan. 11	148, 150	-:-	91, 92
	Isa. 55:3-9	Col. 3:1-17	John 14:6-14
Jan. 12	98, 99, [100]	-:-	---------
	Gen. 49:1-2, 8-12	Col. 3:18--4:6	John 15:1-16
Eve of 1 Epiphany	--------	-:-	104
	Isa. 61:1-9	Gal. 3:23-29; 4:4-7	

Week of 1 Epiphany

Sunday	146, 147	-:-	111, 112, 113
	Gen. 1:1--2:3	Eph. 1:3-14	John 1:29-34
Monday	1, 2, 3	-:-	4, 7
	Gen. 2:4-9(10-15)16-25	Heb. 1:1-14	John 1:1-18
Tuesday	5, 6	-:-	10, 11
	Gen. 3:1-24	Heb. 2:1-10	John 1:19-28
Wednesday	119:1-24	-:-	12, 13, 14
	Gen. 4:1-16	Heb. 2:11-18	John 1:(29-34)35-42
Thursday	18:1-20	-:-	18:21-50
	Gen. 4:17-26	Heb. 3:1-11	John 1:43-51
Friday	16, 17	-:-	22
	Gen. 6:1-8	Heb. 3:12-19	John 2:1-12
Saturday	20, 21:1-7(8-13)	-:-	110:1-5(6-7),116,117
	Gen. 6:9-22	Heb. 4:1-13	John 2:13-22

* The Psalms and Readings for the dated days after the Epiphany are used only until the following Saturday evening.

Daily Office Year Two

Week of 2 Epiphany

Sunday	148, 149, 150	-:-	114, 115
	Isa. 43:14-44:5	Heb. 6:17-7:10	John 4:27-42
Monday	25	-:-	9, 15
	Isa. 44:6-8, 21-23	Eph. 4:1-16	Mark 3:7-19a
Tuesday	26, 28	-:-	36, 39
	Isa. 44:9-20	Eph. 4:17-32	Mark 3:19b-35
Wednesday	38	-:-	119:25-48
	Isa. 44:24-45:7	Eph. 5:1-14	Mark 4:1-20
Thursday	37:1-18	-:-	37:19-42
	Isa. 45:5-17	Eph. 5:15-33	Mark 4:21-34
Friday	31	-:-	35
	Isa. 45:18-25	Eph. 6:1-9	Mark 4:35-41
Saturday	30, 32	-:-	42, 43
	Isa. 46:1-13	Eph. 6:10-24	Mark 5:1-20

Week of 3 Epiphany

Sunday	63:1-8(9-11), 98	-:-	103
	Isa. 47:1-15	Heb. 10:19-31	John 5:2-18
Monday	41, 52	-:-	44
	Isa. 48:1-11	Gal. 1:1-17	Mark 5:21-43
Tuesday	45	-:-	47, 48
	Isa. 48:12-21	Gal. 1:18--2:10	Mark 6:1-13
Wednesday	119:49-72	-:-	49, [53]
	Isa. 49:1-12	Gal. 2:11-21	Mark 6:13-29
Thursday	50	-:-	[59,60] or 118
	Isa. 49:13-23	Gal. 3:1-14	Mark 6:30-46
Friday	40, 54	-:-	51
	Isa. 50:1-11	Gal. 3:15-22	Mark 6:47-56
Saturday	55	-:-	138, 139:1-17(18-23)
	Isa. 51:1-8	Gal. 3:23-29	Mark 7:1-23

Daily Office Year One

Week of 2 Epiphany

Sunday	148,149,150 Gen. 7:1-10,17-23	-:- Eph. 4:1-16	114, 115 Mark 3:7-19
Monday	25 Gen. 8:6-22	-:- Heb. 4:14-5:6	9, 15 John 2:23--3:15
Tuesday	26, 28 Gen. 9:1-17	-:- Heb. 5:7-14	36, 39 John 3:16-21
Wednesday	38 Gen. 9:18-29	-:- Heb. 6:1-12	119:25-48 John 3:22-36
Thursday	37:1-18 Gen. 11:1-9	-:- Heb. 6:13-20	37:19-42 John 4:1-15
Friday	31 Gen. 11:27-12:8	-:- Heb. 7:1-17	35 John 4:16-26
Saturday	30, 32 Gen. 12:9-13:1	-:- Heb. 7:18-28	42, 43 John 4:27-42

Week of 3 Epiphany

Sunday	63:1-8(9-11), 98 Gen. 13:2-18	-:- Gal. 2:1-10	103 Mark 7:31-37
Monday	41, 52 Gen. 14(1-7)8-24	-:- Heb.8:1-13	44 John 4:43-54
Tuesday	45 Gen. 15:1-11, 17-21	-:- Heb. 9:1-14	47, 48 John 5:1-18
Wednesday	119:49-72 Gen. 16:1-14	-:- Heb. 9:15-28	49, [53] John 5:19-29
Thursday	50 Gen. 16:15-17:14	-:- Heb. 10:1-10	[59, 60] or 118 John 5:30-47
Friday	40, 54 Gen. 17:15-27	-:- Heb. 10:11-25	51 John 6:1-15
Saturday	55 Gen. 18:1-16	-:- Heb. 10:26-39	138,139:1-17(18-23) John 6:16-27

Daily Office Year Two

Week of 4 Epiphany

Sunday	24, 29	-:-	8, 84
	Isa. 51:9-16	Heb. 11:8-16	John 7:14-31
Monday	56,57, [58]	-:-	64, 65
	Isa. 51:17-23	Gal. 4:1-11	Mark 7:24-37
Tuesday	61, 62	-:-	68:1-20(21-23)24-36
	Isa. 52:1-12	Gal. 4:12-20	Mark 8:1-10
Wednesday	72	-:-	119:73-96
	Isa. 54:1-10(11-17)	Gal. 4:21-31	Mark 8:11-26
Thursday	[70], 71	-:-	74
	Isa. 55:1-13	Gal. 5:1-15	Mark 8:27-9:1
Friday	69:1-23(24-30)31-38	-:-	73
	Isa. 56:1-8	Gal. 5:16-24	Mark 9:2-13
Saturday	75, 76	-:-	23, 27
	Isa. 57:3-13	Gal. 5:25--6:10	Mark 9:14-29

Week of 5 Epiphany

Sunday	93, 96	-:-	34
	Isa. 57:14-21	Heb. 12:1-6	John 7:37-46
Monday	80	-:-	77, [79]
	Isa. 58:1-12	Gal. 6:11-18	Mark 9:30-41
Tuesday	78:1-39	-:-	78:40-72
	Isa. 59:1-15a	2 Tim. 1:1-14	Mark 9:42-50
Wednesday	119:97-120	-:-	81, 82
	Isa. 59:15b-21	2 Tim. 1:15-2:13	Mark 10:1-16
Thursday	[83] or 146, 147	-:-	85, 86
	Isa. 60:1-17	2 Tim. 2:14-26	Mark 10:17-31
Friday	88	-:-	91, 92
	Isa. 61:1-9	2 Tim.3:1-17	Mark 10:32-45
Saturday	87, 90	-:-	136
	Isa. 61:10-62:5	2 Tim. 4:1-8	Mark 10:46-52

Daily Office Year One

Week of 4 Epiphany

Sunday	24, 29	-:-	8, 84
	Gen. 18:16-33	Gal. 5:13-25	Mark 8:22-30

Monday	56,57, [58]	-:-	64, 65
	Gen. 19:1-17(18-23)24-29	Heb. 11:1-12	John 6:27-40

Tuesday	61, 62	-:-	68:1-20(21-23)24-36
	Gen. 21:1-21	Heb. 11:13-22	John 6:41-51

Wednesday	72	-:-	119:73-96
	Gen. 22:1-18	Heb. 11:23-31	John 6:52-59

Thursday	[70], 71	-:-	74
	Gen. 23:1-20	Heb. 11:32-12:2	John 6:60-71

Friday	69:1-23(24-30)31-38	-:-	73
	Gen. 24:1-27	Heb. 12:3-11	John 7:1-13

Saturday	75, 76	-:-	23, 27
	Gen. 24:28-38, 49-51	Heb. 12:12-29	John 7:14-36

Week of 5 Epiphany

Sunday	93, 96	-:-	34
	Gen. 24:50-67	2 Tim. 2:14-21	Mark 10:13-22

Monday	80	-:-	77, [79]
	Gen. 25:19-34	Heb. 13:1-16	John 7:37-52

Tuesday	78:1-39	-:-	78:40-72
	Gen. 26:1-6,12-33	Heb. 13:17-25	John 7:53-8:11

Wednesday	119:97-120	-:-	81, 82
	Gen. 27:1-29	Rom. 12:1-8	John 8:12-20

Thursday	[83] or 146,147	-:-	85, 86
	Gen. 27:30-45	Rom. 12:9-21	John 8:21-32

Friday	88	-:-	91, 92
	Gen. 27:46-28:4,10-22	Rom. 13:1-14	John 8:33-47

Saturday	87, 90	-:-	136
	Gen. 29:1-20	Rom. 14:1-23	John 8:47-59

Daily Office Year Two

Week of 6 Epiphany

Sunday	66, 67	-:-	19, 46
	Isa. 62:6-12	1 John 2:3-11	John 8:12-19

Monday	89:1-18	-:-	89:19-52
	Isa. 63:1-6	1 Tim. 1:1-17	Mark 11

Tuesday	97, 99, [100]	-:-	94, [95]
	Isa. 63:7-14	1 Tim. 1:18-2:8	Mark 11:12-26

Wednesday	101, 109:1-4(5-19)20-30	-:-	119:121-144
	Isa. 63:15-64:9	1 Tim. 3:1-16	Mark 11:27--12:12

Thursday	105:1-22	-:-	105:23-45
	Isa. 65:1-12	1 Tim. 4:1-16	Mark 12:13-27

Friday	102	-:-	107:1-32
	Isa. 65:17-25	1 Tim 5:17-22(23-25)	Mark 12:28-34

Saturday	107:33-43, 108:1-6(7-13)	-:-	33
	Isa. 66:1-6	1 Tim. 6:6-21	Mark 12:35-44

Week of 7 Epiphany

Sunday	118	-:-	145
	Isa. 66:7-14	1 John 3:4-10	John 10:7-16

Monday	106:1-18	-:-	106:19-48
	Ruth 1:1-14	2 Cor. 1:1-11	Matt. 5:1-12

Tuesday	[120],121,122,123	-:-	124,125,126, [127]
	Ruth 1:15-22	2 Cor. 1:12-22	Matt. 5:13-20

Wednesday	119:145-176	-:-	128,129, 130
	Ruth 2:1-13	2 Cor. 1:23-2:17	Matt. 5:21-26

Thursday	131,132, [133]	-:-	134,135
	Ruth 2:14-23	2 Cor. 3:1-18	Matt. 5:27-37

Friday	140,142	-:-	141,143:1-11(12)
	Ruth 3:1-18	2 Cor. 4:1-12	Matt. 5:38-48

Saturday	137:1-6(7-9), 144	-:-	104
	Ruth 4:1-17	2 Cor. 4:13-5:10	Matt. 6:1-6

Daily Office Year One

Week of 6 Epiphany

| Sunday | 66, 67
Gen. 29:20-35 | -:-
1 Tim. 3:14-4:10 | 19, 46
Mark 10:23-31 |

Sunday   66, 67   -:-   19, 46

Sunday   66, 67   -:-   19, 46
           Gen. 29:20-35   1 Tim. 3:14-4:10   Mark 10:23-31

Monday   89:1-18   -:-   89:19-52
           Gen. 30:1-24   1 John 1:1-10   John 9:1-17

Tuesday   97, 99, [100]   -:-   94, [95]
           Gen. 31:1-24   1 John 2:1-11   John 9:18-41

Wednesday 101,109:1-4(5-19)20-30 -:-   119:121-144
           Gen. 31:25-50   1 John 2:12-17   John 10:1-18

Thursday   105:1-22   -:-   105:23-45
           Gen. 32:3-21   1 John 2:18-29   John 10:19-30

Friday   102   -:-   107:1-32
           Gen. 32:22-33:17   1 John 3:1-10   John 10:31-42

Saturday   107:33-43,108:1-6(7-13)   -:-   33
           Gen. 35:1-20   1 John 3:11-18   John 11:1-16

Week of 7 Epiphany

Sunday   118   -:-   145
           Prov. 1:20-33   2 Cor. 5:11-21   Mark 10:35-45

Monday   106:1-18   -:-   106:19-48
           Prov. 3:11-20   1 John 3:18-4:6   John 11:17-29

Tuesday   [120],121,122,123   -:-   124,125,126, [127]
           Prov. 4:1-27   1 John 4:7-21   John 11:30-44

Wednesday 119:145-176   -:-   128,129,130
           Prov. 6:1-19   1 John 5:1-12   John 11:45-54

Thursday   131,132, [133]   -:-   134,135
           Prov. 7:1-27   1 John 5:13-21   John 11:55--12:8

Friday   140,142   -:-   141,143:1-11(12)
           Prov. 8:1-21   Philemon 1-25   John 12:9-19

Saturday   137:1-6(7-9),144   -:-   104
           Prov. 8:22-36   2 Tim. 1:1-14   John 12:20-26

Daily Office Year Two

Week of 8 Epiphany

| Sunday | 146, 147 | -:- | 111, 112, 113 |
| | Deut. 4:1-9 | 2 Tim. 4:1-8 | John 12:1-8 |

| Monday | 1, 2, 3 | -:- | 4, 7 |
| | Deut. 4:9-14 | 2 Cor. 10:1-18 | Matt.6:7-15 |

| Tuesday | 5, 6 | -:- | 10,11 |
| | Deut. 4:15-24 | 2 Cor. 11:1-21a | Matt. 6:16-23 |

| Wednesday | 119:1-24 | -:- | 12,13,14 |
| | Deut. 4:25-31 | 2 Cor. 11:21b-33 | Matt. 6:24-34 |

| Thursday | 18:1-20 | -:- | 18:21-50 |
| | Deut. 4:32-40 | 2 Cor. 12:1-10 | Matt. 7:1-12 |

| Friday | 16,17 | -:- | 22 |
| | Deut. 5:1-22 | 2 Cor. 12:11-21 | Matt. 7:13-21 |

| Saturday | 20,21:1-7(8-13) | -:- | 110:1-5(6-7), 116, 117 |
| | Deut. 5:22-33 | 2 Cor. 13:1-14 | Matt. 7:22-29 |

Week of Last Epiphany

| Sunday | 148, 149, 150 | -:- | 114, 115 |
| | Deut. 6:1-9 | Heb. 12:18-29 | John 12:24-32 |

| Monday | 25 | -:- | 9, 15 |
| | Deut. 6:10-15 | Heb. 1:1-14 | John 1:1-18 |

| Tuesday | 26, 28 | -:- | 36, 39 |
| | Deut. 6:16-25 | Heb. 2:1-10 | John 1:19-28 |

| Ash Wednesday | 95* & 32, 143 | -:- | 102, 130 |
| | Jonah 3:1-4:11 | Heb. 12:1-14 | Luke 18:9-14 |

| Thursday | 37:1-18 | -:- | 37:19-42 |
| | Deut. 7:6-11 | Titus 1:1-16 | John 1:29-34 |

| Friday | 95* & 31 | -:- | 35 |
| | Deut. 7:12-16 | Titus 2:1-15 | John 1:35-42 |

| Saturday | 30, 32 | -:- | 42, 43 |
| | Deut. 7:17-26 | Titus 3:1-15 | John 1:43-51 |

* For the Invitatory

Daily Office Year One

Week of 8 Epiphany

Sunday	146, 147	-:-	111, 112, 113
	Prov. 9:1-12	2 Cor. 9:6b-15	Mark 10:46-52
Monday	1, 2, 3	-:-	4, 7
	Prov. 10:1-12	2 Tim. 1:15-2:13	John 12:27-36a
Tuesday	5, 6	-:-	10,11
	Prov. 15:16-33	2 Tim. 2:14-26	John 12:36b-50
Wednesday	119:1-24	-:-	12,13,14
	Prov. 17:1-20	2 Tim. 3:1-17	John 13:1-20
Thursday	18:1-20	-:-	18:21-50
	Prov. 21:30-22:6	2 Tim. 4:1-8	John 13:21-30
Friday	16,17	-:-	22
	Prov. 23:19-21, 29-24:2	2 Tim. 4:9-22	John 13:31-38
Saturday	20,21:1-7(8-13)	-:-	110:1-5(6-7), 116, 117
	Prov. 25:15-28	Phil. 1:1-11	John 18:1-14

Week of Last Epiphany

Sunday	148, 149, 150	-:-	114, 115
	Ecclus. 48:1-11	2 Cor. 3:7-18	Luke 9:18-27
Monday	25	-:-	9, 15
	Prov. 27:1-6, 10-12	Phil. 2:1-13	John 18:15-18, 25-27
Tuesday	26, 28	-:-	36, 39
	Prov. 30:1-4, 24-33	Phil. 3:1-11	John 18:28-38
Ash Wednesday	95* & 32, 143	-:-	102, 130
	Amos 5:6-15	Heb. 12:1-14	Luke 18:9-14
Thursday	37:1-18	-:-	37:19-42
	Hab. 3:1-10(11-15)16-18	Phil. 3:12-21	John 17:1-8
Friday	95* & 31	-:-	35
	Ezek. 18:1-4, 25-32	Phil. 4:1-9	John 17:9-19
Saturday	30, 32	-:-	42, 43
	Ezek. 39:21-29	Phil. 4:10-20	John 17:20-26

* For the Invitatory

Daily Office Year Two

Week of 1 Lent

Sunday	63:1-8(9-11), 98	-:-	103
	Deut. 8:1-10	1 Cor. 1:17-31	Mark 2:18-22
Monday	41, 52	-:-	44
	Deut. 8:11-20	Heb. 2:11-18	John 2:1-12
Tuesday	45	-:-	47, 48
	Deut. 9:4-12	Heb. 3:1-11	John 2:13-22
Wednesday	119:49-72	-:-	49, [53]
	Deut. 9:13-21	Heb. 3:12-19	John 2:23-3:15
Thursday	50	-:-	[59, 60] or 19, 46
	Deut. 9:23-10:5	Heb. 4:1-10	John 3:16-21
Friday	95* & 40, 54	-:-	51
	Deut. 10:12-22	Heb. 4:11-16	John 3:22-36
Saturday	55	-:-	138, 139:1-17(18-23)
	Deut. 11:18-28	Heb. 5:1-10	John 4:1-26

Week of 2 Lent

Sunday	24, 29	-:-	8, 84
	Jer. 1:1-10	1 Cor. 3:11-23	Mark 3:31-4:9
Monday	56, 57, [58]	-:-	64, 65
	Jer. 1:11-19	Rom. 1:1-15	John 4:27-42
Tuesday	61, 62	-:-	68:1-20(21-23)24-36
	Jer. 2:1-13	Rom. 1:16-25	John 4:43-54
Wednesday	72	-:-	119:73-96
	Jer. 3:6-18	Rom. 1:28-2:11	John 5:1-18
Thursday	[70], 71	-:-	74
	Jer. 4:9-10,19-28	Rom. 2:12-24	John 5:19-29
Friday	95* & 69:1-23(24-30)31-38	-:-	73
	Jer. 5:1-9	Rom. 2:25-3:18	John 5:30-47
Saturday	75, 76	-:-	23, 27
	Jer. 5:20-31	Rom. 3:19-31	John 7:1-13

* For the Invitatory

Daily Office Year One

Week of 1 Lent

| Sunday | 63:1-8(9-11), 98 | -:- | 103 |
| | Dan. 9:3-10 | Heb. 2:10-18 | John 12:44-50 |

| Monday | 41, 52 | -:- | 44 |
| | Gen. 37:1-11 | 1 Cor. 1:1-19 | Mark 1:1-13 |

| Tuesday | 45 | -:- | 47, 48 |
| | Gen. 37:12-24 | 1 Cor. 1:20-31 | Mark 1:14-28 |

| Wednesday | 119:49-72 | -:- | 49, [53] |
| | Gen. 37:25-36 | 1 Cor. 2:1-13 | Mark 1:29-45 |

| Thursday | 50 | -:- | [59, 60] or 19, 46 |
| | Gen. 39:1-23 | 1 Cor. 2:14-3:15 | Mark 2:1-12 |

| Friday | 95* & 40, 54 | -:- | 51 |
| | Gen. 40:1-23 | 1 Cor. 3:16-23 | Mark 2:13-22 |

| Saturday | 55 | -:- | 138, 139:1-17(18-23) |
| | Gen. 41:1-13 | 1 Cor. 4:1-7 | Mark 2:23--3:6 |

Week of 2 Lent

| Sunday | 24, 29 | -:- | 8, 84 |
| | Gen. 41:14-45 | Rom. 6:3-14 | John 5:19-24 |

| Monday | 56, 57, [58] | -:- | 64, 65 |
| | Gen. 41:46-57 | 1 Cor. 4:8-20(21) | Mark 3:7-19a |

| Tuesday | 61, 62 | -:- | 68:1-20(21-23)24-36 |
| | Gen. 42:1-17 | 1 Cor. 5:1-8 | Mark 3:19b-35 |

| Wednesday | 72 | -:- | 119:73-96 |
| | Gen. 42:18-28 | 1 Cor. 5:9-6:8 | Mark 4:1-20 |

| Thursday | [70], 71 | -:- | 74 |
| | Gen. 42:29-38 | 1 Cor. 6:12-20 | Mark 4:21-34 |

| Friday | 95* & 69:1-23(24-30)31-38 | -:- | 73 |
| | Gen. 43:1-15 | 1 Cor. 7:1-9 | Mark 4:35-41 |

| Saturday | 75, 76 | -:- | 23, 27 |
| | Gen. 43:16-34 | 1 Cor. 7:10-24 | Mark 5:1-20 |

* For the Invitatory

Daily Office Year Two

Week of 3 Lent

Sunday	93, 96 Jer. 6:9-15	-:- 1 Cor. 6:12-20	34 Mark 5:1-20
Monday	80 Jer. 7:1-15	-:- Rom. 4:1-12	77, [791 John 7:14-36
Tuesday	78:1-39 Jer. 7:21-34	-:- Rom. 4:13-25	78:40-72 John 7:37-52
Wednesday	119:97-120 Jer. 8:18-9:6	-:- Rom. 5:1-11	81, 82 John 8:12-20
Thursday	[83] or 42, 43 Jer. 10:11-24	-:- Rom. 5:12-21	85, 86 John 8:21-32
Friday	95* & 88 Jer. 11:1-8, 14-20	-:- Rom. 6:1-11	91, 92 John 8:33-47
Saturday	87, 90 Jer. 13:1-11	-:- Rom. 6:12-23	136 John 8:47-59

Week of 4 Lent

Sunday	66, 67 Jer. 14:1-9, 17-22	-:- Gal. 4:21-5:1	19, 46 Mark 8:11-21
Monday	89:1-18 Jer. 16:10-21	-:- Rom. 7:1-12	89:19-52 John 6:1-15
Tuesday	97, 99, [100] Jer. 17:19-27	-:- Rom. 7:13-25	94, [95] John 6:16-27
Wednesday	101, 109:1-4(5-19)20-30 Jer. 18:1-11	-:- Rom. 8:1-11	119:121-144 John 6:27-40
Thursday	69:1-23(24-30)31-38 Jer. 22:13-23	-:- Rom. 8:12-27	73 John 6:41-51
Friday	95* & 102 Jer. 23:1-8	-:- Rom. 8:28-39	107:1-32 John 6:52-59
Saturday	107:33-43, 108:1-6(7-13) Jer. 23:9-15	-:- Rom. 9:1-18	33 John 6:60-71

* For the Invitatory

Daily Office Year One

Week of 3 Lent

Sunday	93, 96	-:-	34
	Gen. 44:1-17	Rom. 8:1-10	John 5:25-29

Monday	80	-:-	77, [79]
	Gen. 44:18-34	1 Cor. 7:25-31	Mark 5:21-43

Tuesday	78:1-39	-:-	78:40-72
	Gen. 45:1-15	1 Cor. 7:32-40	Mark 6:1-13

Wednesday	119:97-120	-:-	81, 82
	Gen. 45:16-28	1 Cor. 8:1-13	Mark 6:13-29

Thursday	[83] or 42, 43	-:-	85, 86
	Gen. 46:1-7, 28-34	1 Cor. 9:1-15	Mark 6:30-46

Friday	95* & 88	-:-	91, 92
	Gen. 47:1-26	1 Cor. 9:16-27	Mark 6:47-56

Saturday	87, 90	-:-	136
	Gen. 47:27-48:7	1 Cor. 10:1-13	Mark 7:1-23

Week of 4 Lent

Sunday	66, 67	-:-	19, 46
	Gen. 48:8-22	Rom. 8:11-25	John 6:27-40

Monday	89:1-18	-:-	89:19-52
	Gen. 49:1-28	1 Cor. 10:14-11:1	Mark 7:24-37

Tuesday	97, 99, [100]	-:-	94, [95]
	Gen. 49:29-50:14	1 Cor. 11:17-34	Mark 8:1-10

Wednesday	101, 109:1-4(5-19)20-30	-:-	119:121-144
	Gen. 50:15-26	1 Cor. 12:1-11	Mark 8:11-26

Thursday	69:1-23(24-30)31-38	-:-	73
	Exod. 1:6-22	1 Cor. 12:12-26	Mark 8:27--9:1

Friday	95* & 102	-:-	107:1-32
	Exod. 2:1-22	1 Cor. 12:27-13:3	Mark 9:2-13

Saturday	107:33-43,108:1-6(7-13)	-:-	33
	Exod. 2:23-3:15	1 Cor. 13:1-13	Mark 9:14-29

* For the Invitatory

Daily Office Year Two

Week of 5 Lent

Sunday	118	-:-	145
	Jer. 23:16-32	1 Cor. 9:19-27	Mark 8:31--9:1

Monday	31	-:-	35
	Jer. 24:1-10	Rom. 9:19-33	John 9:1-17

Tuesday	[120],121,122,123	-:-	124, 125, 126, [127]
	Jer. 25:8-17	Rom. 10:1-13	John 9:18-41

Wednesday	119:145-176	-:-	128, 129, 130
	Jer. 25:30-38	Rom. 10:14-21	John 10:1-18

Thursday	131,132, [133]	-:-	140,142
	Jer. 26:1-16	Rom. 11:1-12	John 10:19-42

Friday	95* & 22	-:-	141,143:1-11(12)
	Jer. 29:1, 4-13	Rom. 11:13-24	John 11:1-27,
			or 12:1-10

Saturday	137:1-6(7-9),144	-:-	42, 43
	Jer. 31:27-34	Rom. 11:25-36	John 11:28-44,
			or 12:37-50

Holy Week

Palm Sunday	24, 29	-:-	103
	Zech. 9:9-12**	1 Tim. 6:12-16**	
	Zech. 12:9-11, 13:1, 7-9;***	Matt. 21:12-17***	

Monday	51:1-18(19-20)	-:-	69:1-23
	Jer. 12:1-16	Phil. 3:1-14	John 12:9-19

Tuesday	6, 12	-:-	94
	Jer. 15:10-21	Phil. 3:15-21	John 12:20-26

Wednesday	55	-:-	74
	Jer. 17:5-10, 14-17	Phil.4:1-13	John 12:27-36

Maundy Thursday	102	-:-	142, 143
	Jer. 20:7-11	1 Cor. 10:14-17; 11:27-32	
			John 17:1-11 (12-26)

Good Friday	95* & 22	-:-	40:1-14(15-19), 54
	Wisdom 1:16-2:1,12-22	1 Peter 1:10-20	John 13:36-38**
	or Gen. 22:1-14		John 19:38-42***

Holy Saturday	95* & 88	-:-	27
	Job 19:21-27a	Heb. 4:1-16**	Rom. 8:1-11***

* For the Invitatory ** Intended for use in the morning
*** Intended for use in the evening

Daily Office Year One

The Book of Common Prayer   450

Week of 5 Lent

Sunday	118	-:-	145
	Exod. 3:16-4:12	Rom. 12:1-21	John 8:46-59
Monday	31	-:-	35
	Exod. 4:10-20(21-26)27-31	1 Cor. 14:1-19	Mark 9:30-41
Tuesday	[120], 121, 122, 123	-:-	124,125, 126, [127]
	Exod. 5:1-6:1	1 Cor. 14:20-33a, 39-40	Mark 9:42-50
Wednesday	119:145-176	-:-	128, 129, 130
	Exod. 7:8-24	2 Cor. 2:14-3:6	Mark 10:1-16
Thursday	131, 132, [133]	-:-	140, 142
	Exod. 7:25-8:19	2 Cor. 3:7-18	Mark 10:17-31
Friday	95* & 22	-:-	141, 143:1-11(12)
	Exod. 9:13-35	2 Cor. 4:1-12	Mark 10:32-45
Saturday	137:1-6(7-9), 144	-:-	42, 43
	Exod. 10:21-11:8	2 Cor. 4:13-18	Mark 10:46-52

Holy Week

Palm Sunday	24, 29	-:-	103
	Zech. 9:9-12**	1 Tim. 6:12-16**	
	Zech. 12:9-11; 13:1, 7-9***	Luke 19:41-48***	
Monday	51:1-18(19-20)	-:-	69:1-23
	Lam. 1:1-2,6-12	2 Cor. 1:1-7	Mark 11:12-25
Tuesday	6, 12	-:-	94
	Lam. 1:17-22	2 Cor. 1:8-22	Mark 11:27-33
Wednesday	55	-:-	74
	Lam.2:1-9	2 Cor. 1:23-2:11	Mark 12:1-11
Maundy Thursday	102	-:-	142, 143
	Lam. 2:10-18	1 Cor. 10:14-17; 11:27-32	
			Mark 14:12-25
Good Friday	95* & 22	-:-	40:1-14(15-19),54
	Lam. 3:1-9, 19-33	1 Pet. 1:10-20	John 13:36-38**
			John 19:38-42***
Holy Saturday	95* & 88	-:-	27
	Lam. 3:37-58	Heb. 4:1-16**	Rom. 8:1-11***

* For the Invitatory   ** Intended for use in the morning
*** Intended for use in the evening

Daily Office Year Two

The Book of Common Prayer   451

Easter Week

Easter Day	148, 149, 150	-:-	113,114,or 118
	Exod. 12:1-14**	--------	John 1:1-18
	Isa. 51:9-11***	Luke 24:13-35, or John 20:19-23***	
Monday	93, 98	-:-	66
	Jonah 2:1-9	Acts 2:14, 22-32*	John 14:1-14
Tuesday	103	-:-	111, 114
	Isa. 30:18-21	Acts 2:36-41(42-47)*	John 14:15-31
Wednesday	97, 99	-:-	115
	Micah 7:7-15	Acts 3:1-10*	John 15:1-11
Thursday	146, 147	-:-	148, 149
	Ezek. 37:1-14	Acts 3:11-26*	John 15:12-27
Friday	136	-:-	118
	Dan. 12:1-4,13	Acts 4:1-12*	John 16:1-15
Saturday	145	-:-	104
	Isa. 25:1-9	Acts 4:13-21(22-31)*	John 16:16-33

Week of 2 Easter

Sunday	146, 147	-:-	111, 112, 113
	Isa. 43:8-13	1 Pet. 2:2-10	John 14:1-7
Monday	1, 2, 3	-:-	4, 7
	Dan. 1:1-21	1 John 1:1-10	John 17:1-11
Tuesday	5, 6	-:-	10, 11
	Dan. 2:1-16	1 John 2:1-11	John 17:12-19
Wednesday	119:1-24	-:-	12, 13, 14
	Dan. 2:17-30	1 John 2:12-17	John 17:20-26
Thursday	18:1-20	-:-	18:21-50
	Dan. 2:31-49	1 John 2:18-29	Luke 3:1-14
Friday	16, 17	-:-	134, 135
	Dan. 3:1-18	1 John 3:1-10	Luke 3:15-22
Saturday	20, 21:1-7(8-13)	-:-	110:1-5(6-7),116,117
	Dan. 3:19-30	1 John 3:11-18	Luke 4:1-13

** Intended for use in the morning * Duplicates the First Lesson at the Eucharist.

*** Intended for use in the evening Readings from Year Two may be substituted.

Daily Office Year One

Easter Week

Easter Day	148, 149, 150	-:-	113, 114, or 118
	Exod. 12:1-1 4**	--------	John 1:1-18**
	Isa. 51:9-11***	Luke 24:13-35, or John 20:19-23***	
Monday	93, 98	-:-	66
	Exod. 12:14-27	1 Cor. 15:1-11	Mark 16:1-8
Tuesday	103	-:-	111, 114
	Exod. 12:28-39	1 Cor. 15:12-28	Mark 16:9-20
Wednesday	97, 99	-:-	115
	Exod. 12:40-51	1 Cor. 15:(29)30-41	Matt. 28:1-16
Thursday	146, 147	-:-	148, 149
	Exod. 13:3-10	1 Cor. 15:41-50	Matt. 28:16-20
Friday	136	-:-	118
	Exod. 13:1-2, 11-16	1 Cor. 15:51-58	Luke 24:1-12
Saturday	145	-:-	104
	Exod. 13:17-14:4	2 Cor. 4:16-5:10	Mark 12:1 8-27

Week of 2 Easter

Sunday	146, 147	-:-	111, 112, 113
	Exod. 14:5-22	1 John 1:1-7	John 14:1-7
Monday	1, 2, 3	-:-	4, 7
	Exod. 14:21-31	1 Pet. 1:1-12	John 14:(1-7)8-17
Tuesday	5, 6	-:-	10, 11
	Exod. 15:1-21	1 Pet. 1:13-25	John 14:18-31
Wednesday	119:1-24	-:-	12, 13, 14
	Exod. 15:22-16:10	1 Pet. 2:1-10	John 15:1-11
Thursday	18:1-20	-:-	18:21-50
	Exod. 16:10-22	1 Pet. 2:11-25	John 15:12-27
Friday	16,17	-:-	134, 135
	Exod. 16:23-36	1 Pet. 3:13-4:6	John 16:1-15
Saturday	20, 21:1-7(8-13)	-:-	110:1-5(6-7),116,117
	Exod. 17:1-16	1 Pet. 4:7-19	John 16:16-33

** Intended for use in the morning
*** Intended for use in the evening

Daily Office Year Two

The Book of Common Prayer   453

Week of 3 Easter

Sunday	148, 149, 150	-:-	114, 115
	Dan. 4:1-18	1 Pet. 4:7-11	John 21:15-25

Monday	25	-:-	9, 15
	Dan. 4:19-27	1 John 3:19 4:6	Luke 4:14-30

Tuesday	26, 28	-:-	36, 39
	Dan. 4:28-37	1 John 4:7-21	Luke 4:31-37

Wednesday	38	-:-	119:25-48
	Dan. 5:1-12	1 John 5:1-12	Luke 4:38-44

Thursday	37:1-18	-:-	37:19-42
	Dan. 5:13-30	1 John 5:13-20(21)	Luke 5:1-11

Friday	105:1-22	-:-	105:23-45
	Dan. 6:1-15	2 John 1-13	Luke 5:12-26

Saturday	30, 32	-:-	42, 43
	Dan. 6:16-28	3 John 1-15	Luke 5:27-39

Week of 4 Easter

Sunday	63:1-8(9-11), 98	-:-	103
	Wisdom 1:1-15	1 Pet. 5:1-11	Matt. 7:15-29

Monday	41, 52	-:-	44
	Wisdom 1:16-2:11,21-24	Col. 1:1-14	Luke 6:1-11

Tuesday	45	-:-	47, 48
	Wisdom 3:1-9	Col. 1:15-23	Luke 6:12-26

Wednesday	119:49-72	-:-	49, [53]
	Wisdom 4:16-5:8	Col. 1:24-2:7	Luke 6:27-38

Thursday	50	-:-	[59,60] or 114, 115
	Wisdom 5:9-23	Col. 2:8-23	Luke 6:39-49

Friday	40, 54	-:-	51
	Wisdom 6:12-23	Col. 3:1-11	Luke 7:1-17

Saturday	55	-:-	138, 139:1-17(18-23)
	Wisdom 7:1-14	Col. 3:12-17	Luke 7:18-28, (29-30)31-35

Daily Office Year One

Week of 3 Easter

Sunday	148, 149, 150	-:-	114, 115
	Exod. 18:1-12	1 John 2:7-17	Mark 16:9-20
Monday	25	-:-	9,15
	Exod. 18:13-27	1 Pet. 5:1-14	Matt. (1:1-17); 3:1-6
Tuesday	26, 28	-:-	36, 39
	Exod. 19:1-16	Col. 1:1-14	Matt. 3:7-12
Wednesday	38	-:-	119:25-48
	Exod. 19:16-25	Col. 1:15-23	Matt. 3:13-17
Thursday	37:1-18	-:-	37:19-42
	Exod. 20:1-21	Col. 1:24-2:7	Matt. 4:1-11
Friday	105:1-22	-:-	105: 23 -45
	Exod. 24:1-18	Col. 2:8-23	Matt. 4:12-17
Saturday	30, 32	-:-	42,43
	Exod. 25:1-22	Col. 3:1-17	Matt. 4:18-25

Week of 4 Easter

Sunday	63:1-8(9-11), 98	-:-	103
	Exod. 28:1-4, 30-38	1 John 2:18-29	Mark 6:30-44
Monday	41, 52	-:-	44
	Exod. 32:1-20	Col. 3:18--4:6(7-18)	Matt. 5:1-10
Tuesday	45	-:-	47, 48
	Exod. 32:21-34	1 Thess. 1:1-10	Matt. 5:11-16
Wednesday	119:49-72	-:-	49, [53]
	Exod. 33:1-23	1 Thess. 2:1-12	Matt. 5:17-20
Thursday	50	-:-	[59, 60] or 114, 115
	Exod. 34:1-17	1 Thess. 2:13-20	Matt. 5:21-26
Friday	40, 54	-:-	51
	Exod. 34:18-35	1 Thess. 3:1-13	Matt. 5:27-37
Saturday	55	-:-	138,139:1-17(18-23)
	Exod. 40:18-38	1 Thess. 4:1-12	Matt. 5:38-48

Week of 5 Easter

Sunday
24, 29   -:-   8, 84
Wisdom 7:22-8:1 2 Thess. 2:13-17   Matt. 7:7-14

Monday
56, 57, [58]   -:-   64, 65
Wisdom 9:1,7-18 Col.(3:18--4:1)2-18 Luke 7:36-50

Tuesday
61, 62   -:-   68:1-20(21-23)24-36
Wisdom 10:1-4(5-12)13-21 Rom. 12:1-21 Luke 8:1-15

Wednesday 72   -:-   119:73-96
Wisdom 13:1-9   Rom. 13:1-14   Luke 8:16-25

Thursday   [70], 71   -:-   74
Wisdom 14:27-15:3 Rom. 14:1-12   Luke 8:26-39

Friday
106:1-18   -:-   106:19-48
Wisdom 16:15-17:1 Rom. 14:13-23   Luke 8:40-56

Saturday   75, 76   -:-   23, 27
Wisdom 19:1-8, 18-22 Rom. 15:1-13   Luke 9:1-17

Week of 6 Easter

Sunday
93, 96   -:-   34
Ecclus. 43:1-12, 27-32 1 Tim. 3:14-4:5 Matt. 13:24-34a

Monday
80   -:-   77, [79]
Deut. 8:1-10   James 1:1-15   Luke 9:18-27

Tuesday
78:1-39   -:-   78:40-72
Deut. 8:11-20   James 1:16-27   Luke 11:1-13

Wednesday 119:97-120   -:-   -----------
Baruch 3:24-37   James 5:13-18   Luke 12:22-31

Eve of Ascension --------   -:-   68:1-20
2 Kings 2:1-15   Rev. 5:1-14

Ascension Day 8, 47   -:-   24, 96
Ezek. 1:1-14,24-28b Heb. 2:5-18   Matt. 28:16-20

Friday
85, 86   -:-   91, 92
Ezek. 1:28-3:3   Heb. 4:14--5:6   Luke 9:28-36

Saturday   87, 90   -:-   136
Ezek. 3:4-17   Heb. 5:7-14   Luke 9:37-50

Daily Office Year One

Week of 5 Easter

| Sunday | 24, 29 | -:- | 8, 84 |
| | Lev. 8:1-13, 30-36 | Heb. 12:1-14 | Luke 4:16-30 |

| Monday | 56, 57, [58] | -:- | 64, 65 |
| | Lev. 16:1-19 | 1 Thess. 4:13-18 | Matt. 6:1-6,16-18 |

| Tuesday | 61, 62 | -:- | 68:1-20(21-23)24-36 |
| | Lev. 16:20-34 | 1 Thess. 5:1-11 | Matt. 6:7-15 |

| Wednesday | 72 | -:- | 119:73-96 |
| | Lev. 19:1-18 | 1 Thess. 5:12-28 | Matt. 6:19-24 |

| Thursday | [70], 71 | -:- | 74 |
| | Lev. 19:26-37 | 2 Thess. 1:1-12 | Matt. 6:25-34 |

| Friday | 106:1-18 | -:- | 106:19-48 |
| | Lev. 23:1-22 | 2 Thess. 2:1-17 | Matt. 7:1-12 |

| Saturday | 75, 76 | -:- | 23, 27 |
| | Lev. 23:23-44 | 2 Thess. 3:1-18 | Matt. 7:13-21 |

Week of 6 Easter

| Sunday | 93, 96 | -:- | 34 |
| | Lev. 25:1-17 | James 1:2-8, 16-18 | Luke 12:13-21 |

| Monday | 80 | -:- | 77, [79] |
| | Lev. 25:35-55 | Col. 1:9-14 | Matt. 13:1-16 |

| Tuesday | 78:1-39 | -:- | 78:40-72 |
| | Lev. 26:1-20 | 1 Tim. 2:1-6 | Matt. 13:18-23 |

| Wednesday | 119:97-120 | -:- | 81, 82 |
| | Lev. 26:27-42 | Eph. 1:1-10 | Matt. 22:41-46 |

| Eve of Ascension | -------- | -:- | 68:1-20 |
| | 2 Kings 2:1-15 | Rev. 5:1-14 | |

| Ascension Day | 8, 47 | -:- | 24, 96 |
| | Dan. 7:9-14 | Heb. 2:5-18 | Matt. 28:16-20 |

| Friday | 85, 86 | -:- | 91, 92 |
| | 1 Sam. 2:1-10 | Eph. 2:1-10 | Matt. 7:22-27 |

| Saturday | 87, 90 | -:- | 136 |
| | Num. 11:16-17, 24-29 | Eph. 2:11-22 | Matt. 7:28--8:4 |

Sunday	66, 67	-:-	19, 46
	Ezek. 3:16-27	Eph. 2:1-10	Matt. 10:24-33, 40-42

Monday	89:1-18	-:-	89:19-52
	Ezek. 4:1-17	Heb.6:1-12	Luke 9:51-62

Tuesday	97, 99, [100]	-:-	94, [95]
	Ezek. 7:10-15, 23b-27	Heb. 6:13-20	Luke 10:1-17

Wednesday	101,109:1-4(5-19)20-30	-:-	119:121-144
	Ezek. 11:14-25	Heb. 7:1-17	Luke 10:17-24

Thursday	105:1-22	-:-	105:23-45
	Ezek. 18:1-4,19-32	Heb. 7:18-28	Luke 10:25-37

Friday	102	-:-	107:1-32
	Ezek. 34:17-31	Heb. 8:1-13	Luke 10:38-42

Saturday	107:33-43, 108:1-6(7-13)	-:-	--------
	Ezek. 43:1-12	Heb. 9:1-14	Luke 11:14-23

Eve of Pentecost	-------	-:-	33
	Exod. 19:3-8a, 16-20	1 Pet. 2:4-10	

The Day of Pentecost	118	-:-	145
	Isa. 11:1-9	1 Cor. 2:1-13	John 14:21-29

On the weekdays which follow, the Readings are taken from
the numbered Proper (one through six) which corresponds
most closely to the date of Pentecost.

Eve of Trinity Sunday	------	-:-	104
	Ecclus. 42:15-25	Eph. 3:14-21	

Trinity Sunday	146, 147	-:-	111, 112, 113
	Ecclus.43:1-12(27-33)	Eph.4:1-16	John 1:1-18

On the weekdays which follow, the Readings are taken from
the numbered Proper (two through seven) which corresponds
most closely to the date of Trinity Sunday.

Daily Office Year One

Week of 7 Easter

Sunday	66, 67	-:-	19, 46
	Exod. 3:1-12	Heb. 12:18-29	Luke 10:17-24

Monday	89:1-18	-:-	89:19-52
	Joshua 1:1-9	Eph. 3:1-13	Matt. 8:5-17

Tuesday	97, 99, [100]	-:-	94, [95]
	1 Sam. 16:1-13a	Eph. 3:14-21	Matt. 8:18-27

Wednesday	101, 109:1-4(5-19)20-30	-:-	119:121-144
	Isa. 4:2-6	Eph. 4:1-16	Matt. 8:28-34

Thursday	105:1-22	-:-	105: 23-45
	Zech. 4:1-14	Eph. 4:17-32	Matt. 9:1-8

Friday	102	-:-	107:1-32
	Jer. 31:27-34	Eph. 5:1-20	Matt. 9:9-17

Saturday	107:33-43, 108:1-6(7-13)	-:-	---------
	Ezek. 36:22-27	Eph. 6:10-24	Matt. 9:18-26

Eve of Pentecost	-----	-:-	33
	Exod. 19:3-8a, 16-20	1 Pet. 2:4-10	

The Day of Pentecost	118	-:-	145
	Deut. 16:9-12	Acts 4:18-21,23-33	John 4:19-26

On the weekdays which follow, the Readings are taken from the numbered Proper (one through six) which corresponds most closely to the date of Pentecost.

Eve of Trinity Sunday	------	-:-	104
	Ecclus. 42:15-25	Eph. 3:14-21	

Trinity Sunday	146,147	-:-	111, 112, 113
	Job 38:1-11; 42:1-5	Rev. 19:4-16	John 1:29-34

On the weekdays which follow, the Readings are taken from the numbered Proper (two through seven) which corresponds most closely to the date of Trinity Sunday.

Daily Office Year Two

The Season after Pentecost

Directions for the use of the Propers which follow are on page 158 of the BCP.

Proper 1 Week of the Sunday closest to May 11

Monday	106:1-18	-:-	106:19-48
	Isa. 63:7-14	2 Tim. 1:1-14	Luke 11:24-36
Tuesday	[120],121,122,123	-:-	124,125,126, [127]
	Isa. 63:15-64:9	2 Tim. 1:15-2:13	Luke 11:37-52
Wednesday	119:145-176	-:-	128,129,130
	Isa. 65:1-12	2 Tim. 2:14-26	Luke 11:53-12:12
Thursday	131,132, [133]	-:-	134,135
	Isa. 65:17-25	2 Tim. 3:1-17	Luke 12:13-31
Friday	140,142	-:-	141, 143:1-11(12)
	Isa. 66:1-6	2 Tim. 4:1-8	Luke 12:32-48
Saturday	137:1-6(7-9),144	-:-	104
	Isa. 66:7-14	2 Tim. 4:9-22	Luke 12:49-59

Proper 2 Week of the Sunday closest to May 18

Monday	1, 2, 3	-:-	4, 7
	Ruth 1:1-18	1 Tim. 1:1-17	Luke 13:1-9
Tuesday	5, 6	-:-	10, 11
	Ruth 1:19--2:13	1 Tim. 1:18-2:8	Luke 13:10-17
Wednesday	119:1-24	-:-	12, 13, 14
	Ruth 2:14-23	1 Tim. 3:1-16	Luke 13:18-30
Thursday	18:1-20	-:-	18:21-50
	Ruth 3:1-18	1 Tim. 4:1-16	Luke 13:31-35
Friday	16,17	-:-	22
	Ruth 4:1-17	1 Tim. 5:17-22(23-25)	Luke 14:1-11
Saturday	20,21:1-7(8-13)	-:-	110:1-5(6-7),116,117
	Deut. 1:1-8	1 Tim. 6:6-21	Luke 14:12-24

Daily Office Year One

Directions for the use of the Propers which follow are on page 158 of the BCP.

Proper 1 Week of the Sunday closest to May 11

Monday	106:1-18	-:-	106:19-48
	Ezek. 33:1-11	1 John 1:1-10	Matt. 9:27-34
Tuesday	[120],121,122,123	-:-	124,125,126, [127]
	Ezek. 33:21-33	1 John 2:1-11	Matt. 9:35-10:4
Wednesday	119:145-176	-:-	128,129,130
	Ezek. 34:1-16	1 John 2:12-17	Matt. 10:5-15
Thursday	131,132, [133]	-:-	134,135
	Ezek. 37:21b-28	1 John 2:18-29	Matt. 10:16-23
Friday	140,142	-:-	141, 143:1-11(12)
	Ezek. 39:21-29	1 John 3:1-10	Matt. 10:24-33
Saturday	137:1-6(7-9);144	-:-	104
	Ezek. 47:1-12	1 John 3:11-18	Matt. 10:34-42

Proper 2 Week of the Sunday closest to May 18

Monday	1, 2, 3	-:-	4, 7
	Prov. 3:11-20	1 John 3:18-4:6	Matt. 11:1-6
Tuesday	5, 6	-:-	10, 11
	Prov. 4:1-27	1 John 4:7-21	Matt. 11:7-15
Wednesday	119:1-24	-:-	12, 13, 14
	Prov. 6:1-19	1 John 5:1-12	Matt. 11:16-24
Thursday	18:1-20	-:-	18:21-50
	Prov. 7:1-27	1 John 5:13-21	Matt. 11:25-30
Friday	16,17	-:-	22
	Prov. 8:1-21	2 John 1-13	Matt. 12:1-14
Saturday	20, 21:1-7(8-13)	-:-	110:1-5(6-7),116,117
	Prov. 8:22-36	3 John 1-15	Matt. 12:15-21

Daily Office Year Two

Proper 3 Week of the Sunday closest to May 25

Sunday	148, 149, 150	-:-	114, 115
	Deut. 4:1-9	Rev. 7:1-4, 9-17	Matt. 12:33-45
Monday	25	-:-	9, 15
	Deut. 4:9-14	2 Cor. 1:1-11	Luke 14:25-35
Tuesday	26, 28	-:-	36, 39
	Deut. 4:15-24	2 Cor. 1:12-22	Luke 15:1-10
Wednesday	38	-:-	119:25-48
	Deut. 4:25-31	2 Cor. 1:23-2:17	Luke 15:1-2,11-32
Thursday	37:1-18	-:-	37:19-42
	Deut. 4:32-40	2 Cor. 3:1-18	Luke 16:1-9
Friday	31	-:-	35
	Deut. 5:1-22	2 Cor. 4:1-12	Luke 16:10-17(18)
Saturday	30, 32	-:-	42, 43
	Deut. 5:22-33	2 Cor. 4:13-5:10	Luke 16:19-31

Proper 4 Week of the Sunday closest to June 1

Sunday	63:1-8(9-11), 98	-:-	103
	Deut. 11:1-12	Rev. 10:1-11	Matt. 13:44-58
Monday	41, 52	-:-	44
	Deut. 11:13-19	2 Cor. 5:11-6:2	Luke 17:1-10
Tuesday	45	-:-	47, 48
	Deut. 12:1-12	2 Cor. 6:3-13 (14-7:1)	Luke 17:11-19
Wednesday	119:49-72	-:-	49, [53]
	Deut. 13:1-11	2 Cor. 7:2-16	Luke 17:20-37
Thursday	50	-:-	[59, 60] or 8, 84
	Deut. 16:18-20; 17:14-20	2 Cor. 8:1-16	Luke 18:1-8
Friday	40, 54	-:-	51
	Deut. 26:1-11	2 Cor. 8:16-24	Luke 18:9-14
Saturday	55	-:-	138,139:1-17(18-23)
	Deut. 29:2-15	2 Cor. 9:1-15	Luke 18:15-30

Daily Office Year One

Proper 3 Week of the Sunday closest to May 25

Sunday	148, 149, 150 Prov. 9:1-12	-:- Acts 8:14-25	114, 115 Luke 10:25-28, 38-42
Monday	25 Prov. 10:1-12	-:- 1 Tim. 1:1-17	9, 15 Matt. 12:22-32
Tuesday	26, 28 Prov. 15:16-33	-:- 1 Tim. 1:18-2:8	36, 39 Matt. 12:33-42
Wednesday	38 Prov. 17:1-20	-:- 1 Tim. 3:1-16	119:25-48 Matt. 12:43-50
Thursday	37:1-18 Prov. 21:30-22:6	-:- 1 Tim. 4:1-16	37:19-42 Matt. 13:24-30
Friday	31 Prov. 23:19-21, 29-24:2	-:- 1 Tim. 5:17-22(23-25)	35 Matt. 13:31-35
Saturday	30, 32 Prov. 25:15-28	-:- 1 Tim. 6:6-21	42, 43 Matt. 13:36-43

Proper 4 Week of the Sunday closest to June 1

Sunday	63:1-8(9-11), 98 Eccles. 1:1-11	-:- Acts 8:26-40	103 Luke 11:1-13
Monday	41, 52 Eccles. 2:1-15	-:- Gal. 1:1-17	44 Matt. 13:44-52
Tuesday	45 Eccles. 2:16-26	-:- Gal. 1:18--2:10	47, 48 Matt. 13:53-58
Wednesday	119:49-72 Eccles. 3:1-15	-:- Gal. 2:11-21	49, [53] Matt. 14:1-12
Thursday	50 Eccles. 3:16-4:3	-:- Gal. 3:1-14	[59, 60] or 8, 84 Matt. 14:13-21
Friday	40, 54 Eccles. 5:1-7	-:- Gal. 3:15-22	51 Matt. 14:22-36
Saturday	55 Eccles. 5:8-20	-:- Gal. 3:23-4:11	138,139:1-17(18-23) Matt. 15:1-20

Daily Office Year Two

Proper 5 Week of the Sunday closest to June 8

Sunday   24, 29   -:-   8, 84
            Deut. 29:16-29   Rev. 12:1-12   Matt. 15:29-39

Monday   56, 57, [58]   -:-   64, 65
            Deut. 30:1-10   2 Cor. 10:1-18   Luke 18:31-43

Tuesday   61, 62   -:-   68:1-20(21-23)24-36
            Deut. 30:11-20   2 Cor. 11:1-21a   Luke 19:1-10

Wednesday   72   -:-   119:73-96
            Deut. 31:30-32:14   2 Cor. 11:21b-33   Luke 19:11-27

Thursday   [70], 71   -:-   74
            Ecclus. 44:19-45:5   2 Cor. 12:1-10   Luke 19:28-40

Friday   69:1-23(24-30)31-38   -:-   73
            Ecclus. 45:6-16   2 Cor. 12 ~ 21   Luke 19:41-48

Saturday   75, 76   -:-   23, 27
            Ecclus. 46:1-10   2 Cor. 13:1-14   Luke 20:1-8

Proper 6 Week of the Sunday closest to June 15

Sunday   93, 96   -:-   34
            Ecclus. 46:11-20   Rev. 15:1-8   Matt. 18:1-14

Monday   80   -:-   77, [79]
            1 Samuel 1:1-20   Acts 1:1-14   Luke 20:9-19

Tuesday   78:1-39   -:-   78:40-72
            1 Samuel 1:21--2:11   Acts 1:15-26   Luke 20:19-26

Wednesday   119:97-120   -:-   81, 82
            1 Samuel 2:12-26   Acts 2:1-21   Luke 20:27-40

Thursday   [83] or 34   -:-   85, 86
            1 Samuel 2:27-36   Acts 2:22-36   Luke 20:41-21:4

Friday   88   -:-   91, 92
            1 Samuel 3:1-21   Acts 2:37-47   Luke 21:5-19

Saturday   87, 90   -:-   136
            1 Samuel 4:1b-11   Acts 4:32-5:11   Luke 21:20-28

Daily Office Year One

Proper 5 Week of the Sunday closest to June 8

Sunday	24, 29	-:-	8, 84
	Eccles. 6:1-12	Acts 10:9-23	Luke 12:32-40
Monday	56, 57, [58]	-:-	64, 65
	Eccles. 7:1-14	Gal. 4:12-20	Matt. 15:21-28
Tuesday	61, 62	-:-	68:1-20(21-23)24-36
	Eccles. 8:14-9:10	Gal. 4:21-31	Matt. 15:29-39
Wednesday	72	-:-	119:73-96
	Eccles. 9:11-18	Gal. 5:1-15	Matt. 16:1-12
Thursday	[70], 71	-:-	74
	Eccles. 11:1-8	Gal. 5:16-24	Matt. 16:13-20
Friday	69:1-23(24-30)31-38	-:-	73
	Eccles. 11:9-12:14	Gal. 5:25-6:10	Matt. 16:21-28
Saturday	75, 76	-:-	23, 27
	Num. 3:1-13	Gal. 6:11-18	Matt. 17:1-13

Proper 6 Week of the Sunday closest to June 15

Sunday	93, 96	-:-	34
	Num. 6:22-27	Acts 13:1-12	Luke 12:41-48
Monday	80	-:-	77, [79]
	Num. 9:15-23; 10:29-36	Rom. 1:1-15	Matt. 17:14-21
Tuesday	78:1-39	-:-	78:40-72
	Num. 11:1-23	Rom. 1:16-25	Matt. 17:22-27
Wednesday	119:97-120	-:-	81, 82
	Num. 11:24-33(34-35)	Rom. 1:28-2:11	Matt. 18:1-9
Thursday	[83] or 34	-:-	85, 86
	Num. 12:1-16	Rom. 2:12-24	Matt. 18:10-20
Friday	88	-:-	91, 92
	Num. 13:1-3, 21-30	Rom. 2:25-3:8	Matt. 18:21-35
Saturday	87, 90	-:-	136
	Num. 13:31-14:25	Rom. 3:9-20	Matt. 19:1-12

Daily Office Year Two

Proper 7 Week of the Sunday closest to June 22

Sunday	66, 67	-:-	19, 46
	1 Samuel 4:12-22	James 1:1-18	Matt. 19:23-30
Monday	89:1-18	-:-	89:19-52
	1 Samuel 5:1-12	Acts 5:12-26	Luke 21:29-36
Tuesday	97, 99, [100]	-:-	94, [95]
	1 Samuel 6:1-16	Acts 5:27-42	Luke 21:37-22:13
Wednesday	101,109:1-4(5-19) 20-30 -:-		119:121-144
	1 Samuel 7:2-17	Acts 6:1-15	Luke 22:14-23
Thursday	105:1-22	-:-	105:23-45
	1 Samuel 8:1-22	Acts 6:15-7:16	Luke 22:24-30
Friday	102	-:-	107:1-32
	1 Samuel 9:1-14	Acts 7:17-29	Luke 22:31-38
Saturday	107:33-43, 108:1-6(7-13) -:-		33
	1 Samuel 9:15-10:1	Acts 7:30-43	Luke 22:39-51

Proper 8 Week of the Sunday closest to June 29

Sunday	118	-:-	145
	1 Samuel 10:1-16	Rom. 4:13-25	Matt. 21:23-32
Monday	106:1-18	-:-	106:19-48
	1 Samuel 10:17-27	Acts 7:44-8:1a	Luke 22:52-62
Tuesday	[120],121,122,123	-:-	124,125,126, [127]
	1 Samuel 11:1-15	Acts 8:1-13	Luke 22:63-71
Wednesday	119:145-176	-:-	128, 129,130
	1 Samuel 12:1-6,16-25	Acts8:14-25	Luke 23:1-12
Thursday	131, 132,[133]	-:-	134, 135
	1 Samuel 13:5-18	Acts 8:26-40	Luke 23:13-25
Friday	140, 142	-:-	141, 143:1-11(12)
	1 Samuel 13:19-14:15	Acts 9:1-9	Luke 23:26-31
Saturday	137:1-6(7-9),144	-:-	104
	1 Samuel 14:16-30	Acts 9:10-19a	Luke 23:32-43

Daily Office Year One

Proper 7 Week of the Sunday closest to June 22

Sunday	66, 67	-:-	19, 46
	Num. 14:26-45	Acts 15:1-12	Luke 12:49-56
Monday	89:1-18	-:-	89:19-52
	Num. 16:1-19	Rom.3:21-31	Matt. 19:13-22
Tuesday	97, 99, [100]	-:-	94, [95]
	Num. 16:20-35	Rom. 4:1-12	Matt. 19:23-30
Wednesday	101,109: 1-4(5-19)20-30 -:-		119: 121-144
	Num. 16: 36-50	Rom. 4:13-25	Matt. 20:1-16
Thursday	105:1-22	-:-	105:23-45
	Num. 17:1-11	Rom. 5:1-11	Matt. 20:17-28
Friday	102	-:-	107:1-32
	Num. 20:1-13	Rom. 5:12-21	Matt. 20:29-34
Saturday	107:33-43,108:1-6(7-13) -:-		33
	Num. 20:14-29	Rom. 6:1-11	Matt. 21:1-11

Proper 8 Week of the Sunday closest to June 29

Sunday	118	-:-	145
	Num. 21:4-9, 21-35	Acts 17:(12-21)22-34	Luke 13:10-17
Monday	106:1-18	-:-	106:19-48
	Num. 22:1-21	Rom. 6:12-23	Matt. 21:12-22
Tuesday	[120],121,122,123	-:-	124, 125, 126, [127]
	Num. 22:21-38	Rom. 7:1-12	Matt. 21:23-32
Wednesday	119:145-176	-:-	128, 129, 130
	Num. 22:41-23:12	-:- Rom. 7:13-25	Matt. 21:33-46
Thursday	131, 132, [133]	-:-	134, 135
	Num. 23:11-26	Rom. 8:1-11	Matt. 22:1-14
Friday	140, 142	-:-	141, 143:1-11(12)
	Num. 24:1-13	Rom. 8:12-17	Matt. 22:15-22
Saturday	137:1-6(7-9),144	-:-	104
	Num. 24:12-25	Rom. 8:18-25	Matt. 22:23-40

Daily Office Year Two

Proper 9 Week of the Sunday closest to July 6

Sunday   146, 147   -:-   111, 112, 113
            1 Samuel 14:36-45   Rom. 5:1-11   Matt. 22:1-14

Monday   1, 2, 3   -:-   4, 7
            1Samuel 15:1-3,7-23 Acts 9:19b-31 Luke 23:44-56a

Tuesday   5, 6   -:-   10, 11
            1 Samuel 15:24-35   Acts 9:32-43   Luke 23:56b-24:11

Wednesday   119:1-24   -:-   12, 13, 14
            1 Samuel 16:1-13   Acts 10:1-16   Luke 24:12-35

Thursday   18:1-20   -:-   18:21-50
            1 Samuel 16:14-17:11 Acts 10:17-33 Luke 24:36-53

Friday   16, 17   -:-   22
            1 Samuel 17:17-30   Acts 10:34-48 Mark 1:1-13

Saturday   20,21:1-7(8-13)   -:-   110:1-5(6-7), 116, 117
            1 Samuel 17:31-49   Acts 11:1-18   Mark 1:14-28

Proper 10 Week of the Sunday closest to July 13

Sunday   148, 149, 150   -:-   114, 115
            1 Samuel 17:50-18:4 Rom. 10:4-17   Matt. 23:29-39

Monday   25   -:-   9, 15
            1 Samuel 18:5-16, 27b-30 Acts 11:19-30 Mark 1:29-45

Tuesday   26, 28   -:-   36, 39
            1 Samuel 19:1-18   Acts 12:1-17   Mark 2:1-12

Wednesday   38   -:-   119:25-48
            1 Samuel 20:1-23   Acts 12:18-25 Mark 2:13-22

Thursday   37:1-18   -:-   37:19-42
            1 Samuel 20:24-42   Acts 13:1-12   Mark 2:23-3:6

Friday   31   -:-   35
            1 Samuel 21:1-15   Acts 13:13-25 Mark 3:7-19a

Saturday   30, 32   -:-   42, 43
            1 Samuel 22:1-23   Acts 13:26-43 Mark 3:19b-35

Daily Office Year One

Proper 9 Week of the Sunday closest to July 6

Sunday	146, 147	-:-	111, 112, 113
	Num. 27:12-23	Acts 19:11-20	Mark 1:14-20

Monday	1, 2, 3	-:-	4, 7
	Num. 32:1-6,16-27	Rom. 8:26-30	Mark. 23:1-12

Tuesday	5, 6	-:-	10,11
	Num. 35:1-3, 9-15, 30-34	Rom. 8:31-39	Matt. 23:13-26

Wednesday	119:1-24	-:-	12, 13, 14
	Deut. 1:1-18	Rom. 9:1-18	Matt. 23:27-39

Thursday	18:1-20	-:-	18:21-50
	Deut. 3:18-28	Rom. 9:19-33	Matt. 24:1-14

Friday	16, 17	-:-	22
	Deut. 31:7-13, 24--32:4	Rom. 10:1-13	Matt. 24:15-31

Saturday	20, 21:1-7(8-13)	-:-	110:1-5(6-7),116,117
	Deut. 34:1-12	Rom. 10:14-21	Matt. 24:32-51

Proper 10 Week of the Sunday closest to July 13

Sunday	148, 149, 150	-:-	114, 115
	Joshua 1:1-18	Acts 21:3-15	Mark 1:21-27

Monday	25	-:-	9, 15
	Joshua 2:1-14	Rom. 11:1-12	Matt. 25:1-13

Tuesday	26, 28	-:-	36, 39
	Joshua 2:15-24	Rom. 11:13-24	Matt. 25:14-30

Wednesday	38	-:-	119:25-48
	Joshua 3:1-13	Rom. 11:25-36	Matt. 25:31-46

Thursday	37:1-18	-:-	37:19-42
	Joshua 3:14-4:7	Rom. 12:1-8	Matt. 26:1-16

Friday	31	-:-	35
	Joshua 4:19-5:1,10-15	Rom. 12:9-21	Matt. 26:17-25

Saturday	30, 32	-:-	42, 43
	Joshua 6:1-14	Rom. 13:1-7	Matt. 26:26-35

Daily Office Year Two

Proper 11 Week of the Sunday closest to July 20

Sunday	63:1-8(9-11), 98	-:-	103
	1 Samuel 23:7-18	Rom. 11:33-12:2	Matt. 25:14-30
Monday	41, 52	-:-	44
	1 Samuel 24:1-22	Acts 13:44-52	Mark 4:1-20
Tuesday	45	-:-	47, 48
	1 Samuel 25:1-22	Acts 14:1-18	Mark 4:21-34
Wednesday	119:49-72	-:-	49, [53]
	1 Samuel 25:23-44	Acts 14:19-28	Mark 4:35-41
Thursday	50	-:-	[59, 60] or 66, 67
	1 Samuel 28:3-20	Acts 15:1-11	Mark 5:1-20
Friday	40, 54	-:-	51
	1 Samuel 31:1-13	Acts 15:12-21	Mark 5:21-43
Saturday	55	-:-	138,139:1-17(18-23)
	2 Samuel 1:1-16	Acts 15:22-35	Mark 6:1-13

Proper 12 Week of the Sunday closest to July 27

Sunday	24, 29	-:-	8, 84
	2 Samuel 1:17-27	Rom. 12:9-21	Matt. 25:31-46
Monday	56, 57, [58]	-:-	64, 65
	2 Samuel 2:1-11	Acts 15:36-16:5	Mark 6:14-29
Tuesday	61, 62	-:-	68:1-20(21-23)24-36
	2 Samuel 3:6-21	Acts 16:6-15	Mark 6:30-46
Wednesday	72	-:-	119:73-96
	2 Samuel 3:22-39	Acts 16:16-24	Mark 6:47-56
Thursday	[70], 71	-:-	74
	2 Samuel 4:1-12	Acts 16:25-40	Mark 7:1-23
Friday	69:1-23(24-30)31-38	-:-	73
	2 Samuel 5:1-12	Acts 17:1-15	Mark 7:24-37
Saturday	75, 76	-:-	23, 27
	2 Samuel 5:22-6:11	Acts 17:16-34	Mark 8:1-10

Daily Office Year One

Proper 11 Week of the Sunday closest to July 20

Sunday	63:1-8(9-11),98	-:-	103
	Joshua 6:15-27	Acts 22:30-23:11	Mark 2:1-12
Monday	41, 52	-:-	44
	Joshua 7:1-13	Rom. 13:8-14	Matt. 26:36-46
Tuesday	45	-:-	47, 48
	Joshua 8:1-22	Rom. 14:1-12	Matt. 26:47-56
Wednesday	119:49-72	-:-	49, [53]
	Joshua 8:30-35	Rom. 14:13-23	Matt. 26:57-68
Thursday	50	-:-	[59, 60] or 66, 67
	Joshua 9:3-21	Rom. 15:1-13	Matt. 26:69-75
Friday	40, 54	-:-	51
	Joshua 9:22-10:15	Rom. 15:14-24	Matt. 27:1-10
Saturday	55	-:-	138, 139:1-17(18-23)
	Joshua 23:1-16	Rom. 15:25-33	Matt. 27:11-23

Proper 12 Week of the Sunday closest to July 27

Sunday	24, 29	-:-	8, 84
	Joshua 24:1-15	Acts 28:23-31	Mark 2:23-28
Monday	56, 57, [58]	-:-	64, 65
	Joshua 24:16-33	Rom. 16:1-16	Matt. 27:24-31
Tuesday	61, 62	-:-	68:1-20(21-23)24-36
	Judges 2:1-5, 11-23	Rom. 16:17-27	Matt. 27:32-44
Wednesday	72	-:-	119:73-96
	Judges 3:12-30	Acts 1:1-14	Matt. 27:45-54
Thursday	[70], 71	-:-	74
	Judges 4:4-23	Acts 1:15-26	Matt. 27:55-66
Friday	69:1-23(24-30)31-38	-:-	73
	Judges 5:1-18	Acts 2:1-21	Matt. 28:1-10
Saturday	75, 76	-:-	23,27
	Judges 5:19-31	Acts 2:22-36	Matt. 28:11-20

Daily Office Year Two

Proper 13 Week of the Sunday closest to August 3

Sunday	93, 96	-:-	34
	2 Samuel 6:12-23	Rom. 14:7-12	John 1:43-51
Monday	80	-:-	77, [79]
	2 Samuel 7:1-17	Acts 18:1-11	Mark 8:11-21
Tuesday	78:1-39	-:-	78:40-72
	2 Samuel 7:18-29	Acts 18:12-28	Mark. 8:22-33
Wednesday	119:97-120	-:-	81, 82
	2 Samuel 9:1-13	Acts 19:1-10	Mark 8:34-9:1
Thursday	[83] or 145	-:-	85, 86
	2 Samuel 11:1-27	Acts 19:11-20	Mark 9:2-13
Friday	88	-:-	91, 92
	2 Samuel 12:1-14	Acts 19:21-41	Mark 9:14-29
Saturday	87, 90	-:-	136
	2 Samuel 12:15-31	Acts 20:1-16	Mark 9:30-41

Proper 14 Week of the Sunday closest to August 10

Sunday	66, 67	-:-	19, 46
	2 Samuel 13:1-22	Rom. 15:1-13	John 3:22-36
Monday	89:1-18	-:-	89:19-52
	2 Samuel 13:23-39	Acts 20:17-38	Mark 9:42-50
Tuesday	97, 99, [100]	-:-	94, [95]
	2 Samuel 14:1-20	Acts 21:1-14	Mark 10:1-16
Wednesday	101, 109:1-4(5-19)20-30	-:-	119:121-144
	2 Samuel 14:21-33	Acts 21:15-26	Mark 10:17-31
Thursday	105:1-22	-:-	105:23-45
	2 Samuel 15:1-18	Acts21: 27-36	Mark 10:32-45
Friday	102	-:-	107:1-32
	2 Samuel 15:19-37	Acts 21:37-22:16	Mark 10:46-52
Saturday	107:33-43, 108:1-6(7-13)	-:-	33
	2 Samuel 16:1-23	Acts 22:17-29	Mark 11:1-11

Daily Office Year One

Proper 13 Week of the Sunday closest to August 3

Sunday	93, 96	-:-	34
	Judges 6:1-24	2 Cor. 9:6-15	Mark 3:20-30

Monday	80	-:-	77, [79]
	Judges 6:25-40	Acts 2:37-47	John 1:1-18

Tuesday	78:1-39	-:-	78:40-72
	Judges 7:1-18	Acts 3:1-11	John 1:19-28

Wednesday	119:97-120	-:-	81, 82
	Judges 7:19-8:12	Acts 3:12-26	John 1:29-42

Thursday	[83] or 145	-:-	85, 86
	Judges 8:22-35	Acts 4:1-12	John 1:43-51

Friday	88	-:-	91, 92
	Judges 9:1-16,19-21	Acts 4:13-31	John 2:1-12

Saturday	87, 90	-:-	136
	Judges 9:22-25, 50-57	Acts 4:32-5:11	John 2:13-25

Proper 14 Week of the Sunday closest to August 10

Sunday	66, 67	-:-	19, 46
	Judges 11:1-11, 29-40	2 Cor. 11:21b-31	Mark 4:35-41

Monday	89:1-18	-:-	89:19-52
	Judges 12:1-7	Acts 5:12-26	John 3:1-21

Tuesday	97, 99, [100]	-:-	94, [95]
	Judges 13:1-15	Acts 5:27-42	John 3:22-36

Wednesday	101, 109:1-4(5-19)20-30	-:-	119:121-144
	Judges 13:15-24	Acts 6:1-15	John 4:1-26

Thursday	105:1-22	-:-	105:23-45
	Judges 14:1-19	Acts 6:15-7:16	John 4:27-42

Friday	102	-:-	107:1-32
	Judges 14:20-15:20	Acts 7:17-29	John 4:43-54

Saturday	107:33-43, 108:1-6(7-13)	-:-	33
	Judges 16:1-14	Acts 7:30-43	John 5:1-18

Daily Office Year Two

The Book of Common Prayer 473

Proper 15 Week of the Sunday closest to August 17

Sunday	118	-:-	145
	2 Samuel 17:1-23	Gal. 3:6-14	John 5:30-47

Monday	106:1-18	-:-	106:19-48
	2 Samuel 17:24-18:8	Acts 22:30-23:11	Mark 11:12-26

Tuesday	[120],121,122,123	-:-	124, 125, 126, [127]
	2 Samuel 18:9-18	Acts 23:12-24	Mark 11:27-12:12

Wednesday	119:145-176	-:-	128, 129, 130
	2 Samuel 18:19-33	Acts 23:23-35	Mark 12:13-27

Thursday	131,132, [133]	-:-	134, 135
	2 Samuel 19:1-23	Acts 24:1-23	Mark 12:28-34

Friday	140, 142	-:-	141, 143:1-11(12)
	2 Samuel 19:24-43	Acts 24:24-25:12	Mark 12:35-44

Saturday	137:1-6(7-9), 144	-:-	104
	2 Samuel 23:1-7, 13-17	Acts 25:13-27	Mark 13:1-13

Proper 16 Week of the Sunday closest to August 24

Sunday	146, 147	-:-	111 , 112, 113
	2 Samuel 24:1-2, 10-25	Gal. 3:23-4:7	John 8:12-20

Monday	1, 2, 3	-:-	4, 7
	1 Kings 1:5-31	Acts 26:1-23	Mark 13:14-27

Tuesday	5, 6	-:-	10,11
	1 Kings 1:38-2:4	Acts 26:24-27:8	Mark 13:28-37

Wednesday	119:1-24	-:-	12, 13, 14
	1 Kings 3:1-15	Acts 27:9-26	Mark 14

Thursday	18:1-20	-:-	18:21-50
	1 Kings 3:16-28	Acts 27:27-44	Mark 14:12-26

Friday	16, 17	-:-	22
	1 Kings 5:1-6:1,7	Acts 28:1-16	Mark 14:27-42

Saturday	20, 21:1-7(8-13)	-:-	110:1-5(6-7),116,117
	1 Kings 7:51--8:21	Acts 28:17-31	Mark 14:43-52

Daily Office Year One

The Book of Common Prayer   474

Proper 15 Week of the Sunday closest to August 17

Sunday	118	-:-	145
	Judges 16:15-31	2 Cor. 13:1-11	Mark 5:25-34

Monday	106:1-18	-:-	106:19-48
	Judges 17:1-13	Acts 7:44-8:1a	John 5:19-29

Tuesday	[120], 121, 122, 123	-:-	124, 125, 126, [127]
	Judges 18:1-15	Acts 8:1-13	John 5:30-47

Wednesday	119:145-176	-:-	128, 129, 130
	Judges 18:16-31	Acts 8:14-25	John 6:1-15

Thursday	131, 132, [133]	-:-	134, 135
	Job 1:1-22	Acts 8:26-40	John 6:16-27

Friday	140, 142	-:-	141, 143:1-11(12)
	Job 2:1-13	Acts 9:1-9	John 6:27-40

Saturday	137:1-6(7-9), 144	-:-	104
	Job 3:1-26	Acts 9:10-19a	John 6:41-51

Proper 16 Week of the Sunday closest to August 24

Sunday	146, 147	-:-	111, 112, 113
	Job 4:1-6, 12-21	Rev. 4:1-11	Mark 6:1-6a

Monday	1, 2, 3	-:-	4, 7
	Job 4:1; 5:1-11,17-21, 26-27	Acts 9:19b-31	John 6:52-59

Tuesday	5, 6	-:-	10, 11
	Job 6:1-4, 8-15, 21	Acts 9:32-43	John 6:60-71

Wednesday	119:1-24	-:-	12, 13, 14
	Job 6:1; 7:1-21	Acts 10:1-16	John 7:1-13

Thursday	18:1-20	-:-	18:21-50
	Job 8:1-10, 20-22	Acts 10:17-33	John 7:14-36

Friday	16, 17	-:-	22
	Job 9:1-15, 32-35	Acts 10:34-48	John 7:37-52

Saturday	20, 21:1-7(8-13)	-:-	110:1-5(6-7),116,117
	Job 9:1; 10:1-9,16-22	Acts 11:1-18	John 8:12-20

Daily Office Year Two

Proper 17 Week of the Sunday closest to August 31

Sunday   148, 149, 150   -:-   114, 115
             1 Kings 8:22-30(31-40)   1 Tim. 4:7b-16   John 8:47-59

Monday   25   -:-   9, 15
             2 Chron. 6:32-7:7   James 2:1-13   Mark 14:53-65

Tuesday   26, 28   -:-   36, 39
             1 Kings 8:65-9:9   James 2:14-26   Mark 14:66-72

Wednesday   38   -:-   119:25-48
             1 Kings 9:24--10:13   James 3:1-12   Mark 15:1-11

Thursday   37:1-18   -:-   37:19-42
             1 Kings 11:1-13   James 3:13-4:12 Mark 15:12-21

Friday   31   -:-   35
             1 Kings 11:26-43   James 4:13--5:6 Mark 15:22-32

Saturday   30, 32   -:-   42, 43
             1 Kings 12:1-20   James 5:7-12,19-20   Mark 15:33-39

Proper 18 Week of the Sunday closest to September 7

Sunday   63:1-8(9-11), 98   -:-   103
             1 Kings 12:21-33   Acts 4:18-31   John 10:31-42

Monday   41, 52   -:-   44
             1 Kings 13:1-10   Phil. 1:1-11   Mark 15:40-47

Tuesday   45   -:-   47, 48
             1 Kings 16:23-34   Phil. 1:12-30   Mark 16:1-8(9-20)

Wednesday   119:49-72   -:-   49, [53]
             1 Kings 17:1-24   Phil. 2:1-11   Matt. 2:1-12

Thursday   50   -:-   [59, 60] or 93, 96
             1 Kings 18:1-19   Phil. 2:12-30   Matt. 2:13-23

Friday   40, 54   -:-   51
             1 Kings 18:20-40   Phil. 3:1-16   Matt. 3:1-12

Saturday   55   -:-   138, 139:1-17(18-23)
             1 Kings 18:41-19:8 Phil. 3:17-4:7   Matt. 3:13-17

Daily Office Year One

Proper 17 Week of the Sunday closest to August 31

| Sunday | 148, 149, 150 | -:- | 114, 115 |
| | Job 11:1-9,13-20 | Rev. 5:1-14 | Matt. 5:1-12 |

| Monday | 25 | -:- | 9, 15 |
| | Job 12:1-6,13-25 | Acts 11:19-30 | John 8:21-32 |

| Tuesday | 26, 28 | -:- | 36, 39 |
| | Job 12:1;13:3-17, 21-27 | Acts 12:1-17 | John 8:33-47 |

| Wednesday | 38 | -:- | 119:25-48 |
| | Job 12:1;14:1-22 | Acts 12:18-25 | John 8:47-59 |

| Thursday | 37:1-18 | -:- | 37:19-42 |
| | Job 16:16-22; 17:1,13-16 | Acts 13:1-12 | John 9:1-17 |

| Friday | 31 | -:- | 35 |
| | Job 19:1-7,14-27 | Acts 13:13-25 | John 9:18-41 |

| Saturday | 30, 32 | -:- | 42, 43 |
| | Job 22:1-4,21-23:7 | Acts 13:26-43 | John 10:1-18 |

Proper 18 Week of the Sunday closest to September 7

| Sunday | 63:1-8(9-11), 98 | -:- | 103 |
| | Job 25:1-6; 27:1-6 | Rev. 14:1-7, 13 | Matt. 5 :13-20 |

| Monday | 41, 52 | -:- | 44 |
| | Job 32:1-10,19-33:1,19-28 | Acts 13:44-52 | John 10:19-30 |

| Tuesday | 45 | -:- | 47, 48 |
| | Job 29:1-20 | Acts 14:1-18 | John 10:31-42 |

| Wednesday | 119:49-72 | -:- | 49, [53] |
| | Job 29:1;30:1-2,16-31 | Acts14:19-28 | John 11:1-16 |

| Thursday | 50 | -:- | [59, 60] or 93, 96 |
| | Job 29:1;31:1-23 | Acts 15:1-11 | John 11:17-29 |

| Friday | 40, 54 | -:- | 51 |
| | Job 29:1; 31:24-40 | Acts 15:12-21 | John 11:30-44 |

| Saturday | 55 | -:- | 138, 139:1-17(18-23) |
| | Job 38:1-17 | Acts 15:22-35 | John 11:45-54 |

Daily Office Year Two

Proper 19 Week of the Sunday closest to September 14

Sunday	24, 29	-:-	8, 84
	1 Kings 19:8-21	Acts 5:34-42	John 11:45-57
Monday	56, 57, [58]	-:-	64, 65
	1 Kings 21:1-16	1 Cor. 1:1-19	Matt.4:1-11
Tuesday	61, 62	-:-	68:1-20(21-23)24-36
	1 Kings 21:17-29	1 Cor. 1:20-31	Matt. 4:12-17
Wednesday	72	-:-	119:73-96
	1 Kings 22:1-28	1 Cor. 2:1-13	Matt. 4:18-25
Thursday	[70], 71	-:-	74
	1 Kings 22:29-45	1 Cor. 2:14-3:15	Matt. 5:1-10
Friday	69:1-23(24-30)31-38	-:-	73
	2 Kings 1:2-17	1 Cor. 3:16-23	Matt. 5:11-16
Saturday	75, 76	-:-	23, 27
	2 Kings 2:1-18	1 Cor. 4:1-7	Matt. 5:17-20

Proper 20 Week of the Sunday closest to September 21

Sunday	93, 96	-:-	34
	2 Kings 4:8-37	Acts 9:10-32	Luke 3:7-18
Monday	80	-:-	77, [79]
	2 Kings 5:1-19	1 Cor. 4:8-21	Matt. 5:21-26
Tuesday	78:1-3 9	-:-	78:40-72
	2 Kings 5:19-27	1 Cor. 5:1-8	Matt. 5:27-37
Wednesday	119:97-120	-:-	81, 82
	2 Kings 6:1-23	1 Cor. 5:9-6:8	Matt. 5:38-48
Thursday	[83] or 116, 117	-:-	85, 86
	2 Kings 9:1-16	1 Cor. 6:12-20	Matt. 6:1-6, 16-18
Friday	88	-:-	91, 92
	2 Kings 9:17-37	1 Cor. 7:1-9	Matt. 6:7-15
Saturday	87, 90	-:-	136
	2 Kings 11:1-20a	1 Cor. 7:10-24	Matt. 6:19-24

Daily Office Year One

Proper 19 Week of the Sunday closest to September 14

Sunday	24, 29	-:-	8, 84
	Job 38:1,18-41	Rev. 18:1-8	Matt. 5:21-26
Monday	56, 57, [58]	-:-	64, 65
	Job 40:1-24	Acts 15:36-16:5	John 11:55-12: 8
Tuesday	61, 62	-:-	68:1-20(21-23)24-36
	Job 40:1; 41:1-11	Acts 16:6-15	John 12:9-19
Wednesday	72	-:-	119:73-96
	Job 42:1-17	Acts 16:16-24	John 12:20-26
Thursday	[70], 71	-:-	74
	Job 28:1-28	Acts 16:25-40	John 12:27-36a
Friday	69:1-23(24-30)31-38	-:-	73
	Esther 1:1-4, 10-19	Acts 17:1-15	John 12:36b-43
Saturday	75, 76	-:-	23, 27
	Esther 2:5-8, 15-23*	Acts 17:16-34	John 12:44-50

Proper 20 Week of the Sunday closest to September 21

Sunday	93, 96	-:-	34
	Esther 3:1-4:3*	James 1:19-27	Matt. 6:1-6, 16-18
Monday	80	-:-	77, [79]
	Esther 4:4-17*	Acts 18:1-11	Luke (1:1-4); 3:1-14
Tuesday	78:1-39	-:-	78:40-72
	Esther 5:1-14*	Acts 18:12-28	Luke 3:15-22
Wednesday	119:97-120	-:-	81, 82
	Esther 6:1-14*	Acts 19:1-10	Luke 4:1-13
Thursday	[83] or 116, 117	-:-	85, 86
	Esther 7:1-10*	Acts 19:11-20	Luke 4:14-30
Friday	88	-:-	91, 92
	Esther 8:1-8, 15-17*	Acts 19:21-41	Luke 4:31-37
Saturday	87, 90	-:-	136
	Hosea 1:1-2:1	Acts 20:1-16	Luke 4:38-44

* In place of Esther may be read Judith:
F 4:1-15   Su 5:22-6:4, 10-21 Tu 8:9-17; 9:1, 7-10 Th 12:1-20
Sa 5:1-21   M 7:1-7,19-32   W 10:1-2.3   F 13:1-20

Proper 21 Week of the Sunday closest to September 28

Sunday	66, 67	-:-	19, 46
	2 Kings 17:1-18	Acts 9:36-43	Luke 5:1-11
Monday	89:1-18	-:-	89:19-52
	2 Kings 17:24-41	1 Cor. 7:25-31	Matt. 6:25-34
Tuesday	97, 99, [100]	-:-	94, [95]
	2 Chron. 29:1-3;	1 Cor. 7:32-40	Matt. 7:1-12
	30:1(2-9) 10-27		
Wednesday	101, 109:1-4(5-19)20-30 -:-		119:121-144
	2 Kings 18:9-25	1 Cor. 8:1-13	Matt. 7:13-21
Thursday	105:1-22	-:-	105:23-45
	2 Kings 18:28-37	1 Cor. 9:1-15	Matt. 7:22-29
Friday	102	-:-	107:1-32
	2 Kings 19:1-20	1 Cor. 9:16-27	Matt. 8:1-17
Saturday	107:33-43,108:1-6(7-13) -:-		33
	2 Kings 19:21-36	1 Cor. 10:1-13	Matt. 8:18-27

Proper 22 Week of the Sunday closest to October 5

Sunday	118	-:-	145
	2 Kings 20:1-21	Acts 12:1-17	Luke 7:11-17
Monday	106:1-18	-:-	106:19-48
	2 Kings 21:1-18	1 Cor.10:14-11:1	Matt.8:28-34
Tuesday	[120],121,122,123	-:-	124,125,126, [127]
	2 Kings 22:1-13	1 Cor. 11:2, 17-22	Matt. 9:1-8
Wednesday	119:145-176	-:-	128,129, 130
	2 Kings 22:14-23:3	1 Cor. 11:23-34	Matt. 9:9-17
Thursday	131,132,[133]	-:-	134, 135
	2 Kings 23:4-25	1 Cor. 12:1-11	Matt. 9:18-26
Friday	140, 142	-:- 141, 143:1-11(12)	
	2 Kings 23:36-24:17	1 Cor. 12:12-26	Matt. 9:27-34
Saturday	137:1-6(7-9), 144	-:-	104
	Jer. 35:1-19	1 Cor. 12:27--13:3	Matt. 9:35-10:4

Daily Office Year One

Proper 21 Week of the Sunday closest to September 28

Sunday	66, 67	-:-	19, 46
	Hosea 2:2-14	James 3:1-13	Matt. 13:44-52
Monday	89:1-18	-:-	89:19-52
	Hosea 2:14-23	Acts 20:17-38	Luke 5:1-11
Tuesday	97, 99, [100]	-:-	94, [95]
	Hosea 4:1-10	Acts 21:1-14	Luke 5:12-26
Wednesday	101,109:1-4(5-19)20-30	-:-	119:121-144
	Hosea 4:11-19	Acts 21:15-26	Luke 5:27-39
Thursday	105:1-22	-:-	105:23-45
	Hosea 5:8-6:6	Acts 21:27-36	Luke 6:1-11
Friday	102	-:-	107:1-32
	Hosea 10:1-15	Acts 21:37-22:16	Luke 6:12-26
Saturday	107:33-43,108:1-6(7-13)	-:-	33
	Hosea 11:1-9	Acts 22:17-29	Luke 6:27-38

Proper 22 Week of the Sunday closest to October 5

Sunday	118	-:-	145
	Hosea 13:4-14	1 Cor. 2:6-16	Matt. 14:1-12
Monday	106:1-18	-:-	106:19-48
	Hosea 14:1-9	Acts 22:30-23:11	Luke 6:39-49
Tuesday	[120],121,122,123	-:-	124,125,126, [127]
	Micah 1:1-9	Acts 23:12-24	Luke 7:1-17
Wednesday	119:145-176	-:-	128, 129, 130
	Micah 2:1-13	Acts 23:23-35	Luke 7:18-35
Thursday	131,132, [133]	-:-	134,135
	Micah 3:1-8	Acts 24:1-23	Luke 7:36-50
Friday	140, 142	-:-	141, 143:1-11(12)
	Micah 3:9-4:5	Acts 24:24-25:12	Luke 8:1-15
Saturday	137:1-6(7-9),144	-:-	104
	Micah 5:1-4, 10-15	Acts 25:13-27	Luke 8:16-25

Daily Office Year Two

The Book of Common Prayer 481

Proper 23 Week of the Sunday closest to October 12

Sunday	146, 147	-:-	111, 112, 113
	Jer. 36:1-10	Acts 14:8-18	Luke 7:36-50
Monday	1, 2, 3	-:-	4, 7
	Jer. 36:11-26	1 Cor. 13:(1-3)4-13	Matt. 10:5-15
Tuesday	5, 6	-:-	10, 11
	Jer. 36:27-37:2	1 Cor. 14:1-12	Matt. 10:16-23
Wednesday	119:1-24	-:-	12, 13, 14
	Jer. 37:3-21	1 Cor. 14:13-25	Matt. 10:24-33
Thursday	18:1-20	-:-	18:21-50
	Jer. 38:1-13	1 Cor. 14:26-33a, 37-40	Matt. 10:34-42
Friday	16, 17	-:-	22
	Jer. 38:14-28	1 Cor. 15:1-11	Matt. 11:1-6
Saturday	20,21:1-7(8-13)	-:-	110:1-5(6-7), 116, 117
	2 Kings 25:8-12, 22-26	1 Cor. 15:12-29	Matt. 11:7-15

Proper 24 Week of the Sunday closest to October 19

Sunday	148, 149, 150	-:-	114, 115
	Jer. 29:1, 4-14	Acts 16:6-15	Luke 10:1-12,17-20
Monday	25	-:-	9, 15
	Jer. 44:1-14	1 Cor. 15:30-41	Matt. 11:16-24
Tuesday	26, 28	-:-	36, 39
	Lam. 1:1-5(6-9)10-12	1 Cor. 15:41-50	Matt. 11:25-30
Wednesday	38	-:-	119:25-48
	Lam. 2:8-15	1 Cor. 15:51-58	Matt. 12:1-14
Thursday	37:1-18	-:-	37:19-42
	Ezra 1:1-11	1 Cor. 16:1-9	Matt. 12:15-21
Friday	31	-:-	35
	Ezra 3:1-13	1 Cor. 16:10-24	Matt. 12:22-32
Saturday	30, 32	-:-	42, 43
	Ezra 4:7, 11-24	Philemon 1-25	Matt. 12:33-42

Daily Office Year One

Proper 23 Week of the Sunday closest to October 12

Sunday	146, 147	-:-	111 , 112, 113
	Micah 6:1-8	1 Cor. 4:9-16	Matt. 15:21-28
Monday	1, 2, 3	-:-	4, 7
	Micah 7:1-7	Acts 26:1-23	Luke 8:26-39
Tuesday	5, 6	-:-	10, 11
	Jonah 1:1-17a	Acts 26:24-27:8	Luke 8:40-56
Wednesday	119:1-24	-:-	12, 13, 14
	Jonah 1:17-2:10	Acts 27:9-26	Luke 9:1-17
Thursday	18:1-20	-:-	18:21-50
	Jonah 3:1-4:11	Acts 27:27-44	Luke 9:18-27
Friday	16,17	-:-	22
	Ecclus. 1:1-10,18-27	Acts 28:1-16	Luke 9:28-36
Saturday	20, 21:1-7(8-13)	-:-	110:1-5(6-7),116,117
	Ecclus. 3:17-31	Acts 28:17-31	Luke 9:37-50

Proper 24 Week of the Sunday closest to October 19

Sunday	148,149, 150	-:-	114, 115
	Ecclus. 4:1-10	1 Cor. 10:1-13	Matt. 16:13-20
Monday	25	-:-	9, 15
	Ecclus. 4:20-5:7	Rev. 7:1-8	Luke 9:51-62
Tuesday	26, 28	-:-	36, 39
	Ecclus. 6:5-17	Rev. 7:9-17	Luke 10:1-16
Wednesday	38	-:-	119:25-48
	Ecclus. 7:4-14	Rev. 8:1-13	Luke 10:17-24
Thursday	37:1-18	-:-	37:19-42
	Ecclus. 10:1-18	Rev. 9:1-12	Luke 10:25-37
Friday	31	-:-	35
	Ecclus. 11:2-20	Rev. 9:13-21	Luke 10:38-42
Saturday	30, 32	-:-	42, 43
	Ecclus. 15:9-20	Rev. 10:1-11	Luke 11:1-13

Daily Office Year Two

Proper 25 Week of the Sunday closest to October 26

Sunday	63:1-8(9-11), 98	-:-	103
	Haggai 1:1-2:9	Acts 18:24-19:7	Luke 10:25-37
Monday	41, 52	-:-	44
	Zech. 1:7-17	Rev. 1:4-20	Matt. 12:43-50
Tuesday	45	-:-	47, 48
	Ezra 5:1-17	Rev. 4:1-11	Matt. 13:1-9
Wednesday	119:49-72	-:-	49, [53]
	Ezra 6:1-22	Rev. 5:1-10	Matt. 13:10-17
Thursday	50	-:-	[59, 60] or 103
	Neh. 1:1-11	Rev. 5:11-6:11	Matt. 13:18-23
Friday	40, 54	-:-	51
	Neh. 2:1-20	Rev. 6:12-7:4	Matt. 13:24-30
Saturday	55	-:-	138,139:1-17(18-23)
	Neh. 4:1-23	Rev. 7:(4-8)9-17	Matt. 13:31-35

Proper 26 Week of the Sunday closest to November 2

Sunday	24, 29	-:-	8, 84
	Neh. 5:1-19	Acts 20:7-12	Luke 12:22-31
Monday	56, 57, [58]	-:-	64, 65
	Neh. 6:1-19	Rev. 10:1-11	Matt. 13:36-43
Tuesday	61, 62	-:-	68:1-20(21-23)24-36
	Neh. 12:27-31a, 42b-47	Rev. 11:1-19	Matt. 13:44-52
Wednesday	72	-:-	119:73-96
	Neh. 13:4-22	Rev. 12:1-12	Matt. 13:53-58
Thursday	[70], 71	-:-	74
	Ezra 7:(1-10)11-26	Rev. 14:1-13	Matt. 14:1-12
Friday	69:1-23(24-30)31-38	-:-	73
	Ezra 7:27-28; 8:21-36	Rev. 15:1-8	Matt. 14:13-21
Saturday	75, 76	-:-	23, 27
	Ezra 9:1-15	Rev. 17:1-14	Matt. 14:22-36

Daily Office Year One

Proper 25 Week of the Sunday closest to October 26

| Sunday | 63:1-8(9-11), 98 | -:- | 103 |
| | Ecclus. 18:19-33 | 1 Cor. 10:15-24 | Matt. 18:15-20 |

| Monday | 41, 52 | -:- | 44 |
| | Ecclus. 19:4-17 | Rev. 11:1-14 | Luke 11:14-26 |

| Tuesday | 45 | -:- | 47,48 |
| | Ecclus. 24:1-12 | Rev. 11:14-19 | Luke 11:27-36 |

| Wednesday | 119:49-72 | -:- | 49, [53] |
| | Ecclus. 28:14-26 | Rev. 12:1-6 | Luke 11:37-52 |

| Thursday | 50 | -:- | [59, 60] or 103 |
| | Ecclus. 31:12-18,25-32:2 | Rev.12:7-17 | Luke 11:53-12:12 |

| Friday | 40, 54 | -:- | 51 |
| | Ecclus. 34:1-8,18-22 | Rev. 13:1-10 | Luke 12:13-31 |

| Saturday | 55 | -:- | 138,139:1-17(18-23) |
| | Ecclus. 35:1-17 | Rev. 13:11-18 | Luke 12:32-48 |

Proper 26 Week of the Sunday closest to November 2

| Sunday | 24, 29 | -:- | 8, 84 |
| | Ecclus. 36:1-17 | 1 Cor. 12:27-13:13 | Matt. 18:21-35 |

| Monday | 56, 57, [58] | -:- | 64, 65 |
| | Ecclus. 38:24-34 | Rev. 14:1-13 | Luke 12:49-59 |

| Tuesday | 61, 62 | -:- | 68:1-20(21-23)24-36 |
| | Ecclus. 43:1-22 | Rev. 14:14--15:8 | Luke 13:1-9 |

| Wednesday | 72 | -:- | 119:73-96 |
| | Ecclus. 43:23-33 | Rev. 16:1-11 | Luke 13:10-17 |

| Thursday | [70] 71 | -:- | 74 |
| | Ecclus. 44:1-15 | Rev. 16:12-21 | Luke 13:18-30 |

| Friday | 69:1-23(24-30)31-38 | -:- | 73 |
| | Ecclus. 50:1,11-24 | Rev. 17:1-18 | Luke 13:31-35 |

| Saturday | 75, 76 | -:- | 23,27 |
| | Ecclus. 51:1-12 | Rev. 18:1-14 | Luke 14:1-11 |

Daily Office Year Two

Proper 27 Week of the Sunday closest to November 9

Sunday	93, 96	-:-	34
	Ezra 10:1-17	Acts 24:10-21	Luke 14:12-24
Monday	80	-:-	77, [79]
	Neh. 9:1-15(16-25)	Rev. 18:1-8	Matt. 15:1-20
Tuesday	78:1-39	-:-	78:40-72
	Neh. 9:26-38	Rev. 18:9-20	Matt. 15:21-28
Wednesday	119:97-120	-:-	81, 82
	Neh. 7:73b-8:3, 5-18	Rev. 18:21-24	Matt. 15:29-39
Thursday	[83] or 23, 27	-:-	85, 86
	1 Macc. 1:1-28	Rev. 19:1-10	Matt. 16:1-12
Friday	88	-:-	91, 92
	1 Macc. 1:41-63	Rev. 19:11-16	Matt. 16:13-20
Saturday	87, 90	-:-	136
	1 Macc. 2:1-28	Rev. 20:1-6	Matt. 16:21-28

Proper 28 Week of the Sunday closest to November 16

Sunday	66, 67	-:-	19, 46
	1 Macc. 2:29-43, 49-50	Acts 28:14b-23	Luke 16:1-13
Monday	89:1-18	-:-	89:19-52
	1 Macc. 3:1-24	Rev. 20:7-15	Matt. 17:1-13
Tuesday	97, 99, [100]	-:-	94, [95]
	1 Macc. 3:25-41	Rev. 21:1-8	Matt. 17:14-21
Wednesday	101,109:1-4(5-19)20-30	-:-	119:121-144
	1 Macc. 3:42-60	Rev. 21:9-21	Matt. 17:22-27
Thursday	105:1-22	-:-	105:23-45
	1 Macc. 4:1-25	Rev.21:22--22:5	Matt.18:1-9
Friday	102	-:-	107:1-32
	1 Macc. 4:36-59	Rev. 22:6-13	Matt. 18:10-20
Saturday	107:33-43,108:1-6(7-13)	-:-	33
	Isa. 65:17-25	Rev. 22:14-21	Matt. 18:21-35

Daily Office Year One

Proper 27 Week of the Sunday closest to November 9

Sunday	93, 96	-:-	34
	Ecclus. 51:13-22	1 Cor. 14:1-12	Matt. 20:1-16
Monday	80	-:-	77, [79]
	Joel 1:1-13	Rev. 18:15-24	Luke 14:12-24
Tuesday	78:1-39	-:-	78:40-72
	Joel 1:15-2:2(3-11)	Rev. 19:1-10	Luke 14:25-35
Wednesday	119:97-120	-:-	81, 82
	Joel 2:12-19	Rev. 19:11-21	Luke 15:1-10
Thursday	[83] or 23, 27	-:-	85, 86
	Joel 2:21-27	James 1:1-15	Luke 15:1-2,11-32
Friday	88	-:-	91, 92
	Joel 2:28-3:8	James 1:16-27	Luke 16:1-9
Saturday	87, 90	-:-	136
	Joel 3:9-17	James 2:1-13	Luke 16:10-17(18)

Proper 28 Week of the Sunday closest to November 16

Sunday	66, 67	-:-	19, 46
	Hab. 1:1-4(5-11)12-2:1	Phil. 3:13-4:1	Matt. 23:13-24
Monday	89:1-18	-:-	89:19-52
	Hab. 2:1-4, 9-20	James 2:14-26	Luke 16:19-31
Tuesday	97, 99, [100]	-:-	94, [95]
	Hab. 3:1-10(11-15)16-18	James 3:1-12	Luke 17:1-10
Wednesday	101,109:1-4(5-19)20-30	-:-	119:121-144
	Mal. 1:1,6-14	James 3:13-4:12	Luke 17:11-19
Thursday	105:1-22	-:-	105:23-45
	Mal. 2:1-16	James 4:13-5:6	Luke 17:20-37
Friday	102	-:-	107:1-32
	Mal. 3:1-12	James 5:7-12	Luke 18:1-8
Saturday	107:33-43,108:1-6(7-13)	-:-	33
	Mal. 3:13-4:6	James 5:13-20	Luke 18:9-14

Daily Office Year Two

The Book of Common Prayer 487

Proper 29 Week of the Sunday closest to November 23

Sunday	118	-:-	145
	Isa. 19:19-25	Rom. 15:5-13	Luke 19:11-27
Monday	106:1-18	-:-	106:19-48
	Joel 3:1-2, 9-17	1 Pet. 1:1-12	Matt. 19:1-12
Tuesday	[120],121, 122, 123	-:-	124,125,126, [127]
	Nahum 1:1-13	1 Pet. 1:13-25	Matt. 19:13-22
Wednesday	119:145-176	-:-	128, 129,130
	Obadiah 15-21	1 Pet. 2:1-10	Matt. 19:23-30
Thursday	131,132, [133]	-:-	134,135
	Zeph. 3:1-13	1 Pet. 2:11-25	Matt. 20:1-16
Friday	140, 142	-:-	141, 143:1-11(12)
	Isa. 24:14-23	1 Pet. 3:13-4:6	Matt. 20:17-28
Saturday	137:1-6(7-9),144	-:-	104
	Micah 7:11-20	1 Pet. 4:7-19	Matt. 20:29-34

Daily Office Year One

The Book of Common Prayer   488

Sunday	118 Zech. 9:9-16	-:- 1 Pet. 3:13-22	145 Matt. 21:1-13
Monday	106:1-18 Zech. 10:1-12	-:- Gal. 6:1-10	106:19-48 Luke 18:15-30
Tuesday	[120],121,122,123 Zech. 11:4-17	-:- 1 Cor. 3:10-23	124,125,126, [127] Luke 18:31-43
Wednesday	119:145-176 Zech. 12:1-10	-:- Eph. 1:3-14	128,129,130 Luke 19:1-10
Thursday	131,132, [133] Zech. 13:1-9	-:- Eph. 1:15-23	134,135 Luke 19:11-27
Friday	140, 142 Zech. 14:1-11	-:- Rom. 15:7-13	141,143:1-11(12) Luke 19:28-40
Saturday	137:1-6(7-9),144 Zech. 14:12-21	-:- Phil. 2:1-11	104 Luke 19:41-48

Daily Office Year Two

	Morning Prayer	Evening Prayer
St. Andrew November 30	34 Isaiah 49:1-6 1 Corinthians 4:1-16	96,100 Isaiah 55:1-5 John 1:35-42
St. Thomas December 21	23,121 Job 42:1-6 1 Peter 1:3-9	27 Isaiah 43:8-13 John 14:1-7
St. Stephen December 26	28,30 2 Chronicles 24:17-22 Acts 6:1-7	118 Wisdom 4:7-15 Acts 7:59-8:8
St. John December 27	97,98 Proverbs 8:22-30 John 13:20-35	145 Isaiah 44:1-8 1 John 5:1-12
Holy Innocents December 28	2,26 Isaiah 49:13-23 Matthew 18:1-14	19,126 Isaiah 54:1-13 Mark 10:13-16
Confession of St. Peter January 18	66,67 Ezekiel 3:4-11 Acts 10:3 44	118 Ezekiel 34:11-16 John 21:15-22
Conversion of St. Paul January 25	19 Isaiah 45:18-25 Philippians 3:4b-11	119:89-112 Ecclesiasticus 39:1-10 Acts 9:1-22
Eve of the Presentation		113,122 1 Samuel 1:20-28a Romans 8:14-21
The Presentation February 2	42,43 1 Samuel 12:1-10 John 8:31-36	48, 87 Haggai 2:1-9 1 John 3:1-8
St. Matthias February 24	80 1 Samuel 16:1-13 1 John 2:18-25	33 1 Samuel 12:1-5 Acts 20:17-35
St. Joseph March 19	132 Isaiah 63:7-16 Matthew 1:18-25	34 2 Chronicles 6:12-17 Ephesians 3:14-21

Daily Office

Holy Days

	Morning Prayer	Evening Prayer
Eve of the Annunciation		8,138 Genesis 3:1-15 Romans 5:12-21 or Galatians 4:1-7
Annunciation March 25	85 , 87 Isaiah 52:7-12 Hebrews 2:5-10	110:1-5(6-7),132 Wisdom 9:1-12 John 1:9-14
St. Mark April 25	145 Ecclesiasticus 2:1-11 Acts 12:25-13:3	67,96 Isaiah 62:6-12 2 Timothy 4:1-11
SS Philip & James May 1	119:137-160 Job 23:1-12 John 1:43-51	139 Proverbs 4:7-18 John 12:20-26
Eve of the Visitation		132 Isaiah 11:1-10 Hebrews 2:11-18
The Visitation May 31	72 1 Samuel 1:1-20 Hebrews 3:1-6	146,147 Zechariah 2:10-13 John 3:25-30
St. Barnabas June 11	15,67 Ecclesiasticus 31:3-11 Acts 4:32-37	19,146 Job 29:1-16 Acts 9:26-31
Eve of St. John the Baptist		103 Ecclesiasticus 48:1-11 Luke 1:5-23
Nativity of St. John the Baptist June 24	82,98 Malachi 3:1-5 John 3:22-30	80 Malachi 4:1-6 Matthew 11:2-19
SS Peter & Paul June 29	66 Ezekiel 2:1-7 Acts 11:1-18	97,138 Isaiah 49:1-6 Galatians 2:1-9

Daily Office

	Morning Prayer	Evening Prayer
Independence Day July 4	33 Ecclesiasticus 10:1-8,12-18 James 5:7-10	107:1-32 Micah 4:1-5 Revelation 21:1-7
St. Mary Magdalene July 22	116 Zephaniah 3:14-20 Mark 15:37-16:7	30,149 Exodus 15:19-21 2 Corinthians 1:3-7
St. James July 25	34 Jeremiah 16:14-21 Mark 1:14-20	33 Jeremiah 26:1-15 Matthew 10:16-32
Eve of the Transfiguration		84 1 Kings 19:1-12 2 Corinthians 3:1-9,18
The Transfiguration August 6	2,24 Exodus 24:12-18 2 Corinthians 4:1-6	72 Daniel 7:9-10,13-14 John 12:27-36a

St.Mary
the Virgin
August 15
	113,115
	1 Samuel 2:1-10
	John 2:1-12
		45, or 138, 149
		Jeremiah 31:1-14
		  or Zechariah 2:10-13
		John 19:23-27
		  or Acts 1:6-14

St. Bartholomew August 24	86 Genesis 28:10-17 John 1:43-51	15,67 Isaiah 66:1-2,18-23 1 Peter 5:1-11
Eve of Holy Cross		46, 87 1 Kings 8:22-30 Ephesians 2:11-22
Holy Cross Day September 14	66 Numbers 21:4-9 John 3:11-17	118 Genesis 3:1-15 1 Peter 3:17-22
St. Matthew September 21	119:41-64 Isaiah 8:11-20 Romans 10:1-15	19,112 Job 28:12-28 Matthew 13:44-52

Daily Office

Holy Days

	Morning Prayer	Evening Prayer
St.Michael & All Angels September 29	8,148 Job 38:1-7 Hebrews 1:1-14	34, 150, or 104 Daniel 12:1-3 or 2 Kings 6:8-17 Mark 13:21-27 or Revelation 5:1-14
St. Luke October 18	103 Ezekiel 47:1-12 Luke 1:1-4	67,96 Isaiah 52:7-10 Acts 1:1-8
St. James of Jerusalem October 23	119:145-168 Jeremiah 11:18-23 Matthew 10:16-22	122, 125 Isaiah 65:17-25 Hebrews 12:12-24
SS. Simon & Jude October 28	66 Isaiah 28:9-16 Ephesians 4:1-16	116,117 Isaiah 4:2-6 John 14:15-31
Eve of All Saints		34 Wisdom 3:1-9 Revelation 19:1,4-10
All Saints' Day November 1	111,112 2 Esdras 2:42-47 Hebrews 11:32-12:2	148,150 Wisdom 5:1-5,14-16 Revelation 21:1-4,22--22:5
Thanksgiving Day	147 Deuteronomy 26:1-11 John 6:26-35	145 Joel 2:21-27 1 Thessalonians 5:12-24

Special Occasions

	Morning Prayer	Evening Prayer
Eve of the Dedication		48,122 Haggai 2:1-9 1 Corinthians 3:9-17
Anniversary of the Dedication of a Church	132 1 Kings 8:1-13 John 10:22-30	29,46 1 Kings 8:54-62 Hebrews 10:19-25

Eve of the
Patronal Feast
		27, or 116,117
		Isaiah 49:1-13
		or Ecclesiasticus 51:6b-12
		Ephesians 4:1-13
		  or Revelation 7:9-17
		  or Luke 10:38-42

The Patronal Feast	92,93,or 148,149 Isaiah 52:7-10 or Job 5:8-21 Acts 4:5-13 or Luke 12:1-12	96,97,or 111,112 Jeremiah 31:10-14 or Ecclesiasticus 2:7-18 Romans 12:1-21 or Luke 21:10-19
Eves of Apostles and Evangelists		48, 122, or 84, 150 Isaiah 43:10-15* or Isaiah 52:7-10** Revelation 21:1-4,9-14 or Matthew 9:35--10:4

* Except on the Eve of St Thomas
** Except on the Eves of St. Mark and St. Luke

Daily Office

Bibliography

The Anglican Service Book [1979 in Traditional English, with supplements]. The Church of the Good Shepherd, Rosemont, Pennsylvania, 1991.

The Book of Common Prayer [1662]. Introduction by Diarmaid MacCulloch, Everyman's Library, 1999

The Book of Common Prayer [1928]. The Church Pension Fund, NY, 1945.

The Book of Common Prayer [1979]. Oxford University Press, NY, 2007.

Common Worship. Church House Publishing, London, 2000.

Commentary on the American Prayer Book [1979]. by Marion Hatchett, Seabury Press, NY, 1981

The First English Prayer Book [1549]. by Thomas Cranmer (Ed. by Robert Van de Weyer), Morehouse Publishing, Harrisburg PA, 1999

Handbook of Prayers, ed. James Socias, Princeton, NJ: Sceptor Publishers, 1997

The Holy Bible, English Standard Version. by Crossway Bibles, a division of Good News Publishers, Wheaton, IL, 2001.

My Prayer-Book – Happiness in Goodness – Reflections, Counsels, Prayers, and Devotions. Lasance, F.L., NY: Benziger Brothers, 1944

The Oxford American Prayer Book Commentary [1928], by Massey Hamilton Shepherd, Oxford University Press, NY, 1973

The Practice of Religion – A Short Manual of Instructions and Devotions. by Archibald Campbell Knowles, Morehouse-Gorham Co. NY, 1950

Saint Augustine's Prayer Book – A Book of Devotions for Members of the Episcopal Church [1947]. Ed. by Loren Gavitt, Holy Cross Publications, West Park, NY, 1999

Contact:

*If you discover errors, or have any comments or questions —
including matters regarding your personal faith and
relationship with Christ that you wish to explore, please contact
the editor at*

Saint Austin's Press
info@austinspress.com

or

Fr. Van McCalister
fr.mccalister@gmail.com

Made in United States
North Haven, CT
27 November 2022

27349130R00302